IET COMPUTING SERIES 53

Nature-Inspired Optimization Algorithms and Soft Computing

Other volumes in this series:

Nature-Inspired Optimization Algorithms and Soft Computing

Methods, technology and applications for IoTs, smart cities, healthcare and industrial automation

Edited by
Rajeev Arya, Sangeeta Singh, Maheshwari P. Singh, Brijesh R. Iyer and Venkat N. Gudivada

The Institution of Engineering and Technology

Published by The Institution of Engineering and Technology, London, United Kingdom

The Institution of Engineering and Technology is registered as a Charity in England & Wales (no. 211014) and Scotland (no. SC038698).

© The Institution of Engineering and Technology 2023

First published 2023

The Institution of Engineering and Technology
Futures Place
Kings Way, Stevenage
Hertfordshire SG1 2UA, United Kingdom

www.theiet.org

British Library Cataloguing in Publication Data
A catalogue record for this product is available from the British Library

ISBN 978-1-83953-516-1 (hardback)
ISBN 978-1-83953-517-8 (PDF)

Typeset in India by MPS Limited

Cover credit: Starling murmuration/PHOTOSTOCK-ISRAEL/SCIENCE PHOTO LIBRARY/ Science Photo Library

Contents

About the editors

Rajeev Arya is an assistant professor in the Department of Electronics & Communication Engineering at the National Institute of Technology, Patna, India. His research interests cover the fields of wireless communication and security issues, device-to-device communication based IoT System, UAV communications in 5G and beyond networks, soft computing techniques and applications. He has published in international journals and conferences. He is a member of IEI, IEEE ISRD-, and IAENG. He received his Ph.D. degree in Communication Engineering from the Indian Institute of Technology (IIT Roorkee), India.

Sangeeta Singh is an assistant professor in the Department of Electronics and Communication Engineering at the National Institute of Technology, Patna, India. Her research interests include soft computing techniques and applications and beyond CMOS Devices Green Electronics steep switching transistors. She has actively participated in technical courses, workshops, and seminars at the NITs. She is a member of IEEE and IEEE EDS Society. She received her Ph.D. degree in Electronics and Communication Engineering from PDPM-IIITDM Jabalpur, India.

Maheshwari P. Singh is a professor in the Department of Computer Science and Engineering at NIT Patna, India. He has written and edited several research books. His research interests include machine learning and wireless sensor networks, fuzzy set, social media and security. He has actively participated in technical courses, workshops and seminars at the IITs and NITs. He is a member of IE (Fellow), ACM (Senior), IEEE (Senior), and ISTE (Life Member). He received his Ph.D. degree in Computer Science and Engineering from MNNIT Allahabad, India.

Brijesh Iyer holds a Ph.D. degree in Electronics and Telecommunication Engineering from Indian Institute of Technology, Roorkee, India. He is presently a senior faculty member in the Department of E&TC Engineering, Dr Babasaheb Ambedkar Technological University, India (a state technological University of Maharashtra-India). His research interests include RF front end design for 5G and beyond, IoT, biomedical imaging and signal processing. He has two patents to his credit, has authored five books on cutting edge technologies, and published over 40 research papers in peer-reviewed journals and conference proceedings. He has served as a program committee member of various international conferences. He is a member of IEEE MTTS, ISTE, IEANG, and IETE.

Venkat N. Gudivada is the chairperson of and a professor in the Computer Science Department at East Carolina University, USA. His research has been funded by NSF, NASA, U.S. Department of Energy, US Department of Navy, US Army Research Office, Marshall University Foundation, and West Virginia Division of Science and Research. His research interests include cognitive computing, computational linguistics/NLP, information retrieval, automated question generation, data management and NoSQL systems, and personalization of learning. He has published over 110 articles in peer reviewed journals, book chapters, and conference proceedings. He is an IEEE Senior Member, and member of IARIA) and the Honor Society of Phi Kappa Phi. He received his PhD degree in Computer Science from the University of Louisiana – Lafayette, Louisiana, The USA.

Foreword

The objective of this book series is to enlighten researchers with the current trends in the field of blockchain technology and its integration with distributed computing and systems. Blockchains show riveting features such as decentralization, verifiability, fault tolerance, transparency, and accountability. The technology enables more secure, transparent, and traceable scenarios to assist in distributed applications. We plan to bring forward the technological aspects of blockchain technology for Internet of Things (IoTs), cloud computing, edge computing, fog computing, wireless sensor networks (WSNs), peer-to-peer (P2P) networks, mobile edge computing, and other distributed network paradigms for real-world enhanced and evolving future applications of distributed computing and systems.

We are honoured to write the foreword of this first book in our book series. This valuable contribution to the field of blockchain technology and social media computing will serve as a useful reference for those seeking to deepen their understanding of this rapidly evolving field and inspire further research and innovation. The authors have provided insightful and thought-provoking perspectives on the current state and future potential of blockchain technology in social media computing, and we are confident that this book will be a valuable resource for years to come.

As the world becomes more interconnected and reliant on technology, social media has emerged as a ubiquitous tool for communication, entertainment, and commerce. However, the centralized nature of many social media platforms has led to concerns about data privacy, security, and content moderation. With the rise of fake news, privacy breaches, and centralized control, the need for a more secure and decentralized social media platform has never been greater. In recent years, blockchain technology has emerged as a potential solution to many of these challenges, offering a decentralized and secure platform for social media computing.

The book *"Blockchain Technology for Secure Social Media Computing"* provides a comprehensive overview of blockchain technology's use in social media computing. With contributions from experts in the field, the book covers a wide range of topics, from the basics of blockchain technology to its applications in social media computing and emerging trends in the field. In addition, this book provides a comprehensive overview of the latest technologies, and applications of blockchain in online social media. From blockchain-based security for social media computing to emerging trends in social networking design, models, and handling, the authors cover a broad range of topics to address the challenges and opportunities of blockchain technology in the social media sphere.

The chapters are written by leading researchers and academics who share their experience and knowledge to provide readers with a practical understanding of how blockchain technology can be leveraged to build a more secure, transparent, and decentralized social media platform. It is an essential guide for researchers, practitioners, and students who are interested in learning more about blockchain technology and its potential to transform social media computing.

Dr. Brij B. Gupta, Director, CCRI & Professor, CSIE, Asia University, Taiwan

Professor Gregorio Martinez Perez, Department of Information and Communication Engineering, University of Murcia, Spain

Dr. Tu N. Nguyen, Department of Computer Science, Kennesaw State University, Georgia, USA

Preface

Recently, the field of bio-inspired computing applications for practical industrial uses has seen a surge in research activity. Most of the time, it is impractical to solve issues with large data sets using an exhaustive data search. Powerful tools are available thanks to optimization methods for handling data analysis and learning problems. Several techniques are used to design and put optimization algorithms into practice, and they all work better. However, the search area expands exponentially with problem size in a number of applications. Sets of more adaptable and flexible algorithms are required to overcome constraints and handle larger scale combinatorial and highly nonlinear optimization problems efficiently. Research at the nexus of biomedical imaging, data analysis, and system development is motivated by new optimization research trends that are primarily founded on machine learning and artificial intelligence. The goal of nature-inspired computing is to transfer the exceptional information-processing skills of the natural world to the computational sphere. Due to its efficacy and distinctiveness, it forges close ties with computational biology and other computing models that are motivated by biology. Numerous fields, including engineering, medicine, industry, education, and the military, can handle optimization in high-dimensional real-world issues thanks to some metaheuristic search algorithms with population-based frameworks.

A significant area of computational intelligence, soft computing, and optimization in general is the study of nature-inspired optimization methods. Since algorithms do not necessitate the fulfilment of any mathematical conditions, they offer effective tools for issues that cannot be solved using conventional and classical mathematical methods. The Internet of Things (IoTs), which uses smart devices, smart sensors, and machine learning, and cloud computing are other popular subjects. They encompass all kinds of systems, including business, finance, industry, manufacturing, management, and the environment, in addition to information and communication technology. IoT creates a significant quantity of data and links the physical world to the Internet. Big data processing is made easier by a cloud computing environment, which also uses machine learning and big data analysis to make wise choices. Additionally, the fusion of intellect and technology enables the reduction of human effort while increasing the precision and efficacy of the latter. By connecting innovative thinking with innovative action and innovative execution in nearly every aspect of human life, smart devices, and systems are revolutionizing the world. A system becomes intelligent when it has the ability to collect data, process it, analyse it, and make decisions. Sensors are typically used for data capture and gathering, and processing converts raw data into usable information. The task of making decisions is ultimately assisted by the analysis of data using clever algorithms.

This edited book's general goal is to compile the most recent chapter reviews on the interrelated fields of biomedical imaging, soft computing, and data analysis. This book is dedicated to the analysis, modeling, simulation, and applications in the interdisciplinary fields of these cutting-edge technologies, from challenges and current issues to foundations, latest research and development, and opportunities. We will attempt to cover every facet of the interplay between metaheuristics and complex systems, including evolutionary algorithms, swarm intelligence, etc. We intend to offer a thorough platform for researchers to present novel methods for handling various types of uncertainties in practical issues using cutting-edge machine learning algorithms. We will examine the potential future work in IoTs and its novel approach to bridging the divide between theory and day-to-day practical problems. Additionally, we will present a unified manifesto for applied scientists to use machine learning methods in many different engineering fields, such as IoTs and healthcare, as well as the difficulties they will encounter in the process. This book will investigate new learning domains and include case studies based on both synthetic and actual data from various domains. We anticipate that it will act as a one-stop resource for field researchers, scholars, scientists, and industrialists.

Chapter 1 discusses various optimization techniques, search for optimality, need for optimization, brief history of metaheuristics optimization, difference between metaheuristics and heuristics optimization. It represents a confounded arrangement of prerequisites to understand the implications for metaheuristic optimization, theoretical analyses, and systematic approaches for the selection of optimization algorithms. It is difficult to choose an optimization algorithm that will find the best solution to the issue while considering all the limitations. There is not a single algorithm that can fix every optimization issue.

Chapter 2 represents an in-depth view of the nature-inspired optimization algorithms, search for an ideal algorithm, evolutionary algorithms, chemistry-based algorithms, physics-based algorithms, and various other algorithms. This chapter shows the path to general strategies and frameworks for efficiency improvement of nature-inspired algorithms, applications on single objective and multi objective problems and finally some concluding remarks.

Chapter 3 attempts to address the application aspects of nature-inspired optimization algorithms. It begins with the definition of nature-inspired optimization algorithms. In addition to that, it also deals with its implementation, and parameter tunning. Furthermore, it also presents a study on constrained and unconstrained optimization. Later, it covers the feature selection and practical engineering applications of nature-inspired optimization algorithms.

Chapter 4 is dedicated for the particle swarm optimization applications and implications. It starts with the outline of swarm intelligence, PSO for single objective problem, and PSO for multi objective problem. It also covers the different approaches of multi objective PSO, different variants of PSO, PSO in hybrid environment, and many other computational experiments.

Chapter 5 covers the advanced optimization by nature-inspired algorithms. It will give a comprehensive review of the latest optimization techniques; cat swarm optimization, cuckoo optimization, mine blast optimization, water cycle algorithm-based optimization, anarchic society optimization, teaching-learning-based optimization, ant lion optimizer, and crow search algorithm.

Chapter 6 deals with the applications and challenges of optimization in Internet of Things (IoTs). It starts with the network optimization in IoT and then it covers the nature-inspired optimization in IoT. It also includes the evolutionary algorithms in IoT and bio-inspired heuristic algorithms in IoT.

In Chapter 7, the role of optimization in healthcare systems, medical diagnosis, biomedical informatics, biomedical image processing, ECG classification, feature extraction and classification, and intelligent detection of disordered systems have been discussed in detail. Different techniques have been used to explore methods for predictive analytics in healthcare as well as innovations and technologies for smart healthcare. This chapter provides examples of some of the problems and difficulties that can arise when using optimization methods for wearable technology and smart healthcare.

Chapter 8 focuses on the need of the industrial automation and its optimization as if the companies want to keep their stock cheap while also being more responsive and cutting delivery times, they must make the best use of their industrial and logistics capacities, optimize and streamline flows throughout the supply chain, and get the most out of their resources. It covers the various aspects of the applications and challenges of optimization in industrial automation, factory digitalization, product flow monitoring, inventory management, safety and security, quality control, and packaging optimization.

Chapter 9 deals with the expectations from modern evolutionary approaches for image processing. This chapter covers how the complex optimization issues in image processing could be solved using environmentally inspired optimization algorithms like genetic algorithms, particle swarm optimization, and ant colony optimization.

Finally, Chapter 10 gives the detailed concluding remarks of the study present in the earlier chapters. It highlighted the various challenges and potentials of bio-inspired optimization algorithms for IoT applications, challenges, and opportunities of bio-inspired optimization algorithms for biomedical applications, recent trends in smarty cities planning based on nature-inspired computing, and lastly future perspectives of nature-inspired computing.

Chapter 1

Introduction to various optimization techniques

Trishna Saikia[1], Koushlendra Kumar Singh[1],
Sergey Vityazev[2] and Akbar Sheikh Akbar[3]

1.1 Introduction

Today in every field, there is a desire to get maximum profit with the least investment. Efficiency and utilization with a minimum investment are key requirements. And here comes the idea of optimization. Optimization is a process of choosing the best available options from given alternatives which, as a result, gives us the best solution. For example, in the design of a bridge, civil engineers must make many decisions in various stages of construction. So, optimization is nothing but making the best feasible decision. The goal of such decisions is either to maximize the profit or to minimize the effort. It is a crucial tool for analyzing systems. Both maximizing and minimizing are two categories of optimization problems. Optimization methods are applied to many problems in various fields to handle practical problems. It is not limited to some fields only; the idea is used widely in all fields. With the advancement in computing techniques, optimization has become an important part of problem solving. Many optimization techniques have been proposed in the last few years by researchers. However, despite many optimization algorithms, no method is suitable for all optimization problems. The most appropriate method is selected based on the specific problem.

1.2 Optimization

Optimization is finding the condition that maximizes or minimizes the value of a function. In mathematical terms, an optimization problem is a problem of finding the best optimum solution from the given set of solutions. Classification of optimization problems is based on several factors, such as it is based on the existence of constraints, also based on the nature of variables, and depending on the structure of the problem. Operations research is a field of mathematics that deals with the

[1]Machine Vision and Intelligence Lab, National Institute of Technology Jamshedpur, India
[2]Ryazan State Radio Engineering University, Russia
[3]Leeds Beckett University, UK

application of different methods and techniques to solve problems by bringing the best or optimal solutions. Mathematical optimization techniques such as linear and nonlinear programming and network flow theory were developed during World War II. Mathematical optimization is useful in many different fields. Some of the fields are engineering, manufacturing, policy modeling, transportation, economics, genetics, etc.

An optimization algorithm is used to find the best optimal solution. Many optimization algorithms can be used based on the aim and characteristics of the problem. If the aim is to find the derivative of a function, optimization can be classified as gradient-based optimization and if the function requires only a random value that gets maximized or minimized, it is classified as gradient-free optimization. Optimization algorithms can also be classified into trajectory-based and population-based. A trajectory-based algorithm uses one solution at a time to find the path with continuous iteration. And population-based algorithms use multiple solutions which, in combination, find multiple paths [1].

Looking from another perspective, optimization algorithms are also classified as deterministic algorithms and stochastic algorithms. These are the two types of optimization algorithms that are mostly used in most fields to perform optimization. Deterministic algorithms use specific rules and have predefined outputs. Stochastic algorithms use random conditions to find the optimal solution. Algorithms with stochastic behavior are also known as metaheuristics. In the past, stochastics was referred to as heuristics. The performance of metaheuristics is considered better than simple heuristics. So, no algorithm is a perfect match for a given problem. A combination of one algorithm with another algorithm is used to design a more efficient algorithm.

The first step in the optimization process is to make a model. A model consists of the objective function, variables, and constraints. An objective function is a function that is maximized or minimized. It is the output. Variables are those components that act as the parameter of a model. Variables are the input to the model. Constraints are used to put limits on the variables. They describe the relationship between various inputs. And the second step is to determine the category of the model. Some problems have constraints, and some have not. Problems can also be static or dynamic.

1.3   Search for optimality

Optimization is all about finding the best solution from the given set of feasible solutions. For example, selecting a site for an industry, finding the optimum design of a system, or planning the best strategy to get maximum profit. Reaching optimality is the key reason for performing optimization techniques on various problems. Optimality is the conditions that a function must satisfy to get an optimum or best solution. Local optimum is a point that gives an optimal, either maximal or minimal solution to the optimization problem. We can find the optimum point for a given problem in two separate ways. First, by optimizing the parameters and constants of the system. And the second method is by optimizing all variables or selected variables of the system.

There are several methods used for solving optimization problems. For example, the hill climbing method starts from a basic approach and then moves to improve solutions. This method solves global problems by using the information on local optimum solutions. The optimum point is dependent on nearby points as defined by the method.

1.4   Needs for optimization

There are several activities taking place every day around the world; these activities can be considered as a system (whether it can be theoretical entities or physical entities). The performance of these systems depends on the working principles of various indices of the system, which means the efficient operation of various indices makes the system efficient. This is only possible when the optimization of various indices has been performed. While representing a system in a mathematical model, algebraic variables are used to represent these indices. These variables depend upon many factors [2]. After representing the system in a mathematical model, some optimization techniques are applied. As a result of this, the values of those variables are found, which either maximize or minimize the system. In the case of maximization, it must maximize the profit or gain of the system and in the case of minimization, it must minimize the loss or waste of the system. Optimization is needed in many fields, such as in electrical engineering to minimize total harmonic distortion in the multilevel inverter; in civil engineering, optimization techniques are used in every step of a project life cycle; in mechanical engineering also, optimization is used for mechanical design, similarly, in computer science, there are many areas where optimization being used, etc. [3].

Let us take an example for a better understanding of the importance of optimization. These days cloud computing has become the latest computing model for a variety of applications. It can allow access to shared resources immediately after receiving a request from clients and also discharged with a little administration. In cloud computing, all the applications keep running on a virtual platform and all the resources are distributed among the virtual machines [4]. Due to these kinds of user-friendly applications, the number of clients using cloud services increased drastically. The main goal of a cloud service provider is to create an illusion among clients that they have an infinite number of resources but in reality, they do not have one. So, creating this kind of illusion is possible only with the help of efficient scheduling. So if we can develop such a scheduling algorithm that can utilize the resources which are being provided by the service provider in a better manner or an optimal manner then it would immensely end in a better performance by the service provider. A good task scheduler should adapt its scheduling strategy to the changing environment and the type of tasks. Therefore, a dynamic task scheduling algorithm is appropriate for cloud environments such as ant colony optimization, particle swarm optimization, etc.

1.5   A brief history of metaheuristics optimization

People knowingly or unknowingly used metaheuristic techniques from ancient days to solve enormous backbreaking optimization problems. Nevertheless, huge progress has been made since the establishment of the first metaheuristics concepts. Though in the third period of 1980s, the word "metaheuristic" was first thought up, people were applying heuristic (even metaheuristic) techniques before 1940, but they did not formally study this. For humans, heuristics are so natural, but for human minds having only the heuristic strategy to solve a diversity of problems without having any prior experience is doubtful. The human mind must solve those problems by using the derived heuristic form, which is nothing but the metaheuristic strategies. In the period from 1940 to 1960, several applications used heuristic strategies. In 1958, to solve "ill-structured" problems, problems that cannot be formulated explicitly or solved by known and feasible computational techniques, Simon and Newell used a heuristics strategy. In 1958, their prediction slightly emerged optimistically. From that, we can surely accept that problem solving becomes more flexible with heuristic strategy than with exact methods. In 1963, the evolutionary strategy was developed by Ingo Rechenberg and Hans Paul Schwefel at the Technical University of Berlin. Moreover, in 1966, evolutionary programming was developed by L.J. Fogel *et al.* In evolutionary programming, solutions are represented as finite state machines, but the concept of a population and crossover was missing there. In 1975, the real start of this field was started by John Holland; he was the first who acknowledged the importance of both population and crossover through his seminal book on genetic algorithms [5].

The development of evolutionary strategies as well as evolutionary programming became the first turning point in the field of metaheuristics. The period from 1980 to 1990 was considered the most electrifying time for the development of metaheuristics algorithms. In 1983, the development of simulated annealing was the key step in the development of metaheuristics. It is an optimization technique that was developed by S. Kirkpatrick *et al.* In 1986, an artificial immune system was developed by Farmer *et al.*, which was also considered a major step in the development of metaheuristics. In 1980, Glover constituted the use of memory in metaheuristics, which was published later in 1997 in his seminal book on "Tabu Search" (Glover and Laguna). In 1992, Marco Dorigo described the innovative work on ant colony optimization, which is a swarm intelligence-inspired search technique, in his Ph.D. thesis on optimization and natural algorithms. In 1992, after publishing a book on genetic programming by John R. Koza, a new field of machine learning began.

The development of particle swarm optimization is also significant progress in the development of metaheuristics, which was developed by James Kennedy and Russell C. Eberhart later in 1995. The vector-based evolutionary algorithm called differential evolution proved to be more efficient than genetic algorithms in many applications. This vector-based evolutionary algorithm was developed by R. Storn and K. Price later in 1997. In 2001, harmony search, a music-inspired algorithm, was developed by Zong Woo Geem *et al.* Around 2002, Passino developed a bacteria foraging algorithm, and, in 2004, the honey bee algorithm was developed by S. Nakrani and C. Tovey. Based on this algorithm, in 2005, novel bee algorithm was developed by D.T. Pham *et al.*, and the artificial bee colony was also developed by D. Karaboga. An efficient cuckoo search algorithm was proposed by Yang and Deb during the period from 2009 to 2010 [6]. Nevertheless, so many metaheuristics algorithms are now being developed to use for optimization.

1.6 Difference between metaheuristics optimization and heuristic optimization

There are so many problems in the world. Among those, some problems are very hard to solve, which we consider as NP-problems. For these problems, finding the exact solution is very difficult by using conventional methods. Either it fails to solve the problems or it becomes too time consuming. So, to solve these kinds of problems, researchers used approximate methods to find approximate solutions. Both metaheuristics and heuristics are approximate approaches that are used to solve different optimization problems [3]. Simply, we can define a heuristic approach as a method that uses local information to find the solution to a given problem and a reverse metaheuristics approach as a method that uses global information to solve any given problem. In addition to this, both these optimization techniques differ from each other in many ways.

Naturally, heuristic methods are deterministic. On the other hand, metaheuristics methods are an extended form of heuristic approach along with randomization.

Most of the heuristics methods are algorithmic or iterative types, but most of the metaheuristics methods are nature-inspired; they are also iterative types. In both methods, the nature of the solution is inexact and gives a near-optimal solution.

Metaheuristics methods are also called guided random search techniques, as it does a random search to explore the entire search space. It is an advantage over heuristic methods because metaheuristics methods avoid getting trapped in local optima and always drive the search toward global optima. In metaheuristics methods, there is a starting point for the search process, which must be specified, as well as a stopping condition must also be set to stop the search process. Both these methods are generally easy to implement, and usually, they can be assimilated efficiently.

1.7 Implications of metaheuristic optimization

The application of metaheuristic optimization algorithms is growing with time, as they are quite attractive algorithms, which are having some distinct advantages over conventional optimization algorithms. Metaheuristic optimization algorithms can solve complex real-world problems by finding high-quality solutions [7]. There are some problems regarding parameter adaptation in metaheuristic optimization. Researchers are trying to reduce this problem. After trying so many approaches, they proposed a modification of these methods by using fuzzy logic to obtain better results than the original methods [8]. Many researchers used these metaheuristic optimization algorithms with some modifications to find more efficient solutions throughout their research work. There is an efficient ant colony optimization algorithm, which is also a metaheuristic optimization algorithm that can take all types of optimization problems like linear, non-linear, and mixed integer [9]. A good balance is needed for all metaheuristics algorithms. Every metaheuristic algorithm follows different strategies to balance mainly two factors: one is to identify the high-quality search space for finding better results and another factor is not wasting unnecessary time in the already explored search space or the search space, which does not give a promising solution.

Metaheuristic optimization methods can mainly be classified into two parts: one is single-solution-based metaheuristics and the other is population-based metaheuristics. Single-solution-based algorithms are also called trajectory-based algorithms. Those algorithms work on a single solution at any point in time, while population-based metaheuristic algorithms work on the whole population or a whole bundle of solutions at a time. Metaheuristic algorithms are mainly inspired by nature. For example, evolutionary algorithms are inspired by biology, particle swarm optimization, and ant colony optimization, these swarm intelligence-based algorithms are inspired by ant or bee colonies, and the simulated annealing algorithm is inspired by physics, etc. Metaheuristic optimization algorithms can also be classified into two categories: one is deterministic and the other is stochastic. A deterministic optimization algorithm follows a deterministic decision approach to solve a given optimization problem, e.g., tabu search and local search. While stochastic optimization algorithms follow random rules to solve a given optimization problem, e.g., simulated annealing and evolutionary algorithms. There are different criteria based on which metaheuristic optimization algorithms can be classified, but here we have discussed a few.

1.8   Heuristic optimization algorithms

Heuristic methods involve using iterative computational procedures to improve a candidate solution toward an optimal solution with respect to a given quality measure [10]. These methods can explore vast spaces of candidate solutions to find near-optimal solutions at a reasonable computational cost without making any significant assumptions about the problem being optimized. Despite their practicality, heuristic algorithms cannot guarantee feasibility or optimality and, in some cases, may need help to determine how close a feasible solution is to optimality. Over the years, various heuristic tools have been developed to solve optimization problems that were previously challenging or even impossible to solve. The primary advantage of these tools is that they offer quick solutions that are easy to comprehend and implement [11].

Heuristic algorithms are useful in providing fast and practical short-term solutions to planning and scheduling issues. However, the main drawback of heuristic approaches is their inability to guarantee optimal solutions to problems.

While heuristic methods may offer a quick fix to specific planning or scheduling challenges, they are only sometimes effective in delivering the best possible results. Moreover, heuristic approaches need more flexibility to create lasting, optimal solutions that enhance productivity and profitability.

This section provides an overview of various heuristic optimization techniques, including fundamental constructive algorithms such as evolutionary programming and greedy strategies and local search algorithms like hill climbing.

1.8.1 Constructive heuristic optimization algorithms

Constructive heuristic algorithms consist of three phases:

1. Index development, where jobs are sorted based on a specific attribute of the problem instance [12].
2. Solution construction, where a solution is built recursively by trying unscheduled jobs at different positions in a partial schedule until the schedule is complete [12].
3. Improvement, where the existing solution is modified to enhance its quality [12].

Many well-known problems, such as the traveling salesman problem, are tackled using these approaches. Construction heuristics create a complete tour by iteratively extending a connected partial tour. Another method builds several tour fragments and combines them to form a complete tour. One example of a construction heuristic is the greedy heuristic. In this approach, all edges in Graph G are sorted by weight, and then each edge is examined sequentially, starting from the edge with the least weight. If the edge does not result in a cycle of less than n edges or vertices of a degree greater than two, it is added to the current partial candidate solution. The greedy heuristic has several variations that use different criteria to select the edge to add. One of these is the Quick-Borůvka Heuristic. This approach is based on Borůvka's minimum spanning tree algorithm and sorts the vertices in G arbitrarily. It then processes each vertex in the specified order and adds the minimum weight edge that does not result in a cycle of less than n edges or vertices of a degree greater than two. The savings heuristic, on the other hand, builds multiple partial tours by selecting a base vertex and cyclic paths. It then combines two cyclic paths at each construction step by removing an edge incident to the base vertex in both paths and connecting the resulting paths into a new cyclic path. This process continues until a single cyclic path is left. The edges to remove are chosen to minimize the total cost. Greedy tours are at most $(1 + \log n)/2$ times longer than optimal tours, while the length of a savings tour is at most a factor of $(1 + \log n)$ above the optimal length. No worst-case bounds on solution quality are known for Quick-Borůvka tours [13].

1.9 Metaheuristics optimization algorithms

In the realm of computer science and mathematics, a metaheuristic is a heuristic or procedure that operates on a higher level than a partial search algorithm. Its goal is to find, generate, tune, or select an algorithm that can provide a satisfactory solution to optimization problems or machine learning problems. Metaheuristics explore a subset of solutions that would otherwise be too vast to be completely enumerated or explored. In the realm of computer science and mathematics, a metaheuristic is a heuristic or procedure that operates on a higher level than a partial search algorithm. These methods do not rely on many assumptions about the problem at hand, which makes them applicable to various problems. However, unlike iterative methods and optimization algorithms, metaheuristics cannot guarantee that a globally optimal solution can be found for some problems. Although most literature on metaheuristics is experimental in nature, providing empirical results from computer experiments with the algorithms, some formal theoretical results are also available, typically concerning convergence and the potential to find the global optimum.

The field of metaheuristics has produced many algorithms that claim novelty and practical efficacy. While high-quality research can be found in the field, many publications suffer from flaws such as vagueness, lack of conceptual elaboration, poor experiments, and disregard for previous literature. Metaheuristic algorithms belong to the category of computational intelligence paradigms, mainly used for solving complex optimization problems. This section aims to provide an overview of metaheuristic optimization algorithms. There are two main categories of metaheuristic algorithms: trajectory-based and population-based.

1.9.1 Trajectory-based metaheuristic algorithms

A trajectory-based metaheuristic algorithm employs a single agent or solution to move through the search space in a piecewise manner. These algorithms accept better solutions while also allowing for the possibility of accepting suboptimal solutions with a certain probability. By tracing a trajectory through the search space, these algorithms may reach the global optimum.

One example of a trajectory-based metaheuristic algorithm is simulated annealing, which is a probabilistic optimization method that efficiently finds solutions close to the global maximum. Simulated annealing accepts neighboring states probabilistically, even if they result in worse outcomes, which sets it apart from search algorithms like hill climbing and beam search.

Other trajectory-based metaheuristic algorithms include tabu search (TS), iterated local search (ILS), and guided local search (GLS). TS is an iterative neighborhood search algorithm that dynamically changes the neighborhood to enhance local search [14]. By actively avoiding points in the search space already visited, loops in search trajectories can be avoided, and local optima can be escaped. TS combines local search (LS) and memory structures with the main feature being the use of explicit memory. Memory is used to achieve two goals: to prevent the search from revisiting previously visited solutions and to explore unvisited areas of the solution space.

The ILS metaheuristic employs a LS strategy that utilizes a single solution throughout the iterative process [15]. It is a computationally efficient method that improves the quality of local optima, which is particularly beneficial in high-dimensional problems. The ILS method typically starts with a randomly generated initial solution (in binary encoding) within the predefined search space, and the stopping criterion is often a specified number of iterations. The fundamental concept of ILS revolves around the steps of local search, perturbation, and the stopping criterion.

GLS is a metaheuristic algorithm that accumulates penalties during a search to assist LS algorithms in escaping local minima and plateaus [16]. If the LS algorithm settles in a local optimum, GLS modifies the objective function using a specific approach. The LS then operates using an augmented objective function, which is tailored to bring the search out of the local optimum.

1.9.2 Population-based metaheuristic algorithms

In optimization problems with a high-dimensional search space, exact optimization algorithms are inadequate in providing a suitable solution. As the problem size increases, the search space grows exponentially, making an exhaustive search impractical. Furthermore, classical approximate optimization methods, such as greedy-based algorithms, rely on several assumptions to solve problems. However, validating these assumptions can be difficult in some cases. As a result, meta-heuristic algorithms have been extensively developed to solve optimization problems. These algorithms make few or no assumptions about a problem and can explore very large spaces of candidate solutions. Population-based meta-heuristic algorithms, such as genetic algorithm (GA), ant colony optimization (ACO), particle swarm optimization (PSO), and artificial bee colony (ABC), are particularly useful for global searches due to their ability to explore worldwide and exploit locally.

GA is an evolutionary algorithm that takes inspiration from Darwin's theory of natural selection [17]. GA broadly involves the following steps:

Initialization: The algorithm starts with a population of potential solutions to the problem.
Selection: A fitness function is applied to evaluate the fitness of everyone in the population, and the fittest individuals are selected for reproduction.
Crossover: The selected individuals are used to create new solutions by exchanging genetic information through different crossover points and mating techniques.
Mutation: To maintain diversity in the population, some individuals undergo small mutations after crossover.

The above process continues until convergence, i.e., the population becomes highly like its previous state. The converged population is used as the solution to the given problem. Despite criticisms of the evolutionary theory, GA can provide good enough solutions for complex problems, including NP-complete problems such as the Knapsack Problem, Bin Packing, and Graph Coloring.

ACO is a technique used to solve computational problems, particularly those that involve finding good paths through graphs [18]. It is based on the behavior of real ants and uses pheromone-based communication, where ants leave pheromone trails along paths to find food. The ACO algorithm can be described as follows:

- Every ant starts from a random vertex or city.
- For each iteration, each ant visits a city along the edge of the graph and keeps the route in memory.
- The ants avoid previously visited cities but travel to every city in the graph by probabilistically choosing the edge, depending on the amount of pheromone associated with the path. Higher pheromone values increase the chance of the ant choosing the path.
- The pheromone value is decreased by a percentage for each iteration.
- A solution is generated for every ant upon completing its visit, and pheromones are assigned to routes depending on the quality of the solution.
- The process is repeated until a solution converges, or the termination condition is met.

ACO algorithms are commonly used in various fields, especially in vehicle routing, scheduling, and set problems. The combination of artificial ants and local search algorithms has proven effective for numerous optimization tasks.

PSO is a bio-inspired optimization algorithm that aims to find optimal solutions in a solution space [19]. Unlike other optimization algorithms, PSO does not depend on the gradient or any differential form of the objective; only the objective function is required. PSO works by initializing a swarm of candidate solutions, referred to as particles, and moving them around in the search space based on simple formulae. Each particle's movement is guided by its own best-known position in the search space, as well as the entire swarm's best-known position. As improved positions are discovered, they guide the swarm's movements in subsequent iterations. This process is repeated until a satisfactory solution is found, although it is not guaranteed to converge to an optimal solution. PSO is a straightforward algorithm that is widely used in various fields, such as engineering, economics, and finance.

The ABC optimization technique is a swarm intelligence algorithm that mimics the foraging process of honeybee swarms. It is a stochastic search method that uses the quality of nectar as a fitness evaluator for candidate solutions represented as food sources in the search space [20]. The algorithm involves three types of bees: employed bees, onlookers, and scouts. The number of employed bees is equal to the number of food sources around the hive. Each employed bee goes to its assigned food source and returns to the hive to dance on the location. If an employed bee's food source is abandoned, it becomes a scout and searches for a new food source.

In the ABC algorithm, the position of a food source represents a possible solution to the optimization problem, and the nectar amount of a food source corresponds to the quality (fitness) of the associated solution. The initial population (food source positions) is randomly distributed. The population then undergoes cycles of search processes by employed, onlooker, and scout bees. Employed bees modify the position of their food source and discover new positions. They keep the new position if their nectar amount is higher than the previous one. Onlooker bees evaluate the nectar information from all employed bees and choose a food source to modify. If the new nectar amount is higher, the onlooker keeps the new position. The abandoned sources are replaced with new sources by artificial scouts.

The ABC algorithm is a powerful optimization technique that has been successfully used in various domains, such as image processing, classification, and feature selection.

1.10   Theoretical analysis

The objective of optimization is to minimize the system or to maximize the system. An optimization algorithm is used to find an optimal solution by choosing from various solutions. Based on the behavior of problems, an appropriate algorithm is selected. There are various criteria used to select an algorithm. These are the computational time of the algorithm, capability to find near optimum solutions, ease of use, etc. [21]. The property of the algorithm is also an important criterion for selection. Some of the characteristics are the need for computational resources, level of complexity, performance, robustness, etc. The two main stochastic methods used to solve nonconvex problems are heuristics and metaheuristics algorithms. Both algorithms speed up the process of finding the optimal solution [22]. While in some cases where finding an optimal solution is extremely hard, these methods work fine. Heuristics are problem-dependent methods, whereas metaheuristics are problem-independent methods. Heuristics find good solutions for larger problems. And they also provide acceptable solutions for a wide range of problems. But they do not guarantee the solution. Metaheuristic algorithms are just more powerful mechanisms to solve optimization problems with better solutions. Most of the metaheuristic methods are nature-inspired and iterative. But the heuristics method is algorithmic or iterative.

1.11   Systematic approach for the selection of optimization algorithms

Many optimization algorithms can be used based on the aim and characteristics of the problem. But it is important to select the appropriate algorithm from the available algorithms. The general criteria used for selecting an algorithm are based on the problem characteristics. If the problem is convex, then we can use a simplex algorithm, interior-point methods, and various gradient-based methods. Newton's algorithm is a classic example of a gradient-based optimization algorithm. It is an unconstrained algorithm. Fletcher–Reeves and the Broyde Fletcher–Goldfarb–Shanno (BFGS) methods are popularly used for unconstrained problems. The Fletcher–Reeves method works well for quadratic functions. The BFGS method uses previous information from iterations to find the optimum. The sequential unconstrained minimization techniques (SUMT) approach can be used for unconstrained problems [23]. If the characteristic of the problem is unknown, then a direct search method is used. This type of method is based on metaheuristics and heuristics. Algorithms with stochastic behavior are known as metaheuristics.

Various methods can be used to find the unconstrained maxima and minima of a function. Problems having equality constraints can be optimized by using the Lagrange multiplier method, and similarly, the problems with inequality constraints can be optimized by using Kuhn–Tucker conditions. Most of the methods use numerical techniques where the approximate solutions are found by following an iterative approach starting from a basic solution. Therefore, selecting an optimization algorithm to find the best solution to the problem while satisfying all constraints is a challenging task. There is no single algorithm available that solves all optimization problems.

References

[1] https://en.wikipedia.org/wiki/Mathematical_optimization#Classification_ of_critical_points_and_extrema

[2] Foulds, L.R., *Optimization Techniques: An Introduction*, New York, Heidelberg, Berlin: Springer-Verlag, 1981.

[3] C. Bastien and T. Marco. *An Introduction to Metaheuristics for Optimization*, Springer, 2018.

[4] Arunarani, D.M. and V. Sugumaran. Task scheduling techniques in cloud computing: a literature survey. *Future Generation Computer Systems*, 91407, 415, 2019.

[5] Kenneth, S., S. Marc, and G. Fred. A history of metaheuristics. cs.AI, 4 Apr 2017.

[6] Yang, X.-S. Metaheuristic optimization. *Scholarpedia*, 6(8), 11472, 2011.

[7] Eden, M.R., I. Marianthi, and G.P. Towler (eds.). *Proceedings of the 13th International Symposium on Process Systems Engineering – PSE*, 2018, https://doi.org/10.1016/B978-0-444-64241-7.50129-4

[8] Fevrier, V., M. Patricia, and C. Oscar. A survey on nature-inspired optimization algorithms with fuzzy logic for dynamic parameter adaptation. *Expert Systems with Applications*, 41, 6459–6466, 2014, https://doi.org/10.1016/j. eswa.2014.04.015

[9] Omid, B.-H., S. Mohammad, and H.A. Loáiciga. *Meta-Heuristic and Evolutionary Algorithms for Engineering Optimization*, WILEY, 2017.

[10] Zanakis, S.H. and R.E. James. Heuristic "optimization": why, when, and how to use it. *Interfaces*, 11(5), 84–91, 1981.

[11] Lee, K.Y. and A. El-Sharkawi Mohamed (eds.). *Modern Heuristic Optimization Techniques: Theory and Applications to Power Systems*, vol. 39, New York, NY: John Wiley & Sons, 2008.

[12] Framinan, J.M., N.D.G. Jatinder, and R. Leisten. A review and classification of heuristics for permutation flow-shop scheduling with makespan objective. *Journal of the Operational Research Society*, 55(12), 1243–1255, 2004.

[13] Christofides, N. and S. Eilon. Algorithms for large-scale traveling salesman problems. *Journal of the Operational Research Society*, 23(4), 511–518, 1972.

[14] Lourenço, H.R., O.C. Martin, and T. Stützle. *Iterated Local Search*, New York, NY: Springer US, 2003.

[15] Voudouris, C., P.K.T. Edward, and A. Alsheddy. Guided local search. In *Handbook of Metaheuristics*, Boston, MA: Springer, pp. 321–361, 2010.

[16] Glover, F. Tabu search: a tutorial. *Interfaces*, 20(4), 74–94, 1990.

[17] Mirjalili, S. Genetic algorithm. In *Evolutionary Algorithms and Neural Networks: Theory and Applications*, Cham: Springer, pp. 43–55, 2019.

[18] Dorigo, M., M. Birattari, and T. Stutzle. Ant colony optimization. *IEEE Computational Intelligence Magazine*, 1(4), 28–39, 2006.

[19] Kennedy, J. and R. Eberhart. Particle swarm optimization. In *Proceedings of ICNN'95 – International Conference on Neural Networks*, vol. 4, pp. 1942–1948, IEEE, 1995.

[20] Karaboga, D. and B. Akay. A comparative study of artificial bee colony algorithm. *Applied Mathematics and Computation,* 214(1), 108–132, 2009.

[21] Entner, D., P. Fleck, T. Vosgien, *et al.* A systematic approach for the selection of optimization algorithms including end-user requirements applied to box-type boom crane design. *Applied System Innovation*, 2, 20, 2019. 10.3390/asi2030020.

[22] Stojanović, I., I. Brajević, P.S. Stanimirović, L.A. Kazakovtsev, and Z. Zdravev. Application of heuristic and metaheuristic algorithms in solving constrained weber problem with feasible region bounded by arcs. *Mathematical Problems in Engineering*, 2017, Article ID 8306732, 13 pages, 2017. https://doi.org/10.1155/2017/8306732

[23] Venter, G. Review of Optimization Techniques, 2010. 10.1002/9780470686652. eae495.

Chapter 2

Nature-inspired optimization algorithm: an in-depth view

Ankit Gambhir[1], Ajit Kumar Verma[2], Ashish Payal[3] and Rajeev Kumar Arya[4]

This chapter deals in an in-depth view of nature-inspired optimization algorithms. It provides a comprehensive overview of optimization methods influenced by nature. It also reflects the ideal search for the optimum nature-inspired algorithm. The general categorization of such algorithms is demonstrated in this chapter. Analysis and various classes of nature-inspired algorithms are revealed in detail. Various optimization algorithms such as evolutionary algorithm and genetic algorithm; bio-inspired algorithm such as particle swarm optimization (PSO), ant colony optimization (ACO), bat algorithm, and crow search algorithm; bio-inspired algorithm but not swarm intelligence such as water cycle algorithm (WCA) and mine blast algorithm; chemistry-based algorithm; physics-based algorithm; and many other algorithms are extensively surveyed in the general framework and strategies for efficiency improvement are reviewed in detail in this chapter. In addition, the distinctions between single-objective and multi-objective problems are discussed in detail. Lastly, the application of such algorithms and concluding remarks are presented.

2.1 Introduction to nature-inspired algorithm

Numerous scientists, academics, and academicians have been inspired by nature in a variety of ways, making it an abundant foundation of motivation. Currently, many novel algorithms are inspired by nature, as these were produced by emulating nature's inspiration [1]. Numerous applications in the real world involve the optimization of diverse objectives, such as the minimizing consumption of energy and expenses and maximizing performance and efficiency [2].

[1]Delhi Technical Campus, India
[2]Western Norway University of Applied Sciences, Norway
[3]Guru Gobind Singh Indraprastha University, India
[4]National Institute of Technology – Patna, India

The optimization algorithms that imitate the behavior of natural and biological systems are referred to as nature-inspired algorithms. These algorithms are also known as intelligent optimization algorithms or nature-inspired metaheuristic algorithms. Heuristic algorithms generate innovative solutions through trial and error, but meta-heuristic algorithms employ memory and other forms of knowledge and strategy. These algorithms are well-known, efficient methods for handling a variety of challenging optimization issues [2]. Consequently, the vast majority of natural algorithms are bio-inspired. Over a hundred distinct algorithms and variants are existing today. There are many classification levels for highlighting the source of inspiration. For convenience, we employ the most evolved sources, such as biology, physics, and chemistry [3].

2.2   Search for an ideal algorithm

Real-world optimization issues are extremely exigent to address, and numerous systems need to cope with them. For addressing such issues various optimization tools must be employed, despite the fact that there is no assurance that an optimal solution can be obtained. Optimization is an emerging field of study that provides optimal solutions to complex real problems. Despite much research and advancements, there are still a number of difficulties and limitations with nature-inspired algorithms [4–6]. A few of these concerns are highlighted below:

1. Absence of a coherent mathematical framework and a lack of an in-depth understanding of how and at what rate such algorithms may converge.
2. There are numerous nature-inspired algorithms, and their comparative analyses are primarily based on numerical experiments or simulation models on a certain set of performance criteria; hence, it is difficult to demonstrate that such comparisons are always objective.
3. Since the majority of research focuses on small-scale problems, it is uncertain if these approaches may scale up to large-scale optimization problems.
4. It is also unclear what the prerequisites are for the development of swarming and intelligent behavior.

2.3   Extensive review of nature-inspired algorithm

Some of the most significant nature-inspired algorithms are PSO based on swarm intelligence, genetic algorithms (GA) [7,8], and differential evolution [9] based on evolution, PSO based on flocks of a bird moving in search of food [10,11], ACO [12] based on intelligent behavior of ants, firefly algorithm (FFA) [13] based on intelligent behavior of firefly, cuckoo search algorithm (CSA) [14] inspired by search intelligence of cuckoo, harmony search [15] based on the pursuit of the ideal harmony is the goal of music, artificial bee colony (ABC) [16] chicken swarm optimization [17] based on the foraging actions of a chicken swarm that had been partitioned into several different subgroups based on the intelligence of bee, glowworm algorithm (GWA) [18] mimics the behavior of glow worms. Bat

Table 2.1 Chronology of optimization algorithm

Year	Optimization algorithm
1975	GA
1992	ACO
1995	PSO
1996	Differential evolution
2001	Harmony search
2005	ABC
2007	FFA
2009	CSA
2010	BA
2012	WCA
2012	FPA
2013	Mine blast algorithm
2015	Water wave optimization

algorithm (BA) [19] based on behavior of bats, flower pollination algorithm (FPA) [20] based on biological evolution of plants, WCA [21] inspired by the nature's process of evaporation, condensation, and precipitation. Mine blast algorithm [22] based on the mine bomb explosion concept, water wave optimization [23] inspired by the shallow water wave theory, to find the optimal solution these algorithms are significantly used. Initially, the search space is a randomly initialized population. For every round, present population is swapped by a newly created population. Table 2.1 reflects the chronological timeline of various nature-inspired algorithms.

2.4 Analysis of nature-inspired algorithms

These algorithms possess three major features, as shown in Table 2.2 [3]:

(a) Investigation (population initiation and global/local search)
(b) Adaption and adjustment (randomness)
(c) Key operators (selection, mutation, crossover, and algorithm formulas)

Table 2.2 Analysis of nature-inspired algorithms

S. no.	Component	Role
1	Population	Population contain samples, performs both local and worldwide searches
2	Randomness	Adjustment as per global and local search. Also get far from local minima
3	Selection	Vital constituents for convergence
4	Mutation, crossover, and algorithmic formulas	Create new solutions and their assessment iteratively

2.5   Classes of optimization algorithm

Nature-inspired algorithms apply to a broader range of problems without the need for specialized knowledge. Nature-inspired algorithms, unlike classical algorithms, are typically designed for global search. Heuristic algorithms generate innovative solutions through trial and error, but metaheuristic algorithms employ memory and other forms of knowledge and strategy. These algorithms are well-known, effective techniques for dealing with a variety of complex optimization problems [5,6].

A heuristic is a rational strategy for logically moving through the solution space to generate an estimated solution in a stipulated time. However, on the other hand, the prime objective of a metaheuristic is to unearth a global optimum. These algorithms are mainly inspired by nature.

Heuristic algorithms are rather informed search technique, which analytically investigates a state space; on the other hand metaheuristic comprises two or more orders, such that the overall seeking performance keeps fluctuating while surveying the state space. As opposed to the problem-independent approach used by meta-heuristics, the heuristic approach relies on the experience of previous solutions to arrive at the best possible one [1].

2.6   General classification of nature-inspired algorithms

Classifications of nature depend on the actual perspective and motivations. Nature-inspired algorithms can be broken down into several different categories according to their primary point of inspiration from the natural world (Figure 2.1).

- Evolutionary algorithms
- Bio-inspired algorithms
- Bio-inspired but not swarm intelligence-based algorithms
- Algorithms based on chemistry and physics
- Additional algorithms

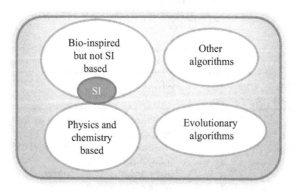

Figure 2.1   Classification of nature-inspired algorithms

It is pertinent to mention that the classification presented here is not exclusive as some algorithms could also be classified into distinct categories at the same time as classification mainly depends on emphasis and perspective.

2.7 Evolutionary algorithms

Evolutionary algorithm (EA) replicates Darwin's idea of evolution. They are founded on the natural law of evolution. In each generation, the fittest individual is chosen. The population of individuals and their representation, the fitness function, the parent selection mechanism, crossover and mutation operators, the survivor selection mechanism (replacement), and the initialization and termination condition procedures are their constituent parts. Evolutionary algorithms select the fittest members of the current population to continue to the next generation. In the sections that follow, we'll break down some of the most notable algorithms that use natural evolution as their foundation.

2.7.1 Genetic algorithm

John Holland invented genetic algorithm (GA) in 1975 using binary representations of individuals [7]. It mimics the process of natural selection, in which only those organisms that can adapt to changes in their ecosystem survive and reproduce. In straightforward terms, they assume "survival of the fittest" amid successive generations. Each generation consists of a population of people, and each person symbolizes a point in the search space and a potential answer [8].

GA is based on the chromosomal performance and genetic structure similarity among populations. Following are the GA foundation:

- Individuals within a population compete for resources and mates
- Individuals who are prosperous (healthiest) mate to produce more progeny than others
- The "fittest" parent's genes proliferate across the generation
- Thus, each succeeding generation is better adapted to its ecosystem

Each individual is assigned a fitness score that reflects his or her ability to "compete." The individual with the highest (or nearly ideal) fitness score is obtained.

The GA maintains the population (chromosomes/solutions) and fitness scores. Individuals with higher fitness scores have greater reproductive opportunities than those with lower fitness scores. There must be room created for incoming residents because the population size is predetermined. Therefore, once all available mating chances in the existing population have been used up, some people pass away and are replaced by newcomers, giving rise to a new generation [8].

Each next generation has more "superior genes" than its predecessor. Consequently, each innovative generation has better "partial solutions" than its predecessors. The population is converged when progenies produced have no significant differences from progenies produced by preceding populations. The algorithm is eventually transformed into a set of solutions for the problem.

2.7.2 Differential evolution

Storn and Price introduced the algorithm in 1996 [9]. For nonlinear optimization issues, it is a population-based stochastic optimization approach. It only makes a few, if any, assumptions about the core optimization issue and is capable of quickly examining enormous strategy spaces. One of the most flexible and trustworthy population-based search algorithms, differential evolution (DE) demonstrates the robustness of multimodal problems.

The main benefit of standard DE is that only three control settings need to be changed. The trial vector generation method and the control settings used have a significant impact on the performance of DE in a specific optimization problem. One must first select a trial vector generation approach and then adjust the control parameters of the optimization problem in order to achieve desirable optimization results. Finding the ideal values for the control parameters is often difficult, time-consuming, and complex, especially for particular challenging circumstances [9]

2.8 Bio-inspired algorithms

These algorithms are based on certain admirable characteristics of the biological system (Figure 2.2). These algorithms are further divided into two categories: bio-inspired algorithms based on swarm intelligence and bio-inspired algorithms that are not based on swarm Intelligence [10] (Figure 2.3).

2.8.1 Swarm intelligence-based bio-inspired algorithms

Swarm algorithms have been magnetizing great interest in the last two decades and got enormous recognition. There are many reasons for such acknowledgment and attention. Two major reasons are: (a) these algorithms are adaptable and

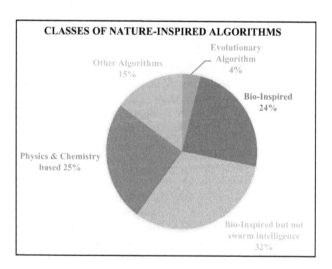

Figure 2.2   Classes of bio-inspired algorithms

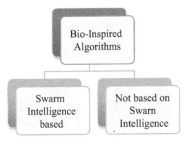

Figure 2.3   Classes of bio-inspired algorithms

multipurpose; (b) they are very competent in solving nonlinear design problems. This section discusses the mathematical context of the algorithms, without covering mathematical proofs of these algorithms. Just to aid the reader to comprehend a particular optimization algorithm. Further, techniques have been explored to improve these algorithms for better results.

Swarm intelligence relates to the cooperative, emerging performance of several, cooperating agents who track some simple guidelines. By the inspiration from swarm behavior in nature, various swarm algorithms have been developing in the last decades. The swarm agents are the core concept of the swarm algorithm. However, every agent might be treated as obtuse. The comprehensive association of various agents might display some self-organization pattern. Moreover, this can act like some kind of supportive intelligence. Self-organization and disseminated control are astonishing elements of swarm systems in nature, leading to an emit behavior. Arise from native communication among the system agents is known as emit behavior and it is unlikely to be accomplished by any of the agents of the system performing unaided.

The collective behavior of natural agents, like particles, pollens of flower's, bees, and fish have been used to design the multi-agent system. Since 1991, swarm-based algorithms have been proposed by adopting distinctive swarm behaviors of ants, particles, flies, bees, cats, etc. These algorithms are formulated by mimicking the intelligent behavior of the organisms like fishes, fireflies, ants, bees, birds, and bats. A huge number of algorithms come under this group. Such kinds of algorithms are mostly population-based stimulated by the cooperative behavior of social insects as well as animal societies some algorithms such as PSO, FFA, and CSA [10–19]. This section explores various types of multi-agent systems known as metaheuristics and focuses on swarm-based algorithms only. The standard PSO [11] adopts the collective behavior of birds, while the FFA [13] focuses on the flashing behavior of fireflies. However, BA [19] uses the echolocation of foraging bats. Swarm algorithms are the widely held and widely used algorithms for various optimization problems. There are several reasons for such attractiveness: firstly, swarm algorithms commonly share information between multiple agents; secondly, several agents can be parallelized naturally so that complex optimization turns out to be more practical as per the implementation scenario. Several well-known swarm algorithms have been explained in this subsection to understand their brief mathematical background and list out the well-known variant of every algorithm.

These algorithms have produced better results for most of the problems and hence grabbed the attention of investigators, while some other algorithms have had enquiries raised on their presence due to insignificant results or less visibility to a majority of authors. A few of them are elaborated in next section. Most of the researched swarm algorithms are listed below regardless of their recognition. Twenty-five algorithms are listed in Table 2.3 and shown in Figure 2.4, mentioning name of founder/author/ pioneer, the year of development, behavior pattern of swarm, and the number of citations from Google Scholar. However, a higher number of citations of an algorithm do not directly translate to a better capability of that algorithm.

Table 2.3   Year-wise citation of bio-inspired swarm-based algorithms

S. no.	Algorithm	Author	Year	Citations
1	ACO	Colorni *et al.* [12]	1991	3,989
2	PSO	Eberhart and Kennedy [11]	1995	12,958
3	HS	Geem *et al.* [15]	2001	4,017
4	ABC	Karaboga [16]	2005	4,731
5	FFA	Yang [13]	2008	3,035
6	CSA	Yang [14]	2009	3,034
7	BA	Yang [19]	2009	2,086
8	Chicken swarm optimization	Xianbing Meng *et al.* [17]	2014	563

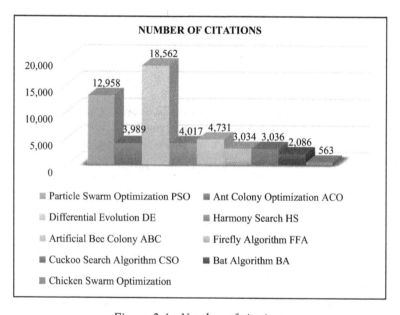

Figure 2.4   Number of citations

2.8.1.1 PSO

This algorithm is inspired by nature whose basis is swarm intelligence. Observing the behavior of a swarm of birds seeking food leads to the manifestation of PSO [11]. The primary objective of the method is to determine the particle locations which will yield the optimal solution of the specified cost function. The PSO algorithm is based on the examination of a group of birds, in which a bird that has located food will guide the others to the food source [24].

The initialization is arbitrary, and multiple iterations are then performed, with the particles position and velocity getting updated at the completion of each iteration [25].

Algorithm for PSO

1. Initialize a S particle with arbitrarily chosen CHs
   $Xij(0) = (x\ i,j(0)\ ,\ y\ i,j(0))$
   The placement of the sensor nodes
2. Determine each particle cost function:
   (a) $\forall ki, i = 1,2,\ldots,N$
       Calculate the distance d (ki,CHp,q) between nodes ki and nodes CHp, q..
       Assign node kii to CHp,q:
       $d(ki,CHp,\ q) = min\ q\ 1,2,\ldots,\ \{d(ki,CHp,q)\ \}$
   (b) Calculate the cost function:
       cost function = $.C1 + (1-a).C2$
       $C1 = max\ q = 1,2,\ldots,q\ \{\ \Sigma d(ki,CHp,\ q)/CHp,q\ \}$
       $C2=i=1NE(ki)/\ q=1QE(CHp,q)$
3. Find the local and global optimal conditions for each particle
4. Alter the position and velocity of the particle by
   $Vid\ (t) = W.Vid\ (t) + L1.\ H1\ (Pbestid - Xid\ (t)+ L2.H2(Gbest-Xid(t))$
   $Xid(t)=Xid(t-1)+Vid\ (t)$
   Or
   $Vid\ (t+1) = W.Vid\ (t-1) + L1.H1\ (Pbestid - Xid\ (t-1)+ L2.H2\ (Gbest-Xid(t-1))$
   $Xid(t+1)=Xid(t)+Vid(t+1)$

Where V and X represent the velocity and position of the particle, respectively, t represents time, L1 and L2 stand for learning factors or acceleration coefficients, 1 and 2 are arbitrary values between 0 and 1, W is the inertia weight such that $(0<W<1)$, and Pbestid and Gbest are particle's best and global position.

Until a satisfactory value for the global position best is reached, the procedure of updating V and X is repeated (Gbest). The particle then uses the below equations to recalculate Pbestid and Gbest based on the cost function.

Pbestid = Pid if cost function of Pi<cost function of Pbesti
Pbestid   else
Gbest = Pid if cost function of Pi<cost function of Gbest
Gbest   else

5. The closest (x,y) coordinates are used to re-map the new locations.

Repeat steps 2–5 until the maximum number of iterations has been reached.

2.8.1.2   ABC optimization

An example of a bio-inspired algorithm is the ABC optimization algorithm. Honey bee behavior is used as a basis for the model [16]. Workers, observers, and scouts are the three types of bees. Half of the colony initially consists of worker bees, while the other half consists of observer bees. Bees with a job are tasked with finding new food sources in the area and spreading the word to their fellow bees. An observer bee follows a new arrival from the area where food is plentiful. The term "Scout bee" refers to a certain species of bee that searches for food in a random fashion. When the nectar supply from a new source is greater than that of the previous source, the worker bees will switch to the new source. Observer bees, after exhausting all other options, settle on the food source with the highest likelihood and relocate it. The contest between the new and old cost functions is maintained, with the best solution being saved until the maximum number of cycles has been reached [24,26]. The procedure for the algorithm is as follows.

1. Generate the starting population Yi, i = 1...M
2. Determine the population
3. Set the cycle's value equal to 1; repeat
   (a) For each employed bee in the workforce,
       (i)   Create new solutions Ki by
             Kij= yij + αij (yij-ykj)
       (ii) Where α is an arbitrary number between [−1,1], Ki is candidate solution, yi is present solution, and yk is neighbor solution
             j = {1,2...N}
       (iii) Examine the price function
       (iv) Execute the greedy selection process

   (b) For every onlooker bee
       (i)   Select a solution yi on the basis of Gi
       (ii) Gi = CSi / k = 1MCSk
       (iii) Where CSi is the cost function of solution i, M = number of food source = number of employed bee
       (iv) Find new solutions Ki by
       (v)   Kij = yij + αij (yij - ykj)
       (vi) Determine the cost function and apply the greedy selection procedure. If a solution exists, we can replace it with the scout's finding, i.e.,
       (vii) yij = yj min + arb(0,1) (yj max − yj min)
             j = {1,2...N}
       where, N is the dimension of the solution vector.

4. Construct the most effective solution until.
       Cycle = cycle + 1, cycle = maximum cycle number.

2.8.1.3 Chicken swarm optimization

It is also a bio-inspired swarm-based algorithm that was developed by studying the foraging actions of a chicken swarm that had been partitioned into several different subgroups, as shown in Figure 2.2. Every single individual in each subgroup worked their way closer and closer to the ideal one [17]. Rooster involves the uppermost position in the hierarchical order, as they possess the finest food-searching capacity. The roosters will likewise battle with different chickens who attack their region. Hens possess the subsequent position and they obey their gathering mate roosters in the food-hunting procedure [27]. There is likewise rivalry among the chickens in the food-searching process. Chicks possess the most reduced position and they follow their mom while searching for food. In this way, the chickens arrange themselves in the food-hunting procedure. This natural conduct of chickens is related to the competence to optimize the problem. To encourage the depiction of CSO, we have to idealize the conduct of the group [28].

1. Few gatherings of chickens in the swarm of chickens. Each gathering of chickens incorporates a rooster, various hens, and various chickens.
2. As per the fitness value of the chicken, chicken is affirmed as a rooster, a hen, and a chicken.

$$\mu^2 = \begin{cases} 1 & \text{If } fm \leq fk \\ \dfrac{fk - fm}{e^{|fm + \in|}} & else \end{cases}$$

We expect some portion of the finest fitness value as a rooster, i.e., leader of a gathering, and the piece of the most noticeably worst fitness as the chicken, and the different as a hen, hen arbitrarily joining a gathering, chicken arbitrarily discover a hen as a mother.

3. The chicken follows a gathering of partners to discover food, they may need to avert other chicken to have their possessed food, and chicken are additionally liable to eat food, which has not been found by them but other chicken [29].

The algorithm depends on the following presumptions:

- The quantity of hens is most elevated in the gathering.
- All the hens do not hatch eggs together. Only some hens are mother hens.
- The mother hens are chosen arbitrarily from the arrangement of hens.
- There is a difference between the number of chicks and hens.

Mathematical modeling is shown below.

Rooster position update:

$$X_{m,n}^{t+1} = X_{m,n}^t * \left(1 + randn\left(0, \mu^2\right)\right)$$

Where $k \in [1,$ Number of rooster node], $k \neq m$ and X_{mn} denotes the position of rooster m in nth dimension during t and $t + 1$ itertion, $randn(0, \mu^2)$ is Gaussian random variable with variance μ^2 (which is a small constant) and mean value is 0. fm is the fitness value for the subsequent rooster m. $\in$ is a low value constant.

Hens' position update:

$$X_{m,n}^{t+1} = X_{m,n}^t + K1 \, randn\left(X_{p1,n}^t - X_{m,n}^t\right) + K2 \, randn\left(X_{p2,n}^t - X_{m,n}^t\right)$$

Where

$$K1 = e^{\frac{fm-fp1}{|fm+\in|}}$$

$$K2 = e^{fp2-fm}$$

p1 is the index of a rooster, and p2 is a chicken from the group that can be a hen or rooster and a uniform random number between 0 and 1 generated by *randn*.

Chicks' position update:

$$X_{m,n}^{t+1} = X_{m,n}^t + AB\left(X_{q,n}^t - X_{m,n}^t\right)$$

$X_{m,n}^t$ denotes position of chicken's mother, AB is arbitrary number between 0 and 2 to obtain the optimum position.

2.8.1.4   ACO

Dorigo first suggested ACO in his PhD thesis in 1992 [12]. The swarming nature established by ACO is modeled after ant colonies. It provides a sufficient solution to the engineering optimization issue. Ants typically leave behind pheromone trails that lead one another to food sources as they scout the area. The stimulated or computer-generated "ants" also keep track of their locations and the qualities of their resolves, enabling additional ants in later simulation cycles to find better solutions. Artificial "ants" navigate within a constrained location while displaying all potential resolutions to find the best possible resolutions [30]. It demonstrates the ACO pseudo code, which calls for two-step calculations.

Create ants solutions as shown in equation below.

To understand the mathematics of ACO, let us consider probability p_{ab}^k of an ant to move from a state to b state.

$$p_{ab}^k = \frac{\left(M_{ab}^\alpha\right)\left(N_{ab}^\beta\right)}{\sum_{z\varepsilon}\left(M_{ac}^\alpha\right)\left(N_{ac}^\beta\right)}$$

Update pheromones:

$$M_{ab}^{new} \leftarrow E.M_{ab}^{old} + \sum_{k=1}^{j}\triangle M_{ab}^k$$

where M_{ab} is the amount of pheromone deposited for a state transition ab, E is the pheromone evaporation coefficient.

$\triangle M_{ab}^k$ is the amount of pheromone deposited by kth ant.

Pseudo code of ACO

Objective function (a), $a = (a_1, ... a_n)^T$

Describe pheromone rate evaporation rate γ

while (Max_number_of_iteration)

{

*for*loop_over_all_n_dimensions

{

Generate novel solutions using Equation

Calculate the newly generated solutions

Revise pheromone using Equation (3.2)

}

Find out the current best

}

Output the finest results and pheromone dispersal.

2.8.1.5   FFA

The flashing pattern of tropical fireflies serves as the basis for the FFA. It was created in 2007 by Xin-She Yang [13]. This algorithm applied three fundamental rules. First, because fireflies have no sexual preference, they are all attracted to each other. Second, when the distance between fireflies grows, the attraction, which is proportionate to the luminosity, decreases. The less bright firefly will therefore move toward the more brightly lit one for any pair of flashing fireflies. Last but not the least, a firefly's brightness is determined by how the objective function is perceived, and brightness is correlated with the cost of the objective function [31–33].

Pseudo Code of Firefly Algorithm

Objective function (a), $a = (a1, ... ad)^t$

Reset algorithm parameters:

MaxGen: the maximal number of generations

∂: the light absorption coefficient

ω: the particular distance from the light source

d: the domain space

Generate the initial population of fireflies or ai ($i = 1, 2, ..., k$)

calculate the intensity of light íi at ai via f(ai)

while ($t < Max\_number\_of\_iteration$)

{

for i = 1 *to* k

{

for j = 1 *to* k

{

If (íj > íi

{

Move firefly *i* towards *j* by using Equation

Attractiveness changes as a function of distance ω via $e^{-\partial\omega^2}$

Assess novel solutions and update the intensity of light

}

}

reorder the fireflies according to intensity of light and find the value current fitness function;

}

Output the best results.

$$a_i^t = a_i^t + \beta 0 e^{-\partial\omega^2}(aj - ai) + \alpha\varepsilon_i$$

2.8.1.6   CSA

This method is based on the cuckoo parasites' breeding behavior. These natural processes are ingrained by the algorithm [14].

In this algorithm, a few following presumptions are made:

Assumption 1: One egg is laid by a cuckoo at a time, and it is then dropped into a different nest each time.

Assumption 2: The nest that produces the highest caliber eggs will be passed down to succeeding generations.

Assumption 3: The number of host nests is fixed, and each nest holds only one egg.

Assumption 4: There is a pa chance that the host bird will find a foreign egg.

A cuckoo egg stands for a fresh solution, and each nest represents a solution. The algorithm's goal is to employ novel, possibly superior solutions [34,35]. Pseudo Code of CSO:

Objective function (x), $x = (x_1, \ldots \ldots x_n)^T$

Generate initial population of *n* host nests x_i

while (*t* < *Max_number_of_iteration*)

{

t=t+1

Get a cuckoo that has been randomly created using Levy's flights as a solution, and then assess its fitness function (i.e., F_i).

$F_i > F_j$

Replace j by new solution.

The worst nets are uncontrolled to a certain degree (pa), and new ones are generated.

Maintain the best nests. g^*. }

Output the best results g^* and x^{t+1}.

2.8.2   *Variants of swarm algorithms*

Table 2.4 is a presented list of swarm algorithms. Using a variety of methods, such as parameter tweaking, Gaussian distribution, Levy's distribution, chaotic distribution, and others, one can find a better version of any swarm algorithm. New swarm algorithms that consider changing swarm behaviors have been developed since the original swarm algorithm was created and are still in use today [36]. Additionally, several aspects of the above-discussed methods are already present in these algorithms [37]. For instance, Levy's flight distribution is used by the FPA and the BA, respectively [38]. Any algorithm that has been hybridized has been done so primarily to increase performance. The performance of swarm algorithms has been improved using a variety of methods.

The mathematical structure of the algorithm has a significant impact on the choice of a swarm algorithm and the corresponding improvement technique [39]. For instance, whereas FPA can be searched both locally and globally, it may become snared in a local optimum. The use of chaotic distribution can make this better.

Following an examination of swarm algorithms and their variations, the following conclusion has been reached:

1. Only a small number of the many developed swarm algorithms have been the focus of additional study.
2. Techniques including parameter adjustment, Levy's distribution, chaotic distribution, and Gaussian distribution have all been shown to improve algorithm performance.
3. The mathematical structure of the algorithm has a significant impact on the performance of a swarm algorithm and each version.

2.8.3   *Bio-inspired but not swarm intelligence based*

2.8.3.1   FPA

In order to improve the ability of optimization algorithms to explore in global space, Yang employed the pollination concept in optimization problems in 2012 [40]. Pollination is the process by which plants reproduce and are fertilized. It entails transferring pollen, a sticky substance made from the flower's male stamen, to the stigma (i.e., top of female part called PISTIL). Pollinating agents like the wind, animals (such as insects, birds, and bats), or the plant itself can spread pollen. Stamen and filament are collectively referred to as such, and pistil refers to the stigma, style, ovary, and ovules [41]. In nature, flower pollination serves to promote plant reproduction and the survival of the fittest.

Table 2.4 Summary of swarm-based nature-inspired algorithms

S. no.	Algorithm	Author	Year	Behavior
1	ACO	Colorni et al. [12]	1991	In order to solve discrete optimization issues or problems with unknown solutions, a colony of artificial ants collaborates or works together.
2	PSO	Eberhart and Kennedy [10]	1995	Interaction of the particles in the swarm.
3	HS	Geem et al. [15]	2001	The pursuit of the ideal harmony is the goal of music.
4	ABC	Karaboga [16]	2005	Based on honey bees' clever foraging techniques.
5	FFA	Yang [13]	2008	A firefly's flash serves as a signaling mechanism to draw in other fireflies.
6	CSA	Yang [14]	2009	Inspired by the eco-location of bats. Inspired by the obligate brood parasitism of some cuckoo species, which deposit their eggs in the nests of other host birds (of different species).
7	BA	Yang [19]	2009	Inspired by the eco location of bats.
8	Chicken swarm algorithm	Xianbing Meng et al. [17]	2014	Dividing the hens into several subgroups and watching the foraging behavior of the swarm.
9	Glow worm swarm optimization (GWSO)	Krishnanand and Ghose [18]	2005	Mimics the behavior of glow worms.
10	Wasp swarm algorithm (WSA)	Pinto [68]	2007	Wasp colonies establish a hierarchy among themselves through communication among the individuals.
11	Lion optimization algorithm (LOA)	Wang et al. [69]	2012	Lion prides promote the principle of group living and evolution.
12	Spider monkey algorithm	Bansal et al. [70]	2014	Stimulates spider monkeys' foraging behavior.
13	Whale optimization algorithm (WOA)	Mirjalili and Lewis [71]	2016	Mimics humpback whales' social behavior.
14	Wolf pack algorithm	Hu-Sheng et al. [72]	2014	To find prey on the Tibetan Plateau, the wolf pack joins forces and collaborates closely.

With reference to natural processes, FPA can be idealized as follows: self-pollination is seen as local pollination, whereas cross pollination is regarded as global pollination. Both local and global pollination are governed by a switch probability, p. The value of p is affected by variables like wind and pollinator availability, among others.

2.9 Physics- and chemistry-based algorithm

2.9.1 WCA

Engineering problems have been sorted using conventional search methods for the past few decades. Numerous promising algorithms have produced promising outcomes. In 2012, Hadi Eskandar *et al.* [21] proposed WCA. The fundamental principle of WCA is inspired by nature and motivated by the natural water cycle process, which includes how streams and rivers are formed and water drains to the sea. It simulates the evaporation, condensation, and precipitation processes that make up the fundamental hydrological cycle. In the atmosphere, water evaporates to create clouds, which then further condenses to produce rain and release water back onto the land. We refer to this as precipitation. If a river does not enter the sea, every time two streams converge, they create a new, higher order stream. On constrained benchmark issues and engineering design optimization, WCA is also validated. The idea of evaporation rate for rivers and streams is also considered in WCA in some articles. WCA's comprehensive MATLAB codes were presented in [42]. Additionally, it is used to solve issues that are confined and uncontrolled. The stated results were highly encouraging. WCA's comprehensive review were presented in [43].

2.10 Application of nature-inspired optimization algorithm on constraints engineering problem

2.10.1 Nature-inspired optimization algorithm (NIOA)-based clustering routing protocols

Engineering constraint issues were reformulated throughout the past 10 years using optimization methods that were influenced by nature. Many encouraging computations have found potential results (Figure 2.5). Numerous bio-inspired algorithms have been discovered to execute competitively on a variety of optimization problems in recent study.

Figure 2.5 Application of NIOA in WSN

Tillet *et al.* [44] have provided the first study based on the application of evolutionary algorithms on cluster head selection. PSO has been used for cluster head (CH) detection.

It is an evolutionary algorithm technique in which test answers are allowed to interact and work together to find the optimal answer to the problem at hand, much like a natural swarm of birds. The wireless sensor network (WSN) algorithm can be broken down into three logical parts. The clusters are produced in the first section. Each cluster's cluster heads are chosen in the second section. The third section assigns cluster heads to each of the network's nodes. Each phase in this situation uses PSO. A succinct overview of the use of PSO in WSN to handle a variety of difficulties, including optimal deployment, node localization, clustering, and data aggregation, was presented by Kulkarni *et al.* [45]. An energy-efficient CH selection approach based on PSO has been presented by Srinivasa Rao *et al.* [46], employing an effective particle model and fitness function. They have taken into account a number of factors, including residual energy, intra-cluster distance, and sink distance, for the energy efficiency of the suggested approach. The technique was tested using several WSN scenarios, sensor node counts, and CHs. By utilizing the PSO-based methodology within the cluster as opposed to the base station, Buddha Singh *et al.* [47] had transformed it into a semi-distributed method. Their suggested method's main goal is to locate the head nodes close to the cluster density's center. On the basis of the optimal CH position, they have also calculated the estimated distance travelled by packet transmission from node to BS. Additionally, they have computed the anticipated number of retransmissions along the path to CH and examined the impact of link failure. Last but not the least, power computation is performed to assess the energy savings, and the results are compared with LEACH-C and procedures.

Latiff *et al.* [48] defined a new cost function in their research titled "Energy-aware clustering for wireless sensor networks using particle swarm optimization." The proposed protocol creates clusters evenly distributed over the whole WSN field by choosing a high-energy node as the CH.

To determine the maximum quality thresholding potential for cluster generation in WSNs, Jenn-Long Liu *et al.* [49] developed a genetic algorithm (GA)-based entirely adaptive clustering procedure. The results of the simulation show that the most likely distribution closely reflects the analytical conclusions made by the authors' updated formulas. Given that it uses the most effective probability, power-efficient clustering algorithm, the suggested LEACH-GA method exceeds LEACH in terms of network lifetime.

Complex combinatorial problems can be solved using swarm intelligence techniques like ACO [50]. It is a cleverly devised approach for resolving challenging integration issues. To resolve the routing issue in sensor networks, Tiago Camilo, Carlos Carreto, and others [51] discovered the usefulness of the Ant Colony Optimization metaheuristic. The energy-efficient ant-based routing (EEABR) protocol finds paths between nerves and node nodes using "lightweight" ants, which can be improved by grade and energy levels. The experimental findings demonstrated that the set of rules produces excellent outcomes in various WSNs

A novel WSN router operating protocol was introduced by Selcuk Okdem *et al.* [52]. The protocol is implemented by offering a potent multi-course data transfer technique and using the ACO algorithm to enhance route paths and obtain dependable connections in the event of node faults. The suggested approach is contrasted with EEABR, an event-based template-based set of fashion ant-based rules. The results show that their approach significantly reduces the amount of energy consumed, which is utilized as a performance indicator for unique-sized WSNs.

The improvement of artificial bee colonies is suggested by Karaboga *et al.* [53]. Bees are divided into three groups: employed, spectator, and scout. In the beginning, one type of bee—an employed bee—makes up half of the colony, and another—an onlooker bee—makes up the other half. Employed bees scout out potential food sources in the area and advise curious bees of new food sources. According to the knowledge they have, spectator bees search for a fresh one in the vicinity of food supplies that are nearby. A scout bee is a bee that searches at random. Employed bees switch to a new food source if the new food source's nectar content is greater than the previous one. After conducting all possible searches, observer bees select the food source with the highest probability and move it to a new location. Up until the maximum number of cycles is reached, the cost function of the new one is compared to the old one, and the best solution is stored.

In their article, "A comprehensive survey: ABC algorithm and applications," Dervis Karaboga *et al.* [54] gave a thorough assessment of the application of ABC in numerous disciplines.

PSO with time variable acceleration constants, hierarchical PSO with time varying acceleration constants, PSO with time varying inertia weight, and PSO with supervisor student mode are the four PSO variations that Guru *et al.* [55] presented for energy aware clustering. In wireless sensor networks, four PSO techniques were used to group sensors into clusters. Based on integration criteria, it operates. The inertia w weight drops in line during the correction from 0.9 during the first multiplication to 0.4 during the last repetition. The PSO determines the inertia gravity in the acceleration times, and the acceleration constants c1 and c2 change sequentially throughout the multiplication, causing the particles to travel in huge steps at first but then smaller steps in each repetition.

Various authors have applied PSO in various areas of WSN.

- PSO in node deployment
- PSO in node localization
- PSO in energy aware clustering
- PSO in data aggression

Brief summaries of various well-known nature-inspired algorithms used in clustering routing protocols are shown in Table 2.5.

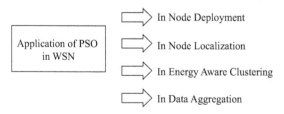

Figure 2.6 Application of PSO in WSN

Table 2.5   Summary of some of the prominent NIOA applied on clustering routing protocols

S. no.	Author	Optimization algorithm used	Available information	Year
1	Tillet et al. [73]	PSO	Reduces energy consumption and speeds up data transfer Use of basic PSO	2003
2	Latiff et al. [74]	PSO	1. Established a new cost function. 2. Clusters are evenly distributed	2011
3	Guru et al. [55]	Variant of PSO	Only the physical distance between the CH and node is considered for application of PSO	2005
4	Yubin Xu et al. [75]	PSO	Improve the LEACH-based method. Improve clustering and identify the CH node	2011
5	Thilagavathi et al. [76]	PSO	1. Performance evaluation of LEACH in WSNs 2. Optimal number of clusters and cluster head	2015
6	Cao et al. [77]	PSO	Shown an analysis of CH election for multi-hop communication	2008
7	Jin et al. [78]	GA	Clustering teaches about the sensor network's communication distance	2003
8	Hussain et al. [79]	GA	1. Energy-efficient clusters for routing in WSNs are proposed 2. Examined the progressive loss of energy	2009
9	Norouzi et al. [80]	GA	A mathematical formula that increases the protection against lifetime risk was proposed	2011
10	Luo et al. [81]	QGA	Quantum GA (QGA)-based QoS routing protocol, a proposed technique, is effective with best-effort traffic	2010
11	Seo et al. [82]	2D GA	1. Using GA, achieved the ideal cluster formation 2. Developed an algorithm known as the location-aware two-dimensional GA (LA2D-GA).	2009
12	Salehpour et al. [83]	ACO	Presented a useful routing strategy for large-scale WSNs based on clusters	2008
13	Camilo et al. [51]	ACO	Suggested EEABR algorithm to increase the lifetime of WSNs	2006

(Continues)

Table 2.5   (Continued)

S. no.	Author	Optimization algorithm used	Available information	Year
14	Mao *et al.* [84]	ACO	To achieve network load balancing, it is advised that high-density WSNs use a non-uniform clustering protocol that is energy cognizant	2013
15	Almshreqi *et al.* [85]	ACO	Projected an algorithm for balanced energy consumption	2012
16	Dervis Karaboga *et al.* [86]	ABCO	The ABCO algorithm's search characteristics, which are very effective and optimizing, were used to enhance CH selection Compared with the other protocols based on LEACH and PSO	2012
17	Kumar *et al.* [87]	Two-step ABCO	A two-step ABCO algorithm is suggested for issues with data clustering. K-means algorithm is utilized to construct the initial food source position for the ABC algorithm Comparison of the traditional ABCO algorithm and its variations, including ACO, PSO GA, and K-means algorithms	2015
18	Pawandeep *et. al.* [88]	ABCO	It was suggested that an ABC-based energy efficient adaptive clustering hierarchy protocol might effectively increase the network life and stability of WSNs	2016
19	Potthuri *et al.* [89]	Differential evolution (DE) and simulated annealing algorithm	1. First, initializing the population using the opposite point method 2. Self-adaptive control parameters for the DE are taken into consideration 3. Cost function evaluation 4. Distribution of CH	2016
20	Kaur *et al.* [90]	Hybrid PSO & ACO	1. Clustering protocol for WSNs based on ACOPSO 2. Discovered the quickest route between CH and BS 3. Compressive sensing is used to reduce packet size	2017

For the performance study of appropriate routing protocols and clustering strategies in sensor networks, a number of methodologies have been put out in the literature. Although the literature has documented substantial advancements in wireless sensor network life extension, there are still a number of problems that need to be resolved. While numerous studies and methodologies have shown strong agreement for improving both, due to various problems and difficulties of infrastructure less mobile wireless networks, it is more difficult to provide a suitable routing protocol and clustering scheme than it is in fixed networks, and this problem is perpetually open in infrastructure less ad hoc wireless networks. A thorough study of the literature is followed by the identification of the research gaps.

Due to node mobility, a major problem in wireless sensor networks is that communication must be conducted while the network architecture is changing (dynamically). In a wireless sensor network, each node communicates with its neighbors directly within its transmission range, but it must use intermediary nodes to send its messages hop by hop with the aid of a routing protocol in order to communicate with nodes that are located outside of this range. In order to find effective and appropriate routing protocols for various sensor network applications, research is required.

Common network management systems available today were often created to operate on wireless networks that were static or relatively small. Numerous ad hoc network applications involve large networks with thousands of nodes, like in the case of sensor networks and tactical networks, which are exceedingly difficult to administer. Clustering is a crucial field of research for wireless sensor networks since it increases network size, lowers overheads, and makes the network more manageable when there is both extreme mobility and a significant number of mobile nodes. Therefore, a new clustering technique must be found and created in order to divide the enormous network into smaller, more manageable networks. In clustering, the gateway node facilitates inter-cluster communication while the cluster head oversees and retains recent routing information. The loss of stored routing information and reduced battery life of nodes, as well as the modification of the route between two nodes, has all been linked to the frequent switching of the cluster head and gateway node. This instability also affects the performance of the routing protocol and the cluster structure. To choose a new CH, communication overhead in the form of message switching is necessary.

To retain the cluster head and gateway node change as little as possible and to increase the stability of the cluster structure, it is crucial to prevent the loss of routing information. The majority of the clustering literature reviews rely on choosing the cluster head and gateway node independently. Therefore, there is a huge need to find innovative clustering methods for wireless sensor networks.

2.10.2   *Implementation of WCA on leach routing protocol*

Another possible interpretation of the consonance is as follows: in this scenario, the initial population consists of all nodes, and fitness function is determined by their individual energies [56]. During the startup phase, the LEACH Protocol is used to elect CH, and the node that has the highest energy is known as the sea or CH. More energy-efficient nodes are clustered at the cluster's epicenter (where the rivers empty into the sea), while less efficient nodes are located further from the center (streams farthest from the sea). After some iterations, the energy of each node will be computed, and its new positions will be decided. Rivers are selected from nodes with the optimal amount of energy, while less energetic nodes are rejected. We select high-energy nodes as rivers and low-energy ones as streams. Similarly, to how the locations of rivers and streams are revised at each energy assessment, a new CH is selected at regular intervals. The same procedure is carried out repeatedly till the maximum number of rounds has been reached [57]. In the end, the WCA reduces the expense of selecting the best node that can serve as the cluster head in the WSN's hierarchical routing protocol. The acquired findings showed that the suggested technique outperforms traditional LEACH in terms of results.

2.10.3   *Nature-inspired optimization algorithm applied in solid-state wielding*

This study examines how the mechanical characteristics of the AA 6082-T6 joint are affected by underwater friction stir welding (UFSW) process parameters and to simulate this process using a variety of evolutionary optimization strategies. The impact of differences in these parameters on the ultimate tensile strength (UTS in MPa), percentage elongation (E in%), and impact strength (IS in J) of the welded joint was studied using experimental measurements and records. To model this UFSW process, two evolutionary optimization algorithms were used, namely, PSO and FFA. In these simulations, the cost function was an artificial neural network with two layers that resembled a nonlinear function, and it was used to forecast the values of the response variables, UTS, E, and IS, which had previously been measured experimentally. These simulations involved multiple experiments with various randomly chosen data sets, and the accuracy of each simulation was then compared. Results showed that, while predicting the values of the response variable, the FFA-based simulation outperformed the PSO with the least mean square error (MSE). For UTS, E, and IS, it was found that the minimum MSE for the FFA-based simulation was as low as 0.009%, 0.004%, and 0.017%, respectively.

There are now several joining techniques available, but joining aluminum alloys (AAs) remain difficult due to their high heat conductivity and low melting point [58]. During fusion welding (FW) of AAs, porosity, solidification cracking, residual strains, oxidation, and other discontinuities are also formed, reducing the aesthetics and practical weld qualities. Friction stir welding (FSW) is an effective method for combining similar and dissimilar materials because it does not require melting and recasting the material [59–61]. This 1990s-era method relies heavily on frictional heating and severe plastic deformation of the foundation. Because of the thermo-mechanical cycles created during the process, welding some AAs with FSW causes the strengthening precipitates to dissolve or become coarser, which reduces the mechanical performance of the joints [62]. In earlier investigations, external cooling was used to solve this issue.

One such procedure that uses water to adjust the temperature in joints is UFSW [63]. Underwater, which may be still or may be continuously flowing across the surface of the samples to be welded, is where the welding is done. Underwater, which may be still or may be continuously flowing across the surface of the samples to be welded, is where the welding is done. Due to the extensive circulation and high heat-capturing capabilities of the water, the coarsening and dissolving of precipitates are controlled [60]. Over FSW and FW, UFSW has the capacity to offer better mechanical qualities and fine-grain structural features. Heat circulation, material movement, and intermixing during UFSW are significantly influenced by the various welding settings as well as varied joint designs and tool features. This alters the joint's mechanical characteristics and produces change in the macro- and microstructural aspects [59–63]. Therefore, choosing the best parameter combination and optimizing it are crucial for enhancing the mechanical properties of the joints. Sharma *et al.* [64] investigated multi-response optimization using the TOPSIS technique for different FSW joints. They discovered that the rotating speed has a significant impact on micro hardness and UTS. Palanivel *et al.* [65] used central composite face-centered factorial during dissimilar joining of AAs utilizing FSW to establish empirical modeling between the FSW parameters and the UTS. The literature that is now accessible also shows a dearth of research into the simulation of the UFSW process for using various evolutionary optimization techniques. Motivated by these knowledge gaps, the following goals were systematically designed and accomplished by various authors: (i) to investigate the impact of three UFSW input parameters on the UTS, E%, and IS of marine grade AA 6082-T6 joints using the Taguchi's L18 standard orthogonal array and (ii) to compare the simulation abilities of these optimization algorithms.

2.10.3.1   Experimental details

Butt welding AA 6082-T6 with dimensions of $200 \times 50 \times 3$ mm was done using UFSW. The tool's material of choice was H 13 tool steel. In this work, tri-flute profiled tools with a 6-mm pin diameter and 2.7-mm pin height were used. The welding tools were angled at 20 degrees. An UFSW-specific vertical milling machine was used to accomplish a single-pass run. The tool shoulder diameter (A), rotational speed (B), and traverse speed ranges for three UFSW parameters were established using the trial run results (C). Table 2.6 lists the UFSW process parameters and their levels. Taguchi's L18 orthogonal array (OA) was used to construct the 18 runs that are listed in Table 2.7. Using wire EDM, the tensile and impact parts were cut. A tensometer was used to measure the UTS and% E at room temperature and at a crosshead speed of 2 mm/min. The IS was computed using the Charpy Impact test.

Table 2.6   Parameter (designation)

Parameter (designation)	Unit	Level 1	Level 2	Level 3
A	mm	17	20	–
B	rpm	710	900	1,120
C	mm/min	50	63	80

In order to achieve better results from the chosen prediction mode, the parameter values were normalized to a range of (0, 1).

Five independent experiments were carried out for each set of input parameters to analyze the data using each optimization procedure. The following sections include the findings of top three runs (experiments) for selected optimization algorithm.

The values of numerous parameters or constraints that must be established in each method, such as the number of iterations, population or swarm size, and number of elements or particles taken into account, are described in Table 2.8. This table's values were determined through a series of exploratory trials. Table 2.9 also

Table 2.7   Taguchi L18 OA

S. no.	A	B	C
1	17	710	50
2	17	710	63
3	17	710	80
4	17	900	50
5	17	900	63
6	17	900	80
7	17	1,120	50
8	17	1,120	63
9	17	1,120	80
10	20	710	50
11	20	710	63
12	20	710	80
13	20	900	50
14	20	900	63
15	20	900	80
16	20	1,120	50
17	20	1,120	63
18	20	1,120	80

Table 2.8   Additional parameters that are stated for each algorithm

S. no.	PSO parameters		Firefly parameters	
1	Max. no. of iterations	25,000	Max. no. of iterations	5,000
2	Size of the swarm	96, 192,96[a]	Size of the swarm	96, 192,96[a]
3	Number of particles (elements)	32, 36[a], 32	Number of particles (elements)	32, 36[a], 32
3	Correction factor (C_1)	1.2	Coefficient of light absorption	1.50
4	Correction factor (C_1)	2.4	Value of attraction coefficient	2.30
5	Weight damping ratio	0.99	Mutation coefficient	0.25

[a]Refers to separate values for UTS, E, and IS response variables.

Table 2.9   Values of input and the response parameter

S. no.	Input parameters			Response parameters		
	A	B	C	UTS (MPa)	E (%)	IS (J)
1	17	710	50	224	11.12	8
2	17	710	63	228	9.67	7
3	17	710	80	223	8.67	6
4	17	900	50	226	12.11	9
5	17	900	63	236	9.78	7
6	17	900	80	241	9.76	7
7	17	1120	50	222	12.89	8
8	17	1,120	63	231	9.87	8
9	17	1,120	80	235	9.67	7
10	20	710	50	208	12.67	8
11	20	710	63	214	12.33	8
12	20	710	80	219	11.54	7
13	20	900	50	227	12.89	9
14	20	900	63	232	12.87	8
15	20	900	80	232	10.43	9
16	20	1,120	50	218	12.89	9
17	20	1,120	63	221	9.34	8
18	20	1,120	80	228	12.56	7

shows that different parameters were required to simulate UTS, E%, and IS. To simulate the E% parameter, the model required more parameters than the other response parameters, particularly for the PSO and FFA algorithms [66,67].

2.10.3.2   Results of the PSO algorithm

It is evident from the results obtained (Table 2.6) that PSO correctly anticipated the response (UTS) values. For all 18 samples, the total range of highest and lowest error was found as 0.015–1.575% (Table 2.10). However, the error was just around 2% for the majority of the samples.

The projected values were reasonably similar to the experimental values anticipated for (%E) as shown in Table 2.11. The difference or error between forecasted and experiments values for each of the 18 samples range between 0.126% and 8.370%.

The data in Table 2.12 showed that projected values are really quite close to experimental values. In other instances, the divergence is found as 0.002%. The total measured range of error was 6.607–0.002%.

2.10.3.3   Results of the FFA

The results of the best three experiments are shown in Tables 2.13–2.15.

Table 2.13 findings demonstrate that the FFA was successful in estimating the UTS values. For all 18 samples, the total range of maximum and minimum error was found to be 0.009–0.836%. However, this discrepancy was only around 1% for the vast majority of the samples.

Table 2.10   Experimental and predicted values from PSO algorithm for the UTS parameter

S. no.	Experimental value (MPa)	Prediction 1 (MPa)	Prediction 2 (MPa)	Prediction 3 (MPa)	Max. error (%)	Min. error (%)
1	224.000	223.383	222.219	222.326	0.795	0.275
2	228.000	228.038	229.088	228.280	0.477	0.017
3	223.000	223.319	223.530	223.187	0.238	0.084
4	226.000	228.472	227.938	229.560	1.575	0.857
5	236.000	235.632	237.248	237.304	0.553	0.156
6	241.000	239.596	238.930	240.229	0.859	0.320
7	222.000	221.604	221.878	220.295	0.768	0.055
8	231.000	229.784	228.657	228.840	1.014	0.526
9	235.000	236.359	236.694	234.623	0.721	0.160
10	208.000	208.045	208.132	208.924	0.444	0.021
11	214.000	214.448	215.555	214.523	0.726	0.209
12	219.000	218.602	217.574	218.429	0.651	0.182
13	227.000	227.035	225.704	225.067	0.851	0.015
14	232.000	229.778	231.452	229.147	1.230	0.236
15	232.000	233.908	232.561	233.538	0.822	0.242
16	218.000	217.204	218.092	218.930	0.427	0.042
17	221.000	222.109	222.755	223.480	1.122	0.502
18	228.000	227.625	226.993	228.237	0.442	0.104
	Experiment wise mean error (%)	0.377	0.517	0.590		

Table 2.11   Experimental and predicted values from PSO algorithm for the % elongation parameter

S. no.	Experimental value (%)	Prediction 1 (%)	Prediction 2 (%)	Prediction 3 (%)	Max. error (%)	Min. error (%)
1	11.120	11.172	11.540	11.177	3.774	0.471
2	9.670	9.658	9.092	9.500	5.982	0.126
3	8.670	8.731	8.901	8.852	2.670	0.698
4	12.110	11.806	12.047	12.068	2.509	0.348
5	9.780	10.361	10.355	10.156	5.942	3.846
6	9.760	9.148	9.168	9.049	7.280	6.069
7	12.890	13.130	12.763	13.024	1.862	0.985
8	9.870	9.211	9.363	9.226	6.672	5.141
9	9.670	10.179	10.132	10.412	7.678	4.777
10	12.670	12.693	12.652	12.586	0.662	0.142
11	12.330	12.263	12.448	12.573	1.970	0.546
12	11.540	11.457	11.398	11.342	1.713	0.718
13	12.890	13.058	12.490	13.087	3.106	1.305
14	12.870	12.443	12.440	12.092	6.048	3.321
15	10.430	11.097	11.121	11.239	7.760	6.392
16	12.890	12.649	13.125	12.701	1.868	1.469
17	9.340	10.114	10.074	10.122	8.370	7.864
18	12.560	11.900	11.961	11.823	5.864	4.767
	Experiment wise mean error (%)	3.205	3.647	3.693		

Table 2.12   Experimental and predicted results from PSO algorithm for the IS parameter

S. no.	Experimental value (J)	Prediction 1 (J)	Prediction 2 (J)	Prediction 3 (J)	Max. error (%)	Min. error (%)
1	8.000	7.958	7.927	7.964	0.912	0.455
2	7.000	7.084	6.953	6.948	1.199	0.669
3	6.000	5.947	6.098	5.949	1.629	0.858
4	9.000	8.908	8.977	8.701	3.322	0.251
5	7.000	7.159	7.210	7.353	5.047	2.276
6	7.000	6.964	6.905	7.144	2.054	0.520
7	8.000	8.037	7.984	8.473	5.912	0.195
8	8.000	7.948	8.045	7.471	6.607	0.569
9	7.000	7.012	6.930	6.846	2.195	0.177
10	8.000	8.056	8.010	7.981	0.704	0.122
11	8.000	7.912	8.034	8.026	1.096	0.323
12	7.000	7.050	6.945	7.053	0.783	0.718
13	9.000	9.054	9.000	9.177	1.972	0.002
14	8.000	7.881	8.098	8.176	2.196	1.219
15	9.000	9.035	8.951	8.780	2.448	0.394
16	9.000	8.988	9.061	8.785	2.387	0.139
17	8.000	8.041	7.771	7.799	2.869	0.509
18	7.000	6.972	7.098	7.378	5.406	0.393
	Experiment wise mean error (%)	0.764	0.979	2.524		

Table 2.13   Experimental and predicted values from FFA for the UTS parameter

S. no.	Experimental value (MPa)	Prediction 1 (MPa)	Prediction 2 (MPa)	Prediction 3 (MPa)	Max. error (%)	Min. error (%)
1	224.000	223.653	222.611	223.296	0.620	0.155
2	228.000	228.248	228.403	228.626	0.275	0.109
3	223.000	223.095	223.021	223.030	0.042	0.009
4	226.000	226.218	226.503	227.264	0.559	0.096
5	236.000	235.878	236.475	235.701	0.201	0.052
6	241.000	240.811	240.730	240.332	0.277	0.079
7	222.000	222.216	222.616	221.626	0.278	0.097
8	231.000	230.804	230.233	229.934	0.461	0.085
9	235.000	235.068	235.203	236.032	0.439	0.029
10	208.000	207.785	208.088	207.973	0.104	0.013
11	214.000	214.653	214.683	214.364	0.319	0.170
12	219.000	218.457	218.640	218.701	0.248	0.137
13	227.000	227.116	227.179	227.433	0.191	0.051
14	232.000	231.503	231.231	230.569	0.617	0.214
15	232.000	232.570	232.906	232.709	0.391	0.246
16	218.000	217.399	217.497	217.312	0.316	0.231
17	221.000	221.650	221.353	222.847	0.836	0.160
18	228.000	227.856	227.622	227.267	0.322	0.063
	Experiment wise mean error %	0.141	0.218	0.308		

Table 2.14   Experimental and predicted values from FFA for the % elongation parameter

S. no.	Experimental value (%)	Prediction 1 (%)	Prediction 2 (%)	Prediction 3 (%)	Max. error (%)	Min. error (%)
1	11.120	11.809	11.615	11.520	6.194	3.598
2	9.670	9.278	9.248	9.303	4.360	3.797
3	8.670	8.669	8.861	8.827	2.205	0.015
4	12.110	11.798	11.870	12.074	2.576	0.297
5	9.780	10.083	10.012	10.257	4.880	2.374
6	9.760	9.604	9.368	9.364	4.059	1.595
7	12.890	12.890	12.921	12.853	0.288	0.004
8	9.870	9.487	9.627	9.332	5.448	2.462
9	9.670	9.945	10.024	9.954	3.665	2.844
10	12.670	12.625	12.653	12.690	0.355	0.131
11	12.330	12.210	12.191	12.043	2.331	0.972
12	11.540	11.636	11.103	11.106	3.785	0.829
13	12.890	12.619	12.770	12.599	2.254	0.935
14	12.870	12.608	12.639	12.544	2.532	1.794
15	10.430	10.630	11.617	11.645	11.645	1.920
16	12.890	13.003	12.901	12.974	0.877	0.082
17	9.340	9.928	9.806	9.986	6.920	4.984
18	12.560	12.226	11.841	12.005	5.728	2.659
	Experiment wise mean error %	2.350	3.095	3.433		

Table 2.15   Experimental and predicted results from FFA for the IS parameter

S. no.	Experimental value (J)	Prediction 1 (J)	Prediction 2 (J)	Prediction 3 (J)	Max. error (%)	Min. error (%)
1	8.000	7.903	8.010	7.783	2.715	0.121
2	7.000	6.991	6.862	7.085	1.968	0.123
3	6.000	6.178	6.001	5.954	2.958	0.017
4	9.000	9.111	9.005	8.947	1.239	0.050
5	7.000	6.877	7.183	7.250	3.568	1.757
6	7.000	6.965	6.849	7.151	2.160	0.501
7	8.000	7.994	8.004	7.985	0.184	0.054
8	8.000	8.011	8.024	8.079	0.992	0.135
9	7.000	6.986	6.982	6.827	2.476	0.206
10	8.000	7.997	8.029	8.028	0.360	0.036
11	8.000	8.260	7.980	8.009	3.249	0.109
12	7.000	6.791	7.040	7.045	2.987	0.570
13	9.000	8.944	8.927	8.978	0.814	0.250
14	8.000	8.146	8.242	8.274	3.426	1.824
15	9.000	8.758	8.871	8.565	4.839	1.436
16	9.000	9.006	9.055	9.050	0.608	0.071
17	8.000	7.919	7.677	7.814	4.040	1.007
18	7.000	7.184	7.266	7.156	3.797	2.235
	Experiment wise mean error (in %)	1.295	1.246	1.633		

Table 2.14 shows that the predicted values obtained were quite close to the expected experimental results. The entire error range was discovered to be between 0.004% and 11.645%.

The results show that projected values are very close to experiment data. In other cases, the variation can be as low as 0.002%. The complete error range was discovered to be between 0.017% and 4.839%.

The evaluation of prediction error for the various UFSW process parameters and the different optimization strategies is shown in Tables 2.16–2.18.

The three runs of the PSO- and FFA-based simulations are shown along with the maximum, lowest, and mean values for the maximum and minimum prediction errors for the UTS. Table 2.16 shows that the FFA-based simulation forecasted the data the most accurately, with an average maximum and minimum error of 0.541%

Table 2.16   Maximum and minimum prediction errors for the UTS

	PSO algorithm			Firefly algorithm		
	Max. error	Min. error	Avg. error	Max. error	Min. error	Avg. error
Highest value among experiments	1.575	0.857	1.216	0.836	0.246	0.541
Lowest value among experiments	0.238	0.015	0.126	0.042	0.009	0.026
Mean value among experiments	0.762	0.223	0.492	0.361	0.111	0.236

Table 2.17   Maximum and minimum prediction errors for the elongation %

	PSO algorithm			Firefly algorithm		
	Max. error	Min. error	Avg. error	Max. error	Min. error	Avg. error
Highest value among experiments	8.370	7.864	8.117	11.645	4.984	8.314
Lowest value among experiments	0.662	0.126	0.394	0.288	0.004	0.146
Mean value among experiments	4.541	2.721	3.631	3.895	1.738	2.816

Table 2.18   Maximum and minimum prediction errors for the impact strength

	PSO algorithm			Firefly algorithm		
	Max. error	Min. error	Avg. error	Max. error	Min. error	Avg. error
Highest value among experiments	6.607	2.276	4.442	4.839	2.235	3.537
Lowest value among experiments	0.704	0.002	0.353	0.184	0.017	0.100
Mean value among experiments	2.708	0.544	1.626	2.354	0.583	1.469

and 0.026%, respectively. The overall mean prediction error remained as low as 0.236% in this simulation. Experiment 1 demonstrated the FFA algorithm's best mean error values, with a mean error percentage of 0.141%. The top-performing PSO experiment had average errors of 0.377% and 1.142%, respectively. The FFA-based simulation achieved a small error value of 0.009% over the three trials mentioned.

In this case, the PSO and FFA-based models both performed reasonably well; however, the FFA-based simulation yielded the lowest mean average prediction error of 2.816%. Experiment 1 of the FFA technique had the lowest mean error values, with an average error of 2.35%. The FFA-based prediction model achieved an error value of 0.004%.

Table 2.18 shows the mean, maximum, and minimum impact strength predicted errors for tests performed with PSO and FFA. The FFA-based simulation performed admirably in this case as well, with prediction error% ranging from 0.1 to 3.537 and the lowest mean average prediction error of 1.469%. In experiment 2, the mean error values were 1.246%, with an average error percentage of 1.246%. The FFA-based prediction model achieved an error value of 0.017% across the three experiments shown in Table 2.12. PSO produced a minimum error value of 0.002% for impact strength.

2.11 Conclusion

For the last few decades, traditional search algorithms have been used to sort out engineering problems. Many promising algorithms have found potential results. This chapter presented an in-depth view of nature-inspired optimization algorithm and its application in engineering constraint problems. Various nature-inspired optimization algorithms were considered for extensive review. Different classes of such algorithms are presented. Some of the popular and widely used NIOA were elaborated and their applications on different domains are also discussed. Application on clustering routing protocols and solid-state wielding is elucidated in details. The WCA-based clustering routing protocol eventually lessens the cost of determining the best node as the cluster head. This novel energy-efficient clustering mechanism sustains the network lifetime. Similarly, PSO and FFA evolutionary optimization algorithms are used to simulate the UFSW process. The results strongly suggest that the FFA technique can be successfully used to simulate a highly efficient model for predicting the parameters of the UFSW process. The findings and results drawn from the study of NIOA are of great relevance to researchers of optimization algorithms and also help in optimizing engineering problems and practical application hence therefore has been adequately detailed. There are a variety of research directions that could be well thought of as a helpful expansion of this analysis.

References

[1]   A. Singh, S. Sharma, and J. Singh, "Nature-inspired algorithms for wireless sensor networks: a comprehensive survey," *Comput. Sci. Rev.*, vol. 39, no. 100342, p. 100342, 2021.

[2] K. G. Dhal, S. Ray, A. Das, and S. Das, "A survey on nature-inspired optimization algorithms and their application in image enhancement domain," *Arch. Comput. Methods Eng.*, vol. 26, no. 5, pp. 1607–1638, 2019.

[3] X.-S. Yang, "Nature-inspired optimization algorithms: challenges and open problems," *J. Comput. Sci.*, vol. 46, no. 101104, p. 101104, 2020.

[4] S. R. Kumar and K. D. Singh, "Nature-inspired optimization algorithms: research direction and survey," arXiv [cs.NE], 2021.

[5] N. E. L. Y. Kouba and M. Boudour, "A brief review and comparative study of nature-inspired optimization algorithms applied to power system control," in *Natural Computing for Unsupervised Learning*, Cham: Springer International Publishing, 2019, pp. 35–49.

[6] R. Rajakumar, P. Dhavachelvan, and T. Vengattaraman, "A survey on nature inspired metaheuristic algorithms with its domain specifications," in *2016 International Conference on Communication and Electronics Systems (ICCES)*, 2016.

[7] D. E. Goldberg and J. H. Holland, "Genetic algorithms and machine learning," *Mach Learn*, vol. 3, no. 2, pp. 95–99, 1988.

[8] J. Koza, "Genetic programming as a means for programming computers by natural selection," *Stat. Comput.*, vol. 4, no. 2, pp. 87–112, 1994.

[9] R. Storn and K. Price, "Differential evolution: a simple and efficient heuristic for global optimization," *J. Global Optim*, vol. 11, pp. 341–359, 1997.

[10] X.-S. Yang, S. Deb, S. Fong, X. He, and Y.-X. Zhao, "From swarm intelligence to metaheuristics: nature-inspired optimization algorithms," *Computer (Long Beach Calif.)*, vol. 49, no. 9, pp. 52–59, 2016.

[11] J. Kennedy and R. Eberhart, "Particle swarm optimization," in *Proceedings of ICNN'95 – International Conference on Neural Networks*, 2002.

[12] M. Dorigo, "Optimization, learning, and natural algorithms," PhD Thesis, Politecnico di Milano, 1992.

[13] X.-S. Yang, "Firefly algorithms for multimodal optimization," in *Stochastic Algorithms: Foundations and Applications*, Berlin, Heidelberg: Springer Berlin Heidelberg, 2009, pp. 169–178.

[14] X.-S. Yang and S. Deb, "Cuckoo search via Lévy flights," in *Proceedings of World Congress on Nature and Biologically Inspired Computing*, USA: IEEE Publications, 2009, pp. 210–214.

[15] Z. W. Geem, J. H. Kim, and G. V. Loganathan, "A new heuristic optimization algorithm: Harmony Search," *Simulation*, vol. 76, no. 2, pp. 60–68, 2001.

[16] D. Karaboga, "An idea based on honey bee swarm for numerical optimization", Technical report-tr06; Erciyes university, engineering faculty, computer engineering department," *Tech. Rep*, 2005.

[17] X. Meng, Y. Liu, X. Gao, and H. Zhang, "A new bio-inspired algorithm: chicken swarm optimization," in *Lecture Notes in Computer Science*, Cham: Springer International Publishing, 2014, pp. 86–94.

[18] K. Krishnanand and D. Ghose, "Detection of multiple source locations using a glowworm metaphor with applications to collective robotics"," in *Swarm Intelligence Symposium*, 2005, pp. 84–91.

[19] X.-S. Yang, "A new metaheuristic bat-inspired algorithm," in *Nature Inspired Cooperative Strategies for Optimization (NICSO 2010)*, Berlin, Heidelberg: Springer Berlin Heidelberg, 2010, pp. 65–74.

[20] S. Łukasik and P. A. Kowalski, "Study of flower pollination algorithm for continuous optimization", in *Intelligent Systems*, Springer, 2014.

[21] H. Eskandar, A. Sadollah, A. Bahreininejad, and M. Hamdi, "Water cycle algorithm – a novel metaheuristic optimization method for solving constrained engineering optimization problems," *Comput. Struct.*, vol. 110–111, pp. 151–166, 2012.

[22] A. Sadollah, A. Bahreininejad, H. Eskandar, and M. Hamdi, "Mine blast algorithm for optimization of truss structures with discrete variables," *Comput. Struct.*, vol. 102–103, pp. 49–63, 2012.

[23] Y.-J. Zheng, "Water wave optimization: a new nature-inspired metaheuristic," *Comput. Oper. Res.*, vol. 55, pp. 1–11, 2015.

[24] A. Gambhir and A. Payal, "Analysis of particle swarm and artificial bee colony optimisation-based clustering protocol for WSN," *Int. J. Comput. Syst. Eng.*, vol. 5, no. 2, p. 77, 2019.

[25] A. Gambhir, A. Payal, and R. Arya, "Analysis of PSO based clustering protocol in assorted scenarios of WSN," in *Communication and Computing Systems*, London: CRC Press, 2019, pp. 400–405.

[26] A. Gambhir, A. Payal, and R. Arya, "Performance analysis of artificial bee colony optimization based clustering protocol in various scenarios of WSN," *Procedia Comput. Sci.*, vol. 132, pp. 183–188, 2018.

[27] A. Gambhir, A. Payal, and R. Arya, "Chicken swarm optimization algorithm perspective on energy constraints in WSN," in *2020 IEEE 7th Uttar Pradesh Section International Conference on Electrical, Electronics and Computer Engineering (UPCON)*, 2020.

[28] S. Deb, X.-Z. Gao, K. Tammi, K. Kalita, and P. Mahanta, "Recent studies on chicken swarm optimization algorithm: a review (2014–2018)," *Artif. Intell. Rev.*, vol. 53, no. 3, pp. 1737–1765, 2020.

[29] W. Osamy, A. A. El-Sawy, and A. Salim, "CSOCA: chicken swarm optimization based clustering algorithm for wireless sensor networks," *IEEE Access*, vol. 8, pp. 60676–60688, 2020.

[30] C. Blum, "Ant colony optimization: introduction and recent trends," *Phys. Life Rev.*, vol. 2, no. 4, pp. 353–373, 2005.

[31] S. Tripathi, "A brief review of Firefly Algorithm: application in structural optimization problem," *J. Inst. Eng.*, vol. 15, no. 2, pp. 183–191, 2019.

[32] V. Kumar and D. Kumar, "A systematic review on firefly algorithm: past, present, and future," *Arch. Comput. Methods Eng.*, vol. 28, no. 4, pp. 3269–3291, 2021.

[33] J. Nayak, B. Naik, D. Pelusi, and A. V. Krishna, "A comprehensive review and performance analysis of firefly algorithm for artificial neural networks," in *Nature-Inspired Computation in Data Mining and Machine Learning*, Cham: Springer International Publishing, 2020, pp. 137–159.

[34] A. B. Mohamad, A. M. Zain, and N. E. Nazira Bazin, "Cuckoo search algorithm for optimization problems—a literature review and its applications," *Appl. Artif. Intell.*, vol. 28, no. 5, pp. 419–448, 2014.

[35] S. Walton, O. Hassan, K. Morgan, and M. R. Brown, "A review of the development and applications of the cuckoo search algorithm," in *Swarm Intelligence and Bio-Inspired Computation*, New York, NY: Elsevier, 2013, pp. 257–271.

[36] Y. Song, Z. Chen, and Z. Yuan, "New chaotic pso-based neural network predictive control for nonlinear process"," *IEEE Transactions on Neural Networks*, vol. 18, pp. 595–601, 2007.

[37] J. Cai, X. Ma, L. Li, Y. Yang, H. Peng, and X. Wang, "Chaotic ant swarm optimization to economic dispatch," *Electric Power Systems Research*, vol. 77, no. 10, pp. 1373–1380, 2007.

[38] K. Gopal Dhal, "A chaotic lévy flight approach in bat and firefly algorithm for gray level image enhancement," *Int. J. Image Graph. Signal Process.*, vol. 7, no. 7, pp. 69–76, 2015.

[39] B. Alatas, "Chaotic harmony search algorithms," *Applied Mathematics and Computation*, vol. 216, no. 9, pp. 2687–2699, 2010.

[40] X.-S. Yang, "Flower pollination algorithm for global optimization," in *Unconventional Computation and Natural Computation*, Berlin, Heidelberg: Springer Berlin Heidelberg, 2012, pp. 240–249.

[41] A. Fouad and X.-Z. Gao, "A novel modified flower pollination algorithm for global optimization," *Neural Comput. Appl.*, vol. 31, no. 8, pp. 3875–3908, 2019.

[42] A. Sadollah, H. Eskandar, H. M. Lee, D. G. Yoo, and J. H. Kim, "Water cycle algorithm: a detailed standard code," *SoftwareX*, vol. 5, pp. 37–43, 2016.

[43] M. Nasir, A. Sadollah, Y. H. Choi, and J. H. Kim, "A comprehensive review on water cycle algorithm and its applications," *Neural Comput. Appl.*, vol. 32, no. 23, pp. 17433–17488, 2020.

[44] J. Tillett, T. Rao, F. Sahin, and R. Rao, "Darwinian particle swarm optimization," in *Proceedings of the 2nd Indian International Conference on Artificial Intelligence (IICAI-05)*, 2005.

[45] R. V. Kulkarni and G. K. Venayagamoorthy, "Particle swarm optimization in wireless-sensor networks: a brief survey," *IEEE Trans. Syst. Man Cybern. C Appl. Rev.*, vol. 41, no. 2, pp. 262–267, 2011.

[46] P. C. S. Rao, P. K. Jana, and H. Banka, "A particle swarm optimization based energy efficient cluster head selection algorithm for wireless sensor networks," *Wirel. Netw.*, vol. 23, no. 7, pp. 2005–2020, 2017.

[47] B. Singh and D. K. Lobiyal, "A novel energy-aware cluster head selection based on particle swarm optimization for wireless sensor networks," *Hum.-Centric Comput. Inf. Sci.*, vol. 2, no. 1, p. 13, 2012.

[48] N. M. A. Latiff, C. C. Tsimenidis, and B. S. Sharif, "Energy-aware clustering for wireless sensor networks using particle swarm optimization," in *2007 IEEE 18th International Symposium on Personal, Indoor and Mobile Radio Communications*, 2007.

[49] J.-L. Liu and C. V. Ravishankar, "LEACH-GA: genetic algorithm-based energy-efficient adaptive clustering protocol for wireless sensor networks," *Int. J. Mach. Learn. Comput.*, pp. 79–85, 2011.

[50] T. Liao, T. Stützle, M. A. Montes de Oca, and M. Dorigo, "A unified ant colony optimization algorithm for continuous optimization," *Eur. J. Oper. Res.*, vol. 234, no. 3, pp. 597–609, 2014.

[51] T. Camilo, C. Carreto, J. S. Silva, and F. Boavida, "An energy-efficient ant-based routing algorithm for wireless sensor networks," in *Ant Colony Optimization and Swarm Intelligence*, Berlin, Heidelberg: Springer Berlin Heidelberg, 2006, pp. 49–59.

[52] S. Okdem and D. Karaboga, "Routing in wireless sensor networks using an ant colony optimization (ACO) router chip," *Sensors (Basel)*, vol. 9, no. 2, pp. 909–921, 2009.

[53] D. Karaboga and B. Basturk, "Artificial bee colony (ABC) optimization algorithm for solving constrained optimization problems," in *Lecture Notes in Computer Science*, Berlin, Heidelberg: Springer Berlin Heidelberg, 2007, pp. 789–798.

[54] D. Karaboga, B. Gorkemli, C. Ozturk, and N. Karaboga, "A comprehensive survey: artificial bee colony (ABC) algorithm and applications," *Artif. Intell. Rev*, vol. 42, no. 1, pp. 21–57, 2014.

[55] S. M. Guru, S. K. Halgamuge, and S. Fernando, "Particle swarm optimisers for cluster formation in wireless sensor networks," in *2005 International Conference on Intelligent Sensors, Sensor Networks and Information Processing*, 2005.

[56] A. Gambhir, A. Payal, and R. Arya, "Water cycle algorithm based optimized clustering protocol for wireless sensor network," *J. Interdiscip. Math.*, vol. 23, no. 2, pp. 367–377, 2020.

[57] A. Gambhir, R. Arya, and A. Payal, "Performance analysis of SEP, I-SEP, PSO and WCA-based clustering protocols in WSN," *Int. J. Intell. Eng. Inform.*, vol. 7, no. 6, p. 545, 2019.

[58] M. A. Wahid, A. N. Siddiquee, and Z. A. Khan, "Aluminum alloys in marine construction: characteristics, application, and problems from a fabrication viewpoint," *Mar. Syst. Ocean Technol.*, vol. 15, no. 1, pp. 70–80, 2020.

[59] M. A. Wahid, Z. A. Khan, A. N. Siddiquee, R. Shandley, and N. Sharma, "Analysis of process parameters effects on underwater friction stir welding of aluminum alloy 6082-T6," *Proc. Inst. Mech. Eng. Pt. B: J. Eng. Manuf.*, vol. 233, no. 6, pp. 1700–1710, 2019.

[60] M. A. Wahid, Z. A. Khan, and A. N. Siddiquee, "Review on underwater friction stir welding: a variant of friction stir welding with great potential of improving joint properties," *Trans. Nonferrous Met. Soc. China*, vol. 28, no. 2, pp. 193–219, 2018.

[61] M. A. Wahid, S. Masood, Z. A. Khan, A. N. Siddiquee, I. A. Badruddin, and A. Algahtani, "A simulation-based study on the effect of underwater friction stir welding process parameters using different evolutionary optimization algorithms," *Proc Inst Mech Eng Part C*, vol. 234, no. 2, pp. 643–657, 2020.

[62] M. A. Wahid, P. Goel, Z. A. Khan, K. M. Agarwal, and E. Hasan Khan, "Underwater friction stir welding of AA6082-T6: thermal analysis," in *Advances in Engineering Materials*, Singapore: Springer Singapore, 2021, pp. 365–375.

[63]   M. A. Wahid, S. K. Shihab, R. Shandley, A. Jacob, and T. Majeed, "Friction stir welding process vis-a-vis human health," in *Design Science and Innovation*, Singapore: Springer Singapore, 2021, pp. 1003–1010.

[64]   N. Sharma, Z. A. Khan, A. N. Siddiquee, and M. A. Wahid, "Multi-response optimization of friction stir welding process parameters for dissimilar joining of Al6101 to pure copper using standard deviation based TOPSIS method," *Proc. Inst. Mech. Eng. Part C*, vol. 233, no. 18, pp. 6473–6482, 2019.

[65]   R. Palanivel, R. F. Laubscher, S. Vigneshwaran, and I. Dinaharan, "Prediction and optimization of the mechanical properties of dissimilar friction stir welding of aluminum alloys using design of experiments," *Proc. Inst. Mech. Eng. Pt. B: J. Eng. Manuf.*, vol. 232, no. 8, pp. 1384–1394, 2018.

[66]   R. L. Malghan, K. M. C. Rao, A. K. Shettigar, S. S. Rao, and R. J. D'Souza, "Application of particle swarm optimization and response surface methodology for machining parameters optimization of aluminium matrix composites in milling operation," *J. Braz. Soc. Mech. Sci. Eng.*, vol. 39, no. 9, pp. 3541–3553, 2017.

[67]   A. Majumder, A. Das, and P. K. Das, "A standard deviation based firefly algorithm for multi-objective optimization of WEDM process during machining of Indian RAFM steel," *Neural Comput. Appl.*, vol. 29, no. 3, pp. 665–677, 2018.

[68]   P. C. Pinto, T. A. Runkler, and J. M. Sousa, "Wasp swarm algorithm for dynamic max-sat problems," in *International Conference on Adaptive and Natural Computing Algorithms*, Springer, 2007, pp. 350–357.

[69]   B. Wang, X. Jin, and B. Cheng, "Lion pride optimizer: an optimization algorithm inspired by lion pride behavior," *Science China Information Sciences*, vol. 55, no. 10, pp. 2369–2389, 2012.

[70]   J. C. Bansal, H. Sharma, S. S. Jadon, and M. Clerc, "Spider monkey optimization algorithm for numerical optimization," *Memetic Computing*, vol. 6, no. 1, pp. 31–47, 2014.

[71]   S. Mirjalili and A. Lewis, "The whale optimization algorithm," *Adv. Eng. Softw.*, vol. 95, pp. 51–67, 2016.

[72]   H.-S. Wu and F.-M. Zhang, "Wolf pack algorithm for unconstrained global optimization," *Math. Probl. Eng.*, vol. 2014, pp. 1–17, 2014.

[73]   J. C. Tillett, R. M. Rao, F. Sahin, and T. M. Rao, "Particle swarm optimization for the clustering of wireless sensors," in *Proc. SPIE 5100, Digital Wireless Communications V*, 2003.

[74]   N. A. A. Latiff, N. M. Abdullatiff, and R. B. Ahmad, "Extending wireless sensor network lifetime with base station repositioning," in *2011 IEEE Symposium on Industrial Electronics and Applications*, IEEE, 2011, pp. 241–246.

[75]   Y. Xu and Y. Ji, "A clustering algorithm of wireless sensor networks based on PSO," in *Artificial Intelligence and Computational Intelligence*, Berlin, Heidelberg: Springer Berlin Heidelberg, 2011, pp. 187–194.

[76]   S. Thilagavathi and B. G. Geetha, "Energy aware swarm optimization with intercluster search for wireless sensor network," *Scientific World Journal*, vol. 2015, p. 395256, 2015.

[77] X. Cao, H. Zhang, J. Shi, and G. Cui, "Cluster heads election analysis for multi-hop wireless sensor networks based on weighted graph and particle swarm optimization," in *2008 Fourth International Conference on Natural Computation*, 2008.

[78] S. Jin, M. Zhou, and A. S. Wu, "Sensor network optimization using a genetic algorithm," in *Proceedings of the 7th World Multiconference on Systemics, Cybernetics and Informatics*, 2003, pp. 109–116.

[79] D. S. Hussain and O. Islam, "Genetic algorithm for energy-efficient trees in wireless sensor networks," in *Advanced Intelligent Environments*, Boston, MA: Springer US, 2009, pp. 139–173.

[80] A. Norouzi, F. S. Babamir, and A. H. Zaim, "A new clustering protocol for wireless sensor networks using genetic algorithm approach," *Wirel. Sens. Netw.*, vol. 03, no. 11, pp. 362–370, 2011.

[81] W. Luo, "A quantum genetic algorithm based QoS routing protocol for wireless sensor networks," in *2010 IEEE International Conference on Software Engineering and Service Sciences*, 2010.

[82] H.-S. Seo, S.-J. Oh, and C.-W. Lee, "Evolutionary genetic algorithm for efficient clustering of wireless sensor networks," in *2009 6th IEEE Consumer Communications and Networking Conference*, 2009.

[83] A.-A. Salehpour, B. Mirmobin, A. Afzali-Kusha, and S. Mohammadi, "An energy efficient routing protocol for cluster-based wireless sensor networks using ant colony optimization," in *2008 International Conference on Innovations in Information Technology*, 2008.

[84] S. Mao, C. Zhao, Z. Zhou, and Y. Ye, "An improved fuzzy unequal clustering algorithm for wireless sensor network," *Mob. Netw. Appl.*, vol. 18, no. 2, pp. 206–214, 2013.

[85] A. M. S. Almshreqi, B. M. Ali, M. F. A. Rasid, A. Ismail, and P. Varahram, "An improved routing mechanism using bio-inspired for energy balancing in wireless sensor networks," in *The International Conference on Information Network 2012*, 2012.

[86] D. Karaboga, S. Okdem, and C. Ozturk, "Cluster based wireless sensor network routing using artificial bee colony algorithm," *Wirel. Netw.*, vol. 18, no. 7, pp. 847–860, 2012.

[87] Y. Kumar and G. Sahoo, "A two-step artificial bee colony algorithm for clustering," *Neural Comput. Appl.*, vol. 28, no. 3, pp. 537–551, 2017.

[88] P. P, M. Garg, and N. Jain, "An energy efficient routing protocol using ABC to increase survivability of WSN," *Int. J. Comput. Appl.*, vol. 143, no. 2, pp. 37–42, 2016.

[89] S. Potthuri, T. Shankar, and A. Rajesh, "Lifetime improvement in wireless sensor networks using hybrid differential evolution and simulated annealing (DESA)," *Ain Shams Eng. J.*, vol. 9, no. 4, pp. 655–663, 2018.

[90] S. Kaur and R. Mahajan, "Hybrid metaheuristic optimization based energy efficient protocol for wireless sensor networks," *Egypt. Inform. J.*, vol. 19, no. 3, pp. 145–150, 2018.

Chapter 3

Application aspects of nature-inspired optimization algorithms

Abhinav Kumar[1], Subodh Srivastava[1], Vinay Kumar[1] and Niharika Kulshrestha[2]

In today's time, there are numerous nature-inspired optimization algorithms (NIOAs) that help to achieve fast computation with maximum profit and minimum cost. They are widely used in various fields of engineering, management, and science due to their effectiveness in solving complex optimization problems. This chapter attempts to address the application aspects of NIOAs. It begins with the definition of NIOAs. In addition to that, it also deals with its implementation and parameter tunning. Furthermore, it also presents a study on constrained and unconstrained optimization. Later, it covers the feature selection and practical engineering applications of NIOAs.

3.1 Introduction

NIOAs are sets of nature-based computational algorithms [1]. Basically, these are a type of metaheuristic algorithms that are adapted or governed by natural phenomena. It is categorized as bio-inspired (BIOAs), evolution based, and natural science inspired (physics and chemistry) optimization algorithms (NSIOAs) [2] as shown in Figure 3.1.

BIOAs are divided into evolution and swarm intelligence-based optimization algorithm (OA). Genetic algorithm (GA) [3] and differential evolution (DE) [4] fall under evolution-based OA. Swarm intelligence-based OAs are particle swarm optimization (PSO) algorithm [5], fire fly (FF) [6], artificial bee colony (ABC) [7], bacterial foraging (BF) [8], ant colony optimization (ACO) [9], bat algorithm (BA) [10], cuckoo search (CS) [11], and so on. NSIOAs include simulated annealing (SA) [12], gravitational search (GS) [13], and big bang big crunch (BBBC) [14]. As shown in Figure 3.2, NIOAs [15] can be significantly used for engineering, finance

[1]Department of Electronics and Communication Engineering, National Institute of Technology – Patna, India
[2]Department of Physics, GLA University, India

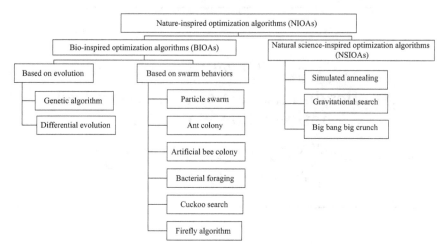

Figure 3.1   Different categories of nature-inspired optimization algorithms

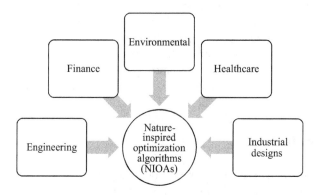

Figure 3.2   Different applications of NIOAs

business activities, environmental management, healthcare, and industrial designs. NIOAs offer a best possible or optimal solution to an application that maximize the performance in terms of profit, output, and efficiency. Furthermore, it minimizes the overall time and energy consumption. It works on set of mathematical models or algorithms that helps to tune the parameters used in the application.

In engineering section, OAs deals with problems of electrical, electronics and communication, mechanical, civil engineering, and power systems. However, the growth of engineering domain is not limited to core section only. The NIOAs are also a solution provider in other aspects of engineering such as, expert systems, artificial intelligence (AI) [16], robotics, machine learning (ML) [17], deep learning (DL) [18], social media, pattern recognition, speech processing, bioinformatics, biomedical, computer vision, and signal and image processing [19]. NIOAs assist to optimize the issues of industrial designs such as manufacturing, operation research, and maintenance. In healthcare, NIOAs club with internet of things (IoT) [20], and big cloud to readdress the current issues and challenges like its scheduling and management [21]. Furthermore, stock prediction, portfolio, and risk management optimization are the main areas of financials activities where NIOAs play an important role. NOAs have been applied in environmental management for solving complex optimization problems related to water resources, air quality index, and logistic and waste management. For instance, GA and PSO algorithms have been used for water resources management, and ABC algorithm has been used for air quality management. Thus, optimization is necessary part of our day-to-day life like from engineering design and development to business setup and from internet browsing to vacation planning, as real-world applications usually have limited resources, time, and money. With a variety of constraints, we need to develop ways to use these precious resources as efficiently as possible.

Before dive into chapter, some common terminologies related to NIOAs [15] are defined. After that, some of the most commonly used NOAs such as DE [4], GA [3], PSO [5], ACO [22], ABC [7], CS [11], and [12] SA are discussed.

(A) Common terminologies
   (a) Objective function (OF): The function that is being minimized or maximized. Sometimes it may be known as the cost function, loss function, or fitness function.
   (b) Constraints: The limitations or restrictions that must be satisfied for the solution to be valid. Constraints can be equality constraints or inequality constraints.
   (c) Decision variables: The elements that can be adjusted to optimize the objective function. These variables are often denoted as x, y, or z.
   (d) Feasible solution: A solution that satisfies all the constraints or restrictions.
   (e) Infeasible solution: A solution that violates one or more constraints.
   (f) Global optimum: The best possible solution to the optimization problem.
   (g) Local optimum: A solution that is optimal within a local neighborhood but may not be the best overall solution.
   (h) Gradient: The direction and magnitude of the steepest increase or decrease of the objective function. It is often used to guide the search for the optimal solution.
   (i) Convergence or stopping criteria: The process of getting closer and closer to the optimal solution. Convergence criteria are used to determine when the optimization algorithm has found a satisfactory solution.
   (j) Iterations: The number of times the optimization algorithm evaluates the objective function and adjusts the decision variables to search for the optimal solution.
   (k) Candidate solution: Candidate solution reflects a member, which is the part of set of all possible feasible solution.

(B) Some of the most commonly used NOAs

    (a) Differential evolution

        DE [4] is an evolution-based metaheuristic algorithm that uses the alterations amid arbitrarily chosen solutions in the population to generate new solutions. It originates with a population of candidate solutions, called "individuals or entities" [23]. Then, it arbitrarily selects three entities from the population and produces a new entity by adding a weighted difference among two of the selected entities to a third selected entity. The resulting entity is equated to its parent in the population, and the better of the two is retained for the next generation.

    (b) Genetic algorithm

        GA [24] is a type of evolution-based NIOAs that simulates the progression of natural selection. It utilizes the principle of survival of the fittest to choose the utmost optimal solution from a set of solutions. It works by generating a population of potential solutions to a problem and continually applying genetic operators or parameters such as mutation, crossover, and selection to evolve the population until an optimal solution is obtained.

    (c) Ant colony optimization

        ACO [9] algorithms are a type of BIOAs that follows the behavior of ants in finding the shortest path between their colony and a food source. Primarily, it uses a pheromone as a biochemical messenger and the concentration of pheromone indicates the quality of solutions to the issue. The greater pheromone concentrations indicate routes and paths that are better at providing answers to issues like discrete combinatorial problems. This is because solutions are tied to the pheromone concentration from an implementation objective. The choice is subtly influenced by some a priori information about the route, including how frequently the distance is used.

    (d) Artificial bee colony

        ABC mimic the foraging behavior of honey bees [7]. It is constituted of three kinds of bees: employed, onlooker, and scout bees. The employed bees explore for food sources (i.e., potential solutions) in the vicinity of their current food source, while the onlooker bees observe the waggle dance of the employed bees to select a promising food source to explore. The scout bees search for new food sources in areas of the solution space that have not been explored yet. The algorithm works by iteratively updating the positions of the employed, onlooker, and scout bees in the solution space, with the goal of finding the optimal solution.

    (e) Particle swarm optimization

        PSO [5] follows the principle of swarm intelligence that includes the natures of bird, flocks, and fish schools. In PSO, a population of particles is used to explore the solution space of an optimization problem. Each particle signifies a possible solution, and its position in the solution space corresponds to the parameters of the solution. The particles move over the solution space and update their positions and velocities according to their own best-known position and the best-known position of the swarm. The velocity update is regulated by the particle's own experience (i.e., its personal best position) and the experience of the swarm as a whole (i.e., the global best position). The particle's position is then updated based on the new velocity. This process is repeated iteratively, with the goal of finding the optimal solution.

(f) Cuckoo search

CS [11] follows the brood mechanism of cuckoo species. In CS [25], a population of cuckoos represents potential solutions to an optimization problem. Each cuckoo lays an egg, which represents a potential new solution. The cuckoo then discards its own egg and replaces it with the new egg if the new solution is better than its own. The algorithm also includes a local search mechanism to explore the solution space around the current solution.

(g) Fire fly

In FF [6], a population of fireflies represents potential solutions to an optimization issue. Each firefly is attracted to other fireflies in the population based on their brightness (i.e., fitness). The firefly moves to the brighter firefly and updates its position accordingly. The brightness of each firefly is estimated by the objective function being optimized.

(h) Simulated annealing

SA [12] is based on the characteristics of the metal annealing process. It originated with an initial solution and iteratively produces new candidate solutions by randomly perturbing the recent solution. The candidate solution is then acknowledged or disallowed based on a probability function that depends on the quality of the candidate solution and a temperature parameter that decreases over time. The acknowledged probability function is founded on the Metropolis-Hastings algorithm [26] from statistical mechanics. At higher temperatures, the algorithm is more likely to accept solutions that are worse than the current solution, which allows the algorithm to escape from local optima. As the temperature decreases, the algorithm becomes less likely to accept worse solutions, which allows it to converge towards the optimal solution.

As mentioned above, there are many applications that can be optimized with the aid of NIOAs. Since the role of image processing is very vast in the areas such as diagnosis of disease through medical images [27], forgery detection [28], crowd management [29], and so on. So, this chapter presents an overview of optimization algorithms in image processing.

3.2   Application domains of nature-inspired optimization algorithms

Image is a collection of pixel values [30]. Image processing is a process of image manipulation where an image is transformed into digital form by a suitable means to extract the required information from it. As shown in Figure 3.3, pre-processing,

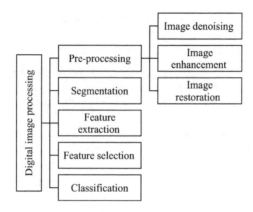

Figure 3.3 Basic building of digital image processing

segmentation, feature extraction, feature selection, and classification are the basic building blocks of image processing [31]. Pre-processing refers to the task of image resizing, normalization, cropping, noise removal, image quality improvement, and image restoration [32]. Pre-processing steps enhance the features of image. Segmentation helps to find the region of interests (ROIs) by dividing the images into a group of segments [33]. ROIs indicate the abnormal region in the case of medical images. Feature extraction is the procedure of mining the features of an image that assists in differentiation between two objects [34]. It is derived from the internal attributes and the characteristics of the image. Feature selection is a statistical approach which finds the redundant and non-redundant features related to the image [35]. It is usually used for dimension deduction. Classification [36] describes the class or label of the image. It is estimated on the basis of extracted and selected features. For example, in the case of image cancer classification, the classification process categorized the images as cancerous or non-cancerous.

Nowadays, the steps involved in image processing are clubbed with ML and DL to accelerate the accuracy and computation rate. Yet, it cannot be done without the aid of an optimization technique. OAs are employed in various image processing application like to increase image quality, lessen noise, improve segmentation, to optimize the feature set and classifications parameters. For instance, DE [37], GA [38], PSO [39], ACO [40,41], and ABC [42] algorithms have been used for image enhancement, segmentation [37,43], feature selection, classification [40], and clustering, respectively.

3.2.1 Optimization in image denoising

Image denoising is a means to eliminate the noise from an image [31]. Noise can be caused at the time of image acquisition or transmission by various factors such as sensor noise, compression artifacts, or environmental factors. The general mathematical model of an image [32] can be read as:

$$y = m\eta_1.x + a\eta_2 \tag{3.1}$$

Here, y is the observed image; x is the noiseless image; $a\eta_2$ is additive noise, which due to machine calibration or sensors; and $m\eta_1$ is inherent characteristic of image known as multiplicative noise.

Based on the evolution of imaging modalities [27] like mammography (X-ray) [32], ultrasound [44], magnetic resonance imaging (MRI) [45], computed tomography (CT) [42], positron emission tomography (PET), and micro biopsy [33], the noises can be categorized as Quantum (Poisson) [32], Speckle (Rayleigh) [44], Rician [46], and Gaussian, respectively. The most commonly used denoising filters [31] are median [47], wiener [48], wavelet [49], bilateral [50], non-local means [51], total variation (TV) [52], anisotropic diffusion [53], fourth-order partial differential equation [54], and complex diffusion [55]. All these filters are constituted with a number of image parameter. The parameters are selected manually, which increases the time complexity and affects the denoising filters accuracy. So, there is a need of optimization that can improve the efficiency of denoising filters by selecting the optimal filter parameters and denoising rules, and also minimize the error between the noisy and denoised image.

3.2.2 Optimization in image enhancement

Image enhancement [31] is a procedure of refining the quality of an image by increasing its contrast, sharpness, brightness, color balance, and other visual features. Histogram equalization [56], unsharp masking [55], high boost filtering [57], contrast limited adaptive histogram [31], equalization, contrast stretching [30], and so on are primarily developed image enhancement techniques. The purpose of any enhancement techniques is to redefine or restore the pixel values. Since, the enhancement techniques comprise manual tuned parameters. Thus, optimization is essential in order to advance the efficacy of enhancement techniques by choosing the optimal parameters values. The NIOAs like GA, PSO, ABC, and ACO may be used for contrast, brightness, color image enhancement, and image sharpening, respectively. Upendra *et al.* [56] have proposed an image enhancement technique that combined GA with histogram equalization to enhance the contrast of images.

The idea behind of ACO for image contrast enhancement is as follows:

(i) It searches for the best values of the contrast parameters by mimicking the foraging behavior of ants.

(ii) The algorithm's pheromone trail is a representation of the contrast level, and the ants' behavior is based on the intensity of the pheromone trail.

(iii) By applying this method, the algorithm can enhance the image's contrast by increasing the brightness level of the pixels in the image.

3.2.3 Optimization in image segmentation

Image segmentation [31] is a method of partitioning an image into several segments or regions that is governed by certain characteristics, such as color, texture, or shape. It is crucial in image processing as it enables the identification of ROIs in an image. The image segmentation techniques [30] are categorized as thresholding, edge detection, region growing, clustering, watershed, and graph-based segmentation techniques. These techniques can be castoff individually or in combination with each other to attain the expected segmentation results. The selection of technique depends on the specific requirements of the application and the characteristics of the image being segmented. But due to complex image structures, segmentation fails to segment desired ROIs. Therefore, OAs can play a vital role.

The optimization problem can be expressed as an objective function that measures the quality of the segmentation and NIOAs can be applied to optimize this function. In simple words, the fitness function is designed to measure the similarity between the segmented image and the ground truth. The NIOAs advances the accuracy and proficiency of image segmentation by choosing the optimal threshold values, clustering parameters, and region growing rules. Bahadur *et al.* [45] have demonstrated MRI brain tumor image segmentation and classification using GA.

3.2.4   *Optimization in image feature extraction and selection*

Image feature extraction and selection have played a significant role in many computer vision applications [58], such as object detection, recognition, and tracking [31]. The goal of feature extraction is to draw out relevant and discriminative features from the image, while feature selection aims to choose the most informative features for the task at hand. The features can be extracted by using image properties loke texture, shape, and size. Some common techniques for image feature extraction and selection [59] are scale-invariant feature transform (SIFT) [60], local binary patterns [34], histogram of oriented gradients [61], speeded-up robust features [62], principal component analysis [63], recursive feature elimination [64], linear discriminant analysis [65], and mutual information (MI) [66]. The choice of feature extraction and selection techniques depends on the specific task and the characteristics of the image data. It is often necessary to experiment with different techniques and combinations of techniques to find the best approach for a particular application. NIOAs plays a crucial role in image feature extraction and selection because it can significantly improve the performance, accuracy, efficiency, and scalability of computer vision [58] algorithms making them more suitable for real-world applications. NIOAs can be used to find the best subset of features that maximizes the objective function with the aid of parameter tuning, dimensionality reduction. For example, the SIFT algorithm [60] has parameters that control the size of the key points, the number of orientations, and the threshold for eliminating low-contrast key points. OAs such as grid search, random search, or Bayesian optimization can be used to find the optimal values for these parameters [67].

3.2.5   *Optimization in image classification*

Image classification [31] is the procedure of assigning a label or a class to an image based on its features. Its goal is to accurately identify and classify images into predefined categories, such as objects, scenes, or activities. Furthermore, the extended form of classification helps in localization and detection of abnormalities from medical images, object recognition from day-to-day activity, and face detection [38] from crowd management. The traditional approach of image classi-fication is to draw out the features from the image and then use a ML algorithm to learn a mapping between the features and the labels. However, this approach requires domain expertise in feature engineering and may not generalize well to new data. Support vector machine (SVM) [35], K-nearest neighbor [68], decision tree, random forest, convolutional neural network (CNN) [69], mask regional convolutional neural network [70], and so on are classification techniques.

Classification techniques have some limitations in handling complex and non-linear relationships between the features and the labels. So, the OAs like GA, PSO, CS, and ACO can be used to optimize the classification parameters where the fitness function can be defined as the classification accuracy of a classifier trained on the extracted features.

3.3   Implementation

NIOAs have several parameters that need to be set correctly to ensure good per-formance. These parameters [71] include the population size, crossover with mutation rates (for GA), inertia weight with learning factors (for PSO), and pher-omone evaporation and deposition rates (for ACO). Implementation of NIOAs involves parameter tuning, representation of the solution, fitness function, and stopping criteria [72]. Parameter tuning helps to find the best values for these above-mentioned parameters. It relies on the specific issues being solved, and different values can lead to different solutions. The solution representation is another crucial aspect of implementing these NIOAs. The solution needs to be encoded in a way that is suitable for the specific algorithm being used. For exam-ple, in GA, solutions are typically exhibited as binary strings, while in PSO, solu-tions are represented as vectors. The solution representation can greatly affect the performance of the algorithm, and different representations can lead to different solutions. The fitness function is the objective function that the OAs are trying to optimize. It evaluates how good a particular solution is. It needs to be expressed in a way that exactly captures the problem being solved. In some cases, it can be difficult to design, and it may require domain-specific knowledge. Furthermore, stopping criteria determine when the OAs should stop searching for a solution. It may be the number of assigned iterations, the maximum time allowed, or when a specific solution is found. Choosing the right stopping criteria is crucial to prevent overfitting or underfitting the problem being solved.

Figure 3.4 demonstrates the generalized implementation steps to perform an optimization in image denoising. It starts from input noisy image followed by the definition objective function; choosing of an OAs; initialization of the OAs; itera-tion of the OAs; determination of stopping criteria; and it ends with output denoised image. Table 3.1 illustrates the implementation steps of PSO-based TV denoising filter. The optimization begins with defining an objective function. The OF is defined in terms of noisy and denoised image. After that, the PSO particles are initialized and its fitness is evaluated. Based on the fitness evaluation, PSO

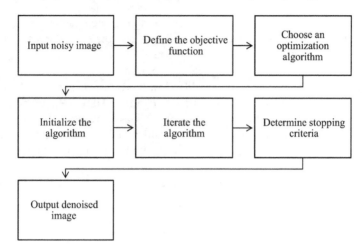

Figure 3.4   Generalized implementation steps of optimization algorithms for image denoising

Table 3.1   Generalized implementation steps of PSO in TV denoising filter

Step I: Define the objective function
The goal is to find an image that is close to the noisy image while also being smooth. The objective function in PSO consists two terms: (I) a data fidelity term that measures the difference among the noisy image and the denoised image and (II) a regularization term that promotes smoothness.
Step II: Initialize the particles
The population of particles in PSO represents potential solutions to the optimization problem. Each particle has a position and a velocity vector that are initialized randomly.
Step III: Evaluate the fitness
The fitness of each particle is estimated by using its position vector, which corresponds to a denoised image. The fitness is computed using the objective function.
Step IV: Update the particles
Each particle's velocity and position vectors which are updated based on its own best position so far (i.e., the position with the best fitness that this particle has reached) and the global best position so far (i.e., the position with the best fitness among all particles in the population). The velocity update is done by the particle's previous velocity, the difference among its recent position and its best position, and the difference between the global best position and its recent position.
Step V: Evaluate the fitness of the updated particles
After the particles' positions and velocities have been updated, their fitness is re-evaluated based on the updated position vectors.
Step VI: Repeat the update and evaluation steps
Steps 4 and 5 are repeated until a stopping criterion is met. This criterion can be based on a maximum number of iterations, a minimum change in the objective function or the fitness of the particles, or some other criterion.
Step VII: Output the denoised image
Once the PSO algorithm has converged, the best particle (i.e., the one with the best fitness) represents the denoised image, and its position vector can be outputted as the final estimate.

particles are updated. These steps are repeated until the matching of stopping criteria. At the end, the optimized denoised image is obtained as output. PSO particles are categorized as position and velocity vector as stated in the definition.

The implementation of the NIOAs needs to be carefully designed and optimized to ensure a good performance. Furthermore, the algorithm needs to be designed to take advantage of parallel processing when available, as well as other optimizations such as local search and hybridization with other algorithms. It also needs to be scalable and adaptable to different problem sizes and types.

3.3.1 Parameter tuning

NIOAs are broadly used to solve complex optimization issues. The performance of NIOAs is highly reliant on the values of their parameters [71]. Because, parameters control the behavior of the search process, such as the rate of mutation in GA or the velocity update in PSO. The choice of appropriate parameter values can significantly affect the convergence rate and the quality of the solutions obtained by the algorithm. Therefore, parameter tuning is a critical step in the application of these algorithms. The parameters include population size, mutation, crossover rate, selection strategy, and convergence criteria.

(a) **Population Size (PS):** It determines the quantity of candidate solutions that are evaluated in every iteration. A larger PS can improve the accuracy of the search but also increases the computational cost. While a smaller PS can reduce the computational cost but may lead to premature convergence. The PS should be selected according to the problem's complexity, the available computational resources, and the algorithm's performance.

(b) **Mutation Rate (MR):** MR controls the degree of randomness in the search process. A higher MR increases the diversity of the population that leads the algorithm escape local optima. However, a high mutation rate can also reduce the convergence rate and lead to a longer search time. The mutation rate should be selected based on the problem's landscape and the algorithm's performance.

(c) **Crossover Rate:** Crossover rate is a parameter that determines the frequency of recombination between candidate solutions. A higher crossover rate explores the search space more efficiently, but it may also increase the probability of premature convergence. A lower crossover rate may improve convergence but may also decrease the diversity of the population. The crossover rate should be selected based on the problem's landscape and the algorithm's performance.

(d) **Selection Strategy:** Selection strategy is a parameter that determines how candidate solutions are selected for the next iteration. The most common selection strategies are roulette wheel and tournament selection strategies. Roulette wheel selection selects solutions based on their fitness, whereas tournament selection selects solutions based on their ranking. The selection strategy should be selected based on the problem's characteristics and the algorithm's performance.

(e) **Convergence Criteria**: Convergence criteria is a parameter that determines when the algorithm should stop. The most common convergence criteria are the maximum number of iterations and the target fitness value. The convergence criteria should be selected based on the problem's complexity and the algorithm's performance.

The parameters of NIAOs are of two kinds: global and local parameters. Global parameters affect the behavior of the entire algorithm, such as the PS in GA or the number of iterations in ACO. Furthermore, local parameters affect the behavior of individual components of the algorithm, such as the crossover probability in GA or the pheromone evaporation rate in ACO. There are various methods for parameter tuning [67] in NIOAs, including manual tuning, grid search, random search, and metaheuristic optimization. Each of these methods has its advantages and disadvantages, and the selection of the technique depends on the specific problem at hand. A well-tuned NIOAs can significantly improvise the proficiency and exactness of the optimization process.

3.3.2   Manual tuning

Manual tuning is the most straightforward and commonly used technique for parameter tuning. In this technique, the parameters are selected by the domain knowledge and experience of the user. The user adjusts the parameters of the algorithm iteratively until the desired performance is achieved. It is a time-consuming process and may require multiple trials and errors to obtain the optimal parameter values.

3.3.3   Grid search

It is a simple and organized approach for parameter tuning. In this technique, a range of parameter values is defined for each parameter, and the algorithm is run for all combinations of parameter values. The performance is evaluated for each combination, and the optimal parameter values are selected based on the results. It is a computationally expensive technique and may not be feasible for problems with a large number of parameters or a high computational cost.

3.3.4   Random search

It is a stochastic approach for parameter tuning. In this technique, the parameters are selected randomly within predefined ranges. The algorithm is run for each combination of parameter values, and the performance is evaluated. The optimal parameter values are selected based on the results. It is less computationally expensive than grid search but may require more iterations to obtain the optimal parameter values.

3.3.5   Metaheuristic optimization

It is a powerful technique for parameter tuning. In this technique, a metaheuristic algorithm searches the optimal parameter values. The metaheuristic algorithm can be any NIOAs, such as GA, PSO, ACO, and CS. The metaheuristic algorithm optimizes a fitness function that evaluates the performance of the original algorithm for each parameter combination. It can be computationally expensive but can provide better results than manual tuning, grid search, or random search.

Table 3.2   Time complexity relationship with the parameters

Parameters tuning methods	Time complexity
Manual tuning	It may be linear to exponential, depending on the number of hyperparameters and the number of values each hyperparameter can take.
Grid search	The time complexity is $O(n^m)$, where n is the number of hyperparameters and m is the number of values each hyperparameter can take.
Random search	The time complexity is $O(k)$, where k is the number of samples taken. It depends on the number of samples taken and the size of the search space.
Metaheuristic optimization	The time complexity can range from $O(n \log n)$ to $O(n^2)$, where n is the number of hyperparameters.

Table 3.2 shows the time complexity chart of manual tuning, grid search, random search, and metaheuristic optimization-based parameters tuning.

3.4   Constrained and unconstrained optimization

Optimization problems can be categorized into two types: constrained [73] and unconstrained optimization [74]. Constraints are set of circumstances that must be satisfied in order to achieve a valid solution. In both cases, NIOAS have become popular due to their effectively solving procedure. Figure 3.5 exhibits the categorization of NIOAs problems according to constrained- and unconstrained-based optimization.

3.4.1   Constrained optimization

It refers to the problem of finding the optimal solution subject to one or more constraints. The constraints may be in the form of equalities or inequalities. The main challenge in constrained optimization is to find a feasible solution that satisfies all the constraints and is also optimal [75].

NIOAs are well-suited for constrained optimization problems because they can efficiently search the solution space and find feasible solutions that satisfy the constraints. The constraint-based algorithms [73] can be classified into two groups: penalty function and constraint handling methods.

3.4.1.1   Penalty function methods

It adds a penalty term to the OF to penalize violations of the constraints. The penalty term is designed to be large when the constraints are violated, and it decreases as the constraints are satisfied. The algorithm then searches for the solution that minimizes the penalized objective function.

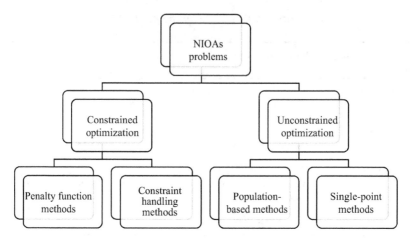

Figure 3.5   Categorization NIOAs on the basis of constrained and unconstrained optimization problems

3.4.1.2   Constraint handling methods

It uses specific techniques to handle the constraints directly. These techniques may include repairing infeasible solutions, transforming the constraints into the objective function, or incorporating the constraints into the search process. NIAOs that are commonly used for constrained optimization problems [76] include GA, PSO, DE, and ACO.

3.4.2   Unconstrained optimization

It refers to the problem of finding the optimal solution without any constraints. The main challenge in unconstrained optimization is to find the global optimum, which is the point that minimizes the objective function.

The unconstrained-based OAs are population-based methods and single-point methods.

3.4.2.1   Population-based methods

It maintains a population of candidate solutions and search for the global optimum by evolving the population through selection, crossover, and mutation operations. Examples of population-based methods include GA, PSO, and ACO.

3.4.2.2   Single-point methods

It searches for the global optimum by iteratively updating a single candidate solution. Examples of single-point methods include gradient descent, Newton's method, and SA.

3.5   How to deal with constraints

Constraints are restrictions on the decision variables that must be satisfied in an optimization problem [75]. For example, in a manufacturing process, there may be constraints on the production capacity, material availability, and energy consumption. In financial planning, there may be constraints on the investment portfolio, interest rates, and inflation. In biology, there may be constraints on the nutrient availability, population growth, and predation. NIOAs such as GA [77], PSO [78], and ACO [79] are based on imitating the behavior of natural systems to find optimal solutions to optimization problems. However, these algorithms may not be suitable for problems with constraints, as they may violate the constraints while searching for solutions. Therefore, special techniques are needed to deal with constrained optimization problems [73]. There are several approaches to handling constraints in nature-inspired optimization algorithms.

3.5.1 Penalty functions

The penalty function [80] adds a penalty term to the OF whenever a constraint is violated, thereby discouraging the optimization algorithm from producing solutions that violate the constraints. There are several types of penalty functions that can be used to deal the constraints.

(a) **L1 Penalty (Lasso):** The L1 penalty function adds the absolute values of the coefficients to the OF [81]. It is used to encourage sparse solutions, where many of the coefficients are zero.

(b) **L2 Penalty (Ridge):** The L2 penalty function adds the squared values of the coefficients to the OF [81]. It is used to prevent overfitting by reducing the magnitude of the coefficients.

(c) **Elastic Net Penalty:** It is a combination of the L1 and L2 penalties [82]. It is used to achieve both sparsity and regularization.

(d) **Huber Penalty:** The Huber penalty function is a combination of the L1 and L2 penalties, which is less sensitive to outliers in the data [83].

(e) **Penalty Barrier Method:** It is a type of penalty function that adds a barrier term to the OF [73]. It is used to constrain the variables to a feasible region.

(f) **Augmented Lagrangian Method:** The augmented Lagrangian method is a penalty function that adds a Lagrangian multiplier term to the OF [76]. It is used to impose constraints on the optimization problem.

(g) **Trust-Region Penalty Method:** This penalty method is a penalty function that adds a penalty term to the OF [84]. It is used to impose constraints on the optimization problem by defining a trust region around the current iterate.

These penalty functions may be used in several optimization issues that includes linear [85] and nonlinear programming [86], and may offers a well optimized answer. The penalty function can be designed in different ways, such as a linear or quadratic penalty function, or a more complex function that depends on the degree of constraint violation.

3.5.2 Linear penalty function

A linear penalty function is a function that increases linearly with the violation of the constraints [85]. For example, if the optimization problem has a constraint that a variable x must be greater than or equal to some value b, then a linear penalty function might add a term of the form. It may be mathematically noted as:

$$P(x) = \max(0, b - x) \tag{3.2}$$

This penalty function is zero when x is greater than or equal to b, and is equal to $(b - x)$ when x is less than b. The linear penalty function increases proportionally with the amount of constraint violation.

3.5.3   Quadratic penalty function

A quadratic penalty function is a function that increases quadratically with the violation of the constraints [87]. For example, a quadratic penalty function might add a term as shown in (3.3):

$$P(x) = \max\left(0, (b - x)^2\right) \tag{3.3}$$

This penalty function is zero when x is greater than or equal to b and is equal to $(b - x)^2$ when x is less than b. The quadratic penalty function increases much faster than the linear penalty function with the amount of constraint violation.

3.5.4   Constraint handling techniques

Constraint handling techniques [79] include methods such as repair, feasibility-based selection, and constraint domination. Actually, repair, feasibility-based selection, and constraint domination are not considered as constraint handling techniques in optimization, but they are related concepts that are used in constraint satisfaction problems (CSPs) [88] and constraint programming (CP) [89]. In CSPs, repair methods are used to modify the current solution by repairing the violated constraints.

(i)   Repair methods use heuristics to modify the current solution and make it feasible, without requiring a complete search of the solution space. Repair methods can be used iteratively until a feasible solution is found, or until a maximum number of iterations is reached. Feasibility-based selection is a technique used in CSPs [90] to select variables for assignment based on their feasibility.

(ii) Feasibility-based selection selects variables that are more likely to lead to a feasible solution, based on the constraints that have already been assigned. Constraint domination is a technique used in CP to simplify the constraint graph by removing redundant constraints.

(iii) Constraint domination identifies constraints that are dominated by other constraints and removes them from the constraint graph, reducing the size of the search space and improving the efficiency of the algorithm.

While these techniques are not considered as constraint handling techniques in optimization, they are still important in solving optimization problems with constraints. In some cases, they can be combined with constraint handling techniques to improve the overall performance of the optimization algorithm. Some of the constraint handling [73] techniques along with penalty function method are listed below:

(a) **Lagrange Multiplier Methods**: Lagrange multiplier methods add a Lagrange multiplier term to the OF that enforces the constraints as equality constraints [76]. The Lagrange multiplier is a scalar parameter that is adjusted during optimization to ensure that the constraints are satisfied.

(b) **Sequential Quadratic Programming (SQP):** SQP methods solve a sequence of sub-problems that approximate the original problem while satisfying the constraints [91]. The sub-problems are solved using quadratic programming, which can handle nonlinear constraints.

(c) **Interior Point Methods:** Interior point methods solve the optimization problem by moving towards the interior of the feasible region [92]. The constraints are handled by adding barrier functions to the OF, which ensures that the optimization variables remain within the feasible region.

(d) **Active Set Methods:** Active set methods involve solving a sequence of sub-problems in which some of the constraints are active (i.e., they are satisfied with equality) and others are inactive (i.e., they are satisfied with inequality) [93]. The active set is updated iteratively until a feasible solution is found.

3.5.5   Hybrid constraint handling techniques

Hybrid constraint handling techniques (HCHTs) [94] are a combination of different constraint handling techniques used in NIOAs to improve the optimization performance. For example, a GA can be combined with a local search method that repairs solutions that violate constraints. Some examples of HCHTs [95] used in nature-inspired optimization algorithms are:

(a) **Penalty-Based Hybrid Constraint Handling:** This approach combines a penalty function with other techniques, such as active set methods, to handle constraints. Penalty function, penalizes constraint violations, while the active set method is used to update the constraints and determine which constraints are active.

(b) **Barrier-Based Hybrid Constraint Handling:** This approach combines a barrier method with other techniques, such as augmented Lagrangian methods [76], to handle constraints. The barrier method is used to prevent the optimization solution from violating the constraints, while the augmented Lagrangian method is used to handle nonlinear constraints.

(c) **Hybrid Genetic Algorithm:** This method combines GA with other techniques, such as penalty functions, to handle constraints [96]. The genetic algorithm is used to generate a set of feasible solutions, while the penalty function is used to penalize constraint violations and improve the quality of the solutions.

(d) **Hybrid Particle Swarm Optimization:** This technique combines PSO with other methods, such as active set methods, to handle constraints [97]. The particle swarm optimization algorithm is used to search for the optimal solution, while the active set method is used to update the constraints and ensure feasibility.

(e) **Hybrid Ant Colony Optimization:** This approach combines ACO with other techniques, such as penalty functions, to handle constraints [98]. The ant colony optimization algorithm is used to generate a set of feasible solutions, while the penalty function is used to penalize constraint violations and improve the quality of the solutions.

HCHTs can be effective in improving the optimization performance of nature-inspired optimization algorithms, and the selection of which HCHT to use depends on the explicit problem and the desired level of constraint satisfaction.

3.6   Feature selection

Feature selection is a vital step in many ML [59] and DL [99] tasks, as it can significantly advance the accuracy of the resulting models by deducting the number of features that are irrelevant or redundant. Feature selection algorithms aim to identify the subset of features that are most informative for the given task [31]. The traditional methods for feature selection like the sequential forward selection and backward elimination, have limitations in handling high-dimensional data. NIOAs have been successfully implemented to feature selection problems, as they can effectively explore the search space and identify relevant feature subsets [100].

3.6.1   Feature selection based on GA

Feature set is obtained after the process of feature extraction. Since, these features set contains all redundant and non-redundant information. So, such features which are utmost required for classification or detection purposes that are designated with the aid of feature selection. But all these processes are complex in nature, so to deduce complexity and increase accuracy, it must be optimized. GA uses the genetic operators to optimize the feature set [101]. The steps involved to optimize the feature set with GA is demonstrated in Table 3.3.

Table 3.3   GA-based generalized feature selection step

Initialization: Initialize a population of individuals, where each individual signifies a potential solution (i.e., a subset of features).

Fitness evaluation: Evaluate the fitness of each individual by using the quality of the selected features.

Selection: Select the fittest individuals to form a mating pool for the next iteration.

Crossover: Perform crossover between pairs of parents to create offspring, where the offspring inherit some of the features from each parent.

Mutation: Mutate some of the offspring to introduce new features or remove existing features.

Evaluation: Evaluate the fitness of the offspring.

Replacement: Replace the least fit individuals in the population with the offspring.

Termination: The algorithm stops when a stopping criterion is met, such as a maximum number of iterations or a convergence criterion.

Once the optimization process is completed, the subset of features with the highest fitness value is selected as the optimal subset.

Table 3.4 Overview of feature selection steps with the aid of PSO

Initialization: Initialize a swarm of particles, where each particle signifies a potential solution (i.e., a subset of features).
Velocity and position update: Each particle adjusts its velocity and position based on its recent position, its best position so far, and the best position found by the swarm. This update is based on a set of equations that balance exploration and exploitation.
Fitness evaluation: Evaluate the fitness of each particle by using the quality of the selected features.
Local search: Each particle performs a local search to improve its solution by adding or removing features.
Global update: After each iteration, the best solution found so far is communicated to all particles to update their search behavior.
Termination: The algorithm stops when a stopping criterion is matched like total number of iterations or a convergence norm.
Once the optimization process is completed, the subset of features with the highest fitness value is selected as the optimal subset.

3.6.2   Feature selection based on PSO

PSO can be used to optimize the selection of features based on different criteria, such as mutual information, correlation, or classification error. For example, PSO has been used to optimize the selection of features for classification of medical images [102]. The primarily steps to readdress the issues of feature selection by PSO is presented in Table 3.4.

3.6.3   Feature selection based on ACO

In the context of feature selection by ACO, each feature is represented as a node in a graph, and the pheromone trail represents the importance of each feature [103]. Table 3.5 demonstrates the generalized steps used by ACO to perform feature selection.

3.6.4   Feature selection based on ABC

ABC can be used to perform feature selection by optimizing a fitness function that evaluates the quality of the selected features [104]. ABC mimics the behavior of ants. Table 3.6 exhibits the basic steps for feature selection using ABC.

3.6.5   Feature selection based on CS

CS has a widespread range of applications in feature selection [105]. Many MLs and DLs [20] follow the CS for the feature selection. The generalized feature selection steps based on CS are shown in Table 3.7.

Table 3.5   Steps involved in feature selection by ACO

Initialization: Initialize the population of ants, where each ant signifies a potential solution (i.e., a subset of features).
Pheromone trails: Each ant constructs a pheromone trail that exhibits the quality of its solution, where the pheromone level increases with the fitness value of the solution.
Probabilistic transition: Each ant probabilistically selects the next feature to include in its solution based on the pheromone level and the importance of the feature.
Local search: Each ant performs a local search to improve its solution by adding or removing features.
Global update: After each iteration, the pheromone levels are updated based on the best solution found so far.
Termination: The algorithm stops when a stopping criterion is satisfied in terms of number of iterations.
Once the optimization process is completed, the subset of features with the highest fitness value is selected as the optimal subset.

Table 3.6   Basic steps for feature selection using ABC

Initialization: Initialize the population of bees, where each bee characterizes a potential solution (i.e., a subset of features).
Employed bees: Each employed bee evaluates a fitness function for its solution and then searches for a neighboring solution to improve its fitness. The neighboring solution is generated by randomly selecting a feature to add or remove from the current solution.
Onlooker bees: It select a solution based on its fitness value and then search for a neighboring solution to improve its fitness. The selection probability is relative to the fitness value of the solution.
Scout bees: If an Employed or onlooker bee has not found a better solution after a certain number of iterations, it becomes a scout bee and generates a new solution randomly.
Termination: The algorithm stops when a stopping criterion matched.
Once the optimization process is completed, the subset of features with the highest fitness value is selected as the optimal subset.

Table 3.7   Steps performed for feature selection by CS

Initialization: Initialize the population of cuckoos, where each cuckoo signifies a potential solution (i.e., a subset of features).
Levy Flight: Each cuckoo generates a new solution by performing a random walk in the feature space, which is modelled by a Levy Flight distribution.
Evaluate fitness: Each cuckoo evaluates a fitness function for its solution and compares it to the fitness values of the other cuckoos in the population.
Replace eggs: If a cuckoo's solution is better than another cuckoo's solution, it replaces the other cuckoo's solution with a new solution generated by a Levy Flight.
Abandon eggs: Some cuckoos may lay eggs in the nests of other cuckoos. If a cuckoo finds a better solution by laying an egg in another cuckoo's nest, it abandons its own nest and adopts the other cuckoo's nest.
Termination: The algorithm iterates until stopping condition is matched.
Once the optimization process is completed, the subset of features with the highest fitness value is selected as the optimal subset.

Table 3.8   FF-based feature selection steps

Initialization: Initialize the population of fireflies, where each firefly represents a potential solution (i.e., a subset of features).
Attraction: Each firefly moves towards other fireflies that have a higher fitness value, which is modelled by an attractiveness function that depends on the distance between the fireflies and their fitness values.
Randomization: Each firefly also moves randomly to explore the search space and escape from local optima.
Intensity: The intensity of each firefly's light is relative to its fitness value, and the intensity decreases with distance from the firefly.
Absorption: If a firefly's light intensity is greater than another firefly's light intensity, it absorbs the other firefly's position and updates its solution.
Termination: It will terminate after the matching of convergence norm.
Once the optimization process is completed, the subset of features with the highest fitness value is selected as the optimal subset.

3.6.6   Feature selection based on FF

FF exhibits the properties of natural fire flies. FF can be used for dimension reduction [106]. Table 3.8 shows the steps involved in feature selection by FF.

Additionally, GA, PSO ACO, ABC, CS, and FF may require a large number of iterations to converge to an optimal solution, which can increase the computational cost of the algorithm.

3.7   Practical engineering applications

The applications of NIOAs are numerous and varied, ranging from power distribution networks to building energy systems. As such, they are an essential tool in the toolbox of modern engineers. Some of the practical engineering applications of NIOAs [71,107] are listed below. Furthermore, Table 3.9 demonstrates an overview on the practical engineering applications with the aid of NIOAs.

(a) ACO: It is enthused by the foraging behavior of ants. This algorithm has been broadly used in engineering applications such as optimization of tele-communication networks, vehicle routing, and job scheduling. One practical application of ACO is in the optimization of power distribution networks. ACO can be used to find the shortest path between power stations, reducing energy losses, and improving the efficiency of the network.

(b) PSO: It is governed by the flocking behavior of birds and the schooling behavior of fish. It has been used in a several engineering applications, including antenna design, robot control, and image processing. The real-time example of PSO is in the optimization of wind turbines. PSO can be used to optimize the blade shape and angle of attack, improving the efficiency and power output of the wind turbine.

Table 3.9   Overview on the practical engineering applications with the aid of NIOAs

NIOAs	Practical engineering applications
DE	• Parameter tuning of electric motors • Design of heat exchangers • Optimization of gearboxes • Process control of wastewater treatment plants
GA	• Structural design of aircraft components • Optimization of power generation systems • Design of control systems for autonomous vehicles • Optimization of manufacturing processes
PSO	• Optimization of water distribution networks • Design of antenna arrays • Scheduling of production systems • Optimization of energy consumption in buildings
ACO	• Routing of vehicles in transportation networks • Optimization of wireless sensor networks • Design of electrical power networks • Optimization of logistics and supply chain management
ABC	• Optimization of wind farm layout • Design of power systems • Optimization of wireless communication systems • Parameter estimation in chemical processes
FF	• Optimization of structural design • Optimization of machine learning algorithms • Scheduling of transportation systems • Optimization of neural networks
CS	• Design of power systems • Optimization of artificial neural networks • Image processing and analysis • Optimization of medical diagnosis models
BF	• Signal and Image processing • Sensor networks • Control systems • Electrical power systems • Chemical and mechanical engineering • Bioinformatics
SA	• Optimization of supply chain management systems • Design of artificial neural networks

(Continues)

Table 3.9 (*Continued*)

NIOAs	Practical engineering applications
	• Optimization of renewable energy systems • Scheduling of production systems
GS	• Optimization of robot path planning • Optimization of hydrodynamic flow control systems • Design of communication networks • Optimization of machine learning algorithms
BBBC	• Optimization of water resource management systems • Design of flexible manufacturing systems • Optimization of supply chain networks • Parameter estimation in hydrological models

(c) GA: It is inspired by the process of natural selection and genetics. Its working areas in engineering applications include structural design, material selection, and manufacturing optimization. The practical example of GA is in the optimization of aircraft wing design. GA can be used to optimize the wing shape and size, reducing drag, and improving the lift-to-drag ratio of the aircraft.

(d) ABC: It is evolved by the foraging behavior of honey bees. It has been used in a variety of engineering areas like image processing, power system optimization, and parameter tuning. One practical real application of ABC is in the optimization of water distribution networks. ABC can be used to optimize the placement and sizing of pipes, reducing leaks, and improving the efficiency of the network.

(e) FA: It is originated by the flashing behavior of fireflies. It can be used in robotics, power system optimization, and signal processing. One of the most common practical applications of FA is in the optimization of building energy systems. FA can be used to optimize the control of heating, ventilation, and air conditioning systems, reducing energy consumption, and improving the comfort of the occupants.

(f) BF: It mimics the behavior of bacteria foraging for food. Some examples of practical engineering applications are signal-image processing, sensor networks, control systems, electrical power systems, bioinformatics, environmental, chemical, and mechanical engineering. For instance, it can be used to optimize the load dispatch problem, which involves scheduling the generation and distribution of electrical power in a system. In transportation engineering, it optimizes the traffic signal timings and routing in transportation networks.

3.8 Conclusion

NIOAs have been shown to be effective in solving a wide range of engineering problems. These algorithms take inspiration from natural phenomena and use them to create optimization algorithms that can be used to find the best solution to a problem.

The application areas of these algorithms include engineering optimization, robotics, finance, image processing, machine learning, and environmental management. These can solve complex optimization problems and finding the optimal solution.

In this chapter, various application aspects of NIOAs in the area of image processing like denoising, enhancement, segmentation, feature extraction-selection, and classification have been discussed. Furthermore, parameter tuning is essential for the performance of NIOAs. The optimal values for the algorithm's parameters depend on the problem's characteristics and the available computational resources. A well-tuned algorithm can significantly improve the efficiency and accuracy of the optimization process. In addition to that, NIOAs have become popular in solving constrained and unconstrained optimization problems due to their effectiveness in efficiently searching the solution space and finding the global optimum. The algorithms can be adapted to handle constraints in constrained optimization problems through penalty function methods and constraint handling methods. In unconstrained optimization problems, the algorithms can be classified into population-based methods and single-point methods. Overall, NIOAs provides a powerful tool for solving a wide range of optimization problems.

List of Abbreviations

ABC   Artificial Bee Colony

ACO   Ant Colony Optimization

AI   Artificial Intelligence

BA   Bat Algorithm

BBBC   Big Bang Big Crunch

BIOAs   Bio-Inspired Optimization Algorithms

CNN   Convolutional Neural Network

CP   Constraint Programming

CS   Cuckoo Search

CSPs   Constraint Satisfaction Problems

DE   Differential Evolution

DL   Deep Learning

FF   Firefly

GA   Genetic Algorithm

GS   Gravitational Search

HCHTs   Hybrid Constraint Handling Techniques

IoT   Internet of Things

ML   Machine Learning

MR   Mutation Rate

MI   Mutual Information

NIOAs   Nature-Inspired Optimization Algorithms

NSIOAs   Natural Science Inspired Optimization Algorithms
OF   Objective Function
OAs   Optimization Algorithms
PSO   Particle Swarm Optimization
PS   Population Size
ROIs   Region of Interests
SA   Simulated Annealing
SIFT   Scale-Invariant Feature Transform
SQP   Sequential Quadratic Programming
TV   total variation

References

[1]   W. R. Ashby, *Principles of Self-Organizations: Transaction*. Pergamon Press, 1962.

[2]   I. Fister Jr, X.-S. Yang, I. Fister, J. Brest, and D. Fister, "A brief review of nature-inspired algorithms for optimization," *arXiv Prepr. arXiv1307.4186*, 2013.

[3]   S. Forrest, "Genetic algorithms," *ACM Comput. Surv.*, vol. 28, no. 1, pp. 77–80, 1996.

[4]   S. Das and P. N. Suganthan, "Differential evolution: a survey of the state-of-the-art," *IEEE Trans. Evol. Comput.*, vol. 15, no. 1, pp. 4–31, 2010.

[5]   J. Kennedy and R. Eberhart, "Particle swarm optimization," in *Proceedings of ICNN'95-International Conference on Neural Networks*, 1995, vol. 4, pp. 1942–1948.

[6]   X.-S. Yang, "Firefly algorithms for multimodal optimization," in *Stochastic Algorithms: Foundations and Applications: 5th International Symposium*, SAGA 2009, Sapporo, Japan, October 26–28, 2009. Proceedings 5, 2009, pp. 169–178.

[7]   D. Karaboga and B. Basturk, "A powerful and efficient algorithm for numerical function optimization: artificial bee colony (ABC) algorithm," *J. Glob. Optim.*, vol. 39, pp. 459–471, 2007.

[8]   S. Das, A. Biswas, S. Dasgupta, and A. Abraham, "Bacterial foraging optimization algorithm: theoretical foundations, analysis, and applications," *Found. Comput. Intell. Glob. Optim.*, vol. 3, pp. 23–55, 2009.

[9]   M. Dorigo, M. Birattari, and T. Stutzle, "Ant colony optimization," *IEEE Comput. Intell. Mag.*, vol. 1, no. 4, pp. 28–39, 2006.

[10] X.-S. Yang and A. Hossein Gandomi, "Bat algorithm: a novel approach for global engineering optimization," *Eng. Comput.*, vol. 29, no. 5, pp. 464–483, 2012.

[11] A. H. Gandomi, X.-S. Yang, and A. H. Alavi, "Cuckoo search algorithm: a metaheuristic approach to solve structural optimization problems," *Eng. Comput.*, vol. 29, pp. 17–35, 2013.

[12]   S. Kirkpatrick, C. D. Gelatt Jr, and M. P. Vecchi, "Optimization by simulated annealing," *Science (80-.).*, vol. 220, no. 4598, pp. 671–680, 1983.

[13]   E. Rashedi, H. Nezamabadi-Pour, and S. Saryazdi, "GSA: a gravitational search algorithm," *Inf. Sci. (Ny).*, vol. 179, no. 13, pp. 2232–2248, 2009.

[14]   O. K. Erol and I. Eksin, "A new optimization method: big bang–big crunch," *Adv. Eng. Softw.*, vol. 37, no. 2, pp. 106–111, 2006.

[15]   X.-S. Yang, *Nature-Inspired Optimization Algorithms*. Academic Press, 2020.

[16]   E. V. Onet and E. Vladu, "Nature inspired algorithms and artificial intelligence," *J. Comput. Sci. Control. Syst.*, no. 1, pp. 66, 2008.

[17]   X.-S. Yang and X.-S. He, *Nature-Inspired Computation in Data Mining and Machine Learning*, 1st Edition. Springer Cham Publishers, ISBN: 978-3-030-28555-5, September 2020, https://doi.org/10.1007/978-3-030-28553-1.2020.

[18]   H. Chiroma, A. Gital, N. Rana, *et al.*, "Nature inspired meta-heuristic algorithms for deep learning.: no recent progress and novel perspective," in *Advances in Computer Vision: Proceedings of the 2019 Computer Vision Conference (CVC)*, 2020, vol 1 1, pp. 59–70.

[19]   S. R. Jino Ramson, K. Lova Raju, S. Vishnu, and T. Anagnostopoulos, "Nature inspired optimization techniques for image processing—a short review," in *Nature Inspired Optimization Techniques for Image Processing Applications*. Cham: Springer, 2019, pp. 113–145.

[20]   R. J. S. Raj, S. J. Shobana, I. V. Pustokhina, D. A. Pustokhin, D. Gupta, and K. Shankar, "Optimal feature selection-based medical image classification using deep learning model in internet of medical things," *IEEE Access*, vol. 8, pp. 58006–58017, 2020.

[21]   V. Sharma and A. K. Tripathi, "A systematic review of meta-heuristic algorithms in IoT based application," *Array*, vol. 14, p. 100164, 2022.

[22]   M. Dorigo and G. Di Caro, "Ant colony optimization: a new meta-heuristic," in *Proceedings of the 1999 Congress on Evolutionary Computation-CEC99 (Cat. No. 99TH8406)*, 1999, vol. 2, pp. 1470–1477.

[23]   M. F. Ahmad, N. A. M. Isa, W. H. Lim, and K. M. Ang, "Differential evolution: a recent review based on state-of-the-art works," *Alexandria Eng. J.*, vol. 61, no. 5, pp. 3831–3872, 2022.

[24]   J. H. Holland, *Adaptation in Natural and Artificial Systems: an Introductory Analysis with Applications to Biology, Control, and Artificial Intelligence*. MIT Press, 1992.

[25]   X.-S. Yang and S. Deb, "Cuckoo search via Lévy flights," in *2009 World Congress on Nature and Biologically Inspired Computing (NaBIC)*, 2009, pp. 210–214.

[26]   S. Chib and E. Greenberg, "Understanding the metropolis-hastings algorithm," *Am. Stat.*, vol. 49, no. 4, pp. 327–335, 1995.

[27]   P. Kumar, S. Srivastava, and R. Srivastava, "Basic understanding of medical imaging modalities," in *High-Performance Medical Image Processing*, Apple Academic Press, 2021, pp. 1–17.

[28]   A. K. Rai and S. Srivastava, "A thorough investigation on image forgery detection," *C. Model. Eng. \& Sci.*, vol. 134, no. 3, pp. 1489–1528, 2023.

[29] D. Sharma, A. P. Bhondekar, A. K. Shukla, and C. Ghanshyam, "A review on technological advancements in crowd management," *J. Ambient Intell. Humaniz. Comput.*, vol. 9, no. 3, pp. 485–495, 2018.

[30] K. R. Castleman, *Digital Image Processing.* Prentice Hall Press, 1996.

[31] R. C. Gonzalez, *Digital Image Processing.* Pearson Education India, 2009.

[32] R. Srivastava and S. Srivastava, "Restoration of Poisson noise corrupted digital images with nonlinear PDE based filters along with the choice of regularization parameter estimation," *Pattern Recognit. Lett.*, vol. 34, no. 10, pp. 1175–1185, 2013.

[33] R. Kumar, R. Srivastava, and S. Srivastava, "Microscopic biopsy image segmentation using hybrid color K-means approach," *Int. J. Comput. Vis. Image Process.*, vol. 7, no. 1, pp. 79–90, 2017.

[34] V. P. Singh, S. Srivastava, and R. Srivastava, "Effective mammogram classification based on center symmetric-LBP features in wavelet domain using random forests," *Technol. Heal. Care*, vol. 25, no. 4, pp. 709–727, 2017.

[35] S. Srivastava, N. Sharma, and S. K. Singh, "Empirical analysis of supervised and unsupervised filter based feature selection methods for breast cancer classification from digital mammograms," *Int. J. Comput. Appl.*, vol. 88, no. 8, 2014.

[36] K. Jani, R. Srivastava, and S. Srivastava, "Computer aided medical image analysis for capsule endoscopy using multi-class classifier," in *2019 IEEE 5th International Conference for Convergence in Technology (I2CT)*, 2019, pp. 1–5.

[37] S. Sarkar, S. Das, and S. S. Chaudhuri, "Multi-level thresholding with a decomposition-based multi-objective evolutionary algorithm for segmenting natural and medical images," *Appl. Soft Comput.*, vol. 50, pp. 142–157, 2017.

[38] P. Sukhija, S. Behal, and P. Singh, "Face recognition system using genetic algorithm," *Procedia Comput. Sci.*, vol. 85, pp. 410–417, 2016.

[39] M. Sabeti, R. Boostani, and B. Davoodi, "Improved particle swarm optimisation to estimate bone age," *IET Image Process.*, vol. 12, no. 2, pp. 179–187, 2018.

[40] G. JayaBrindha and E. S. G. Subbu, "Ant colony technique for optimizing the order of cascaded SVM classifier for sunflower seed classification," *IEEE Trans. Emerg. Top. Comput. Intell.*, vol. 2, no. 1, pp. 78–88, 2017.

[41] H.-F. Kuo and Frederick, "Ant colony optimization-based freeform sources for enhancing nanolithographic imaging performance," *IEEE Trans. Nanotechnol.*, vol. 15, no. 4, pp. 599–606, 2016.

[42] A. Mostafa, A. Fouad, M. A. Elfattah, *et al.*, "CT liver segmentation using artificial bee colony optimisation," *Procedia Comput. Sci.*, vol. 60, pp. 1622–1630, 2015.

[43] A. K. Bhandari, A. Kumar, and G. K. Singh, "Tsallis entropy based multi-level thresholding for colored satellite image segmentation using evolutionary algorithms," *Expert Syst. Appl.*, vol. 42, no. 22, pp. 8707–8730, 2015.

[44] A. Kumar and S. Srivastava, "Restoration and enhancement of breast ultra-sound images using extended complex diffusion based unsharp masking," *Proc. Inst. Mech. Eng. Part H J. Eng. Med.*, vol. 236, no. 1, pp. 12–29, 2022.

[45] N. B. Bahadure, A. K. Ray, and H. P. Thethi, "Comparative approach of MRI-based brain tumor segmentation and classification using genetic algorithm," *J. Digit. Imaging*, vol. 31, pp. 477–489, 2018.

[46] V. Kumar and S. Srivastava, "Performance analysis of reshaped Gabor filter for removing the Rician distributed noise in brain MR images," *Proc. Inst. Mech. Eng. Part H J. Eng. Med.*, vol. 236, no. 8, pp. 1216–1231, 2022.

[47] P. M. Narendra, "A separable median filter for image noise smoothing," *IEEE Trans. Pattern Anal. Mach. Intell.*, no. 1, pp. 20–29, 1981.

[48] F. Jin, P. Fieguth, L. Winger, and E. Jernigan, "Adaptive Wiener filtering of noisy images and image sequences," in *Proceedings 2003 International Conference on Image Processing (Cat. No. 03CH37429)*, 2003, vol. 3, pp. III–349.

[49] J. D. Villasenor, B. Belzer, and J. Liao, "Wavelet filter evaluation for image compression," *IEEE Trans. Image Process.*, vol. 4, no. 8, pp. 1053–1060, 1995.

[50] M. Elad, "On the origin of the bilateral filter and ways to improve it," *IEEE Trans. Image Process.*, vol. 11, no. 10, pp. 1141–1151, 2002.

[51] A. Buades, B. Coll, and J.-M. Morel, "Non-local means denoising," *Image Process. Line*, vol. 1, pp. 208–212, 2011.

[52] S. Srivastava, N. Sharma, R. Srivastava, and S. K. Singh, "Restoration of digital mammographic images corrupted with quantum noise using an adaptive total variation (TV) based nonlinear filter," in *2012 International Conference on Communications, Devices and Intelligent Systems (CODIS)*, 2012, pp. 125–128.

[53] R. R. Kumar, A. Kumar, and S. Srivastava, "Anisotropic diffusion based unsharp masking and crispening for denoising and enhancement of MRI images," in *2020 International Conference on Emerging Frontiers in Electrical and Electronic Technologies (ICEFEET)*, 2020, pp. 1–6.

[54] S. Srivastava, R. Srivastava, N. Sharma, S. K. Singh, and S. Sharma, "A fourth-order PDE-based non-linear filter for speckle reduction from optical coherence tomography images," *Int. J. Biomed. Eng. Technol.*, vol. 10, no. 1, pp. 55–69, 2012.

[55] A. Kumar, P. Kumar, and S. Srivastava, "A skewness reformed complex diffusion based unsharp masking for the restoration and enhancement of Poisson noise corrupted mammograms," *Biomed. Signal Process. Control*, vol. 73, pp. 103421, 2022.

[56] U. K. Acharya and S. Kumar, "Genetic algorithm based adaptive histogram equalization (GAAHE) technique for medical image enhancement," *Optik (Stuttg).*, vol. 230, pp. 166273, 2021.

[57] R. Srivastava, J. R. P. Gupta, H. Parthasarthy, and S. Srivastava, "PDE based unsharp masking, crispening and high boost filtering of digital images," in *Contemporary Computing: Second International Conference, IC3 2009, Noida, India, August 17–19, 2009. Proceedings 2*, 2009, pp. 8–13.

[58] S. Winkler, "Vision models and quality metrics for image processing applications," Verlag nicht ermittelbar, 2001.

[59] S. Khalid, T. Khalil, and S. Nasreen, "A survey of feature selection and feature extraction techniques in machine learning," in *2014 Science and Information Conference*, 2014, pp. 372–378.

[60] Z. Daixian, "SIFT algorithm analysis and optimization," in *2010 International Conference on Image Analysis and Signal Processing*, 2010, pp. 415–419.

[61] N. Dalal and B. Triggs, "Histograms of oriented gradients for human detection," in *2005 IEEE Computer Society Conference on Computer Vision and Pattern Recognition (CVPR'05)*, 2005, vol. 1, pp. 886–893.

[62] H. Bay, A. Ess, T. Tuytelaars, and L. Van Gool, "Speeded-up robust features (SURF)," *Comput. Vis. image Underst.*, vol. 110, no. 3, pp. 346–359, 2008.

[63] H. Abdi and L. J. Williams, "Principal component analysis," *Wiley Interdiscip. Rev. Comput. Stat.*, vol. 2, no. 4, pp. 433–459, 2010.

[64] B. F. Darst, K. C. Malecki, and C. D. Engelman, "Using recursive feature elimination in random forest to account for correlated variables in high dimensional data," *BMC Genet.*, vol. 19, no. 1, pp. 1–6, 2018.

[65] S. Balakrishnama and A. Ganapathiraju, "Linear discriminant analysis—a brief tutorial," *Inst. Signal Inf. Process.*, vol. 18, no. 1998, pp. 1–8, 1998.

[66] A. Kraskov, H. Stögbauer, and P. Grassberger, "Estimating mutual information," *Phys. Rev. E*, vol. 69, no. 6, pp. 66138, 2004.

[67] P. Liashchynskyi and P. Liashchynskyi, "Grid search, random search, genetic algorithm: a big comparison for NAS," *arXiv Prepr. arXiv1912.06059*, 2019.

[68] R. Kumar, R. Srivastava, and S. Srivastava, "Detection and classification of cancer from microscopic biopsy images using clinically significant and biologically interpretable features," *J. Med. Eng.*, vol. 2015, Article no. 457906, 2015.

[69] P. Kumar, S. Srivastava, R. K. Mishra, and Y. P. Sai, "End-to-end improved convolutional neural network model for breast cancer detection using mammographic data," *J. Def. Model. Simul.*, vol. 19, no. 3, pp. 375–384, 2022.

[70] P. Kumar, A. Kumar, S. Srivastava, and Y. Padma Sai, "A novel bi-modal extended Huber loss function based refined mask RCNN approach for automatic multi instance detection and localization of breast cancer," *Proc. Inst. Mech. Eng. Part H J. Eng. Med.*, vol. 236, no. 7, pp. 1036–1053, 2022.

[71] X.-S. Yang and X. He, "Nature-inspired optimization algorithms in engineering: overview and applications," *Nat.-Inspired Comput. Eng.*, pp. 1–20, 2016.

[72] A. M. Hemeida, S. Alkhalaf, A. Mady, E. A. Mahmoud, M. E. Hussein, and A. M. B. Eldin, "Implementation of nature-inspired optimization algorithms in some data mining tasks," *Ain Shams Eng. J.*, vol. 11, no. 2, pp. 309–318, 2020.

[73] X.-S. Yang (Ed.), "Chapter 14 — How to deal with constraints," in *Nature-Inspired Optimization Algorithms (Second Edition)*, Academic Press, 2021, pp. 207–220. https://doi.org/10.1016/B978-0-12-821986-7.00021-4.

[74] J. Nocedal, "Theory of algorithms for unconstrained optimization," *Acta Numer.*, vol. 1, pp. 199–242, 1992.

[75] M. J. Box, "A new method of constrained optimization and a comparison with other methods," *Comput. J.*, vol. 8, no. 1, pp. 42–52, 1965.

[76] D. P. Bertsekas, *Constrained Optimization and Lagrange Multiplier Methods*. Academic Press, 2014.

[77] K. Deb, "An efficient constraint handling method for genetic algorithms," *Comput. Methods Appl. Mech. Eng.*, vol. 186, no. 2–4, pp. 311–338, 2000.

[78] P. E. Gill, W. Murray, and M. H. Wright, *Practical Optimization*. SIAM, 2019.

[79] E. Mezura-Montes and C. A. C. Coello, "Constraint-handling in nature-inspired numerical optimization: past, present and future," *Swarm Evol. Comput.*, vol. 1, no. 4, pp. 173–194, 2011.

[80] C. A. C. Coello, "Use of a self-adaptive penalty approach for engineering optimization problems," *Comput. Ind.*, vol. 41, no. 2, pp. 113–127, 2000.

[81] L. Jacob, G. Obozinski, and J.-P. Vert, "Group lasso with overlap and graph lasso," in *Proceedings of the 26th Annual International Conference on Machine Learning*, 2009, pp. 433–440.

[82] H. Zou and T. Hastie, "Regularization and variable selection via the elastic net," *J. R. Stat. Soc. Ser. B (Statistical Methodol.)*, vol. 67, no. 2, pp. 301–320, 2005.

[83] A. B. Owen, "A robust hybrid of lasso and ridge regression," *Contemp. Math.*, vol. 443, no. 7, pp. 59–72, 2007.

[84] A. R. Conn, N. I. M. Gould, and P. L. Toint, *Trust Region Methods*. SIAM, 2000.

[85] D. Bertsimas and J. N. Tsitsiklis, *Introduction to Linear Optimization*, vol. 6. Athena Scientific Belmont, MA, 1997.

[86] W. I. Zangwill, "Non-linear programming via penalty functions," *Manage. Sci.*, vol. 13, no. 5, pp. 344–358, 1967.

[87] C. A. Floudas and V. Visweswaran, "Quadratic optimization," in *Handbook of Global Optimization*. Springer, 1995, pp. 217–269.

[88] V. Kumar, "Algorithms for constraint-satisfaction problems: a survey," *AI Mag.*, vol. 13, no. 1, pp. 32, 1992.

[89] F. Rossi, P. Van Beek, and T. Walsh, *Handbook of Constraint Programming*. Elsevier, 2006.

[90] S. C. Brailsford, C. N. Potts, and B. M. Smith, "Constraint satisfaction problems: algorithms and applications," *Eur. J. Oper. Res.*, vol. 119, no. 3, pp. 557–581, 1999.

[91] P. T. Boggs and J. W. Tolle, "Sequential quadratic programming for large-scale nonlinear optimization," *J. Comput. Appl. Math.*, vol. 124, no. 1–2, pp. 123–137, 2000.

[92] S.-J. Kim, K. Koh, M. Lustig, S. Boyd, and D. Gorinevsky, "An interior-point method for large-scale l1-regularized least squares," *IEEE J. Sel. Top. Signal Process.*, vol. 1, no. 4, pp. 606–617, 2007.

[93] E. Wong, *Active-set Methods for Quadratic Programming*. San Diego: University of California, 2011.

[94] Y. Wang, Z. Cai, Y. Zhou, and Z. Fan, "Constrained optimization based on hybrid evolutionary algorithm and adaptive constraint-handling technique," *Struct. Multidiscip. Optim.*, vol. 37, pp. 395–413, 2009.

[95] C. A. C. Coello, "Theoretical and numerical constraint-handling techniques used with evolutionary algorithms: a survey of the state of the art," *Comput. Methods Appl. Mech. Eng.*, vol. 191, no. 11–12, pp. 1245–1287, 2002.

[96] A. Mani and C. Patvardhan, "A novel hybrid constraint handling technique for evolutionary optimization," in *2009 IEEE Congress on Evolutionary Computation*, 2009, pp. 2577–2583.

[97] H. Garg, "A hybrid PSO-GA algorithm for constrained optimization problems," *Appl. Math. Comput.*, vol. 274, pp. 292–305, 2016.

[98] B. Meyer, "Hybrids of constructive metaheuristics and constraint programming: a case study with aco," in *Hybrid Metaheuristics: An Emerging Approach to Optimization*, 2008, pp. 151–183.

[99] G. Chandrashekar and F. Sahin, "A survey on feature selection methods," *Comput. Electr. Eng.*, vol. 40, no. 1, pp. 16–28, 2014.

[100] B. Xue, M. Zhang, W. N. Browne, and X. Yao, "A survey on evolutionary computation approaches to feature selection," *IEEE Trans. Evol. Comput.*, vol. 20, no. 4, pp. 606–626, 2015.

[101] C.-L. Huang and C.-J. Wang, "A GA-based feature selection and parameters optimization for support vector machines," *Expert Syst. Appl.*, vol. 31, no. 2, pp. 231–240, 2006.

[102] M. Rostami, S. Forouzandeh, K. Berahmand, and M. Soltani, "Integration of multi-objective PSO based feature selection and node centrality for medical datasets," *Genomics*, vol. 112, no. 6, pp. 4370–4384, 2020.

[103] L. G. Fahad, S. F. Tahir, W. Shahzad, M. Hassan, H. Alquhayz, and R. Hassan, "Ant colony optimization-based streaming feature selection: an application to the medical image diagnosis," *Sci. Program.*, vol. 2020, pp. 1–10, 2020.

[104] M. S. Uzer, N. Yilmaz, and O. Inan, "Feature selection method based on artificial bee colony algorithm and support vector machines for medical datasets classification," *Sci. World J.*, vol. 2013, Article ID 419187, 2013.

[105] M. N. Sudha and S. Selvarajan, "Feature selection based on enhanced cuckoo search for breast cancer classification in mammogram image," *Circuits Syst.*, vol. 7, no. 4, pp. 327–338, 2016.

[106] R. Sawhney, P. Mathur, and R. Shankar, "A firefly algorithm based wrapper-penalty feature selection method for cancer diagnosis," in *Computational Science and Its Applications–ICCSA 2018: 18th International Conference, Melbourne, VIC, Australia, July 2–5, 2018, Proceedings, Part I 18*, 2018, pp. 438–449.

[107] J. Nayak, B. Naik, A. K. Das, and D. Pelusi, "Nature inspired optimization and its application to engineering," *Evol. Intell.*, vol. 14, pp. 1–3, 2021.

Chapter 4

Particle swarm optimization applications and implications

Sapna Katiyar[1] and Aakansha Garg[2]

4.1 Introduction to PSO

The particle swarm optimization (PSO) algorithm was developed by Kennedy and Eberhart in 1995 [1]. PSO algorithm is swarm-based algorithm, which mimics the social behavior of animals like flocks, birds, fish, and insect. Swarms tend to vary their search pattern corresponding to their own learning experience or from others. Therefore, they use collaborative approach to search food [2,3].

PSO algorithm design key idea is strongly associated with two studies:

- **Evolutionary algorithm:** Swarm approach used in PSO, facilitates searching larger regions in solution space to get optimized objective function.
- **Artificial life cycle:** PSO analyses the artificial structure with life traits.

There are five fundamental principles, derived from the social animal behaviors including artificial life cycle. These principles are proximity, quality, stability, diverse response, and adaptability. In PSO algorithm, particles have the tendency to update their velocity and position as environment varies. The swarm movement is not restricted; however, they constantly search for optimal solution in search space [4].

In standard PSO model, every bird is characterized as a point in cartesian coordinate system. Some initial velocity and position are arbitrary assigned to each bird. Nearest proximity velocity match rule is applied to execute the program and hence every entity has similar speed as its closest neighbor. With multiple iterations, suddenly all points have equal velocity. To make the entire simulation in real situation, a random variable is added up to the velocity element in each iteration [2,5].

[1]Impledge Technologies, India
[2]ABES Institute of Technology – Ghaziabad, India

4.1.1 PSO elements

Standard PSO is implemented by considering many elements. Few key elements are [3,6] the following:

- **Particle:** Describe particles in real numbers as Pi.
- **Fitness Function:** Generally, it is objective function and used to determine fitness function.
- **Local Best (pbest):** It is particle best position among all positions visited by particle.
- **Global Best (gbest):** Particle visits many positions; among those positions wherever best fitness is attained.
- **Velocity Update:** It is a vector, which determines the particle velocity and direction.
- **Position Update:** For optimal fitness, all particles tend to move for best position. In PSO to get global optima, every particle updates their position.

4.1.2 PSO algorithm

Let us assume position and velocity coordinates of each bird as (x,y) and (Vx, Vy). If the corn field position coordinate is $(x0, y0)$, current position and velocity performance are measured by the distance between corn field and current position [7,8]. It is assumed that each bird can memorize the best position reached (pbest) due to their memory. Other parameters are velocity adjusting constant (a) and random number on [0,1] (rand). Set of rules are there to establish the change in velocity item:

if $x >$ pbest$x$, $v_x = v_x -$ rand $\times$ a, otherwise, $v_x = v_x +$ rand $\times$ a
if $y >$ pbest$y$, $v_y = v_y -$ rand $\times$ a, otherwise, $v_y = v_y +$ rand $\times$ a

Another assumption about the swarm is that they can communicate. Every particle memorizes their best location as gbest. If velocity adjusting constant is b, then adjusted velocity item must be updated as per the mentioned rules:

if $x >$ gbest$x$, $v_x = v_x -$ rand $\times$ b, otherwise, $v_x = v_x +$ rand $\times$ b
if $y >$ gbest$y$, $v_y = v_y -$ rand $\times$ b, otherwise, $v_y = v_y +$ rand $\times$ b

In PSO algorithm, every particle is considered without mass and volume, so it is known as particle swarm optimization algorithm [2,6]. Figure 4.1 illustrates the flowchart of the PSO algorithm. From simulation result of PSO algorithm, it is observed that if the value of

- a/b is small, particles will gather nearby corn field slowly and wobblingly.
- a/b is comparatively large, all particles will gather in corn field speedily.

For PSO in continuous D-dimension space coordinates, let us assume:

- Swarm size is N
- Position vector of individual particle is $Xi = (xi1, xi2, \ldots, xid, \ldots, xiD)$
- Velocity vector is $Vi = (vi1, vi2, \ldots, vid, \ldots, viD)$
- Individual particle optimal position is $Pi = (pi1, pi2, \ldots, pid, \ldots, piD)$
- Swarm's optimal position is characterized as $Pg = (pg1, pg2, \ldots, pgd, \ldots, pgD)$

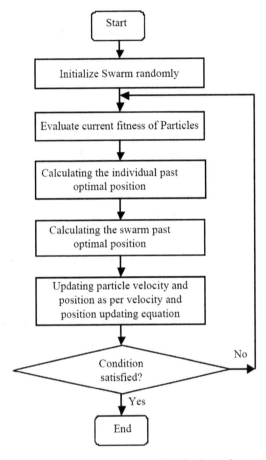

Figure 4.1 Flowchart of PSO algorithm

In the original PSO algorithm, individual particle optimal position is modified by (4.1).

$$p_{i,t+1}^d = \begin{cases} x_{i,t+1}^d, & \text{if} f(X_{i,t+1}) < f(P_{i,t}) \\ p_{i,t}^d, & \text{otherwise} \end{cases} \quad (4.1)$$

The optimal position of swarm is the overall distinct optimal solutions. Velocity and position are updated by (4.2).

$$v_{i,t+1}^d = v_{i,t}^d + c_1 * rand * (p_{i,t}^d - x_{i,t}^d)$$
$$+ c_2 * rand * (p_{g,t}^d - x_{i,t}^d) \quad (4.2)$$
$$x_{i,t+1}^d = x_{i,t}^d + v_{i,t+1}^d$$

For optimization problems, the original version of PSO is not very efficient. Therefore, it is modified by introducing inertia weight in the velocity vector updating equation. This updated algorithm is known as canonical PSO algorithm. So now, (4.2) can be written as follows:

$$v_{i,t+1}^d = \omega * v_{i,t}^d + c_1 * rand * (p_{i,t}^d - x_{i,t}^d) \\ + c_2 * rand * (p_{g,t}^d - x_{i,t}^d)$$

(4.3)

Further, PSO algorithm is modified by considering constriction factor (χ). This factor guarantees convergence and advance convergence rate. Therefore velocity update equation can be written as follows:

$$v_{i,t+1}^d = \chi(v_{i,t}^d + \phi_1 * rand * (p_{i,t}^d - x_{i,t}^d) \\ + \phi_2 * rand * (p_{g,t}^d - x_{i,t}^d)$$

(4.4)

In the above two equations, there is a very slight difference. Both equations would be identical if suitable parameters are chosen.

4.1.3   Standard pseudo code

Researchers have made several attempts to modify the PSO algorithm to improve the overall performance [3,9]. The pseudo code for standard PSO is "initialize population at random."
While (Size of Population)
{
Loop
Evaluate fitness
If fitness value is superior to p_{best} (best fitness value) in record, then
Update p_{best} with latest value of p_{best}
end loop
Choose best fitness value of particle among all g_{best}
While max. iterations or min. error criteria is not reached
{
Update particle velocity as per equation:

$$V_i^{t+1} = W \cdot V_i^t + c_1 U_1^t (P_{b_1}^t - P_i^t) + c_2 U_2^t (g_b^t - P_i^t)$$

(4.5)

Move the particles to the latest position

$$P_i^{t+1} = P_i^t + v_i^{t+1}$$

(4.6)

Next
}
}

4.1.4   PSO advantages and disadvantages

Since there are many optimization algorithms, particle swarm optimization algorithm is relatively cheaper, fast, and efficient. Few parameters are involved in the

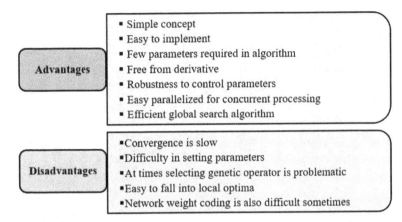

Figure 4.2   Advantages and disadvantages of PSO algorithm

algorithm, which makes it simple [1,5]. It is best fit for discrete, continuous, non-linear, and non-convex kind of problems. Figure 4.2 illustrates various advantages and disadvantages of PSO.

4.1.5   PSO applications

Table 4.1 summarizes the PSO applications in various fields for optimization. PSO has the capability to simulate the motion of particle swarm, so it can also be applied for visual effects such as specialized effects in Hollywood film [10,11]. Different fields where PSO has successfully applied in real-world applications are industrial automation, robotics, combinatorial problems, signal processing, image processing, healthcare, networking, biomedical, power generation, path planning and optimization, environmental applications, smart cities, commercial applications, and prediction and forecasting [6].

4.2   Outline of swarm intelligence

Swarm intelligence (SI), which falls into the umbrella of Artificial Intelligence [50], has always drawn the attention of researchers. In early 1960s itself many swarm-based optimization algorithms have been proposed. In 1980, the word SI was envisioned as a buss word and slowly it has covered broad category. A swarm can be observed as a collection of several thousands of individuals, which have decided their own desire to converge for a common goal. SI depicts the self-configured, coordinated, complex clustered, flexible, and robust action of a group. SI systems comprises many entities and the individuals are somewhat consistent. In such systems, interactions among the entities are established on the basis of simple behavioral rules and overall system behavior is the outcome of group behavior, i.e., individual interaction along with surrounding environment. The two fundamentals and essential properties of SI are:

- **Self-organization:** It is characterized as the system ability to grow its components or agents into appropriate manner without any outside support.

Table 4.1 Summary of PSO applications for different application areas

Reference	Authors	Application Area	Strength	Limitations
[12]	Pashaei et al.	Healthcare (medical image segmentation and disease diagnosis)	Better performance due to hybrid algorithm	Computation time is not considered
[13]	Zeng et al.		Accomplished using SVM model and deep learning algorithm	Experimental analysis is done with one data set only
[14]	Jain et al.		Quicker and more reliable approach with good local optimum solution in standard BPSO	Computation time is not considered
[15]	Li et al.		Improved performance with superior contextual details	Restricted activity of image segmentation problems
[16]	Raj and Ray		High accuracy, better sensitivity with improved productivity	Lack of real-time analysis and more computation time
[17]	Srisukkham et al.		Expedited chaotic investigation. Modified BBPSO algorithm is applied	Only particle's position is updated. Velocity is not considered here
[18]	Kumar et al.	Environmental applications (agricultural and environmental forecasting, prediction, and flood routing)	Improved accuracy and overall performance with the help of hybrid model	Lack of investigation in real-time environment
[19]	Zarel et al.		Hybrid evolutionary algorithm is used, which gives high reliability and improved water release values	Computation time can be reduced further, and monetary cost can be estimated
[20]	Chen et al.		Hybrid forecasting model is used, which gives improved accuracy with less run time	Certain emergencies like major holidays and few influential factors are missing
[21]	Rahgoshay et al.		Uses support vector method. Better accuracy and less computation time	Very simple structure and complex parameters are missing
[4]	Kour and Arora		Hybrid PSO-SVM algorithm is used for plants classification and segmentation. Higher accuracy with less computation time	Plants having medicinal values are not considered, which have major significance

Ref	Author	Applications	Description	Limitation
[22]	Cao et al.		Modified BPSO is used to monitor water quality. Fast convergence and good stability	Hyper-spectral sensors are used, which has low spectral resolution. Other lakes can also be investigated with same approach
[23]	Ghorbani et al.		Hybrid ANN-QPSO gives better accuracy in forecasting	Doubtfulness in the forecasting evaporation data
[24]	Etheram et al.		Uses hybrid BA and PSO algorithm for flood routing. Best solution is obtained with reduced computation time	Creating Muskingum model with few parameters only
[25]	Camci et al.		Achieved improved performance for rice farm inspection using Quadcopter. Capable to handle uncertainties and noise also	Inefficient control of quadcopter for natural landscapes
[26]	Maiyar and Thakkar	Industrial applications (nuclear power plants, wind turbines, TV panels, food transportation, airborne system platforms)	Decision support tool helps to reduce food grain wastage. Economic system	Perishable food grain products have not taken into consideration
[27]	Alnaqi et al.		Hybrid algorithm is used for prediction. Provides good performance and reliability	Consideration for scalability of such systems is missing
[28]	Wang et al.		Hybrid algorithm and fault diagnosis method gives better accuracy with less training time and noise	Real time data is not evaluated so that estimation is missing
[29]	Liu et al.		Hybrid algorithm is used for design optimization, which offers better platform stability and decreases mechanical resonance	It is a multi-objective optimization problem but only three targets were considered

(Continues)

Table 4.1 (Continued)

Reference	Authors	Application Area	Strength	Limitations
[30]	Ghorbani et al.		Hybrid algorithm is applied for PV-WT generation unit. It gives better reliability with reduced cost	Overall system accuracy is not evaluated
[31]	Jiang et al.		Decision support system works well for online customer reviews. It is low cost and less time consuming	Not capable to detect spam review and decision can be biased by sentimental reviews
[32]	Song et al.		Proper positioning of wind turbines gives more production of power with less system cost	Optimization for tedious and practical wind farms assessment is missing
[33]	Qi et al.		This approach offers better accuracy with less cost and response time	Long-term capability is not anticipated
[6]	Lopes et al.		Hybrid algorithm is developed for electric load distribution. It gives good quality solutions and reduces industry production cost	Investigation is done on tiny data set. Computation time is not calculated
[34]	Jiao et al.	Commercial applications	Hybrid algorithm for location estimation is deployed. It provides better transportation facility with reduced cost	Concept of multi objective is not incorporated
[35]	Tang et al.		Building materials price forecasting is done via hybrid approach. Offers fast convergence with better stability	Computation time evaluation is missing
[36]	Shen and Han		Provides real time profit calculation for accounting information system	Computational cost is not considered in overall profit calculation
[37]	Yi et al.		It offers many advantages so can be successfully applied practically. Accuracy is also improved	For such systems, scalability must be computed

Ref	Author	Domain	Description	Limitation
[7]	Kumar et al.		NN model provides statistically prominent results. Offers improved accuracy	Overall system computation time calculation is missing
[38]	Abid et al.	Smart city (highways, smart homes, residential areas)	Algorithm is used for energy management. Offers low cost and low power consumption	Accuracy needs to be calculated and present techniques can be compared with others
[39]	Zhang et al.		Locations for electric vehicles charging stations are identified using PSO. Creates more revenue and provides more coverage	Only two scenarios have been taken for testing, which can be increased
[40]	Li et al.		Hybrid model-based algorithm is applied for traffic forecasting. It provides good stability with improved accuracy	This procedure is very time consuming and data set is also very small
[41]	Jordehi		Hybrid algorithm is used, which reduces daily consumer bill	For such systems scalability can be considered
[42]	Le et al.		Robust hybrid PSO algorithm is applied for investigating building heating load. It offers good reliability	Cost calculation can be done, and accuracy can be further improved
[43]	Ma et al.		Scheduling model is developed for appliance, which provides good coverage and profits by selling electricity	Sometimes doubtful for renewable energy generation
[5]	Hu et al.		Hybrid algorithm is applied to schedule traffic light in urban area	Cost and scalability are not estimated. Some case studies of organized cities can also be included
[44]	Sato et al.		Quality of solution is improved for power grids in smart cities	Less stability and no cost estimation. Robustness needs to be proved

(Continues)

Table 4.1 (Continued)

Reference	Authors	Application Area	Strength	Limitations
[45]	Zarrouk et al.	Scheduling	PSO algorithm provides better quality solutions with lower CPU time	Cost factor is not taken into consideration, which is a very important factor in such type of problems
[46]	Mokhtari and Noroozi		Jobs are done punctually without any delay	Problem size is small. Only commercial optimization is considered, which can be extended further
[47]	Nouiri et al.		Approach is very effective for real time scenario. Decision making is decentralized	Every entity does not participate in final decision. Very high energy consumption
[48]	Zhong et al.	Path planning and optimization	PSO is implemented for Traveling salesman problem. It offers good balance between distance travelled and time	Can be compared with another significant optimization algorithm
[49]	Thabit and Mohades		Path planning is done for multi robots. This algorithm provides risk free, short, and smooth paths	It can be investigated for real time scenario

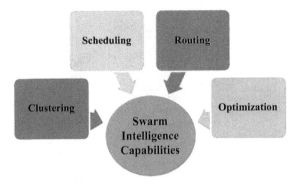

Figure 4.3   Capabilities of SI

Self-organization always depends on positive and negative feedbacks, numerous interactions, and variations.

• **Division of Work:** This property defines synchronized execution of multiple viable and straight forward jobs by individuals. It allows swarms to deal with complicated nature problem, where individuals are working collectively.

Depending upon the interesting properties of SI systems, many capabilities are offered.

Figure 4.3 shows the following SI capabilities:

Clustering: It is the procedure of automatic grouping. In SI, cluster is the group of like and unlike agents in another cluster.

Scheduling: The focus is on job's relative position instead of its direct successor or predecessor in the process of scheduling. Finally, summation assessment rule or global pheromone assessment rule is applied.

Routing: It is meant for end to end deliver and enhanced connectivity. As in the case of ants, backward moving ants utilize the information collected by forward ants about their route from source to destination.

Optimization: It is defined as a process of any problem to determine the best possible solution or minimum cost function among all feasible solutions.

4.2.1   General swarm principles

To frame the wide behavior arises from the swarm and to establish the relationship between swarm and PSO, various principles of SI are presented in Figure 4.4:

• **Proximity Principle:** Every entity of swarm should react back to environmental fluctuations initiated by agents' interaction. Nest building and living resource searching are the basic behavior of agents.
• **Stability Principle:** Every time when environment changes, mode of behavior of population should not change.
• **Adaptability Principle:** Swarm is sensitive for environmental changes, which may depict varied swarm behavior.

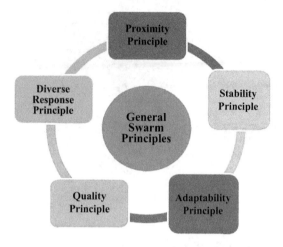

Figure 4.4   General principles of SI

- **Quality Principle:** Swarm should have the capability to react for quality factors like deciding safe location.
- **Diverse Response Principle:** Resources must note be accumulated into narrowing area. Distribution must be planned so that each agent can be highly protected against environmental fluctuations.

In 1989, the concept of SI was presented by Gerardo Beni and Jing Wang. It is a rising field of biologically inspired artificial intelligence, which is based on the behavior theory of social insects like bat, bees, ants, wasps etc. Advantages and disadvantages of Swarm Intelligence is listed in Figure 4.5. Multiple SI-based algorithms were developed and applied effectively multi-domain problems. There are many ways to classify the Swarm based algorithm, but one significant categorization is based on insect, bacteria, bird, wild, and amphibious. Figure 4.6 shows some well-known and proven optimization algorithms.

- Ant colony optimization (ACO) is truly inspired by the searching behavior of actual ants. It is a population-based metaheuristic approach, and the idea was proposed by Marco Dorigo in his PhD thesis in 1992 [51]. Several real-life examples of ACO are job scheduling, travelling salesman problem, path optimization, timetable scheduling, distribution planning, etc. [52].
- Cuckoo search (CS) algorithm was proposed in 2009 by Xin-She Yang and Deb. It is nature-inspired metaheuristic algorithm, encouraged by the brood parasitism of certain cuckoo varieties by leaving their eggs in the nest of host birds of other varieties [53].
- Teaching learning-based optimization (TLBO) algorithm was developed in 2011 by Rao *et al.* This algorithm mimics the classroom environment of teacher and learners, for optimizing any given objective function. There are two phases: teacher phase and learner phase [54,55].
- Particle swarm optimization (PSO) algorithm has many similarities with genetic algorithm and evolutionary computation. It is an iterative approach; its

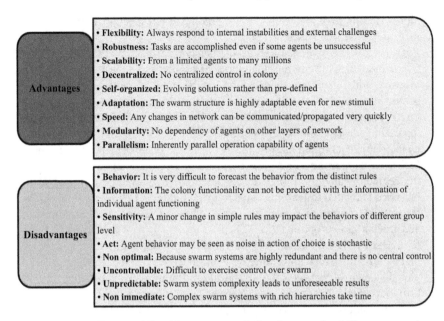

Figure 4.5 *Advantages and disadvantages of SI*

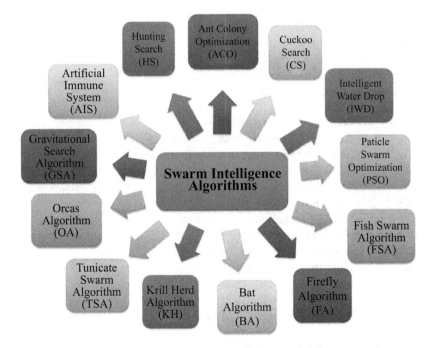

Figure 4.6 *Different types of SI algorithms*

aim is to improve the candidate solution with respect to assigned quality measures in search space [6,11].

- Bat algorithm (BA) is inspired by the behavior of bats, and the idea was proposed in 2012 by Yang and Gandomi. Microbats have the tendency of echolocation with changing loudness and pulse rate of radiation [24,56]. It is somewhat similar with PSO and consist of position and velocity equations.

- Firefly algorithm (FA) was established by Xin-She Yang in 2008. It is created on the flashing designs and behavior of tropical fireflies. Fireflies' fitness is evaluated by their blinking brightness [19,57]. FA is easy to implement and simple in nature.

- Fish swarm algorithm (FSA) was proposed by Li *et al.* in 2002. It is inspired by the regular behavior of fish for food search. In view of optimization, fish behavior is related to learning capacity, which directs fish swarm for searching fresh food sources, i.e., design space. FSA can avoid local minimums to accomplish global optimization [58,59].

- Krill Herd (KH) algorithm is best suitable for continuous optimization problems. In 2012, KH algorithm was introduced by Gandomi and Alavi for global standard function [60,61]. This algorithm mimics the herding actions of krill individuals. In comparison to many SI algorithms, it is robust, efficient, no implementation complexity, and require few control parameters.

- Tunicate swarm algorithm (TSA) is anticipated by Kaur *et al.* in 2020. It is encouraged by the swarm actions of tunicate to live effectively in ocean depth. TSA uses population best solution and works effective for optimizing nonlinear constraint problems [62].

- Orcas algorithm (OA) is encouraged by the lifestyle of Killer Whale or Orca, especially the hunting methods and echolocation actions [63]. It is developed as artificial intelligence grounded on the practical actions for known an ordinary adoption in association with the stages of selection and speeding.

- Gravitational search algorithm (GSA) is extensively applied in machine learning and is proposed by Rashedi *et al.* in 2009. GSA is encouraged by the theory of Newton's Law of Gravity and motion. In this algorithm, the best solution is the solution with the heavier mass [64,65].

- Artificial immune system (AIS) is the computationally intelligent algorithm, resulting from the principles encouraged by human immune system [66,67]. AIS algorithm was proposed by Farmer *et al.* in 1986 and Bersini *et al.* in 1990. This algorithm is very sophisticated and adaptive in nature.

- Hunting search (HS) algorithm is stimulated by the group hunting actions of predatory animals such as wolves, lions, and dolphins. All these hunters have different way of hunting, but one thing is common, which is group prey. The idea of HS algorithm is anticipated by Oftadeh *et al.* in 2010 [68].

4.3 PSO for single-objective problem

When optimization problem involves only one objective function, the task of finding the optimal solution is known as single-objective optimization problem.

PSO is a metaheuristic technique, and at present, it is one of the highly defined and most extensively used SI algorithm. Because of the simplicity of PSO, it has wide range of applications in problems for optimizing single objective [2,4]. PSO is problem independent algorithm, where merely single information is needed to run the algorithm, which is the fitness calculation for candidate solution.

Standard form of PSO is altered and modified, many variants were proposed by researchers to deal with distinct types of problems [5]. Some examples are travelling salesman problem, task planning problem, optimizing logistic planning, UAV mission planning, flood control and routing, and optimizing water harvesting.

4.4 PSO for multi-objective problem

In multi-objective optimization problems, numerous objectives are required to be handed at the same time [9,26]. In many situations, optimization of two or more than two parameters are required so PSO suits well for such multi optimization. Additional situation is when two nondominant solutions are of similarly good quality, then which one is to be chosen to use as best particle position. The range difficulty can be handled by integrating an extra set, known as external repository. This repository stores all nondominant solutions found throughout search. But the choice of highly appropriate repository member depends upon the nature of method. The restricted size of outer repository has certain constraints so that present solutions can be replaced with the new one with the help of specific rules [29].

The common multi-objective PSO structure can be expressed with mentioned pseudocode.

Start
  Initialize parameters (swarm, velocities, and best positions)
  Initialize external repository (initially it must be blank)
  While (criteria to stop in not satisfied) Do
     For every Particle
   Choose a member of external repository (if required)
   Update velocity & position
   Calculate the fresh position
   Updating the best position & external repository
     End For
  End While
End

4.5 Different approaches of multi-objective PSO

Many applications suffer from such problems where two or more than two-objective functions need to be handled simultaneously. Nature of problem may have multiple criteria's; therefore, the concept of Pareto optimality has come up. Many approaches are there for multi-objective PSO based on objective functions and Pareto-based methods separately [31,39].

4.5.1   Objective function aggregation approach

This approach combines all the objective functions over weighted combination into one.

$$F(x) = \sum_{i=1}^{k} w_i f_i(x) \tag{4.7}$$

where w_i is the nonnegative weights such that

$$\sum_{i=1}^{k} w_i = 1$$

Here, optimization is applied to $F(x)$ like single-objective optimization. During algorithm execution, if weights remain stable, then this approach is conventional weighted aggregation (CWA) [69]. It is very simple approach but has many limitations also. For a specific given weight setting when PSO is applied, it gives only one solution. Therefore, this algorithm needs to be repeated and again for different weight settings to have required solutions. CWA method cannot find solutions in concave area of Pareto front. These limitations can be addressed by dealing dynamic weight adjustment. Big-bang weighted aggregation (BWA) is one such approach.

4.5.2   Objective function ordering approach

In this approach, first ranking of objective functions is to be determined. Then each function is minimized separately in the order of priority. In 2002, Hu and Eberhart suggested a scheme based on such ranking. Pareto front puts limits on fitness value space and algorithm keeps easiest objective function fixed and minimizes the remaining objective functions. In such approach, PSO variants with dynamic neighborhoods is used, where controlled solutions are considered as particles best position. Objective function ordering approach works well for two-objective functions only, but its performance is not justified for more than two-objective functions [70,71]. This method is modified by integrating some exterior memory to store nondominated results and, hence decreasing the computational cost. This approach received restricted acceptability and not capable to address the binary string problem.

4.5.3   Non-Pareto, vector-evaluated approach

Vector-evaluated PSO (VEPSO) is a multi-swarm algorithm. It is established on the concept of vector-evaluated genetic algorithm (VEGA). In VEPSO algorithm, one swarm is dedicated to one-objective function and whole estimation is done for that objective function. Then for updating swarm, one swarm best position is utilized for velocity update of other swarm with different objective function [72].

If there are k swarms in a problem with k objectives. Let $vi[s]$ indicates ith particle velocity in the sth swarm, where $s = 1, \ldots, k$; therefore, the velocity is updated using the following equation:

$$v_{ij}^{[s]}(t+1) = w \ v_{ij}^{[s]}(t) + c_1 \ r_1(p_{ij}^{[s]}(t) - x_{ij}^{[s]}(t)) + c_2 \ r_2$$
$$(p_{gj}^{[q]}(t) - x_{ij}^{[s]}(t)), \tag{4.8}$$

where $p_g^{[q]}$ is the best position related to qth swarm, calculated with qth objective function.

A modified version of VEPSO is employed, where one processor indicates each swarm. The total number of swarms need not to be same as overall objective functions. In this system, swarms can communicate with other swarms through Island Migration approach. This algorithm is effectively applied for regulating generator contributions for transmission systems and optimizing radiometer array antenna [73].

One more comparable approach like VEPSO was suggested, known as multi-species PSO. This algorithm was established and linked to robotics for self-sufficient agent response knowledge framework. Subswarms were utilized, which form groups, one is used for every objective function. Then again, every subswarm is estimated with its specific objective function and greatest particle information is conveyed to nearby subswarms for particles velocity update. Therefore, ith particle velocity for sth swarm is modified as per equation:

$$v_{ij}^{[s]}(t+1) = v_{ij}^{[s]}(t) + a_1(p_{ij}^{[s]}(t) - x_{ij}^{[s]}(t)) + a_2$$
$$(p_{gj}^{[s]}(t) - x_{ij}^{[s]}(t))) + A, \tag{4.9}$$

where

$$A = \sum_{l=1}^{H_s} (p_{gj}^{[l]}(t) - x_{ij}^{[s]}(t))$$

H_s is the total number of swarms, which conveys with sth swarm. $p_g^{[l]}$ is the lth swarm's best position.

4.5.4 Algorithms based on Pareto dominance

The approaches that fall into this category apply the idea of Pareto Dominance to identify particle's best position, which will further drive swarm in the course of searching. Therefore, Pareto-based PSO methods turn out to be the budding research area. Some substantial advancements in this field are listed here.

1. Multi-objective PSO (MOPSO) is the initial Pareto-based PSO method. In MOPSO, repository is used to save nondominant results, which particles investigate. Entire search space is split into hypercubes and each hypercube is allocated a fitness value [74]. The fitness value is inversely proportional to the quantity of particles in hypercube. Here Classical Roulette Wheel selection is applied for picking a hypercube. The best particle position is updated after every iteration depending upon current best and its new position. Therefore,

the ith particle velocity update in the form of best position (pi) and repository leader (Rh) will be:

$$vij(t+1) = w \, vij(t) + c1 \, r1(pij(t) - xij(t)) + c2 \, r2(R_h(t) - xij(t))$$

(4.10)

Since the repository has restricted size so when it is full, new solutions can be stored based on retention criteria.

2. Repository insufficiencies to store limited records is overcome in another approach. It uses relatively complicated tree-type structure, known as dominant tree, for addressing the unconstrained repository upkeep. Except for repository upkeep, this algorithm acts like MOPSO. Inclusion of one more feature into this algorithm makes it more efficient, which is mutation, also known as craziness. Mutation acts for particle velocity, which conserves diversity [75].

3. Another algorithm is based on the selection criteria of leaders. More precisely every particle is evaluated for each objective function independently. Swarm global best position is updated as per mean of the best particle for each function. Particle diversity is conserved over the distance calculation. Choice of leader is inclined with respect to non-dominant solution, which promotes the mitigation of particles gathering in groups. This algorithm is examined over the number of problems to estimate efficiency [76].

4. Maximin PSO is one more approach, which utilized maximin fitness function. Fitness function for a particular decision vector (x) with swarm size (N) and number of objective functions (k) is given as follows:

$$\max_{j=1,\ldots,N;x \neq y} \min_{i=1,\ldots,k} \{f_i(x) - f_i(y)\}$$

(4.11)

Those decision vectors whose maximin function value is smaller than zero is considered as nondominant solutions. Swarm diversity is encouraged by maximin function because it corrects particles clusters [77]. There is one debatable point about it that it encourages intermediate solutions in convex faces and severe solutions in concave faces. This point can be handled by using a sufficiently large group of swam.

5. Another MOPSO technique with crowding distance mechanism is developed. It is beneficial for selecting globally the best particle and nondominant solutions removal from outer archive. To maintain diversity, mutation is taken into consideration. For every nondominant solution, crowding distance is calculated individually [78].

Let us assume,

- R as outer archive
- $f1, f2 \ldots, fk$ are objective functions
- then the calculation of crowding distance of p is R
- q is the point on R, which instantly follows p in sorting

By sorting all points in R, w.r.t. their objective value, f_i and taking,

$$CD\text{-}f_j = f_j(q) - f_j(r) \tag{4.12}$$

Therefore, the overall crowding distance of p is written as follows:

$$\sum_{j=1}^{k} CD\text{-}f_j \tag{4.13}$$

Swarm leaders are selected from the fraction of nondominant point of R, which are having maximum crowding distance. Mutation can also be applied upon particles to encourage swarm diversity.

4.6 Variants of PSO algorithm

Particle swarm optimization (PSO) was recommended by Eberhart and Kennedy in 1995. Statistically, it is proven but researchers kept trying efforts to enhance the standard PSO. Therefore, many variants of PSO are there, which are differentiated based on different parameters such as initialization, indolence weight, mutation operator, and constriction factor [10,38,41]. Some types of PSO variants are shown in Figure 4.7. The following are the different PSO variants.

4.6.1 Discrete PSO

The discrete PSO algorithm gives fast convergence and improved performance. Here the position of the particle has a discrete value. This algorithm can be efficiently applied to combinatorial and discrete optimization problems. Generally, when integer solutions are required, an optimal solution can be generated by rounding off the actual best value to the closest integer.

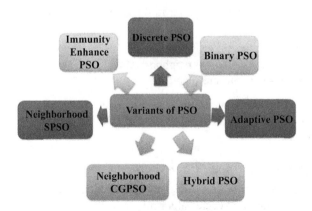

Figure 4.7 Different variants of PSO

4.6.2   Binary PSO

In the binary PSO algorithm, every particle position is represented by either 0 or 1 i.e., in binary value. Every particle in the population takes a binary decision in terms of 1 (True/Yes) or 0 (False/No). Particles value keeps changing from 0 to 1 or 1 to 0. In this algorithm, velocity must be confined in the range of [0, 1].

4.6.3   Adaptive PSO

Adaptive PSO provides improved search efficiency than standard PSO. PSO parameters like acceleration coefficients, inertia weight, etc. are adjusted in real time for finer performance. Though it involves many new parameters, it does not create any implementation complexity. Globally it is observed as the best particle to come out as likely local optima.

4.6.4   Hybrid PSO

Fresh and more refined PSO variants are continuously innovated to achieve better optimization performance. In research, there is always a trend for integrating the capabilities of different evolutionary computational methods, so same can be combined with PSO.

4.6.5   Neighborhood-guaranteed convergence PSO

This variant of PSO models the social networks structuring. Neighborhood guaranteed convergence PSO (GCPSO) permits particles to investigate bigger area of search space. The objective of neighborhood is actually to conserve the heterogeneity within the swarm by impending the information flow through the network.

Velocity update must be done to implement neighborhood in the standard PSO. Equation (4.1) is used to update velocity:

$$vi(t+1) = X(vi(t) + c1r1(pbest(t) - xi(t)) + c2r2(gbest(t) - xi(t)))$$

$$(4.14)$$

where *gbest*: best position found so far in the neighborhood of the *i*th particle.

4.6.6   Neighborhood search strategies PSO

This algorithm applies two global neighborhood searches and one local neighborhood search. Two operations are there:

- For every particle, neighborhood search generates three trial particles.
- Among the three trial particles, the best is selected and that is taken as fresh current particle.

4.6.7   Immunity-enhanced PSO

In this algorithm, a portion of particle population is sampled in workable space. Thereafter the population executes algorithm and PSO variants by updating velocity and position. Then non-uniform mutation is executed in accordance with some probability. So fresh generation is obtained with the help of selection operator when particles fly.

4.7   PSO in hybrid environment

Hybridization is defined as a broad model, which integrates two or more algorithms. The objective is to utilize their advantages and reduce their barriers. Through algorithm hybridization, two important properties of algorithms i.e. exploitation and exploration, can be entirely enhanced. Likewise, the PSO algorithm can be combined with another optimization algorithms [18,20]. PSO in hybridization helps to increase particles quality, algorithm efficiency, and effectiveness. PSO algorithm tends to trap in local optima, so it is unable to discover the entire region of search space. This difficulty can be overcome while combining PSO with others and simultaneously defeating the integral deficiencies of other algorithms [27]. Many hybrid algorithms have been proposed by researchers for solving multiple nature of problems with increased performance. Some of such algorithms have been discussed here.

(A) **PSO with Genetic Algorithm (GA):** Like PSO in case of GA, there is population of possible candidate solutions [21,30]. Every population element has chromosome, which gets mutated depending upon certain probability to preserve population diversity level and solution enhancements. During search process, PSO cannot avoid its trap for local optima though GA algorithm helps to reduce this weakness along with its operator [79].

(B) **PSO with Differential Evolution (DE):** DE falls into the category of evolutionary computation. Candidate solution is improved by iterative process and hence it optimizes any problem. Though DE does not give guarantee optimal solution, it has an excessive capability to preserve population diversity and perform local searches in definite search space. Therefore, hybridization of PSO with DE gives promising results [80,81].

(C) **PSO with Artificial Neural Network (ANN):** In such a hybridization, model PSO can be used to train ANN product unit. When it is compared with other algorithms, it offers less error with improved performance. In another hybrid model, the data set is divided into three: training set, validation set, and testing set. PSO algorithm is used to train the ANN architecture along with all nodes produced when algorithm is initialized [23,82].

(D) **PSO with Bat Algorithm (BA):** Integration of PSO with BA offers great convergence rate and avoid trapping into local minima [24,83].

(E) **PSO with Firefly Algorithm (FA):** Hybrid algorithm of PSO with FA determines global best fitness value so that it can determine when to initiate local search [19,84]. Convergence accuracy is improved.

(F) **PSO with Sine Cosine Algorithm (SCA):** PSO parameters, pbest and gbest are implanted into the traditional SCA algorithm to enhance finding possible candidate solution [85]. Therefore, PSO swarm can exploit the possible search space.

(G) **PSO with Hybrid Whale (HW) Algorithm:** Whale optimization algorithm is popular due to its excellent exploration capability. When it is combined with PSO, it overcomes the PSO phase limitations [86,87]. Forced whale works for exploration and capping phenomenon for exploitation phase to converge global optimum quickly.

(H) **PSO with Many Other Algorithms:** It has been observed that PSO algorithm can be integrated with ant colony optimization (ACO), cuckoo search (CS), artificial bee colony (ABC) algorithms, gray wolf optimization (GWO), cat swarm optimization (CWO), salp swarm algorithm (SSA), etc. for enhanced performance [88–91].

4.8 Computational experiments

Various numerical experiments were performed by integration PSO. Altered version of PSO was used to control inaccurate requirements, operating cost, and data capacity in layered production planning system. It resolved the limitations of production plant prototype by minimizing operating cost and risk involved to attain maximum profit. Such model can be efficiently applied for real-world production scheduling and planning type of problems with poor defined data [92]. In another actual machinery system scenario about cut depth, cutting speed, and feeding rate; process parameters are examined with PSO algorithm for optimizing cutting situations. Results can be observed with minimum considered standards and associated optimal cutting situations [93]. An improved version of PSO algorithm is utilized to resolve the squared error by using joint fitness function. This error is the difference between calculated value and demonstrated value for identification nature problems. Numerical experiments were carried out to verify algorithm performance and authenticating results [94]. Supplementing further improved PSO algorithm was proposed to verify convergence. To do this, very large dimension, benchmark objective function is used. Numerical experiments results depict that the proposed algorithm is very successful [95]. Wireless sensor networks performance optimization is done with total number of active nodes, through improved PSO algorithm. In traditional background, performance of this proposed algorithm is validated [96].

4.9 Convergence

The word convergence can be defined in two distinct forms in relation with PSO [9,10]:

- All particles must converge at a point in search space, which is the convergence of series of solutions. Convergence may be optimum or may not be.
- Irrespective of swarm behavior, all particles personal best (p) and swarm's position best (g) approaches the problem's local optimum. Here convergence is for local optimum.

Series of solutions for convergence has been analyzed for PSO. These analyses give the outcome in selecting PSO parameters, which are required for convergence and avoid particle's divergence. The analysis was criticized because it was too simplified. Assumption was that there is only one particle, which does not use stochastic variable. Reason for attraction was particles best-known position (*p*) and swarm's best-known position (g), remains unchanged throughout the entire optimization process [97]. However, for swarm convergence, it has been observed that such simplifications are not going to impact boundaries defined by this examination for parameters. In recent years, significant efforts have been made for modifying the modelling assumption in stability analysis of PSO [98]. Recently, more generalized results were applied to many PSO variants. It has been observed about the necessary minimum requirement about the modeling assumption. For local optimum, convergence has been investigated for PSO [99,100]. Evidence shows that some modifications are required in PSO for achieving guarantee local optimum. Hence, it can be concluded that PSO parameters and algorithm convergence potentiality depends upon observational and experimental results. Orthogonal learning strategy can also be employed for improving already existing information to achieve quicker global convergence, excellent quality solution, and powerful robustness [101].

If there is a requirement of trade off in between divergence and convergence, some adaptive kind of mechanism needs to be introduced. In comparison to regular PSO, adaptive PSO offers improved search efficiency. Adaptive PSO (APSO) can execute global search in whole search space along with improved convergence rate. Search efficiency and effectiveness can be improved by controlling real time algorithm parameters and acceleration coefficients [25]. Though APSO encloses many new parameters, it does not require additional design and hence no implementation complexity.

4.10 PSO implications on image processing problems

Optimization algorithms are always essential for answering real-time problems, particularly where tuning of parameters is required. PSO is one such algorithm, and it is extensively used in the domain of image processing to determine optimal solution in search space.

- **Image Segmentation:** Multiple approaches are there like thresholding, clustering, edge detection, region growing, compression based, histogram based, watershed algorithms, etc. Standard PSO algorithm and many of its variants are used effectively with improved performance [4]. Incorporating PSO with Markov random field (MRF) can additionally increase the image enhancement performance. Some model of Fuzzy hybrid adaptive PSO along with ant colony optimization is suggested. Identification of cluster partitioning can be done successfully, which gives superior performance in terms of optimal value and fast convergence, compared to existing techniques [102,103].
- **Feature Selection:** Numerous engineering field where image processing is required, selection of suitable feature should be accomplished [5,87]. Feature

selection subfields where feature need to be extracted are text recognition, image recognition, and pattern recognition. Features include contrast, object, size, color change, texture change, cluster importance, etc. Standard techniques are used so far, either for global or local selection. Therefore, feature selection is more of NP hard problem. PSO capability is proven for resolving such problems [5,104]. For clustering, PSO is used to search centroids of clusters, which offers better result.

- **Edge Detection:** Edges play an important role in images. In literature, numerous traditional approaches have been defined, which relies on first order, second order, Laplacian operator, or Canny edge detector, etc. PSO-based approaches have proven their potential to overcome many challenges faced by traditional methods. PSO gives best fitness curve of image, which represents object boundaries. PSO integrated algorithms gives more precise results for highly noisy images too [105,106].
- **Edge Linking:** Many image detection methods undergo for certain limitations like false edge detection, missing actual edge, detecting thin lines, or producing appropriate thickness [89]. Connecting broken edges is also a tedious job. PSO-based techniques are efficient for detecting edges continuous and clear object images, even in the presence of noise also.
- **Image Compression:** The purpose behind the image compression is to remove redundancies available in the image to save storage space and efficient transmission bandwidth. PSO integrated algorithms helps to fulfil the said task and compressed images benefits for time required to CPU execution [107,108].

4.11 PSO implications on optimum route-finding problems

Route planning is a process of determining best route, which can be followed by any object usually robot [24]. Objective is safe travel within two nodes independently without no interventions or restricted interventions of humans. PSO substantially contributes for simple to complex nature route-finding problems [48,49]. Ahmed *et al.* [109] proposed a PSO-based approach for stochastic dynamic environment, where such problems can be carried by keeping a trade off in between short and safest route. Two-objective functions have been introduced, which are dependent on distance and risk.

- Nasrollahy *et al.* suggested PSO algorithm for route finding in dynamic environment along with moving targets and obstacles. PSO tends to identify collision-free path with minimum distance travelled though avoiding local optimums. It is achieved by minimizing the cost function and outcome is enhanced in comparison to other techniques [110].
- Ever *et al.* developed simplified swarm optimization (SSO) algorithm for route planning. Outcomes indicate that it does not gather into obstacle space even it automatically shifted toward obstacle free space [111].
- Li *et al.* recommended improved PSO, which incorporates several factors for improved control of path planning. These factors are learning factor, uniform

distribution, exponential attenuation inertia weight, etc. to attain superior result in lesser iterations [112].

- Standard PSO for path planning has challenges of early convergence, inadequate global search capability, and dropping into local optimum. Cheng *et al.* established integration of improved PSO with Gray wolf optimization (GWO) for route planning [91]. Proposed algorithm achieved the optimal path quickly without any chaos. Global search capability is also enhanced along with particles diversity [113].
- Thammachantuek *et al.* proposed PSO algorithm for route planning with multi-objective. Weight adjustment approach is used for the particle's movement in every iteration so that probability of finding the top fit solution is enhanced. Suggested algorithm determined the shortest path in both static and dynamic environment with lesser processing time [114].

4.12 Implementation and results

Among numerous optimization algorithms, PSO algorithm has obtained extensive attention among researchers in several years. It is very easy and simple to implement. This chapter supports the concept of Swarm Intelligence and particle swarm optimization. Moreover, multi-objective problems solution and various approached have been discussed. To overcome the limitations of PSO, it can be combined with many other algorithms so that better system efficiency, performance, quality, robustness and convergence can be greatly enhanced. PSO algorithms have extensive applications in almost all the fields, but this chapter explains its application for image processing and route-finding problem. Still PSO algorithm continue with many unresolved challenges of arbitrary convergence and convergence rate, determining easy and effective flexible algorithm parameters, and stabilizing global exploration with local exploitation.

References

[1] J. Kennedy and R. C. Eberhart, "Particle swarm optimization", In: *Proceedings of the IEEE International Conference on Neural Networks*, Perth, Australia, pp. 1942–1948, 1995.

[2] T. M. Blackwell, "Particle swarms and population diversity", *Soft Computing*, vol 9(11), pp. 793–802, 2005.

[3] Gad, A. G., "Particle swarm optimization algorithm and its applications: a systematic review", *Archives of Computational Methods in Engineering*, vol 29, pp. 2531–2561, 2022.

[4] V. P. Kour and S. Arora, "Particle swarm optimization-based support vector machine (P-SVM) for the segmentation and classification of plants", *IEEE Access*, vol 7, pp. 29374–29385, 2019.

[5] S. W. Lin, K. C. Ying, S. C. Chen, and Z. J. Lee, "Particle swarm optimization for parameter determination and feature selection of support vector machines", *Expert Systems with Applications*, vol 35, no. 4, pp. 1817–1824, 2008.

[6]   R. F. Lopes, F. F. Costa, A. Oliveira, and A. C. de C. Lima, "Algorithm based on particle swarm applied to electrical load scheduling in an industrial setting", *Energy*, vol 147, pp. 1007–1015, 2018.

[7]   D. P. Kumar and V. Ravi, "Forecasting financial time series volatility using particle swarm optimization trained quantile regression neural network," *Applied Soft Computing*, vol 58, pp. 35–52, 2017.

[8]   W. Hu, H. Wang, Z. Qiu, C. Nie, and L. Yan, "A quantum particle swarm optimization driven urban traffic light scheduling model", *Neural Computing and Applications*, vol 29, pp. 901–911, 2018.

[9]   W. D. Chang, "A modified particle swarm optimization with multiple subpopulations for multimodal function optimization problems", *Applied Soft Computing*, vol 33, pp. 170–182, 2015.

[10] W. Chen, J. Zhang, Y, Lin, *et al.*, "Particle swarm optimization with an aging leader and challenger", *IEEE Transaction of Evolutionary Computing*, vol 17(2), pp. 241–258, 2013.

[11] J. Geng, M. Li, Z. Dong, and Y. Liao, "Port throughput forecasting by MARS-RSVR with chaotic simulated annealing particle swarm optimization algorithm", *Neurocomputing*, vol 147, pp. 239–250, 2014.

[12] E. Pashaei, E. Pashaei, and N. Aydin, "Gene selection using hybrid binary black hole algorithm and modified binary particle swarm optimization", *Genomics*, vol 111(4), pp. 669–686, 2019.

[13] N. Zeng, H. Qiu, Z. Wang, W. Liu, H. Zhang, and Y. Li, "A new switching-delayed-PSO-based optimized SVM algorithm for diagnosis of Alzheimer's disease", *Neurocomputing*, vol 320, pp. 195–202, 2018.

[14] I. Jain, V. K. Jain, and R. Jain, "Correlation feature selection based improved-binary particle swarm optimization for gene selection and cancer classification", *Applied Soft Computing*, vol 62, pp. 203–215, 2018.

[15] Y. Li, X. Bai, L. Jiao, and Y. Xue, "Partitioned-cooperative quantum-behaved particle swarm optimization based on multilevel thresholding applied to medical image segmentation", *Applied Soft Computing*, vol 56, pp. 345–356, 2017.

[16] S. Raj and K. C. Ray, "ECG signal analysis using DCT-based DOST and PSO optimized SVM", *IEEE Transaction on Instruments and Measurement*, vol 66(3), pp. 470–478, 2017.

[17] W. Srisukkham, L. Zhang, S. C. Neoh, S. Todryk, and C. P. Lim, "Intelligent leukaemia diagnosis with bare-bones PSO based feature optimization", *Applied Soft Computing*, vol 56, pp. 405–419, 2017.

[18] S. Kumar, S. K. Pal, R. Singh, "A novel hybrid model based on particle swarm optimization and extreme learning machine for short-term temperature prediction using ambient sensors", *Sustainable Cities and Society*, vol 49, 2019.

[19] X. S. Yang, "Firefly algorithms for multimodal optimization", In: *International Symposium on Stochastic Algorithms*, Springer, pp. 169–178, 2009.

[20] S. Chen, J. Q. Wang, and H. Y. Zhang, "A hybrid PSO-SVM model based on clustering algorithm for short-term atmospheric pollutant concentration

forecasting", *Technology Forecasting and Social Change*, Elsevier, vol 146, pp. 41–54, 2019.

[21] M. Rahgoshay, S. Feiznia, M. Arian, and S. A. A. Hashemi, "Simulation of daily suspended sediment load using an improved model of support vector machine and genetic algorithms and particle swarm", *Arabian Journal of Geoscience*, vol 12(9), 2019.

[22] Y. Cao, Y. Ye, H. Zhao, *et al.*, "Remote sensing of water quality based on HJ-1A HSI imagery with modified discrete binary particle swarm optimization-partial least squares (MDBPSO-PLS) in inland waters: a case in Weishan lake", *Ecological Informatics*, vol 44, pp. 21–32, 2018.

[23] M. A. Ghorbani, R. Kazempour, K. W. Chau, S. Shamshirband, and P. T. Ghazvinei, "Forecasting pan evaporation with an integrated artificial neural network quantum-behaved particle swarm optimization model: a case study in Talesh, Northern Iran", *Engineering Applications of Computational Fluid Mechanics*, vol 12(1), pp. 724–737, 2018.

[24] M. Ehteram, F. B. Othman, Z. M. Yaseen, *et al.*, "Improving the Muskingum flood routing method using a hybrid of particle swarm optimization and bat algorithm", *Water*, vol 10(6), pp. 807, 2018.

[25] E. Camci, D. V. Kripalani, L. Ma, E. Kayacan, and M. A. Khanesar, "An aerial robot for rice farm quality inspection with type-2 fuzzy neural networks tuned by particle swarm optimization-sliding mode control hybrid algorithm", *Swarm and Evolutionary Computation*, vol 41, pp. 1–8, 2017.

[26] M. L. Maiyar and J. J. Thakkar, "Environmentally conscious logistics planning for food grain industry considering wastages employing multi objective hybrid particle swarm optimization", *Transportation Research Part E: Logistics and Transportation Review*, vol 127, pp. 220–248, 2019.

[27] A. Alnaqi, H. Moayedi, A. Shahsavar, and T. K. Nguyen, "Prediction of energetic performance of a building integrated photovoltaic/thermal system thorough artificial neural network and hybrid particle swarm optimization models", *Energy Conversion and Management*, vol 183, pp. 137–148, 2019.

[28] H. Wang, M. j Peng, J. W. Hines, G. Y. Zheng, Y. K. Liu, and B. R. Upadhyaya, "A hybrid fault diagnosis methodology with support vector machine and improved particle swarm optimization for nuclear power plants", *ISA Transaction*, vol 95, pp. 358–371, 2019.

[29] G. Liu, W. Chen, and H. Chen, "Quantum particle swarm with teamwork evolutionary strategy for multi-objective optimization on electro-optical platform", *IEEE Access*, vol 7, pp. 41205–41219, 2019.

[30] N. Ghorbani, A. Kasaeian, A. Toopshekan, L. Bahrami, and A. Maghami, "Optimizing a hybrid wind-PV-battery system using GA-PSO and MOPSO for reducing cost and increasing reliability", *Energy*, vol 154, pp. 581–591, 2018.

[31] H. Jiang, C. Kwong, W. Park, and K. Yu, "A multi-objective PSO approach of mining association rules for affective design based on online customer reviews", *Journal of Engineering Design*, vol 29(7), pp. 381–403, 2018.

[32] M. Song, K. Chen, and J. Wang, "Three-dimensional wind turbine positioning using gaussian particle swarm optimization with differential

evolution", *Journal of Wind Engineering and Industrial Aerodynamics*, vol 172, pp. 317–324, 2018.

[33] C. Qi, A. Fourie, and Q. Chen, "Neural network and particle swarm optimization for predicting the unconfined compressive strength of cemented paste backfill", *Construction and Building Materials*, vol 159, pp. 473–478, 2018.

[34] R. Jiao, X. Huang, H. Ouyang, G. Li, Q. Zheng, and Z. Jiang, "Optimal electric business centre location by centre-decentre quantum particle swarm optimization", *System Science and Control Engineering*, vol 7(1), pp. 222–233, 2019.

[35] B. Tang, J. Han, G. Guo, Y. Chen, and S. Zhang, "Building material prices forecasting based on least square support vector machine and improved particle swarm optimization", *Architectural Engineering and Design Management*, vol 15(3), pp.196–212, 2019.

[36] J. Shen and L. Han, "Design process optimization and profit calculation module development simulation analysis of financial accounting information system based on particle swarm optimization (PSO)", *Information Systems and e-Business Management*, vol 18, pp. 1–14, 2019.

[37] T. Yi, H. Zheng, Y. Tian, and J. p. Liu, "Intelligent prediction of transmission line project cost based on least squares support vector machine optimized by particle swarm optimization", *Mathematical Problems in Engineering*, vol 2018, Article ID 5458696, 2018.

[38] S. Abid, A. Zafar, R. Khalid, *et al.*, "Managing energy in smart homes using binary particle swarm optimization", In: *Conference on Complex, Intelligent, and Software Intensive Systems*, Springer, pp. 189–196, 2017.

[39] Y. Zhang, Q. Zhang, A. Farnoosh, S. Chen, and Y. Li, "GIS-based multi-objective particle swarm optimization of charging stations for electric vehicles", *Energy*, vol 169, pp. 844–853, 2019.

[40] L. Li, L. Qin, X. Qu, J. Zhang, Y. Wang, and B. Ran, "Day-ahead traffic flow forecasting based on a deep belief network optimized by the multi-objective particle swarm algorithm", *Knowledge Based System*, vol 172, pp. 1–14, 2019.

[41] R. Jordehi, "Binary particle swarm optimization with quadratic transfer function: a new binary optimization algorithm for optimal scheduling of appliances in smart homes", *Applied Soft Computing*, vol 78, pp. 465–480, 2019.

[42] L. T. Le, H. Nguyen, J. Zhou, J. Dou, and H. Moayedi, "Estimating the heating load of buildings for smart city planning using a novel artificial intelligence technique PSO-XGBoost", *Applied Sciences*, vol 9(13), p. 2714, 2019.

[43] K. Ma, S. Hu, J. Yang, X. Xu, and X. Guan, "Appliances scheduling via cooperative multi-swarm PSO under day-ahead prices and photovoltaic generation", *Applied Soft Computing*, vol 62, pp. 504–513, 2018.

[44] M. Sato, Y. Fukuyama, T. Iizaka, and T. Matsui, "Total optimization of energy networks in a smart city by multi-swarm differential evolutionary

particle swarm optimization", *IEEE Transactions on Sustainable Energy*, vol 99, p. 1, 2018.

[45] R. Zarrouk, I. E. Bennour, and A. Jemai, "A two-level particle swarm optimization algorithm for the flexible job shop scheduling problem", *Swarm Intelligence*, vol 13, pp. 1–24, 2019.

[46] H. Mokhtari and A. Noroozi, "An efficient chaotic based PSO for earliness/ tardiness optimization in a batch processing flow shop scheduling problem", *Journal of Intelligent Manufacturingr*, Springe, vol 29(5), pp. 1063– 1081, 2018.

[47] M. Nouiri, A. Bekrar, A. Jemai, S. Niar, and A. C. Ammari, "An effective and distributed particle swarm optimization algorithm for flexible job-shop scheduling problem", *Journal of Intelligent Manufacturing*, vol 29(3), pp. 603–615, 2018.

[48] Y. Zhong, J. Lin, L. Wang, and H. Zhang, "Discrete comprehensive learning particle swarm optimization algorithm with metropolis acceptance criterion for traveling salesman problem", *Swarm and Evolutionary Computation*, vol 42, pp. 77–88, 2018.

[49] S. Thabit and A. Mohades, "Multi-robot path planning based on multi-objective particle swarm optimization", *IEEE Access*, vol 7, pp. 2138–2147, 2018.

[50] S. Katiyar and A. Farhana, "Smart agriculture: the future of agriculture using AI and IoT", *Journal of Computer Science*, vol 17(10), pp. 984–999, 2021.

[51] M. Dorigo and T. Stützle, *Ant Colony Optimization*, MIT Press, Cambridge, MA, 2004.

[52] Y. Tamura, T. Sakiyama, and I. Arizono, "Ant colony optimization using common social information and self memory", *Complexity*, vol 2021, pp. 1–7, 2021.

[53] A. S. Joshi, O. Kulkarni, G. M. Kakandikar, and V. M. Nandedkar, "Cuckoo search optimization- a review", *Materials Today: Proceedings*, vol 4, pp. 7262–7269, 2017.

[54] Y. K. Chen, S. X. Weng, and T. P. Liu, "Teaching–Learning Based Optimization (TLBO) with variable neighbourhood search to retail shelf-space allocation", *Mathematics*, vol 8(8), p. 1296, 2020.

[55] D. Wu, S. Wang, Q. Liu, L. Abualigah, and H. Jia, "An improved teaching-learning-based optimization algorithm with reinforcement learning strategy for solving optimization problems", *Computational Intelligence and Neuroscience*, vol 2022, Article ID 1535957, 2022.

[56] C. Enache, V. Sgarciu, and A. P. Nita, "Intelligent feature selection method rooted in Binary Bat Algorithm for intrusion detection", In: *Proceedings of the IEEE International Symposium on Applied Computational Intelligence and Informatics*, Romania, 2015.

[57] R. R. Chhikara, P. Sharma, and L. Singh, "An improved dynamic discrete firefly algorithm for blind image steganalysis", *International Journal of Machine Learning and Cybernetics*, vol 9, pp. 821–835, 2018.

[58] K. C. Lin, S. Y. Chen, and J. C. Hung, "Feature selection and parameter optimization of support vector machines based on modified artificial fish

swarm algorithms", *Mathematical Problem in Engineering*, vol 58, p. 604108, 2015.

[59] Y. Chen, Q. Zhu, and H. Xu, "Finding rough set reduces with fish swarm algorithm", *Knowledge Based Systems*, vol 81, pp. 22–29, 2015.

[60] A. H. Gandomi and A. H. alavi, "Krill Herd Algorithm: a new bio-inspired optimization algorithm", *Communications in Nonlinear Science and Numerical Simulation*, vol 17, pp. 4831–4845, 2012.

[61] A. L. Bolaji, M. A. Al-Betar, M. A. Awadallah, A. T. Khader, and L. M. Abualigah, "A comprehensive review: Krill Herd algorithm (KH) and its applications", *Applied Soft Computing*, vol 49, pp. 437–446, 2016.

[62] S. Kaur, L. K. Awasthi, A. L. Sangal, and G. Dhiman, "Tunicate Swarm Algorithm: a new bio-inspired based metaheuristic paradigm for global optimization", *Engineering Applications of Artificial Intelligence*, vol 90, p. 103541, 2020.

[63] Y. Jiang, Q. Wu, S. Zhu, and L. Zhang, "Orca predation algorithm: a novel bio-inspired algorithm for global optimization problems", *Expert Systems with Applications*, vol 188, p. 116026, 2022.

[64] K. M. Htay, R. R. Othman, A. Amir, and J. M. H. Alkanaani, "Gravitational search algorithm-based strategy for combinatorial t-way test suite generation", *Journal of Computer and Information Sciences*, vol 34(8), pp. 4860–4873, 2022.

[65] R. Shankar, N. Ganesh, R. Čep, R. C. Narayanan, S. Pal, and K. Kalita, "Hybridized particle swarm—gravitational search algorithm for process optimization", *Processes*, vol 10(3), p. 616, 2022.

[66] N. Rashid, J. Iqbal, F. Mahmood, A. Abid, U. S. Khan, and M. I. Tiwana, "Artificial immune system–Negative Selection Classification Algorithm (NSCA) for four class Electroencephalogram (EEG) signals", *Frontier in Human Neuroscience*, vol 12, p. 439, 2018.

[67] S. Aldhaheri, D. Alghazzawi, L. Cheng, A. Barnawi, and B. A. Alzahrani, "Artificial immune systems approaches to secure the internet of things: a systematic review of the literature and recommendations for future research," *Journal of Network and Computer Applications*, vol 157, p. 102537, 2020.

[68] R. Oftadeh, M. J. Mahjoob, and M. Shariatpanahi, "A novel meta-heuristic optimization algorithm inspired by group hunting of animals: hunting search", *Computers & Mathematics with Applications*, vol 60(7), pp. 2087–2098, 2010.

[69] Y. Jin, M. Olhofer, and B. Sendhoff, "Evolutionary dynamic weighted aggregation for multi-objective optimization: why does it work and how?", In: *Proceedings of the GECCO Conference*, San Francisco, CA, pp. 1042–1049, 2001.

[70] X. Hu and R. Eberhart, "Multi-objective optimization using dynamic neighbourhood particle swarm optimization", In: *Proceedings of the IEEE Congress Evolutionary Computation*, IEEE Service Centre, pp. 1677–1681, 2002.

[71] X. Hu, R. C. Eberhart, and Y. Shi, "Particle swarm with extended memory for multi-objective optimization", In: *Proceedings of the IEEE Swarm Intelligence Symposium*, IEEE Service Centre, pp. 193–197, 2003.

[72]   D. Gies and Y. R. Samii, "Vector evaluated particle swarm optimization (VEPSO): optimization of a radiometer array antenna", In: *Proceedings of International Symposium (Digest) of Antennas and Propagation Society*, vol 3, pp 2297–2300, 2004.

[73]   J. G. Vlachogiannis and K. Y. Lee, "Determining generator contributions to transmission system using parallel vector evaluated particle swarm optimization", *IEEE Transactions on Power Systems*, vol 20(4), pp. 1765–1774, 2005.

[74]   C. A. Coello, G. T. Pulido, and M. S. Lechuga, "Handling multiple objectives with particle swarm optimization", *IEEE Transaction of Evolutionary Computing*, vol 8(3), pp. 256–279, 2004.

[75]   J. E. Fieldsend, R. M. Everson, and S. Singh, "Using unconstrained elite archives for multi-objective optimization", *IEEE Transaction on Evolutionary Computing*, vol 7(3), pp. 305–323, 2003.

[76]   X. H. Huo, L. C. Shen, and H. Y. Zhu, "A smart particle swarm optimization algorithm for multi-objective problems", *Lecture Notes in Computer Science*, vol 4115, pp. 72–80, 2006.

[77]   X. Li, "Better spread and convergence: particle swarm multi-objective optimization using the maximin fitness function", *Lecture Notes in Computer Science*, vol 3102, pp. 117–128, 2004.

[78]   C. R. Raquel and P. C. Naval, "An effective use of crowding distance in multi-objective particle swarm optimization", In: *Proceedings of the GECCO*, ACM Press, pp. 257–264, 2005.

[79]   C. F. Juang, "A hybrid of genetic algorithm and particle swarm optimization for recurrent network design", *IEEE Transaction on Systems, Man and Cybernetics*, vol 34, pp. 997–1006, 2004.

[80]   L. Xiao and X. Zuo, "Multi-DEPSO: A DE and PSO based hybrid algorithm in dynamic environments", In: *Proceedings of the IEEE Congress on Evolutionary Computation*, Australia, pp 1–7, 2012.

[81]   M. G. Omran, A. P. Engelbrecht, and A. Salman, "Bare bones differential evolution", *European Journal of Operation Research*, vol 196, pp. 128–139, 2009.

[82]   C. Zhang, H. Shao, and Y. Li, "Particle swarm optimisation for evolving artificial neural network", In: *Proceedings of the IEEE International Conference on Systems, Man and Cybernetics (SMC)*, USA, vol 4, pp. 2487–2490, 2000.

[83]   A. Ferdowsi, S. Farzin, S. F. Mousavi, and H. Karami, "Hybrid bat & particle swarm algorithm for optimization of labyrinth spillway based on half & quarter round crest shapes", *Flow Measurement and Instrumentation*, vol 66, pp. 209–217, 2019.

[84]   I. B. Aydilek, "A hybrid firefly and particle swarm optimization algorithm for computationally expensive numerical problems", *Applied Soft Computing*, vol 66, pp. 232–249, 2018.

[85]   H. Nenavath, R. K. Jatoth, and S. Das, "A synergy of the sine cosine algorithm and particle swarm optimizer for improved global optimization and object tracking", *Swarm Evolutionary Computing*, vol 43, pp. 1–30, 2018.

[86]   N. M. Laskar, K. Guha, I. Chatterjee, S. Chanda, K. L. Baishnab, and P. K. Paul, "HWPSO: a new hybrid whale-particle swarm optimization algorithm and its application in electronic design optimization problems", *Applied Intelligence*, vol 49(1), pp. 265–291, 2019.

[87]   M. M. Mafarja and S. Mirjalili, "Hybrid Whale Optimization Algorithm with simulated annealing for feature selection", *Neurocomputing*, vol 260, pp. 302–312, 2017.

[88]   S. Katiyar, R. Khan, and S. Kumar, "Artificial Bee Colony algorithm for fresh food distribution without quality loss by delivery route optimization", *Journal of Food Quality*, vol 2021, pp. 1–9, 2021.

[89]   M. Schiezaro and H. Pedrini, "Data feature selection based on Artificial Bee Colony algorithm", *EURASIP Journal of Image and Video Processing*, vol 47, pp. 1–8, 2013.

[90]   K. C. Lin, K. Y. Zhang, Y. H. Huang, J. C. Hung, and N. Yen, "Feature selection based on an improved cat swarm optimization algorithm for big data classification", *Journal of Supercomputing*, vol 72, pp. 3210–3221, 2016.

[91]   E. Emary, H. M. Zawbaa, and C. Grosan, "Experienced gray wolf optimization through reinforcement learning and neural networks", *IEEE Transaction of Neural Networks and Learning Systems*, vol 29, pp. 1–14, 2017.

[92]   A. Carlisle and G. Dozier, "An off-the-shelf PSO", In: *Proceedings of the Workshop on Particle Swarm Optimization*, Indiana, USA, 2001.

[93]   M. R. Ganesh, R. Krishna, K. Manikantan, and S. Ramachandran, "Entropy based binary particle swarm optimization and classification for ear detection", *Engineering Applications of Artificial Intelligence*, vol 27, pp. 115–128, 2014.

[94]   J. Lu, H. Hu, and Y. Bai, "Generalized radial basis function neural network based on an improved dynamic particle swarm optimization and ADAboost algorithm," *Neurocomputing*, vol 152, pp. 305–315, 2015.

[95]   M. R. Sierra and C. A. C. Coello, "Improving PSO-based multi-objective optimization using crowding, mutation and epsilon-dominance", *Lecture Notes on Computer Science*, vol 3410, pp. 505–519, 2005.

[96]   S. Salehian and S. K. Subraminiam, "Unequal clustering by improved particle swarm optimization in wireless sensor network", *Procedia Computer Science*, vol 62, pp. 403–409, 2015.

[97]   M. E. H. Pedersen and A. J. Chipperfield, "Simplifying particle swarm optimization", *Applied Soft Computing*, vol 10(2), pp. 618–628, 2010.

[98]   W. C. Cleghorn, "Particle swarm convergence: standardized analysis and topological influence", *Lecture Notes in Computer Science*, vol 8667, pp. 134–145, 2014.

[99]   F. V. D. Bergh and A. P. Engelbrecht, "A convergence proof for the particle swarm optimiser", *Fundamenta Informatics*, vol 105, pp. 1–47, 2010.

[100] M. R. Bonyadi and Z. Michalewicz, "A locally convergent rotationally invariant particle swarm optimization algorithm", *Swarm Intelligence*, vol 8(3), pp. 159–198, 2014.

[101] Z. H. Zhan, J. Zhang, Y. Li, and Y. H. Shi, "Orthogonal learning particle swarm optimization", *IEEE Transactions on Evolutionary Computation*, vol 15(6), pp. 832–847, 2011.

[102] M. Maitra and A. Chatterjee, "A hybrid cooperative comprehensive learning based PSO algorithm for image segmentation using multilevel thresholding", *Expert Systems with Applications*, vol 34(2), pp. 1341–1350, 2008.

[103] A. Chander, A. Chatterjee, and P. Siarry, "A new social and momentum component adaptive PSO algorithm for image segmentation", *Expert Systems with Applications*, vol 38, pp. 4998–5004, 2011.

[104] Z. Xinchao, "A perturbed particle swarm algorithm for numerical optimization", *Applied Soft Computing*, vol 10(1), pp. 119–124, 2010.

[105] N. S. Dagar and P. K. Dahiya, "Edge detection technique using binary particle swarm optimization", *Procedia Computer Science*, vol 67, pp. 1421–1436, 2020.

[106] C. Dongyue, T. Zhou, and X. Yu, "A new method of edge detection based on PSO", In *Advances in Neural Networks*, pp 239–246, 2012.

[107] S. M. Ibrahim, E. A. Zanaty, and H. Alkinani, "Medical image compression based on wavelets and particle swarm optimization", *Computers, Materials and Continua*, vol 67(2), pp. 1577–1593, 2021.

[108] D. E. Touil and N. Terki, "Quality preserved colour image compression using particle swarm optimization algorithm", In: *International Symposium on Modelling and Implementation of Complex Systems*, vol 156, pp. 175–187, 2020.

[109] A. A. Hilli, M. A. Ibadi, A. M. Alfadhel, S. H. Abdulshaheed, and A. H. Hadi, "Optimal path finding in stochastic quasi-dynamic environments using particle swarm optimization", *Expert Systems with Applications*, vol 186, p. 115706, 2021.

[110] A. Z. Nasrollahy and H. H. S. Javadi, "Using particle swarm optimization for robot path planning in dynamic environments with moving obstacles and target," In: *UKSim European Symposium on Computer Modelling and Simulation*, pp 60–65, 2009.

[111] Y. K. Ever, "Using simplified swarm optimization on path planning for intelligent mobile robot", *Procedia Computer Science*, vol 120, pp. 83–90, 2017.

[112] X. Li, D. Wu, J. He, M. Bashir, and M. Liping, "An improved method of particle swarm optimization for path planning of mobile robot", *Journal of Computer Engineering*, vol 2020, Article ID 3857894, 2020.

[113] X. Cheng, J. Li, C. Zheng, J. Zhang, and M. Zhao, "An improved PSO-GWO algorithm with chaos and adaptive inertial weight for robot path planning", *Frontiers in Neurorobotics*, vol 15, 770361, 2021.

[114] I. Thammachantuek and M. Ketcham, "Path planning for autonomous mobile robots using multi-objective evolutionary particle swarm optimization", *PLoS One*, vol 17(8), e0271924, 2022.

Chapter 5

Advanced optimization by nature-inspired algorithm

Altaf Q.H. Badar[1]

5.1 Introduction

The human race is currently witnessing an era where the world is changing at a very fast pace, technologically. The innovations and inventions have been taking place on a daily basis. Also, it is not only engineering field that is experiencing this fast cycle of new incoming technologies but also various fields like medical, social engineering, etc. are also accepting emerging techniques.

One of the most influential reasons for these changes being visible is the advent of Artificial Intelligence (AI). AI is applied and has affected all aspects of life. Some of the examples are presented below:

- AI used to write research papers [1]
- AI's advent into legal services [2]
- AI in medical field [3]
- AI applications in literature [4]
- AI in robots [5]
- AI used in drone swarms [6,7]

The above list is not even the tip of the iceberg, considering the contributions of AI in today's world. Remember that this list does not feature the detailed list of engineering explorations brought about by AI.

Evolutionary optimization algorithms are one of the important components of AI. These optimization techniques are used to find optimal solutions for complex search problems. Another application of the optimization techniques is to obtain feasible solutions for problems, where finding a solution itself is the objective. Such problems have very less number of solutions that are acceptable and thus such a problem is similar to finding a needle in a haystack.

Evolutionary optimization algorithms are usually based on methodologies that are derived from natural processes. These methods are very robust and easily adapt

[1]National Institute of Technology and Science – Warangal, India

to different multidimensional complex problems. Each algorithm has its own merits and demerits.

The initial optimization method, i.e., genetic algorithm was derived from Darwin's theory of "Survival of the fittest." In this theory, the individuals with a better set of genes are able to survive and reproduce. Hence the new generations, have the genes of those individuals from the previous generation that were able to better adapt themselves to the environment. The process repeats and those genes, which are required to survive are passed on and may be modified as per the adaptations.

Evolutionary optimization algorithms were introduced as it was observed that the existing conventional methods applied for solving optimization problems were not capable to obtain optimal solutions. These algorithms are fast, robust, less probable to get trapped in local minima, adaptable, etc. A number of evolutionary optimization algorithms have been introduced over a period of time. Some of these methods have been modified from the base version while some have been combined with other optimization methods to form a hybrid method. Different applications of optimization techniques have been discussed in detail in [8]. Also, step-by-step evaluation of some of these optimization techniques has been presented in [9].

In this chapter, an exhaustive list of evolutionary optimization algorithms is presented first. In the second part of the chapter, some of the advanced evolutionary optimization techniques are discussed.

5.2   List of nature-inspired algorithms

In this section, a table containing a list of more than 200 optimization algorithms is enlisted. Table 5.1 contains the name of the method, author, year of publication, and the reference for each optimization technique. However, for some of the old optimization techniques, there was not a single publication, which introduced the method but a number of publications. For such optimization techniques, one of these publications is listed in the Table 5.1 or the most relevant reference has been cited.

Table 5.1   List of nature-inspired algorithms

Method	Author, Year	Ref.
African Buffalo Optimization Algorithm (ABO)	Odili and Karhar, 2015	[10]
African Vulture Optimization Algorithm (AVOA)	Abdallahzadeh *et al.*, 2021	[11]
Animal Migration Optimization	Li *et al.*, 2014	[12]
Ant Colony Optimization (ACO)	Marco Dorigo, 1996	[13]
Ant Lion Optimizer (ALO)	Mirjalili, 2015	[14]
Aquila Optimizer (AO)	Abualigah *et al.*, 2021	[15]
Archimedes Optimization Algorithm	Hashim *et al.*, 2021	[16]
Arithmetic Optimization Algorithm (AOA)	Laith *et al.*, 2021	[17]

(Continues)

Table 5.1 (*Continued*)

Method	Author, Year	Ref.
Artificial Algae Algorithm (AAA)	Uymaz *et al.*, 2015	[18]
Artificial Bee Colony (ABC)	Dervis Karaboga, 2005	[19]
Artificial Ecosystem-based Optimization (AEO)	Zhao *et al.*, 2020	[20]
Artificial Flora (AF) Optimization Algorithm	Cheng *et al.*, 2021	[21]
Artificial Immune Algorithm (AIA)	Bagheri *et al.*, 2010	[22]
Backtracking Search Optimization Algorithm (BSA)	Pinar Civicioglu, 2013	[23]
Bacterial Foraging Optimization (BFO)	Passino, 2002	[24]
Bald Eagle Search (BES) Optimization Algorithm	Alsattar *et al.*, 2020	[25]
Bat Algorithm (BA)	Xin-She Yang, 2010	[26]
Battle Royale Optimization Algorithm	Rahkar Farshi, 2021	[27]
Bee Colony Optimization Algorithm (BCO)	Teodorovic *et al.*, 2005	[28]
Bee Swarm Optimization	Habiba *et al.*, 2005	[29]
Bees Algorithm	Pham *et al.*, 2006	[30]
Beetle Swarm Optimization Algorithm	Wang and Yang, 2018	[31]
Beluga Whale Optimization (BWO)	Changting Zhong, 2022	[32]
Big Bang Big Crunch (BB-BC)	Erol and Ersking, 2006	[33]
Biogeography-based Optimization (BBO)	Simon, 2008	[34]
Bird Mating Optimizer	Askarzadeh, 2014	[35]
Black Hole Algorithm (BH)	Abdolreza Hatamlou, 2013	[36]
Black Widow Optimization Algorithm	Hayyolalam and Kazem, 2020	[37]
Blind Naked Mole Rats Algorithm (BNMR)	Mohammad, 2013	[38]
Bonobo Optimizer (BO)	Amit and Dilip Kumar, 2019	[39]
Brain Storm Optimization Algorithm (BSO)	Yuhui Shi, 2011	[40]
Bumble Bees Mating Optimization (BBMO)	Marinakis *et al.*, 2010	[41]
Butterfly Mating Optimization Algorithm (BBMO)	Jada *et al.*, 2016	[42]
Butterfly Optimization Algorithm (BOA)	Arora *et al.*, 2019	[43]
Cat Swarm Optimization (CSO)	Chu *et al.*, 2006	[44]
Central Force Optimization (CFO)	Formato, 2008	[45]
Centroid Mutation-Based Search and Rescue (cmSAR) Optimization Algorithm	Houssein *et al.*, 2022	[46]
Chameleon Swarm Algorithm (CSA)	Braik, 2021	[47]
Chaos Optimization Algorithm	Jeng *et al.*, 2017	[48]
Chaos Optimization Method (COM)	Jiang, 1998	[49]
Charged System Search (CSS)	Kaveh and Talatahari, 2010	[50]
Chicken Swarm Optimization	Meng *et al.*, 2014	[51]
Chimp Optimization Algorithm (ChOA)	Khishe and Mosavi, 2020	[52]
Class Topper Optimization Algorithm	Das *et al.*, 2018	[53]
Cognitive Behavior Optimization Algorithm	Li *et al.*, 2016	[54]
Collective Decision Optimization Algorithm	Zhang *et al.*, 2017	[55]
Colliding Bodies Optimization (CBO)	Kaveh and Mahdavi, 2014	[56]
Competition over Resources	Mohseni *et al.*, 2014	[57]
Competitive Optimization Algorithm (COOA)	Sharafi *et al.*, 2016	[58]
Coot Bird Search Algorithm	Mamarzadeh and Keynia, 2021	[59]

(Continues)

Table 5.1   (Continued)

Method	Author, Year	Ref.
Coral Reef Optimization Algorithm	Sanz *et al.*, 2014	[60]
Covariance Matrix Adaptation Evolution Strategy (CMA-ES)	Hansen *et al.*, 2003	[61]
Coyote Optimization Algorithm (COA)	Pierezen and Coelho, 2018	[62]
Crisscross Optimization Algorithm	Meng *et al.*, 2016	[63]
Crow Search Algorithm (CSA)	Askarzadeh, 2016	[64]
Cuckoo Search (CS)	Yang and Deb, 2009	[65]
Cuttle Fish Algorithm (CFA)	Adel Sabry Eesa *et al.*, 2013	[66]
Deer Hunting Optimization Algorithm	Deer Hunting Optimization, 2019	[67]
Differential Evolution (DE)	Storn and Price, 1997	[68]
Dolphin Echolocation (DE)	Kaveh and Farhaundi, 2013	[69]
Dragonfly Algorithm (DA)	Mirjalili, 2016	[70]
Dwarf Mongoose Optimization (DMO) Algorithm	Agushaka *et al.*, 2022	[71]
Ebola Optimization Search Algorithm (EOSA)	Oyelade *et al.*, 2022	[72]
Egret Swarm Optimization Algorithm	Chen *et al.*, 2022	[73]
Electromagnetic Field Optimization (EFO)	Hosein *et al.*, 2016	[74]
Elephant Herding Optimization	Wang *et al.*, 2015	[75]
Emperor Penguin Optimizer (EPO)	Harifi *et al.*, 2019	[76]
Equilibrium Optimizer (EO)	Faramarzi *et al.*, 2020	[77]
Firefly Algorithm (FA)	Xin-She Yang, 2009	[78]
Fireworks Algorithm (FWA)	Tan and Zhu, 2010	[79]
Flower Pollination Algorithm (FPA)	Xin-She Yang, 2012	[80]
Forest Optimization Algorithm	Ghaemi and Feizi-Derakhshi, 2014	[81]
Fruit Fly Optimization Algorithm	Xing and Gao, 2014	[82]
Galactic Swarm Optimization	Muthiah and Mathew, 2016	[83]
Gases Brownian Motion Optimization (GBMO)	Marjan *et al.*, 2013	[84]
Genetic Algorithms (GA)	John Holland, 1970s	[85,86]
Genetic Programming (GP)	John Koza, 1990	[87]
Glowworm Swarm Optimization (GSO)	Krishnanad and Ghose, 2009	[88]
Golden Eagles Optimization (GEO)	Abdolkarim *et al.*, 2021	[89]
Gradient-Based Optimizer (GBO)	Ahmadianfar *et al.*, 2020	[90]
Grass Fibrous Root Optimization Algorithm	Akkar and Mahdi, 2017	[91]
Grasshopper Optimization Algorithm (GOA)	Mirjalili, 2018	[92]
Gravitational Search Algorithm (GSA)	Rashedi *et al.*, 2009	[93]
Greedy Randomized Adaptive Search Procedure (GRASP)	Resende *et al.*, 1994	[94,95]
Grey Wolf Optimizer (GWO)	Mirjalili *et al.*, 2014	[96]
Group Teaching Optimization Algorithm	Zhang and Jin, 2020	[97]
Harmony Search (HS)	Loganathan *et al.*, 2001	[98]
Harris Hawk Optimization (HHO)	Heidari *et al.*, 2019	[99]
Heart Heat Transfer Relation-Based Optimization Algorithm (HOTA)	Asef *et al.*, 2021	[100,101]
Heat Transfer Search (HTS)	Patel and Savsani, 2015	[102]
Henry Gas Solubility Optimization	Hashim *et al.*, 2019	[103]
Honey Badger Algorithm (HBA)	Hashim *et al.*, 2022	[104]

(Continues)

Table 5.1 (*Continued*)

Method	Author, Year	Ref.
Horse Herd Optimization Algorithm	Miar Naeimi *et al.*, 2021	[105]
Human Learning Optimization Algorithm	Wang *et al.*, 2014	[106]
Human Mental Search	Mousavirad *et al.*, 2017	[107]
Hunger Games Search (HGS)	Yang *et al.*, 2021	[108]
Hurricane-Based Optimization Algorithm	Rbouh and El Imrani, 2014	[109]
Imperialist Competitive Algorithm (ICA)	Atashpaz-Gargari and Lucas, 2007	[110]
Inclined Planes System Optimization (IPO) Algorithm	Mozaffari *et al.*, 2016	[111]
Integrated Optimization Algorithm (IOA)	Chen Li *et al.*, 2022	[112]
Interactive Autodidactic School (IAS)	Jahangiri *et al.*, 2020	[113]
Invasive Tumor Growth Optimization (ITGO) Algorithm	Tang *et al.*, 2015	[114]
Invasive Weed Optimization	Rad and Lucas, 2007	[115]
Ions Motion Algorithm	Javidy *et al.*, 2015	[116]
Iterated Local Search (ILS)	Katayama and Narihisa, 1999	[117]
Jaya Optimization Algorithm (JOA)	Venkata Rao, 2016	[118]
Kinetic Gas Molecule Optimization (KGMO)	Moein and Logeswaran, 2014	[119]
Krill Herd Algorithm (KHA)	Gandomi and Alavi, 2012	[120]
Lichtenberg Optimization Algorithm	Pereira *et al.*, 2021	[121]
Lightning Attachment Procedure Optimization Algorithm	Nematollahi *et al.*, 2019	[122]
Lion Optimization Algorithm (LOA)	Yazdani and Jolani, 2016	[123]
Locust Swarm Optimization Algorithm	Cuevas *et al.*, 2020	[124]
Magnetic Optimization Algorithm	Kushwaha *et al.*, 2018	[125]
Magnetic-Inspired Optimization Algorithm	Tayarani and Akbarzadeh, 2014	[126]
Manta Ray Foraging Optimization (MRFO)	Weiguo Zhao *et al.*, 2020	[127]
Marine Predators Algorithm (MPA)	Faramarzi *et al.*, 2020	[128]
Marriage in Honey Bees Optimization (HBO)	Abbass, 2001	[129]
Mayfly Optimization Algorithm	Zervoudakis and Safarakis, 2020	[130]
Mine Blast Algorithm (MBA)	Ali Sadollah *et al.*, 2013	[131]
Monarch Butterfly Optimization (MBO)	Wang *et al.*, 2015	[132]
Monkey King Evolutionary Algorithm	Meng and Pen, 2016	[133]
Monkey Search Algorithm	Seref and Akcali, 2002	[134]
Most Valuable Player Algorithm (MVPA)	Bouchekara, 2020	[135]
Moth-Flame Optimization Algorithm (MFO)	Mirjalili, 2015	[136]
MultiVerse Optimizer (MVO)	Azizi *et al.*, 2019	[137]
Optics Inspired Optimization (OIO)	Kashan, 2015	[138]
Parliamentary Optimization Algorithm (POA)	Borji, 2007	[139]
Particle Swarm Optimization (PSO)	Eberhart and Kennedy, 1995	[140]
Pathfinder Algorithm (PFA)	Yapici and Cetinkayab, 2019	[141]
Pelican Optimization Algorithm (POA)	Trojovsky and Dehghani, 2022	[142]
Pigeon-Inspired Optimization	Duan and Qiao, 2014	[143]
Polar Bear Optimization Algorithm	Polap and Wo'zniak, 2017	[144]
Political Optimizer	Qamar Askari *et al.*, 2020	[145]

(*Continues*)

Table 5.1   (Continued)

Method	Author, Year	Ref.
Poor and Rich Optimization Algorithm	Moosavi and Bardsiri, 2019	[146]
Puzzle Optimization Algorithm (POA)	Zeidabadi and Dehghani, 2022	[147]
Quantum Approximate Optimization Algorithm	Farhi *et al.*, 2014	[148]
Queuing Search Algorithm (QSA)	Zhang *et al.*, 2018	[149]
Raccoon Optimization Algorithm	Koohi *et al.*, 2018	[150]
Rain Optimization Algorithm (ROA)	Moazzeni and Khamehchi, 2020	[151]
Rain-Fall Optimization Algorithm	Kaboli *et al.*, 2017	[152]
Rao Optimization Algorithms (ROA)	Venkata Rao and Pawar, 2020	[153]
Raven Roosting Optimization Algorithm	Brabazon *et al.*, 2016	[154]
Ray Optimization (RO)	Kaveh Khayatazad, 2012	[155]
Red Deer Algorithm (RDA)	Fard and Hajiaghaei-Keshteli, 2016	[156]
Red Fox Optimization Algorithm (RFO)	Polap and Wozniak, 2021	[157]
Reducing Variable Trend Search (RVTS)	Badar *et al.*, 2014	[158]
Remora Optimization Algorithm	Jia *et al.*, 2021	[159]
Reptile Search Algorithm (RSA)	Laith Abualigah *et al.*, 2022	[160]
Rooted Tree Optimization Algorithm	Labbi *et al.*, 2016	[161]
RUNge Kutta optimizer (RUN)	Ahmadianfar *et al.*, 2021	[162]
Salp Swarm Algorithm	Mirjalili *et al.*, 2017	[163]
Sandpiper Optimization Algorithm (SOA)	Kaur *et al.*, 2020	[164]
Satin Bowerbird Optimizer	Moosavi and Bardsiri, 2017	[165]
Scatter Search (SS)	Fred Glover, 1977	[166]
Seagull Optimization Algorithm (SOA)	Dhiman and Kumar, 2019	[167]
Sea Lion Optimization Algorithm	Masadeh *et al.*, 2019	[168]
Search and Rescue Optimization Algorithm	Shabani *et al.*, 2020	[169]
Seasons Optimization Algorithm	Emami, 2020	[170]
Seeker Optimization Algorithm	Dai *et al.*, 2006	[171]
Selfish Herd Optimizer (SHO)	Fausto *et al.*, 2017	[172]
Shark Smell Optimization (SSO)	Oveis Abdinia *et al.*, 2016	[173]
Shuffled Complex Optimizers (SCO)	Duan *et al.*, 1993	[174]
Shuffled Frog-Leaping Algorithm (SFLA)	Eusuff *et al.*, 2006	[175]
Simulated Annealing (SA)	Kirkpatrick *et al.*, 1983	[176]
Sine Cosine Algorithm (SCA)	Seyedali Mirjalili, 2016	[177]
Slime Mold Algorithm (SMA)	Li *et al.*, 2020	[178]
Snake Optimizer	Hashim and Hussien, 2022	[179]
Social Mimic Optimization Algorithm	Bolachian and Baloochian, 2019	[180]
Social Spider Optimization (SSO)	Cuevas *et al.*, 2013 James and Victor, 2015	[181,182]
Socio Evolution and Learning Optimization Algorithm	Kumar *et al.*, 2018	[183]
Sooty Tern Optimization Algorithm (STOA)	Dhiman and Kaur, 2019	[184]
Sparrow Search Algorithm (SSA)	Xue and Shen, 2020	[185]
Sperm Swarm Optimization Algorithm	Hisham *et al.*, 2018	[186]
Spider Monkey Optimization Algorithm	Bansal *et al.*, 2014	[187]

(Continues)

Table 5.1 (*Continued*)

Method	Author, Year	Ref.
Spotted Hyena Optimizer (SHO)	Dhiman *et al.*, 2017	[188]
Squirrel Search Algorithm (SSA)	Jain, 2019	[189]
States of Matter Search (SMS)	Cuevas *et al.*, 2013	[190]
Sunflower Optimization Algorithm (SFO)	Gomes *et al.*, 2019	[191]
Supply–Demand-Based Optimization	Zhao *et al.*, 2019	[192]
Symbiotic Organism Search (SOS)	Cheng and Prayogo, 2014	[193]
Tabu Search (TS)	Fred Glover, 1989	[194,195]
Teaching-Learning-Based Optimization (TLBO)	Venkata Rao, 2011	[196]
Teamwork Optimization Algorithm	Dehghani and Trojovsky, 2021	[197]
Thermal Exchange Optimization (TEO)	Kaveh and Dadras, 2017	[198]
Transient Search Optimization	Qais *et al.*, 2020	[199]
Variable Neighbourhood Search (VNS)	Mladenovi'c and Hansen, 1997	[200]
Virtual Bee Algorithm	Yang, 2005	[201]
Virulence Optimization Algorithm	Jaderyan and Khotanlou, 2016	[202]
Virus Optimization Algorithm	Liang and Cuevas Juarez, 2016	[203]
Vortex Search (VS) Algorithm	Berat and Tamer, 2015	[204]
War Strategy Optimization Algorithm	Tummala *et al.*, 2022	[205]
Water Cycle Algorithm (WCA)	Eskanda *et al.*, 2012	[206]
Water Evaporation Optimization (WEO)	Kaveh and Bakshpoori, 2016	[207]
Water Wave Optimization (WWO)	Zheng, 2015	[208]
Weed Optimization Algorithm	Asgari *et al.*, 2016	[209]
Weighted mean of vectors (INFO)	Ahmandianfar *et al.*, 2022	[210]
Whale Optimization Algorithm (WOA)	Mirjalili and Lewis, 2016	[211]
Wind Driven Optimization	Bayraktar *et al.*, 2010	[212]
Wingsuit Flying Search	Covic and Lacevic, 2020	[213]
World Cup Optimization Algorithm	Shahrezaee, 2017	[214]
Yin-Yang-Pair Optimization	Punnathanam and Kotecha, 2016	[215]

5.3 Optimization techniques

In this section, some of the recent optimization techniques have been discussed. All the necessary equations required to realize these optimization techniques are also presented.

5.3.1 *Anarchic society optimization (ASO)*

ASO is inspired by the anarchic behavior of society members to improve their situation. Anarchic behavior means that the behavior of the members does not follow any controlling rules or principles. In ASO, the members can be fickle minded, i.e., (i) one whose loyalties and affections can change frequently, (ii) adventurous, and (iii) unstable. This kind of behavior of the members can lead to irrational movements which could lead a member to an inferior position. Such anarchic movement of members increases as the difference between them increases or the situation worsens.

The members of the society have the knowledge about the best position attained by any other member of the society till the current iteration is considered. The members are also aware of the member who is occupying the current best position in the society. There are three policies on which a member shall move.

1.   The first policy for movement is based on the current position of a member. This movement is dependent on Fickleness Index (FI). It represents a member's dissatisfaction with its current position in comparison with other members. The FI can be obtained through one of the following equations:

$$FI_i(k) = 1 - a_i \frac{f(Xi_k^*(k))}{f(X_i(k))} - (1 - a_i)_i \frac{f(Pi(k))}{f(X_i(k))}$$

$$FI_i(k) = 1 - a_i \frac{f(G(k))}{f(X_i(k))} - (1 - a_i) \frac{f(Pi(k))}{f(X_i(k))}$$

where a is a number between 0 and 1; "k" is the current iteration; "I" is the member of the society; $Xi(k)$ is the position of ith member for kth iteration; $Pi(k)$ is the personal best position achieved by ith member; $G(k)$ is the global best position; i_k^* is the member holding the best position in the society in the kth iteration; and $f()$ represents the objective function value.

2.   In the second policy, the movement of the member is dependent on other members of the society. The movement under this policy is controlled by external irregularity index (EI). EI is proposed to be evaluated as:

$$EI_i(k) = 1 - e^{-\delta i D(k)}$$

where δi is a positive number. $D(k)$ is a suitable dispersion measure like coefficient of variation.

3.   In the third and last policy of movement, the past positions are considered. It is not necessary that the best position in the past shall be considered. In the movement, internal irregularity index (II) is utilized.

These movement policies are finally combined through the elitism or sequential combination rule.

5.3.2   Antlion optimizer (ALO)

Antlions are also called doodlebugs. The method of foraging used by antlion larvae involves enticing its prey into a cone-shaped pit. The larvae position itself at the bottom of the circular pit and wait for the prey i.e., ant. The cone-shaped pit is so designed that the prey falls into the pit when it crosses the boundary. As the prey falls into the pit, the antlion grabs it and consumes the ant. In case the prey tries to escape, the antlion throws sand on the insect which drags it down to the bottom of the pit. The pit size is observed to be dependent on the amount of hunger and the moon size.

Ants, i.e., the prey, move in a stochastic way in search of food. Its movement is modeled as:

$$X(t) = [0,\ cs(2r(t1) - 1),\ cs(2r(t2) - 1),\ ....cs(2r(tn) - 1]$$

where cs is the cumulative sum; $r(t)$ is evaluated as follows:

$$r(t) = \begin{array}{l} 1\ if\ rand > 0.5 \\ 0\ if\ rand \leq 0.5 \end{array}$$

"n" is the maximum iteration count and "t" is the random walk step.

A pattern of such a random walk is represented through a graph in the reference publication.

The positions of the ants are saved in a matrix called *Mant*, which is given as:

$$\begin{bmatrix} A_{1,1} & A_{1,2} & \cdots & \cdots & A_{1,d} \\ A_{2,1} & A_{2,2} & \cdots & \cdots & A_{2,d} \\ \vdots & \vdots & \cdots & \cdots & \vdots \\ A_{n,1} & A_{n,2} & \cdots & \cdots & A_{n,d} \end{bmatrix}$$

where "d" is the number of dimensions; "n" is the number of ants; and Aij represents a value for ith and for jth dimension.

The ant in the ALO is similar to wolves in Grey Wolf Optimizer or a particle in PSO.

There is another matrix *MOA* which stores the objective function value of each ant. This matrix will be a column matrix of size "n".

Similar to *Mant*, another matrix is formed which is termed as $M_{antlion}$. It is used to store the position of each antlion. Also, corresponding to *MOA*, another matrix is used for storing the objective function value of antlions and is given by *MOAL*.

The movement of the ants should be within the search space. Also, in case the ant gets fitter than the antlion then it means that it has been caught by that antlion.

The random walk is represented as:

$$X_i^t = \frac{(X_i^t - a_i) \times (d_i - c_i^t)}{(d_i^t - a_i)} + c_i$$

where "i" represents the variable/dimension; "t" is the iteration; "a" is the minimum random walk for the variable "i"; "c" and "d" are the minimum and maximum values of ith variable in the tth iteration.

The effect of antlion traps on the random walk of ants is given as:

$$c_i^t = Antlion_j^t + c^t$$
$$d_i^t = Antlion_j^t + d^t$$

where $Antlion_j^t$ gives the position of the jth antlion in the tth iteration.

The sliding of ants toward an antlion is modeled as:

$$c^t = \frac{c^t}{I}$$

$$d^t = \frac{d^t}{I}$$

where I represents a ratio.

The catching of an ant by the antlion is given by the next equation:

$$Antlion_j^t = Ant_i^t \text{ if } f(Ant_i^t) > f(Antlion_j^t)$$

The ant is supposed to walk randomly around a particular antlion, selected through the roulette wheel process, and also toward the best antlion. This is given as:

$$Ant_i^t = \frac{R_A^t + R_E^t}{2}$$

where "R" is the random walk; "t" is the iteration; "A" is the antlion selected through the roulette wheel; "E" is the global best antlion.

5.3.3   Cat swarm optimization

As the name of the optimization is, this algorithm is based on cat behavior. The cat behavior is classified into (i) seeking and (ii) tracking mode. In cat swarm optimization (CSO), the cats play the role of particles in PSO or chromosomes in GA.

Seeking mode represents the lazy mode of cat behavior in which it rests or looks around. This mode introduces four factors:

1. Seeking Memory Pool (SMP): It helps the cat pick a point from the memory.
2. Selected Dimension (SRD): It represents a mutative ratio.
3. Counts of Dimension to Change (CDC): This factor represents the number of dimensions that shall be changed.
4. Self-Position Considering (SPC): This is a Boolean variable that represents whether the cat will move or not.

In CSO, initially, a number of copies are created from the current position of the *cat_k*. Then based on the factors presented above the variations are introduced in them. The objective function value is evaluated for each new candidate position. Any candidate can be selected based on the probability which is obtained as:

$$P_i = \frac{|FS_i - FS_b|}{FS_{max} - FS_{min}}$$

where $FS_b = FS_{max}$ for the minimization problem and $FS_b = FS_{min}$ for the maximization problem.

The new position is randomly picked and *cat_k* has a new position.

In the tracing mode of search, the cat is able to move in all dimensions. The equations applied for the movement of the cat is quite similar to the equations applied in PSO except that the individual best term is not considered.

5.3.4 Crow search algorithm

Crow search algorithm (CSA) exploits the behavior of crows to develop a meta-heuristics technique. The distinct features of crows are:

1. They live in flocks.
2. They can memorize their hiding places.
3. Thievery is prevalent in the flock.
4. They try to protect their catch.

In CSA, the movement of a crow "I" is influenced by the movement of another crow "j," toward its individual best, which it might have achieved in previous iterations. The effect of global best is neglected in the search process, while the movement of a crow is dependent on the individual best of another crow. The movement of a crow is given as:

$$x^{i,it+1} = \begin{cases} x^{i,it} + ri \times fl^{i,it} \times (m^{j,it} - x^{i,it}) & r_j \geq AP^{j,it} \\ a \; random \; position & otherwise \end{cases}$$

where "I" is a particular crow in the flock; "it" is the iteration; "x" represents the position of a crow in the search space; "r" is a random number between 0 and 1; "fl" signifies the flight length. Indirectly, it is a factor which helps control the search process and leads it into an exploration or an exploitation phase; "m" represents the individual best position; "AP" gives awareness probability of a crow.

In CSA, it is required to store the individual best positions of each crow and update them in every iteration.

5.3.5 Cuckoo search

Cuckoos have a special strategy for reproduction. They remove the eggs of other birds and instead put their own eggs in their nest. The cuckoo's chick outgrows the chicks of the host bird and therefore is able to survive. The cuckoo search is based on three rules:

- One egg per cuckoo is laid in a random nest
- Nests with better quality eggs will be considered in the search process
- In case the host is able to discover the cuckoo's egg, it can either discard the egg or build a new nest.

Levy flight which deals with the flight behavior of many animals is also included in this search process.

The equation used in the cuckoo search is:

$$x_i^{(t+1)} = x_i^{(t)} + a \oplus Lévy(\lambda)$$

where "t" is the iteration; "I" is the cuckoo number; a is a constant defined as $a > 0$ or preferably taken as $a = 1$; $\oplus$ represents entry-wise multiplication.

5.3.6   Mine blast algorithm

Mine blast algorithm is based on the process of mine bomb explosion. The shrapnel from the bomb is spread in all directions. This shrapnel then triggers other mine bombs with which they collide. The process represents a minefield being cleared. The aim is to find the mine with the highest explosive capacity and this mine is the optimal solution being searched through the process.

The casualties caused due to a particular bomb is proportional to the objective function value of that mine. Also, a high explosion in a particular area indicates the presence of other mines with high capacity in proximity. In mine blast algorithm, the process starts with one mine which then expands to more number of mines.

The equation that governs the mine blast algorithm is given as:

$$X_{n+1}^f = X_{e(n+1)}^f + \exp\left(-\sqrt{\frac{m_{n+1}^f}{d_{n+1}^f}}\right) X_n^f, \ n = 0, 1, 2, 3, \dots$$

where "X" represents a solution; "f" represents first shot points; "e" represents the explosion point; "m" represents the direction of shrapnel; "d" represents the distance that this shrapnel will cover.

The position of the exploding mine is defined as:

$$X_{e(n+1)}^f = d_{n+1}^f \times \cos(\theta), n = 0, 1, 2, \dots$$

where rand is a random number; θ is angle at which the shrapnel will travel and it is given as $360/N_s$, where N_s is the number of shrapnel pieces.

The distance and the direction of the shrapnel are given as:

$$d_{n+1}^f = \sqrt{(X_{n+1}^f - X_n^f)^2 + (F_{n+1}^f - F_n^f)^2}, \ n = 0, 1, 2, 3, \dots$$

$$m_{n+1}^f = \frac{F_{n+1}^f - F_n^f}{X_{n+1}^f - X_n^f}, n = 0, 1, 2, 3, \dots$$

where "F" is the objective function value.

To promote exploration in the search process, two parameters are considered: (i) exploration factor (μ) and (ii) iteration number index (k). The relationship between these two parameters decides if the exploration process is to be initiated. The equations used for exploration are:

$$d_{n+1}^f = d_n^f \times (|\text{randn}|)^2, \ n = 0, 1, 2, \dots$$

$$X_{e(n+1)}^f = d_{n+1}^f \times \cos(\theta), \ n = 0, 1, 2, \dots$$

where randn is a random number which is normally distributed as in other algorithms, the initial phase of the search process concentrates on exploration, and the later part is directed toward exploitation. Thus, the distance of shrapnel is controlled as:

$$d_n^f = \frac{d_{n-1}^f}{\exp(k/a)}, \ n = 1, 2, 3, \ldots$$

where a is the reduction constant. The value of alpha should be such that the shrapnel distance should reduce with every iteration. This reduction should lead to no distance traveled by the shrapnel in the last iteration.

5.3.7 Water cycle algorithm

A complete water cycle includes the process of evaporation, condensation, transpiration, precipitation, etc. Water cycle algorithm (WCA) is based on the natural process of the formation of streams/rivers as water flows down from hills toward the sea as a part of the water cycle. The small rivulets combine to form a big river as they approach the sea. The population in WCA is made up of raindrops, and the best raindrop is considered as the sea.

The total population is made up of sea, rivers, and raindrops. There can be a single sea in the population, which is represented by the raindrop having the best solution. *Nsr* is used to represent a subset of a population consisting of rivers and sea. *NSn* is used to represent the number of streams that flow into the rivers or sea. It is given as:

$$NS_n = round\left(\left|\frac{Cost_n}{\sum_{i=1}^{N_{sr}} Cost_i}\right| \times N_{Raindrops}\right)$$

where $Cost_n$ is the objective function value of nth raindrops; $N_{Raindrops}$ is given as $N_{POP} - N_{sr}$, where N_{pop} is the population size.

Streams can combine to form a river or can directly flow into the sea. The distance of travel by a stream can be randomly chosen.

The new position of the rivers and streams is represented as:

$$X_{Stream}^{i+1} = X_{Stream}^i + rand \times C \times (X_{River}^i - X_{Stream}^i)$$

$$X_{River}^{i+1} = X_{River}^i + rand \times C \times (X_{Sea}^i - X_{River}^i)$$

where rand is a random number between 0 and 1; "X" is the position.

In case the objective function value of a stream is better than the connecting river then their positions are interchanged. A similar operation can happen between a sea and a river.

In case, the distance between the river and sea is smaller than d_{max}, then the process of evaporation happens after which the raining process will start which is similar to the generation of random solutions within the search space. The value of d_{max} is proposed to increase the search process near the sea. The value of d_{max} can also be made linearly dependent on iterations as:

$$d_{max}^{i+1} = d_{max}^i - \frac{d_{max}^i}{maxiter}$$

The raining process can be used to generate random solutions near the sea for better exploitation in that region.

5.4 Conclusion

The chapter is used to present a vast collection of nature-inspired algorithms along with their references. This information should be very useful for researchers who can access the details of approximately 200 algorithms in a single place.

The chapter also introduces seven recently proposed evolutionary algorithms along with the necessary equations of these methods.

References

[1]   Trends M. AI Writes an Academic Paper About Itself and Researchers Try to Publish It!; 2022. https://www.analyticsinsight.net/ai-writes-an-academic-paper-about-itself-and-researchers-try-to-publish-it/.

[2]   Belton P. Would You Let a Robot Lawyer Defend You?; 2021. https://www.bbc.com/news/ business-58158820.

[3]   Basu K, Sinha R, Ong A, *et al.* Artificial intelligence: How is it changing medical sciences and its future? *Indian Journal of Dermatology.* 2020; 65(5):365.

[4]   Hart M. Google's New AI Helps You Write Poetry Like POE; 2020. https:// nerdist. com/article/google-ai-writes-poetry-like-legendary-poets/#:~:text= Google's%20new%20AI%20tool%2C%20Verse,reading%20the%20poets' %20respective%20oeuvres.

[5]   Moravec H. Rise of the robots – the future of artificial intelligence. In: *Scientific American.* Springer; 2009. p. 23.

[6]   Awasthi S, Balusamy B, and Porkodi V. Artificial intelligence supervised swarm UAVs for reconnaissance. In: *International Conference on Recent Developments in Science, Engineering and Technology.* Springer; 2019. p. 375–388.

[7]   Lomonaco V, Trotta A, Ziosi M, *et al.* Intelligent drone swarm for search and rescue operations at sea, 2018. arXiv preprint arXiv:181105291.

[8]   Badar AQH. In: Mercangöz BA, editor. *Different Applications of PSO.* Cham: Springer International Publishing; 2021. p. 191–208. https://doi.org/ 10.1007/978-3-030-70281-6 11.

[9]   Badar AQ. *Evolutionary Optimization Algorithms.* CRC Press; 2021.

[10] Odili JB and Kahar MNM. Numerical function optimization solutions using the African buffalo optimization algorithm (ABO). *British Journal of Mathematics & Computer Science.* 2015;10(1):1–12.

[11] Abdollahzadeh B, Gharehchopogh FS, and Mirjalili S. African vultures optimization algorithm: a new nature-inspired metaheuristic algorithm for global optimization problems. *Computers & Industrial Engineering.* 2021; 158:107408.

[12] Li X, Zhang J, and Yin M. Animal migration optimization: an optimization algorithm inspired by animal migration behavior. *Neural Computing and Applications.* 2014;24(7):1867–1877.

[13] Dorigo M, Birattari M, and Stutzle T. Ant colony optimization. *IEEE Computational Intelligence Magazine.* 2006;1(4):28–39.

[14] Mirjalili S. The ant lion optimizer. *Advances in Engineering Software.* 2015;83:80–98.

[15] Abualigah L, Yousri D, Abd Elaziz M, *et al.* Aquila optimizer: a novel meta-heuristic optimization algorithm. *Computers & Industrial Engineering.* 2021;157:107250.

[16] Hashim FA, Hussain K, Houssein EH, *et al.* Archimedes optimization algorithm: a new metaheuristic algorithm for solving optimization problems. *Applied Intelligence.* 2021;51(3):1531–1551.

[17] Abualigah L, Diabat A, Mirjalili S, *et al.* The arithmetic optimization algorithm. *Computer Methods in Applied Mechanics and Engineering.* 2021;376:113609.

[18] Uymaz SA, Tezel G, and Yel E. Artificial algae algorithm (AAA) for nonlinear global optimization. *Applied Soft Computing.* 2015;31:153–171.

[19] Karaboga D and Basturk B.. An idea based on honey bee swarm for numerical optimization. *Technical Report – tr06, Erciyes University, Engineering Faculty*; 2005.

[20] Zhao W, Wang L, and Zhang Z. Artificial ecosystem-based optimization: a novel nature-inspired meta-heuristic algorithm. *Neural Computing and Applications.* 2020;32(13):9383–9425.

[21] Cheng L, Wu Xh, and Wang Y. Artificial flora (AF) optimization algorithm. *Applied Sciences.* 2018;8(3):329.

[22] Bagheri A, Zandieh M, Mahdavi I, *et al.* An artificial immune algorithm for the flexible job-shop scheduling problem. *Future Generation Computer Systems.* 2010;26(4):533–541.

[23] Civicioglu P. Backtracking search optimization algorithm for numerical optimization problems. *Applied Mathematics and Computation.* 2013;219 (15):8121–8144.

[24] Passino KM. Biomimicry of bacterial foraging for distributed optimization and control. *IEEE Control Systems Magazine.* 2002;22(3):52–67.

[25] Alsattar HA, Zaidan A, and Zaidan B. Novel meta-heuristic bald eagle search optimisation algorithm. *Artificial Intelligence Review.* 2020;53 (3):2237–2264.

[26] Yang XS. A new metaheuristic bat-inspired algorithm. In: *Nature Inspired Cooperative Strategies for Optimization (NICSO2010).* Springer; 2010. p. 65–74.

[27] Rahkar Farshi T. Battle Royale optimization algorithm. *Neural Computing and Applications.* 2021;33(4):1139–1157.

[28] Teodorovic D and Dell'Orco M. Bee colony optimization – a cooperative learning approach to complex transportation problems. *Advanced OR and AI Methods in Transportation.* 2005;51:60.

[29]   Drias H, Sadeg S, and Yahi S. Cooperative bees swarm for solving the maximum weighted satisfiability problem. In: *International Work-Conference on Artificial Neural Networks*. Springer; 2005. p. 318–325.

[30]   Pham DT, Ghanbarzadeh A, Kǫc E, *et al.* The bees algorithm—a novel tool for complex optimisation problems. In: *Intelligent Production Machines and Systems*. Elsevier; 2006. p. 454–459.

[31]   Wang T, Yang L. Beetle swarm optimization algorithm: theory and application; 2018. arXiv preprint arXiv:180800206.

[32]   Zhong C, Li G, and Meng Z. Beluga whale optimization: a novel nature-inspired metaheuristic algorithm. *Knowledge-Based Systems*. 2022;251: 109215.

[33]   Erol OK and Eksin I. A new optimization method: big bang–big crunch. *Advances in Engineering Software*. 2006;37(2):106–111.

[34]   Simon D. Biogeography-based optimization. *IEEE Transactions on Evolutionary Computation*. 2008;12(6):702–713.

[35]   Askarzadeh A. Bird mating optimizer: an optimization algorithm inspired by bird mating strategies. *Communications in Nonlinear Science and Numerical Simulation*. 2014;19(4):1213–1228.

[36]   Hatamlou A. Black hole: a new heuristic optimization approach for data clustering. *Information Sciences*. 2013; 222:175–184.

[37]   Hayyolalam V and Kazem AAP. Black widow optimization algorithm: a novel meta-heuristic approach for solving engineering optimization problems. *Engineering Applications of Artificial Intelligence*. 2020;87: 103249.

[38]   Taherdangkoo M, Shirzadi MH, Yazdi M, *et al.* A robust clustering method based on blind, naked mole-rats (BNMR) algorithm. *Swarm and Evolutionary Computation*. 2013;10:1–11.

[39]   Das AK and Pratihar DK. A new bonobo optimizer (BO) for real-parameter optimization. In: *2019 IEEE Region 10 Symposium (TENSYMP)*. IEEE; 2019. p. 108–113.

[40]   Shi Y. Brain storm optimization algorithm. In: *International Conference in Swarm Intelligence*. Springer; 2011. p. 303–309.

[41]   Marinakis Y, Marinaki M, and Matsatsinis N. A bumble bees mating optimization algorithm for global unconstrained optimization problems. In: *Nature Inspired Cooperative Strategies for Optimization (NICSO2010)*. Springer; 2010.p. 305–318.

[42]   Jada C, Vadathya AK, Shaik A, *et al.* Butterfly mating optimization. In: *Intelligent Systems Technologies and Applications*. Springer; 2016. p. 3–15.

[43]   Arora S and Singh S. Butterfly optimization algorithm: a novel approach for global optimization. *Soft Computing*. 2019;23(3):715–734.

[44]   Chu SC, Tsai PW, and Pan JS. Cat swarm optimization. In: *Pacific Rim International Conference on Artificial Intelligence*. Springer; 2006. p. 854–858.

[45]   Formato RA. Central force optimization: a new nature inspired computational framework for multidimensional search and optimization. In: *Nature*

Inspired Cooperative Strategies for Optimization (NICSO 2007). Springer; 2008. p. 221–238.

[46] Houssein EH, Saber E, Ali AA, *et al.* Centroid mutation-based Search and Rescue optimization algorithm for feature selection and classification. *Expert Systems with Applications.* 2022;191:116235.

[47] Braik MS. Chameleon Swarm Algorithm: a bio-inspired optimizer for solving engineering design problems. *Expert Systems with Applications.* 2021;174:114685.

[48] Feng J, Zhang J, Zhu X, *et al.* A novel chaos optimization algorithm. *Multimedia Tools and Applications.* 2017;76(16):17405–17436.

[49] Jiang BLW. Optimizing complex functions by chaos search. *Cybernetics & Systems.* 1998;29(4):409–419.

[50] Kaveh A and Talatahari S. A novel heuristic optimization method: charged system search. *Acta Mechanica.* 2010;213(3):267–289.

[51] Meng X, Liu Y, Gao X, *et al.* A new bio-inspired algorithm: chicken swarm optimization. In: *International Conference in Swarm Intelligence.* Springer; 2014. p. 86–94.

[52] Khishe M and Mosavi MR. Chimp optimization algorithm. *Expert Systems with Applications.* 2020;149:113338.

[53] Das P, Das DK, and Dey S. A new class topper optimization algorithm with an application to data clustering. *IEEE Transactions on Emerging Topics in Computing.* 2018;8(4):948–959.

[54] Li M, Zhao H, Weng X, *et al.* Cognitive behavior optimization algorithm for solving optimization problems. *Applied Soft Computing.* 2016;39:199–222.

[55] Zhang Q, Wang R, Yang J, *et al.* Collective decision optimization algorithm: a new heuristic optimization method. *Neurocomputing.* 2017;221: 123–137.

[56] Kaveh A and Mahdavi VR. Colliding bodies optimization: a novel meta-heuristic method. *Computers & Structures.* 2014;139:18–27.

[57] Mohseni S, Gholami R, Zarei N, *et al.* Competition over resources: a new optimization algorithm based on animals behavioral ecology. In: *2014 International Conference on Intelligent Networking and Collaborative Systems.* IEEE; 2014. p. 311–315.

[58] Sharafi Y, Khanesar MA, and Teshnehlab M. COOA: competitive optimization algorithm. *Swarm and Evolutionary Computation.* 2016;30:39–63.

[59] Memarzadeh G and Keynia F. A new optimal energy storage system model for wind power producers based on long short term memory and Coot Bird Search Algorithm. *Journal of Energy Storage.* 2021;44:103401.

[60] Salcedo-Sanz S, Del Ser J, Landa-Torres I, *et al.* The coral reefs optimization algorithm: a novel metaheuristic for efficiently solving optimization problems. *The Scientific World Journal.* 2014;2014:739768.

[61] Hansen N, Müller SD, and Koumoutsakos P. Reducing the time complexity of the derandomized evolution strategy with covariance matrix adaptation (CMA-ES). *Evolutionary Computation.* 2003;11(1):1–18.

[62]   Pierezan J and Coelho LDS. Coyote optimization algorithm: a new meta-heuristic for global optimization problems. In: *2018 IEEE Congress on Evolutionary Computation (CEC)*. IEEE; 2018. p. 1–8.

[63]   Meng A, Ge J, Yin H, *et al.* Wind speed forecasting based on wavelet packet decomposition and artificial neural networks trained by crisscross optimization algorithm. *Energy Conversion and Management*. 2016; 114:75–88.

[64]   Askarzadeh A. A novel metaheuristic method for solving constrained engineering optimization problems: crow search algorithm. *Computers & Structures*. 2016;169:1–12.

[65]   Yang XS and Deb S. Cuckoo search via Lévy flights. In: *2009 World Congress on Nature & Biologically Inspired Computing (NaBIC)*. IEEE; 2009. p. 210–214.

[66]   Eesa AS, Brifcani AMA, and Orman Z. Cuttlefish algorithm – a novel bio-inspired optimization algorithm. *International Journal of Scientific & Engineering Research*. 2013;4(9):1978–1986.

[67]   Brammya G, Praveena S, Ninu Preetha N, *et al.* Deer hunting optimization algorithm: a new nature-inspired meta-heuristic paradigm. *The Computer Journal*. 2019. https://doi.org/10.1093/comjnl/bxy133.

[68]   Storn R and Price K. Differential evolution – a simple and efficient heuristic for global optimization over continuous spaces. *Journal of Global Optimization*. 1997;11(4):341–359.

[69]   Kaveh A and Farhoudi N. A new optimization method: Dolphin echolocation. *Advances in Engineering Software*. 2013;59:53–70.

[70]   Mirjalili S. Dragonfly algorithm: a new meta-heuristic optimization technique for solving single-objective, discrete, and multi-objective problems. *Neural Computing and Applications*. 2016;27(4):1053–1073.

[71]   Agushaka JO, Ezugwu AE, and Abualigah L. Dwarf mongoose optimization algorithm. *Computer Methods in Applied Mechanics and Engineering*. 2022;391:114570.

[72]   Oyelade ON, Ezugwu AES, Mohamed TI, *et al.* Ebola optimization search algorithm: a new nature-inspired metaheuristic optimization algorithm. *IEEE Access*. 2022;10:16150–16177.

[73]   Chen Z, Francis A, Li S, *et al.* Egret swarm optimization algorithm: an evolutionary computation approach for model free optimization. *Biomimetics*. 2022;7(4):144.

[74]   Abedinpourshotorban H, Shamsuddin SM, Beheshti Z, *et al.* Electromagnetic field optimization: a physics-inspired metaheuristic optimization algorithm. *Swarm and Evolutionary Computation*. 2016;26:8–22.

[75]   Wang GG, Deb S, and Coelho LdS. Elephant herding optimization. In: *2015 3rd International Symposium on Computational and Business Intelligence (ISCBI)*. IEEE; 2015. p. 1–5.

[76]   Harifi S, Khalilian M, Mohammadzadeh J, *et al.* Emperor Penguins Colony: a new metaheuristic algorithm for optimization. *Evolutionary Intelligence*. 2019;12(2):211–226.

[77]   Faramarzi A, Heidarinejad M, Stephens B, *et al.* Equilibrium optimizer: a novel optimization algorithm. *Knowledge-Based Systems.* 2020;191:105190.

[78]   Yang XS. Firefly algorithms for multimodal optimization. In: *International Symposium on Stochastic Algorithms.* Springer; 2009. p. 169–178.

[79]   Tan Y and Zhu Y. Fireworks algorithm for optimization. In: *International Conference in Swarm Intelligence.* Springer; 2010. p. 355–364.

[80]   Yang XS. Flower pollination algorithm for global optimization. In: *International Conference on Unconventional Computing and Natural Computation.* Springer; 2012. p. 240–249.

[81]   Ghaemi M and Feizi-Derakhshi MR. Forest optimization algorithm. *Expert Systems with Applications.* 2014;41(15):6676–6687.

[82]   Xing B and Gao WJ. Fruit fly optimization algorithm. In: *Innovative Computational Intelligence: a Rough Guide to 134 Clever Algorithms.* Springer; 2014. p. 167–170.

[83]   Muthiah-Nakarajan V and Noel MM. Galactic swarm optimization: a new global optimization metaheuristic inspired by galactic motion. *Applied Soft Computing.* 2016;38:771–787.

[84]   Abdechiri M, Meybodi MR, and Bahrami H. Gases Brownian motion optimization: an algorithm for optimization (GBMO). *Applied Soft Computing.* 2013;13(5):2932–2946.

[85]   Holland JH. Robust algorithms for adaptation set in a general formal framework. In: *1970 IEEE Symposium on Adaptive Processes (9th) Decision and Control*; 1970. p. 175–175.

[86]   Goldberg DE and Holland JH. Genetic algorithms and machine learning. In: *Machine Learning,* Springer; 1988.

[87]   Koza JR. *Genetic Programming: A Paradigm for Genetically Breeding Populations of Computer Programs to Solve Problems.* vol. 34. Stanford University, Department of Computer Science Stanford, CA; 1990.

[88]   Krishnanand K and Ghose D. Glowworm swarm optimization for simultaneous capture of multiple local optima of multi- modal functions. *Swarm Intelligence.* 2009;3(2):87–124.

[89]   Mohammadi-Balani A, Nayeri MD, Azar A, *et al.* Golden eagle optimizer: a nature-inspired metaheuristic algorithm. *Computers & Industrial Engineering.* 2021;152:107050.

[90]   Ahmadianfar I, Bozorg-Haddad O, and Chu X. Gradient-based optimizer: a new metaheuristic optimization algorithm. *Information Sciences.* 2020;540:131–159.

[91]   Akkar HA and Mahdi FR. Grass fibrous root optimization algorithm. *International Journal of Intelligent Systems and Applications.* 2017; 11(6):15.

[92]   Mirjalili SZ, Mirjalili S, Saremi S, *et al.* Grasshopper optimization algorithm for multi-objective optimization problems. *Applied Intelligence.* 2018;48(4):805–820.

[93]   Rashedi E, Nezamabadi-Pour H, and Saryazdi S. GSA: a gravitational search algorithm. *Information Sciences.* 2009;179(13):2232–2248.

[94] Li Y, Pardalos PM, and Resende MG. A greedy randomized adaptive search procedure for the quadratic assignment. In: *Quadratic Assignment and Related Problems: DIMACS Workshop*, May 20–21, 1993. vol. 16. American Mathematical Soc.; 1994. p. 237.

[95] Feo TA, Resende MG, and Smith SH. A greedy randomized adaptive search procedure for maximum independent set. *Operations Research*. 1994;42(5):860–878.

[96] Mirjalili S, Mirjalili SM, and Lewis A. Grey wolf optimizer. *Advances in Engineering Software*. 2014;69:46–61.

[97] Zhang Y and Jin Z. Group teaching optimization algorithm: a novel metaheuristic method for solving global optimization problems. *Expert Systems with Applications*. 2020;148:113246.

[98] Geem ZW, Kim JH, and Loganathan GV. A new heuristic optimization algorithm: harmony search. *Simulation*. 2001;76(2):60–68.

[99] Heidari AA, Mirjalili S, Faris H, *et al.* Harris hawks optimization: algorithm and applications. *Future Generation Computer Systems*. 2019;97:849–872.

[100] Hatamlou A. Heart: a novel optimization algorithm for cluster analysis. *Progress in Artificial Intelligence*. 2014;2(2):167–173.

[101] Asef F, Majidnezhad V, Feizi-Derakhshi MR, *et al.* Heat transfer relation-based optimization algorithm (HTOA). *Soft Computing*. 2021;25(13):8129–8158.

[102] Patel VK and Savsani VJ. Heat transfer search (HTS): a novel optimization algorithm. *Information Sciences*. 2015;324:217–246.

[103] Hashim FA, Houssein EH, Mabrouk MS, *et al.* Henry gas solubility optimization: a novel physics-based algorithm. *Future Generation Computer Systems*. 2019;101:646–667.

[104] Hashim FA, Houssein EH, Hussain K, *et al.* Honey Badger algorithm: new metaheuristic algorithm for solving optimization problems. *Mathematics and Computers in Simulation*. 2022;192:84–110.

[105] MiarNaeimi F, Azizyan G, and Rashki M. Horse herd optimization algorithm: a nature-inspired algorithm for high-dimensional optimization problems. *Knowledge-Based Systems*. 2021;213:106711.

[106] Wang L, Ni H, Yang R, *et al.* A simple human learning optimization algorithm. In: *Computational Intelligence, Networked Systems and Their Applications*. Springer; 2014, p. 56–65.

[107] Mousavirad SJ and Ebrahimpour-Komleh H. Human mental search: a new population-based metaheuristic optimization algorithm. *Applied Intelligence*. 2017;47(3):850–887.

[108] Yang Y, Chen H, Heidari AA, *et al.* Hunger games search: visions, conception, implementation, deep analysis, perspectives, and towards performance shifts. *Expert Systems with Applications*. 2021;177:114864.

[109] Rbouh I and El Imrani AA. Hurricane-based optimization algorithm. *AASRI Procedia*. 2014;6:26–33.

[110] Khabbazi A, Atashpaz-Gargari E, and Lucas C. Imperialist competitive algorithm for minimum bit error rate beam- forming. *International Journal of Bio-Inspired Computation*. 2009;1(1–2):125–133.

[111] Mozaffari MH, Abdy H, and Zahiri SH. IPO: an inclined planes system optimization algorithm. *Computing and Informatics*. 2016;35(1):222–240.

[112] Li C, Chen G, Liang G, *et al.* Integrated optimization algorithm: a meta-heuristic approach for complicated optimization. *Information Sciences*. 2022;586:424–449.

[113] Jahangiri M, Hadianfard MA, Najafgholipour MA, *et al.* Interactive auto-didactic school: a new metaheuristic optimization algorithm for solving mathematical and structural design optimization problems. *Computers & Structures*. 2020;235:106268.

[114] Tang D, Dong S, Jiang Y, *et al.* ITGO: invasive tumor growth optimization algorithm. *Applied Soft Computing*. 2015;36:670–698.

[115] Rad HS and Lucas C. A recommender system based on invasive weed optimization algorithm. In: *2007 IEEE Congress on Evolutionary Computation*. IEEE; 2007. p. 4297–4304.

[116] Javidy B, Hatamlou A, and Mirjalili S. Ions motion algorithm for solving optimization problems. *Applied Soft Computing*. 2015;32:72–79.

[117] Katayama K and Narihisa H. Iterated local search approach using genetic transformation to the traveling salesman problem. In: *Proceedings of the 1st Annual Conference on Genetic and Evolutionary Computation*, vol. 1; 1999. p. 321–328.

[118] Rao R. Jaya: a simple and new optimization algorithm for solving con-strained and unconstrained optimization problems. *International Journal of Industrial Engineering Computations*. 2016;7(1):19–34.

[119] Moein S and Logeswaran R. KGMO: a swarm optimization algorithm based on the kinetic energy of gas molecules. *Information Sciences*. 2014;275:127–144.

[120] Gandomi AH and Alavi AH. Krill herd: a new bio-inspired optimization algorithm. *Communications in Nonlinear Science and Numerical Simulation*. 2012;17(12):4831–4845.

[121] Pereira JLJ, Francisco MB, da Cunha Jr SS, *et al.* A powerful Lichtenberg Optimization Algorithm: a damage identification case study. *Engineering Applications of Artificial Intelligence*. 2021;97:104055.

[122] Nematollahi AF, Rahiminejad A, and Vahidi B. A novel multi-objective optimization algorithm based on Lightning Attachment Procedure Optimization algorithm. *Applied Soft Computing*. 2019;75:404–427.

[123] Yazdani M and Jolai F. Lion optimization algorithm (LOA): a nature-inspired metaheuristic algorithm. *Journal of Computational Design and Engineering*. 2016;3(1):24–36.

[124] Cuevas E, Fausto F, and González A. The locust swarm optimization algorithm. In: *New Advancements in Swarm Algorithms: Operators and Applications*. Springer; 2020. p. 139–159.

[125] Kushwaha N, Pant M, Kant S, *et al.* Magnetic optimization algorithm for data clustering. *Pattern Recognition Letters*. 2018;115:59–65.

[126] Tayarani-N MH and Akbarzadeh-T MR. Magnetic-inspired optimization algorithms: operators and structures. *Swarm and Evolutionary Computation*. 2014;19:82–101.

[127]   Zhao W, Zhang Z, and Wang L. Manta ray foraging optimization: an effective bio-inspired optimizer for engineering applications. *Engineering Applications of Artificial Intelligence.* 2020;87:103300. https://www.science direct.com/science/article/pii/S0952197619302593.

[128]   Faramarzi A, Heidarinejad M, Mirjalili S, *et al.* Marine Predators Algorithm: a nature-inspired metaheuristic. *Expert Systems with Applications.* 2020;152: 113377.

[129]   Abbass HA. MBO: marriage in honey bees optimization – a haplometrosis polygynous swarming approach. In: *Proceedings of the 2001 Congress on Evolutionary Computation (IEEE Cat. No. 01TH8546).* vol. 1. IEEE; 2001. p. 207–214.

[130]   Zervoudakis K and Tsafarakis S. A mayfly optimization algorithm. *Computers & Industrial Engineering.* 2020;145:106559.

[131]   Sadollah A, Bahreininejad A, Eskandar H, *et al.* Mine blast algorithm: a new population-based algorithm for solving constrained engineering optimization problems. *Applied Soft Computing.* 2013;13(5):2592–2612.

[132]   Wang GG, Zhao X, and Deb S. A novel monarch butterfly optimization with greedy strategy and self-adaptive. In: *2015 Second International Conference on Soft Computing and Machine Intelligence (ISCMI).* IEEE; 2015. p. 45–50.

[133]   Meng Z and Pan JS. Monkey king evolution: a new memetic evolutionary algorithm and its application in vehicle fuel consumption optimization. *Knowledge-Based Systems.* 2016;97:144–157.

[134]   Seref O and Akcali E. Monkey search: a new meta-heuristic approach. In: *INFORMS Annual Meeting*, San Jose, CA; 2002.

[135]   Bouchekara H. Most Valuable Player Algorithm: a novel optimization algorithm inspired from sport. *Operational Research.* 2020;20(1):139–195.

[136]   Mirjalili S. Moth-flame optimization algorithm: a novel nature-inspired heuristic paradigm. *Knowledge-Based Systems.* 2015;89:228–249.

[137]   Azizi M, Ghasemi SAM, Ejlali RG, *et al.* Optimal tuning of fuzzy parameters for structural motion control using multiverse optimizer. *The Structural Design of Tall and Special Buildings.* 2019;28(13):e1652.

[138]   Kashan AH. A new metaheuristic for optimization: optics inspired optimization (OIO). *Computers & Operations Research.* 2015;55:99–125.

[139]   Borji A. A New Global Optimization Algorithm inspired by parliamentary political competitions. In: Gelbukh A, Kuri Morales ÁF, editors. *MICAI 2007: Advances in Artificial Intelligence.* Berlin, Heidelberg: Springer Berlin Heidelberg; 2007. p. 61–71.

[140]   Kennedy J and Eberhart R. Particle swarm optimization. In: *Proceedings of ICNN'95-International Conference on Neural Networks.* vol. 4. IEEE; 1995. p. 1942–1948.

[141]   Yapici H and Cetinkaya N. A new meta-heuristic optimizer: pathfinder algorithm. *Applied Soft Computing.* 2019;78:545–568.

[142]   Trojovský P and Dehghani M. Pelican optimization algorithm: a novel nature-inspired algorithm for engineering applications. *Sensors.* 2022;22 (3):855.

[143] Duan H and Qiao P. Pigeon-inspired optimization: a new swarm intelligence optimizer for air robot path planning. *International Journal of Intelligent Computing and Cybernetics.* 2014;7(1):24–37.

[144] Po-lap D and Wo´zniak M. Polar bear optimization algorithm: meta-heuristic with fast population movement and dynamic birth and death mechanism. *Symmetry.* 2017;9(10):203.

[145] Askari Q, Younas I, and Saeed M. Political optimizer: a novel socio-inspired meta-heuristic for global optimization. *Knowledge-Based Systems.* 2020;195:105709. https://www.sciencedirect.com/science/article/pii/ S09507 05120301350.

[146] Moosavi SHS and Bardsiri VK. Poor and rich optimization algorithm: a new human-based and multi populations algorithm. *Engineering Applications of Artificial Intelligence.* 2019;86:165–181.

[147] Zeidabadi FA and Dehghani M. Poa: puzzle optimization algorithm. *International Journal of Intelligent Systems.* 2022;15:273–281.

[148] Farhi E, Goldstone J, and Gutmann S. A quantum approximate optimization algorithm. arXiv preprint arXiv:14114028. 2014.

[149] Zhang J, Xiao M, Gao L, *et al.* Queuing search algorithm: a novel meta-heuristic algorithm for solving engineering optimization problems. *Applied Mathematical Modelling.* 2018;63:464–490.

[150] Koohi SZ, NAWA H, Othman M, *et al.* Raccoon optimization algorithm. *IEEE Access.* 2018;7:5383–5399.

[151] Moazzeni AR and Khamehchi E. Rain optimization algorithm (ROA): a new metaheuristic method for drilling optimization solutions. *Journal of Petroleum Science and Engineering.* 2020;195:107512.

[152] Kaboli SHA, Selvaraj J, and Rahim N. Rain-fall optimization algorithm: a population based algorithm for solving constrained optimization problems. *Journal of Computational Science.* 2017;19:31–42.

[153] Rao RV and Pawar RB. Self-adaptive multi-population Rao Algorithms for engineering design optimization. *Applied Artificial Intelligence.* 2020;34 (3):187–250. https://doi.org/10.1080/08839514.2020.1712789.

[154] Brabazon A, Cui W, and O'Neill M. The raven roosting optimisation algorithm. *Soft Computing.* 2016;20(2):525–545.

[155] Kaveh A and Khayatazad M. A new meta-heuristic method: ray optimization. *Computers & Structures.* 2012;112:283–294.

[156] Fard A and Hajiaghaei-Keshteli M. Red Deer Algorithm (RDA); a new optimization algorithm inspired by Red Deers' mating. In: *International Conference on Industrial Engineering*, IEEE. vol. 12; 2016. p. 331–342.

[157] Po-lap D and Wo´zniak M. Red fox optimization algorithm. *Expert Systems with Applications.* 2021;166:114107.

[158] Badar AQH, Umre BS, and Junghare AS. Reducing Variable Trend Search algorithm for optimizing non linear multidimensional space search. In: *2014 International Conference on Advances in Engineering Technology Research (ICAETR-2014)*; 2014. p. 1–4.

[159] Jia H, Peng X, and Lang C. Remora optimization algorithm. *Expert Systems with Applications.* 2021;185:115665.

[160] Abualigah L, Abd Elaziz M, Sumari P, *et al.* Reptile Search Algorithm (RSA): a nature-inspired meta-heuristic optimizer. *Expert Systems with Applications.* 2022;191:116158.

[161] Labbi Y, Attous DB, Gabbar HA, *et al.* A new rooted tree optimization algorithm for economic dispatch with valve-point effect. *International Journal of Electrical Power & Energy Systems.* 2016;79:298–311.

[162] Ahmadianfar I, Heidari AA, Gandomi AH, *et al.* RUN beyond the metaphor: an efficient optimization algorithm based on Runge Kutta method. *Expert Systems with Applications.* 2021;181:115079.

[163] Mirjalili S, Gandomi AH, Mirjalili SZ, *et al.* Salp Swarm Algorithm: a bio-inspired optimizer for engineering design problems. *Advances in Engineering Software.* 2017;114:163–191.

[164] Kaur A, Jain S, and Goel S. Sandpiper optimization algorithm: a novel approach for solving real-life engineering problems. *Applied Intelligence.* 2020;50(2):582–619.

[165] Moosavi SHS and Bardsiri VK. Satin bowerbird optimizer: a new optimization algorithm to optimize ANFIS for software development effort estimation. *Engineering Applications of Artificial Intelligence.* 2017;60:1–15.

[166] Glover F. Heuristics for integer programming using surrogate constraints. *Decision Sciences.* 1977;8(1):156–166.

[167] Dhiman G and Kumar V. Seagull optimization algorithm: theory and its applications for large-scale industrial engineering problems. *Knowledge-Based Systems.* 2019;165:169–196.

[168] Masadeh R, Mahafzah BA, and Sharieh A. Sea lion optimization algorithm. *International Journal of Advanced Computer Science and Applications.* 2019;10(5).

[169] Shabani A, Asgarian B, Salido M, *et al.* Search and rescue optimization algorithm: a new optimization method for solving constrained engineering optimization problems. *Expert Systems with Applications.* 2020;161:113698.

[170] Emami H. Seasons optimization algorithm. *Engineering with Computers.* 2020;38:1–21.

[171] Dai C, Zhu Y, Chen W. Seeker optimization algorithm. In: *International Conference on Computational and Information Science.* Springer; 2006. p. 167–176.

[172] Fausto F, Cuevas E, Valdivia A, *et al.* A global optimization algorithm inspired in the behavior of selfish herds. *Biosystems.* 2017;160: 39–55.

[173] Abedinia O, Amjady N, and Ghasemi A. A new metaheuristic algorithm based on shark smell optimization. *Complexity.* 2016;21(5):97–116.

[174] Duan Q, Gupta VK, and Sorooshian S. Shuffled complex evolution approach for effective and efficient global minimization. *Journal of Optimization Theory and Applications.* 1993;76(3):501–521.

[175]   Eusuff M, Lansey K, and Pasha F. Shuffled frog-leaping algorithm: a memetic meta-heuristic for discrete optimization. *Engineering Optimization.* 2006;38(2):129–154.

[176]   Kirkpatrick S, Gelatt Jr CD, and Vecchi MP. Optimization by simulated annealing. *Science.* 1983;220(4598):671–680.

[177]   Mirjalili S. SCA: a sine cosine algorithm for solving optimization problems. *Knowledge-Based Systems.* 2016;96:120–133.

[178]   Li S, Chen H, Wang M, *et al.* Slime mould algorithm: a new method for stochastic optimization. *Future Generation Computer Systems.* 2020;111:300–323.

[179]   Hashim FA and Hussien AG. Snake optimizer: a novel meta-heuristic optimization algorithm. *Knowledge-Based Systems.* 2022;242:108320.

[180]   Balochian S and Baloochian H. Social mimic optimization algorithm and engineering applications. *Expert Systems with Applications.* 2019;134:178–191.

[181]   Cuevas E, Cienfuegos M, Zaldívar D, *et al.* A swarm optimization algorithm inspired in the behavior of the social-spider. *Expert Systems with Applications.* 2013;40(16):6374–6384.

[182]   James J and Li VO. A social spider algorithm for global optimization. *Applied Soft Computing.* 2015;30:614–627.

[183]   Kumar M, Kulkarni AJ, and Satapathy SC. Socio evolution and learning optimization algorithm: a socio-inspired optimization methodology. *Future Generation Computer Systems.* 2018;81:252–272.

[184]   Dhiman G and Kaur A. STOA: a bio-inspired based optimization algorithm for industrial engineering problems. *Engineering Applications of Artificial Intelligence.* 2019;82:148–174.

[185]   Xue J and Shen B. A novel swarm intelligence optimization approach: sparrow search algorithm. *Systems Science & Control Engineering.* 2020;8 (1):22–34.

[186]   Shehadeh HA, Ahmedy I, and Idris MYI. Sperm swarm optimization algorithm for optimizing wireless sensor network challenges. In: *Proceedings of the 6th International Conference on Communications and Broadband Networking*; 2018. p. 53–59.

[187]   Bansal JC, Sharma H, Jadon SS, *et al.* Spider monkey optimization algorithm for numerical optimization. *Memetic Computing.* 2014;6(1):31–47.

[188]   Dhiman G and Kumar V. Spotted hyena optimizer: a novel bio-inspired based metaheuristic technique for engineering applications. *Advances in Engineering Software.* 2017;114:48–70.

[189]   Jain M, Singh V, and Rani A. A novel nature-inspired algorithm for optimization: squirrel search algorithm. *Swarm and Evolutionary Computation.* 2019;44:148–175.

[190]   Cuevas E, Echavarría A, Zaldívar D, *et al.* A novel evolutionary algorithm inspired by the states of matter for template matching. *Expert Systems with Applications.* 2013;40(16):6359–6373.

[191]   Gomes GF, da Cunha SS, and Ancelotti AC. A sunflower optimization (SFO) algorithm applied to damage identification on laminated composite plates. *Engineering with Computers.* 2019;35(2):619–626.

[192]   Zhao W, Wang L, and Zhang Z. Supply-demand-based optimization: a novel economics-inspired algorithm for global optimization. *IEEE Access*. 2019;7:73182–73206.

[193]   Cheng MY and Prayogo D. Symbiotic organisms search: a new metaheuristic optimization algorithm. *Computers & Structures*. 2014;139:98–112.

[194]   Glover F. Tabu search—Part I. *ORSA Journal on Computing*. 1989;1 (3):190–206.

[195]   Glover F. Tabu search—Part II. *ORSA Journal on Computing*. 1990;2 (1):4–32.

[196]   Rao RV, Savsani VJ, and Vakharia D. Teaching – learning-based optimization: a novel method for constrained mechanical design optimization problems. *Computer-Aided Design*. 2011;43(3):303–315.

[197]   Dehghani M and Trojovský P. Teamwork optimization algorithm: a new optimization approach for function minimization/maximization. *Sensors*. 2021;21(13):4567.

[198]   Kaveh A and Dadras A. A novel meta-heuristic optimization algorithm: thermal exchange optimization. *Advances in Engineering Software*. 2017;110:69–84.

[199]   Qais MH, Hasanien HM, and Alghuwainem S. Transient search optimization: a new meta-heuristic optimization algorithm. *Applied Intelligence*. 2020;50(11):3926–3941.

[200]   Mladenovi´c N and Hansen P. Variable neighborhood search. *Computers & Operations Research*. 1997;24(11):1097–1100.

[201]   Yang XS. Engineering optimizations via nature-inspired virtual bee algorithms. In: *International Work-Conference on the Interplay Between Natural and Artificial Computation*. Springer; 2005. p. 317–323.

[202]   Jaderyan M and Khotanlou H. Virulence optimization algorithm. *Applied Soft Computing*. 2016;43:596–618.

[203]   Liang YC and Cuevas Juarez JR. A novel metaheuristic for continuous optimization problems: virus optimization algorithm. *Engineering Optimization*. 2016;48(1):73–93.

[204]   Doğan B and Ölmez T. A new metaheuristic for numerical function optimization: Vortex Search algorithm. *Information Sciences*. 2015;293:125–145.

[205]   Ayyarao TS, RamaKrishna N, Elavarasan RM, *et al.* War strategy optimization algorithm: a new effective meta-heuristic algorithm for global optimization. *IEEE Access*. 2022;10:25073–25105.

[206]   Eskandar H, Sadollah A, Bahreininejad A, *et al.* Water cycle algorithm—A novel metaheuristic optimization method for solving constrained engineering optimization problems. *Computers & Structures*. 2012;110: 151–166.

[207]   Kaveh A and Bakhshpoori T. Water evaporation optimization: a novel physically inspired optimization algorithm. *Computers & Structures*. 2016;167:69–85.

[208]   Zheng YJ. Water wave optimization: a new nature-inspired metaheuristic. *Computers & Operations Research*. 2015;55:1–11.

[209] Asgari HR, Bozorg Haddad O, Pazoki M, *et al.* Weed optimization algorithm for optimal reservoir operation. *Journal of Irrigation and Drainage Engineering.* 2016;142(2):04015055.

[210] Ahmadianfar I, Heidari AA, Noshadian S, *et al.* INFO: an efficient optimization algorithm based on weighted mean of vectors. *Expert Systems with Applications.* 2022;195:116516.

[211] Mirjalili S and Lewis A. The whale optimization algorithm. *Advances in Engineering Software.* 2016;95:51–67.

[212] Bayraktar Z, Komurcu M, and Werner DH. Wind Driven Optimization (WDO): a novel nature-inspired optimization algorithm and its application to electromagnetics. In: *2010 IEEE Antennas and Propagation Society International Symposium.* IEEE; 2010. p. 1–4.

[213] Covic N and Lacevic B. Wingsuit flying search—a novel global optimization algorithm. *IEEE Access.* 2020;8:53883–53900.

[214] Shahrezaee M. Image segmentation based on world cup optimization algorithm. *Majlesi Journal of Electrical Engineering.* 2017;11(2).

[215] Punnathanam V and Kotecha P. Yin-Yang-pair optimization: a novel lightweight optimization algorithm. *Engineering Applications of Artificial Intelligence.* 2016;54:62–79.

Chapter 6

Application and challenges of optimization in Internet of Things (IoT)

Hemlata Sharma[1], Shilpa Srivastava[2] and Varuna Gupta[2]

Optimization is a key part of the Internet of Things (IoT) ecosystem. It is used to make IoT devices, networks, and applications as efficient and effective as possible. In this chapter, a number of optimization algorithms of various technologies have been discussed in IoT like network, nature-inspired, evolutionary, and bio-inspired optimization. In network optimization, IoT devices rely on wireless communication protocols to transmit data, and the optimization of the network can help to reduce latency, improve reliability, and minimize power consumption. Nature-inspired optimization has shown great promise in optimizing various aspects of IoT systems, and their use is likely to become more widespread as IoT continues to grow and evolve. Evolutionary optimization can be used in the IoT to optimize various aspects of the system, including resource allocation, routing, and energy management. Bio-inspired optimization algorithms are designed to solve complex problems by simulating the behavior of natural systems, such as biological organisms, swarms of insects, or ecological systems. In a comparative analysis of various optimization algorithms, it can be safely concluded that optimization plays a vital role in IoT, but it requires careful planning and execution to overcome the associated challenges and realize the benefits of this technology.

6.1 Introduction

Optimization is crucial in the Internet of Things (IoT) to maximize the efficiency of various IoT systems and devices. Some applications of optimization in the IoT include resource optimization, energy optimization, network optimization, and routing optimization. Despite the potential benefits of optimization in IoT, there are also several challenges that need to be addressed like scalability, real-time processing, security, and interoperability.

Overall, optimization is a critical component of IoT systems, and overcoming these challenges will be key to realizing the full potential of this emerging

[1]Sheffield Hallam University, UK
[2]Christ (Deemed to be University) – Delhi, India

technology. To overcome the challenges, a number of optimization algorithms have been proposed in the chapter.

Natural-inspired optimization algorithms have demonstrated considerable promise for enhancing the effectiveness and performance of IoT systems, and their use is anticipated to extend as the IoT develops and expands.

IoT systems that use bio-inspired heuristic algorithms have a number of benefits that make them a desirable option for many optimization issues. In the context of IoT, they provide a reliable, effective, and adaptable method to solve various real-life problems.[1].

Overall, the many evolutionary algorithm types use the principles and procedures of natural selection and evolution to offer adaptable and effective solutions to a variety of optimization challenges in the IoT. These techniques may be used to optimize IoT systems for increased performance, scalability, and reliability.

In general, network optimization is a key component of IoT systems, and the choice of the most suited algorithms relies on the particular needs of the network and the devices involved.

These methods are based on the ideas of genetic algorithms, swarm intelligence, and natural selection. By optimizing numerous factors including energy usage, network traffic, and data processing, they may be utilized to increase the effectiveness and performance of IoT systems.

Comparative examination of several optimization algorithms reveals that optimization plays a crucial role in the IoT, but overcoming the related hurdles and realizing the benefits of this technology needs careful preparation and execution.

This chapter is divided into six sections. Several applications of optimization in IoT are explored in the first section, followed by network optimization methods in the second section. In Sections 3–5, nature-inspired, evolutionary, and bio-inspired algorithms are discussed. Finally, a comparison of all algorithms based on their usefulness has been made.

6.2   Application of optimization in the IoT

Optimization techniques play a crucial role in IoT to ensure efficient resource utilization and enhance system performance [2]. These are some of the key areas where optimization is applied in IoT to ensure efficient, secure, and cost-effective operations [3–5].

Some of the key applications of optimization in IoT are:

Network resource allocation: Optimization algorithms are used to allocate network resources such as bandwidth and power to IoT devices, to ensure effective utilization of these resources.

Data collection: Optimization techniques are applied to minimize data transmission costs in IoT systems by selecting the most cost-effective data collection method and scheduling data transmission to reduce network congestion [6].

Edge computing: Optimization algorithms help in optimizing the distribution of computing tasks between IoT devices and edge servers, reducing the load on the network, and ensuring effective use of computing resources.

Sensor placement: Optimization algorithms are used to determine the optimal placement of sensors in IoT systems, taking into account the trade-off between sensing accuracy and energy consumption.

Security: Optimization algorithms are used to determine the optimal security measures to protect IoT devices and networks, considering the trade-off between security and cost.

6.2.1 Challenges of optimization in IoT

Despite the potential benefits of optimization, there are several challenges associated with implementing it in IoT:

Heterogeneous devices: The wide range of devices and technologies used in IoT presents a significant challenge for optimization algorithms, as they must be able to work effectively with different types of devices and data [7,8].

Network constraints: The limited resources and connectivity issues in IoT networks pose a challenge for optimization algorithms, as they must be able to operate effectively within these constraints.

Real-time processing: IoT systems often require real-time processing of data, which poses a significant challenge for optimization algorithms, as they must be able to make decisions quickly and effectively.

Data privacy and security: Optimization algorithms must be designed to respect the privacy and security of IoT data, as well as the security of the devices and networks themselves.

Complex interactions: The interactions between devices and systems in IoT can be complex and difficult to predict, presenting a challenge for optimization algorithms, as they must be able to make decisions based on these interactions [8].

Overall, optimization in IoT is a crucial area for improving system performance and efficiency, but it also presents significant technical and logistical challenges that must be overcome to achieve these goals.

6.3 Network optimization in IoT

Network optimization in IoT refers to the process of improving the performance, scalability, security, and cost-effectiveness of the communication networks that connect IoT devices and systems [9]. This involves selecting and configuring network technologies, protocols, and services that are suitable for the specific needs and constraints of IoT applications and services. Network optimization can also involve the use of tools and techniques such as traffic management, network virtualization, and network slicing to improve network utilization and reduce network congestion and latency. Overall, the goal of network optimization in IoT is to enable efficient and reliable communication between IoT devices, applications, and services, while minimizing the costs and risks associated with network operations and maintenance. IoT devices rely on wireless communication protocols to transmit data, and the optimization of the network can help to reduce latency, improve reliability, and minimize power consumption.

6.3.1　Types of network optimization in IOT

Here are some strategies for optimizing networks in IoT:

1. **Protocol selection:** IoT devices support various wireless communication protocols, such as Bluetooth, Wi-Fi, ZigBee, and LoRaWAN. Protocol selection depends on the specific use case and the requirements of the application. For example, if the application requires low power consumption, then ZigBee or LoRaWAN would be a better choice.
2. **Traffic shaping and management:** This involves controlling and managing the flow of data and traffic within the IoT network to reduce congestion, minimize latency, and improve reliability.
3. **Network virtualization:** This involves dividing a physical network into multiple virtual networks that can run on the same physical infrastructure, allowing for efficient resource utilization and flexible network configuration.
4. **Network slicing:** This involves creating multiple isolated and dedicated network slices within a common physical network infrastructure, each designed to serve a specific IoT application or use case with guaranteed network performance and quality of service (QoS).
5. **Security optimization:** This involves implementing measures to secure IoT devices, networks, and data from threats such as hacking, unauthorized access, and data breaches.
6. **Energy optimization:** This involves reducing the energy consumption of IoT devices and networks to extend battery life, reduce operational costs, and reduce the environmental impact of IoT.
7. **Cost optimization:** This involves reducing the costs associated with deploying, operating, and maintaining IoT networks by using cost-effective network technologies, infrastructure, and services.
8. **Bandwidth optimization**: IoT devices transmit small amounts of data at regular intervals. By optimizing the bandwidth, we can reduce the amount of data transmitted and extend the battery life of IoT devices. Data compression, traffic shaping, and QoS mechanisms can be used to optimize bandwidth.
9. **Routing optimization:** Routing optimization can be used to minimize the latency and improve the reliability of IoT networks. This can be achieved through the use of efficient routing algorithms, such as shortest path, load balancing, and multipath routing.

In summary, network optimization is a critical aspect of IoT systems, and it is essential to consider the specific requirements of the application and the network to develop an effective optimization strategy (Figure 6.1). By optimizing the network, we can improve the performance, reliability, and security of IoT devices and applications [10].

6.3.2　Algorithms of network optimization in IoT

Network optimization is an important aspect of designing and deploying IoT systems. IoT networks often involve a large number of devices communicating with

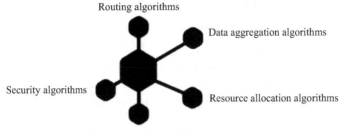

Figure 6.1 Network optimization algorithms in IOT

each other and with the cloud, and optimizing the network can improve efficiency, reduce latency, and increase reliability [11]. Here are some common algorithms used for network optimization in IoT:

- **Routing algorithms:** These algorithms determine the optimal path for data to travel between devices in the network. This can involve selecting the shortest or most reliable path, or balancing the load across different paths [12]. Examples of routing algorithms include Dijkstra's algorithm, A* search, and genetic algorithms.
- **Resource allocation algorithms**: These algorithms manage the allocation of network resources such as bandwidth, power, and memory. They can be used to balance the resources available to different devices in the network and prevent overload or congestion. Examples of resource allocation algorithms include time-division multiple access (TDMA), frequency-division multiple access (FDMA), and code-division multiple access (CDMA) [13].
- **Data aggregation algorithms:** These algorithms reduce the amount of data transmitted across the network by aggregating data from multiple devices before sending it to the cloud. This can reduce network traffic and improve efficiency. Examples of data aggregation algorithms include hierarchical clustering, centroid-based clustering, and k-means clustering.
- **Predictive analytics algorithms:** These algorithms analyze data from the network to predict future trends and patterns. This can be used to optimize the network by anticipating changes in usage and adjusting network resources accordingly. Examples of predictive analytics algorithms include decision trees, random forests, and neural networks.
- **Security algorithms:** These algorithms protect the network from unauthorized access, data breaches, and other security threats [14]. They can be used to encrypt data, authenticate devices, and monitor network activity for anomalies. Examples of security algorithms include AES, RSA, and SHA-256.

Overall, network optimization is a critical component of IoT systems, and the selection of appropriate algorithms depends on the specific requirements of the network and the devices involved.

6.3.3   Advantages of network optimization in IoT

There are several advantages to network optimization in IoT, including:

- *Improved performance:* Network optimization can improve the speed, reliability, and responsiveness of IoT networks, which can lead to better user experience and increased efficiency of IoT applications and services.
- *Increased scalability:* Network optimization can help IoT networks scale up or down as needed to accommodate changes in demand and traffic patterns, allowing for flexible and efficient resource utilization [15].
- *Enhanced security:* Network optimization can help secure IoT networks and devices against cyber threats and attacks, protecting sensitive data and intellectual property.
- *Reduced costs:* Network optimization can help reduce the costs associated with deploying, operating, and maintaining IoT networks by using cost-effective network technologies, infrastructure, and services.
- *Increased energy efficiency:* Network optimization can help reduce the energy consumption of IoT networks, extending battery life and reducing the environmental impact of IoT.
- *Improved quality of service:* Network optimization can help ensure consistent and reliable network performance, reducing network downtime and improving the quality of service for IoT applications and services.
- *Better network utilization:* Network optimization can help improve the utilization of network resources, reducing congestion and latency, and ensuring efficient use of network infrastructure and bandwidth.

6.3.4   Disadvantages of network optimization in IoT

While network optimization in IoT has many benefits, there are also some potential disadvantages that should be considered. Here are some of the key disadvantages of network optimization in IoT:

- **Complexity:** Optimizing IoT networks can be complex, especially when dealing with large numbers of devices and complex data flows. This can lead to increased costs and longer development times.
- **Limited bandwidth:** IoT networks often have limited bandwidth, which can be a major constraint when optimizing the network. This can result in slower transmission speeds and longer processing times.
- **Security concerns:** Optimizing IoT networks can introduce security risks, especially if the network is not properly secured. This can lead to data breaches, unauthorized access, and other security issues.
- **Interoperability issues:** IoT devices often come from different vendors and may use different protocols, which can create interoperability issues when optimizing the network. This can lead to compatibility issues, increased complexity, and higher costs.
- **Reliability issues:** Optimizing IoT networks can sometimes reduce reliability, especially if the network is highly complex or if new technologies are

introduced. This can result in downtime, lost data, and other issues that can impact the overall performance of the network.

- **Privacy concerns**: IoT networks often collect and transmit large amounts of data, which can raise privacy concerns for users. This can result in decreased trust and increased regulatory scrutiny.

Overall, while network optimization in IoT has many benefits, it is important to carefully consider the potential disadvantages before implementing optimization strategies. This will help to ensure that the benefits outweigh the risks and that the network operates effectively and securely.

6.4 Nature-inspired optimization in IoT

Nature-inspired optimization refers to a class of optimization algorithms that are inspired by the mechanisms and processes found in nature, such as evolution, migration, and natural selection. In IoT, nature-inspired optimization techniques, also known as metaheuristics, are a class of algorithms that mimic the behavior of natural systems to solve complex optimization problems [16]. These techniques have been applied to a wide range of fields, including the IoT, to improve performance, reduce power consumption, and enhance overall system efficiency. Some examples of nature-inspired optimization algorithms that are used in IoT include:

6.4.1 Algorithms of nature-inspired optimization in IoT

These nature-inspired optimization algorithms (Figure 6.2) can provide effective and efficient solutions to optimize the deployment of IoT devices, the placement of sensors in a wireless sensor network, the energy consumption of IoT devices, etc. [17].

- **Genetic algorithms**: It is a type of optimization algorithm that is inspired by the process of natural selection and evolution. It uses principles such as inheritance, mutation, and recombination to find the best solution to a problem.

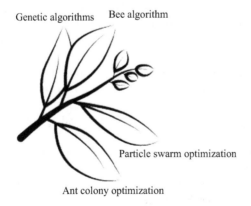

Figure 6.2 Nature-inspired algorithms in IoT

In a genetic algorithm, a set of candidate solutions to a problem, called individuals or chromosomes, are represented as strings of bits or numbers. Each individual represents a potential solution to the problem and is assigned a fitness value that represents how well the solution performs compared to other solutions [18].

The genetic algorithm then iteratively applies genetic operations such as selection, crossover, and mutation to the population of individuals to produce new generations of solutions. The selection operation is used to choose the most fit individuals to survive and propagate to the next generation. The crossover operation combines the genetic information of two individuals to produce a new offspring. The mutation operation randomly changes the genetic information of an individual to introduce diversity into the population. The process continues until a stopping criterion is met, such as a maximum number of generations or a solution with a fitness value that meets a certain threshold. The best solution found by the genetic algorithm is then returned as the final answer to the problem. Genetic algorithms have been applied to various problems in IoT, including network topology design, resource allocation, and traffic management. They offer a flexible and efficient way to find the best solution to optimization problems in IoT, by leveraging the mechanisms and processes found in nature.

- **Ant colony optimization**: It is a type of optimization algorithm that is inspired by the behavior of ant colonies. It uses principles such as cooperation, communication, and self-organization to solve optimization problems.

  In ACO, a set of artificial ants are used to explore the solution space of a problem and find the best solution. Each ant constructs a solution by visiting a set of nodes in a graph and leaving a trail of pheromones, which are used to communicate information about the quality of solutions to other ants. The pheromones represent the strength of the connection between nodes and help guide the ants toward promising areas of the solution space.

  The optimization process consists of multiple iterations, during which the ants construct solutions, update the pheromone trails, and adjust the parameters of the algorithm based on the quality of the solutions found. The process continues until a stopping criterion is met, such as a maximum number of iterations or a solution with a fitness value that meets a certain threshold.

  ACO has been applied to various problems in IoT, including network topology design, resource allocation, and traffic management. It offers a flexible and efficient way to find the best solution to optimization problems in IoT, by leveraging the mechanisms of cooperation and communication found in ant colonies.

- **Particle swarm optimization**: It is a heuristic optimization algorithm inspired by the social behavior of birds or other animals in a flock or swarm. It is used to find the global optimum of a function in a search space. In particle swarm optimization (PSO), each particle represents a candidate solution and moves through the search space guided by its own experience and the experiences of other particles in the swarm. The position and velocity of each particle are updated at each iteration based on its own best solution found so far (pbest) and the best solution found by any particle in the swarm (gbest). PSO has been applied to a wide range of optimization problems and is known for its simplicity and effective convergence characteristics.

- **Bee Algorithm**: It is a metaheuristic optimization algorithm that is inspired by the foraging behavior of honeybees. It is used to find the global optimum of a function in a search space. In BA, the swarm of bees is divided into employed bees, onlooker bees, and scout bees. The employed bees search for nectar sources in their assigned search space and share the information with the onlooker bees. The onlooker bees then choose the best solution based on the information shared by the employed bees. The scout bees, on the other hand, explore new search spaces if the solution quality degrades. The best solution found so far by the swarm is updated at each iteration. BA has been applied to various optimization problems and is known for its fast convergence, robustness, and ability to handle multimodal and complex functions.

6.4.2   Role of nature-inspired algorithms in IoT

Nature-inspired optimization plays a crucial role in the development of IoT systems by providing efficient and effective solutions to various optimization problems in IoT [18]. Some of the key roles of nature-inspired optimization in IoT are:

- **Optimization:** Nature-inspired algorithms can be used to optimize various aspects of IoT systems, including resource allocation, energy management, and routing. For example, algorithms such as genetic algorithms, particle swarm optimization, and ant colony optimization can be used to find the optimal configuration of IoT devices and networks to improve performance and reduce energy consumption [19].
- **Adaptation:** IoT systems often face dynamic and uncertain environments, and nature-inspired algorithms can be used to help these systems adapt to changing conditions. For example, algorithms such as evolutionary programming and artificial immune systems can be used to optimize the behavior of IoT devices in response to changes in the environment.
- **Fault tolerance**: Nature-inspired algorithms can be used to improve fault tolerance in IoT systems. For example, algorithms such as artificial bee colony optimization can be used to improve the robustness of wireless sensor networks against node failures.
- **Security**: Nature-inspired algorithms can also be used to enhance the security of IoT systems. For example, algorithms such as cuckoo search and firefly algorithms can be used to optimize the encryption and decryption of data transmitted by IoT devices.

Overall, nature-inspired algorithms can play a significant role in optimizing, adapting, and securing IoT systems, and their use is likely to become more widespread as IoT continues to grow and evolve.

6.4.3   Advantages of nature-inspired optimization in IoT

Nature-inspired optimization algorithms have several advantages in IoT applications:

- **Flexibility:** Nature-inspired optimization algorithms can be applied to a wide range of optimization problems in IoT, such as network design, resource allocation, traffic management, and security, among others. They can also be easily adapted to handle new problems and changing requirements.
- **Global optimization:** Nature-inspired optimization algorithms are capable of finding the global optimum solution to an optimization problem, rather than just a local optimum. This is important in IoT applications where a globally optimal solution is desired to ensure optimal system performance [20].
- **Efficient exploration:** Nature-inspired optimization algorithms can efficiently explore the solution space of a problem, by using mechanisms such as cooperation, communication, and self-organization. This allows them to quickly find good solutions and avoid getting stuck in local optima [21].
- **Scalability:** Nature-inspired optimization algorithms can be easily scaled to handle large and complex optimization problems in IoT, such as those involving large numbers of nodes and variables. This makes them well-suited to handle the growing complexity of IoT systems.
- **Robustness:** Nature-inspired optimization algorithms are robust to changes in the problem, such as fluctuations in the environment, and can effectively handle uncertainty and incomplete information. This makes them suitable for use in dynamic and unpredictable IoT environments.

Overall, the advantages of nature-inspired optimization algorithms have shown great promise in optimizing various aspects of IoT systems, and their use is likely to become more widespread as IoT continues to grow and evolve [19].

6.4.4   Disadvantages of nature-inspired optimization in IoT

Nature-inspired optimization techniques are increasingly being used in IoT to address the complex optimization problems that arise in these systems. While these techniques have many benefits, there are also some potential disadvantages that should be considered [22]. Here are some of the key disadvantages of nature-inspired optimization in IoT:

- **Computational complexity:** Nature-inspired optimization algorithms can be computationally intensive, especially when dealing with large numbers of devices and complex data flows. This can lead to longer processing times and increased costs.
- **Difficulty of tuning parameters:** Nature-inspired optimization algorithms typically have many parameters that need to be tuned for optimal performance. This can be a complex and time-consuming task, requiring expertise and specialized tools.

- **Lack of transparency:** Nature-inspired optimization algorithms are often black-box models, which can make it difficult to understand how they work and why they make certain decisions. This can lead to reduced trust in the system and difficulty in identifying and fixing problems.
- **Sensitivity to initial conditions:** Nature-inspired optimization algorithms can be sensitive to the initial conditions and the quality of the data used to train them. This can lead to suboptimal results and decreased reliability.
- **Lack of generalizability:** Nature-inspired optimization algorithms are often designed for specific types of problems and may not be easily generalizable to other types of problems. This can limit their usefulness in diverse IoT applications.
- **Ethical considerations:** Some nature-inspired optimization techniques are based on evolutionary principles and may raise ethical concerns related to their impact on natural systems and their potential to reinforce biases or create unintended consequences.

Overall, while nature-inspired optimization techniques have many benefits, it is important to carefully consider the potential disadvantages before implementing them in IoT systems. This will help to ensure that the benefits outweigh the risks and that the system operates effectively and ethically.

6.5 Evolutionary algorithms in IoT

Evolutionary algorithms (EAs) are a class of optimization algorithms that are inspired by the process of natural selection and evolution. EAs are a class of meta-heuristic optimization algorithms inspired by the principles of biological evolution. They can be used in the IoT to optimize various aspects of the system, including resource allocation, routing, and energy management.

In an evolutionary algorithm, a population of candidate solutions is evolved over time by applying genetic operations, such as selection, crossover, and mutation. The best solutions are selected for survival and reproduction, and the population is updated with the new offspring. The process continues until a stopping criterion is met, such as a maximum number of iterations or a solution with a fitness value that meets a certain threshold [23].

The key advantage of EAs in IoT is their ability to find near-optimal solutions to complex and multi-objective optimization problems. EAs can efficiently explore the solution space, handle uncertainty and incomplete information, and adapt to changing environments. They are also well-suited to handle large and complex problems, such as those involving large numbers of nodes and variables [24].

Overall, EAs have shown great promise in optimizing various aspects of IoT systems, and their use is likely to become more widespread as IoT continues to grow and evolve. By leveraging the mechanisms and processes of natural selection and evolution, EAs can help improve the performance, scalability, and robustness of IoT systems.

6.5.1   *Algorithms of evolutionary optimization in the IoT*

There are several types of EAs that are used in the IoT applications:

- **Genetic algorithm (GA):** GA is a type of EA that is inspired by the process of natural selection and evolution. It is based on a population of candidate solutions that are evolved over time through genetic operations, such as selection, crossover, and mutation [25].
- **Differential evolution (DE):** DE is a type of EA that is based on the principle of simulating the process of evolution through the exchange of information between candidate solutions. It is well-suited to problems with many variables and large solution spaces.
- **Particle swarm optimization (PSO):** PSO is a type of EA that is inspired by the behavior of bird flocks and fish schools [26]. It is based on a population of candidate solutions that move in the solution space, guided by the best solutions found so far [27].
- **Artificial bee colony (ABC):** ABC is a type of EA that is inspired by the behavior of bee colonies. It is based on a population of candidate solutions, called bees, that search for food sources, guided by the best solutions found so far.
- **Ant colony optimization (ACO):** ACO is a type of EA that is inspired by the behavior of ant colonies. It is based on a population of candidate solutions, called ants, that search for solutions, guided by a trail of pheromones that are left by previous ants.

Each of these types of EAs has its own strengths and weaknesses, and the best type to use in a specific IoT application depends on the problem at hand, the requirements of the system, and the available computational resources. Overall, the various types of EAs provide flexible and efficient solutions to various optimization problems in IoT, leveraging the mechanisms and processes of natural selection and evolution. By using these algorithms (Figure 6.3), IoT systems can be optimized for improved performance, scalability, and robustness.

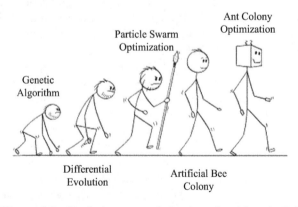

Figure 6.3   Evolutionary optimization algorithms in IoT

6.5.2 Role of evolutionary algorithms in IoT

The role of EAs in the IoT can be significant in various applications. Some of the applications of EAs in IoT are:

- **Network optimization:** EAs can be used to optimize network parameters, such as node placement, resource allocation, and routing, to improve network performance, reduce energy consumption, and increase network lifetime.
- **Machine learning:** EAs can be used to train machine learning models in IoT devices, such as sensor nodes, to make predictions, classify data, and perform other tasks.
- **Parameter tuning:** EAs can be used to automatically tune the parameters of IoT devices, such as sensors, to optimize their performance and reduce the need for manual tuning.
- **Sensor placement:** EAs can be used to determine the optimal placement of sensors in IoT networks to improve coverage, reduce energy consumption, and increase network lifetime.
- **Resource allocation:** EAs can be used to optimize the allocation of resources, such as bandwidth and power, in IoT networks to improve performance, reduce energy consumption, and increase network lifetime [28].

Overall, the use of EAs in IoT can lead to more efficient, effective, and reliable IoT systems [29].

6.5.3 Advantages of evolutionary optimization in IoT

The main advantages of using EAs in the IoT applications are:

- **Flexibility:** EAs are flexible algorithms that can be applied to a wide range of optimization problems in IoT, from network design to resource allocation and traffic management to security. They can handle complex problems with many variables and large solution spaces.
- **Near-optimal solutions:** EAs can efficiently explore the solution space and find near-optimal solutions to complex and multi-objective optimization problems in IoT. They can handle uncertainty and incomplete information and adapt to changing environments.
- **Robustness:** EAs are robust algorithms that can handle large and complex problems, such as those involving many nodes and variables in IoT systems. They can also handle noise and non-linear relationships between variables.
- **Scalability:** EAs can be easily parallelized and scaled to handle large-scale optimization problems in IoT systems. This makes them well-suited to the requirements of large and complex IoT systems.
- **Global optimization:** EAs are capable of global optimization, meaning they can find the best solutions across the entire solution space. This is particularly useful in IoT, where many optimization problems involve global solutions, such as network design and resource allocation.

Overall, EAs provide flexible, efficient, and robust solutions to various optimization problems in IoT. By leveraging the mechanisms and processes of natural selection and evolution, EAs can help improve the performance, scalability, and robustness of IoT systems.

6.5.4 Disadvantages of evolutionary optimization in IoT

Evolutionary algorithms are optimization methods inspired by the process of natural selection and are widely used in various domains, including the IoT. However, despite their advantages, EAs have several limitations in the context of IoT, including:

- **Scalability:** EAs can be computationally intensive and may struggle with large-scale problems, making it difficult to apply them to the huge amounts of data generated by IoT devices.
- **Convergence rate:** EAs can be slow to converge to optimal solutions, especially in complex problems with many variables, which can limit their usefulness in time-sensitive IoT applications.
- **Premature convergence:** EAs can sometimes converge prematurely to suboptimal solutions, which can limit their ability to find globally optimal solutions to IoT problems.
- **Lack of interpretability**: EAs can be difficult to understand and interpret, making it challenging for practitioners to debug and improve them.
- **Data privacy and security:** EAs can be vulnerable to attacks and may not be able to effectively protect the privacy and security of sensitive IoT data.

In conclusion, while EAs have shown great potential in many areas, they have several limitations in the context of IoT and additional research is needed to overcome these challenges and make them more suitable for IoT applications.

6.6 Bio-inspired heuristic algorithms in IoT

Bio-inspired optimization, also known as biologically inspired optimization, is a field of study that draws inspiration from biological systems and processes to develop optimization algorithms. Bio-inspired optimization algorithms are designed to solve complex problems by simulating the behavior of natural systems, such as biological organisms, swarms of insects, or ecological systems [30].

The increasing complexity of real-world problems motivates researchers to search for efficient methods. Divide and conquer techniques are the one way to solve large and complex problems which has been a practice in research for a long time.

Swarms have relatively simple behaviors individually, but with the amazing capability of coordinating and organizing their actions, they represent a complex and highly structured social organization [31]. Examples are bee colonies, ant colonies, mosquito swarms, fish schools, birds, flies, and particle swarms.

Swarm Intelligence is a branch of biologically inspired algorithms, which is focused on the collective behavior of swarms in order to develop some metaheuristics that mimic the swarm's problem-solution abilities. Taking the inspiration from success and efficiency of the distributed, coordinated, and collective behavior of swarms in the real world, researchers have tried to develop sophisticated methods and systems that make use of the techniques of the swarms to find solutions to complex optimization problems.

Bio-inspired algorithms are a type of heuristic algorithms that are inspired by nature and biological systems. In the context of the IoT, bio-inspired algorithms can be used to solve various optimization problems and improve the efficiency of IoT systems.

For example, genetic algorithms (GAs) are popular bio-inspired algorithms that can be used for optimizing complex problems in IoT. In a GA, a population of candidate solutions is evolved over multiple generations using genetic operations such as selection, crossover, and mutation. The solutions are evaluated based on their fitness and the best solutions are selected for the next generation. This process is repeated until a satisfactory solution is found or a stopping criterion is met. Another example is the use of ACO algorithms in IoT. ACO algorithms are inspired by the behavior of ant colonies, where ants work together to find the shortest path between their colony and a food source. In IoT, ACO algorithms can be used to find the shortest path for data transmission or to solve routing problems.

In addition to GAs and ACO, there are other bio-inspired algorithms such as PSO and ABC that can be applied to various optimization problems in IoT.

Overall, the use of bio-inspired algorithms in IoT can help improve the efficiency and performance of IoT systems by providing better solutions to complex problems.

6.6.1   Types of bio-inspired heuristic algorithm in IoT

There are several types of bio-inspired heuristic algorithms that can be used in the context of the IoT:

- **GAs:** They are a type of optimization algorithm inspired by the principles of evolution and natural selection. They can be used in IoT for problems such as network optimization, device placement, and data analysis.
- **ACO:** They are inspired by the behavior of ant colonies and their ability to find the shortest path between their colony and a food source. In IoT, ACO algorithms can be used for routing and data transmission problems.
- **PSO:** It is a heuristic optimization algorithm inspired by the behavior of birds flocking and fish schooling. In IoT, PSO can be used for problems such as device placement, network optimization, and data analysis.
- **ABC:** It is a bio-inspired optimization algorithm inspired by the behavior of honeybees in searching for food. In IoT, ABC can be used for problems such as network optimization, device placement, and data analysis [32].
- **Firefly algorithm (FA):** It is a bio-inspired optimization algorithm inspired by the behavior of fireflies and their ability to communicate and find mates. In IoT, FA can be used for problems such as network optimization, device placement, and data analysis [33].

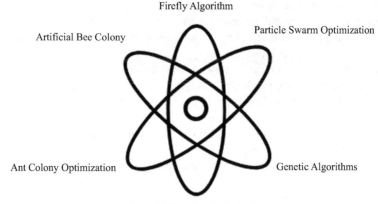

Figure 6.4   Bio-inspired optimization algorithms in IoT

- **Bacterial foraging optimization (BFO):** It is a bio-inspired optimization algorithm inspired by the behavior of bacteria in searching for food. In IoT, BFO can be used for problems such as network optimization, device placement, and data analysis.

These are some of the most commonly used bio-inspired heuristic algorithms in IoT (Figure 6.4). The choice of a specific algorithm will depend on the specific problem being solved and the desired performance characteristics.

In the context of the IoT, bio-inspired optimization algorithms can be used to optimize various aspects of the system, including resource allocation, routing, and energy management.

6.6.2   Role of bio-inspired heuristic algorithm in IoT

The role of bio-inspired heuristic algorithms in the IoT is to provide efficient and effective solutions to complex optimization problems that arise in the context of IoT systems. Some of the key roles of these algorithms in IoT include:

- **Optimization:** Bio-inspired algorithms can be used to optimize network performance in IoT systems by finding the optimal placement of devices, optimizing the routing of data, and reducing energy consumption [34].
- **Device placement:** Bio-inspired algorithms can be used to determine the optimal placement of devices in an IoT system to maximize performance and reduce energy consumption.
- **Data analysis:** Bio-inspired algorithms can be used to analyze large amounts of data generated by IoT devices to identify patterns, relationships, and trends, and to make predictions about future behavior.
- **Resource allocation:** Bio-inspired algorithms can be used to allocate resources in IoT systems such as bandwidth, processing power, and storage, in an efficient and effective manner.

- **Decision making:** Bio-inspired algorithms can be used to make decisions in IoT systems, such as determining the best course of action in response to a change in the environment.

Overall, the role of bio-inspired heuristic algorithms in IoT is to provide efficient and effective solutions to complex problems, while reducing energy consumption and improving performance. They can help optimize the performance of IoT systems, making them more scalable, reliable, and efficient.

6.6.3 Advantages of bio-inspired heuristic algorithm in IoT

The use of bio-inspired heuristic algorithms in the IoT systems provides several advantages, including:

- **Efficiency:** Bio-inspired algorithms are designed to solve complex optimization problems quickly and efficiently. They can provide solutions in a fraction of the time required by traditional algorithms [35].
- **Robustness:** Bio-inspired algorithms are designed to be robust and to provide reliable solutions even in the presence of noise and uncertainty. They are well suited to the dynamic and unpredictable nature of IoT systems.
- **Scalability:** Bio-inspired algorithms can handle large-scale problems and can easily be scaled to meet the needs of growing IoT systems.
- **Adaptability:** Bio-inspired algorithms are designed to be adaptive and can automatically adjust to changing conditions in IoT systems. This allows them to provide optimal solutions even in the face of changing requirements.
- **Global optimization:** Bio-inspired algorithms can find the global optimal solution to a problem, rather than being limited to finding a locally optimal solution.
- **Low complexity**: Bio-inspired algorithms are generally simpler and easier to implement than traditional algorithms, making them a cost-effective solution for many optimization problems in IoT systems.
- **Natural inspiration:** The inspiration from natural systems provides a powerful and intuitive understanding of the optimization process, which can help with problem-solving and design.

Overall, the use of bio-inspired heuristic algorithms in IoT systems provides several advantages that make them an attractive solution for various optimization problems. They offer a robust, efficient, and adaptive approach to problem-solving in the context of IoT [1].

6.6.4 Limitations of bio-inspired heuristic algorithm in IoT

Bio-inspired heuristic algorithms are inspired by biological systems and try to mimic their behaviors to solve problems in computer science. However, despite their success in many applications, they have several limitations in the context of the IoT. Some of these limitations include:

- **Scalability:** Bio-inspired algorithms often struggle with large-scale problems and may not be efficient in handling the huge amounts of data generated by IoT devices.
- **Complexity:** Bio-inspired algorithms can be complex and may require significant computational resources to run, which may not be feasible for resource-constrained IoT devices.
- **Lack of interpretability:** Bio-inspired algorithms can be difficult to understand and interpret, making it challenging for practitioners to debug and improve them.
- **Lack of adaptivity:** Bio-inspired algorithms may not be able to adapt quickly enough to changing conditions in an IoT environment, which can limit their effectiveness in dynamic scenarios.
- **Data privacy and security:** Bio-inspired algorithms can be vulnerable to attacks and may not be able to effectively protect the privacy and security of sensitive IoT data.

In conclusion, while bio-inspired heuristic algorithms have shown great promise in many areas, they have significant limitations in the context of IoT, and additional research is needed to overcome these challenges.

6.7   Load optimization in cognitive IoT

Load optimization in cognitive IoT refers to the process of optimizing the use of resources, such as computing power, bandwidth, and storage, in a cognitive IoT system [36]. Load optimization is important in cognitive IoT to ensure that the system is operating efficiently and effectively while avoiding overloading or underutilizing any of its resources [37].

There are several techniques for optimizing load in cognitive IoT [38], including:

- **Resource allocation:** Allocating resources in an efficient manner to ensure that they are used optimally. This can involve using algorithms such as load balancing or scheduling to determine how resources should be assigned to different tasks.
- **Data reduction:** Reducing the amount of data that needs to be processed by the cognitive IoT system, for example, by compressing or aggregating data.
- **Dynamic resource allocation**: Dynamically allocating resources based on the current load and demand, so that resources can be redirected as needed to meet changing requirements.
- **Edge computing:** Moving processing and storage closer to the source of data, which can reduce the amount of data that needs to be transmitted and processed by the central system.
- **Distributed computing:** Distributing processing and storage across multiple devices, which can improve the overall efficiency of the system.

In conclusion, load optimization is a crucial aspect of cognitive IoT, as it helps to ensure that the system is operating efficiently and effectively while avoiding overloading or underutilizing any of its resources [39]. By implementing techniques such as resource allocation, data reduction, dynamic resource allocation, edge computing, and distributed computing, it is possible to achieve optimal load optimization in cognitive IoT.

6.7.1   Uses of load optimization in cognitive IoT

Load optimization in cognitive IoT is used to improve the performance and efficiency of IoT systems by optimizing the allocation of computing and network resources [40]. Here are some of the key uses of load optimization in cognitive IoT:

- **Improved system performance**: Load optimization can help to improve the overall performance of IoT systems by ensuring that tasks are allocated to the most suitable devices and networks and that the workload is distributed evenly across the system.
- **Efficient use of resources:** Load optimization can help to ensure that resources are used efficiently in IoT systems, by minimizing waste and reducing the need for additional hardware and infrastructure.
- **Increased scalability**: Load optimization can help to increase the scalability of IoT systems, by enabling them to handle a larger number of devices and data flows without becoming overloaded.
- **Reduced energy consumption:** Load optimization can help to reduce the energy consumption of IoT systems, by minimizing the need for devices to operate at full capacity and reducing the overall load on the system.
- **Enhanced reliability:** Load optimization can help to improve the reliability of IoT systems, by reducing the risk of system failures and ensuring that tasks are completed in a timely and efficient manner.

Overall, load optimization is an essential aspect of cognitive IoT, which can help to improve the performance, efficiency, and reliability of these systems, while also reducing costs and energy consumption [41].

6.7.2   Advantages of load optimization in cognitive IoT

Load optimization in cognitive IoT can bring several advantages to the system, including:

- **Improved resource utilization:** Load optimization helps to ensure that all resources in the cognitive IoT system, such as computing power, bandwidth, and storage, are used effectively and efficiently, leading to better utilization of these resources.
- **Better performance:** Load optimization helps to optimize the performance of the cognitive IoT system, ensuring that it is operating at optimal levels and providing the best possible outcomes.
- **Increased efficiency:** Load optimization helps to reduce the amount of data that needs to be processed and transmitted, reducing the overall demand on the system and increasing its efficiency.

- **Increased reliability:** Load optimization helps to ensure that the cognitive IoT system is operating within its capacity and avoiding overloading, which can increase the reliability and stability of the system.
- **Cost savings:** By optimizing the use of resources and reducing the demand on the system, load optimization can help to reduce the overall cost of operating the cognitive IoT system.

In conclusion, load optimization plays a crucial role in ensuring the efficient and effective operation of the cognitive IoT system. By optimizing the use of resources and reducing the demand on the system, load optimization can bring several advantages, including improved resource utilization, better performance, increased efficiency, increased reliability, and cost savings [42].

6.7.3   Disadvantages of load optimization in cognitive IoT

Despite the many advantages that load optimization can bring to cognitive IoT systems, there are also some potential disadvantages that need to be considered, including:

- **Complexity:** Load optimization can be a complex and challenging task, especially in large and dynamic cognitive IoT systems. Implementing load optimization algorithms can require significant expertise and may be difficult for some organizations.
- **Overhead:** Load optimization algorithms can introduce additional overhead into the system, which can reduce its overall efficiency and performance.
- **Flexibility:** Load optimization algorithms may be inflexible and may not be able to effectively handle changes in the system, such as new devices or changes in demand.
- **Accuracy:** Load optimization algorithms may not always provide accurate results, especially in complex and dynamic systems, which can limit their effectiveness.
- **Resource constraints:** Load optimization algorithms may be limited by the available resources in the system, such as computing power, bandwidth, and storage, which can reduce their effectiveness.

In conclusion, while load optimization can bring many advantages to cognitive IoT systems, it is important to consider the potential disadvantages and carefully evaluate the trade-offs before implementing load optimization in a real-world system.

6.8   Comparative analysis

Nature-inspired algorithms, evolutionary algorithms, and bio-inspired algorithms are all types of optimization algorithms that draw inspiration from natural systems and processes to solve complex problems. While there is some overlap between these techniques, they each have their own strengths and weaknesses. In the context of network optimization, these algorithms can be used to optimize various aspects

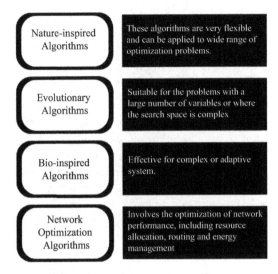

Figure 6.5   Comparative analysis of optimization algorithms

of network performance, including resource allocation, routing, and energy management. Here is a comparative analysis of these algorithms in the context of optimization (Figure 6.5).

- **Network optimization:** Network optimization involves the optimization of various aspects of network performance, including resource allocation, routing, and energy management. Optimization algorithms can be used to optimize these aspects of network performance [43–45].
- **Nature-inspired algorithms:** Nature-inspired algorithms, such as ant colony optimization, particle swarm optimization, and artificial bee colony optimization, are based on the behavior of social animals and other natural phenomena. These algorithms are often well-suited to solving complex optimization problems and can be highly effective at finding near-optimal solutions. However, they can be computationally intensive and may require a large number of iterations to converge to a solution.
- **Evolutionary algorithms:** Evolutionary algorithms are a class of nature-inspired algorithms that simulate the process of natural selection to find optimal solutions to problems. Evolutionary algorithms, such as genetic algorithms and differential evolution, are based on the principles of natural selection and genetics [46,47]. These algorithms are often well-suited to solving complex optimization problems with multiple objectives and can be highly effective at finding near-optimal solutions. However, they can be computationally intensive and may require a large number of iterations to converge to a solution [48].
- **Bio-inspired algorithms:** Bio-inspired algorithms, such as neural networks, fuzzy logic, and swarm intelligence, are based on the behavior of biological systems. These algorithms are often well-suited to solving complex problems

that require intelligence, learning, and adaptation [49,50]. They can be highly effective at finding solutions to complex problems, but may require large amounts of data to train the model and can be computationally intensive. In the context of the IoT, bio-inspired optimization algorithms can be used to optimize various aspects of the system, including resource allocation, routing, and energy management.

In general, nature-inspired algorithms are well-suited to solving problems that require the exploration of large solution spaces, while evolutionary algorithms are well-suited to solving problems with multiple objectives. Bio-inspired algorithms are often used in IoT applications that require learning and adaptation over time. Ultimately, the choice of algorithm will depend on the specific needs and requirements of the IoT system being designed.

References

[1] D. Yadav, "Blood coagulation algorithm: a novel bio-inspired meta-heuristic algorithm for global optimization." *Mathematics*, vol. 9, no. 23, pp. 3011, 2021, https://doi.org/10.3390/math9233011.

[2] E. Kanniga and P. S. Jadhav, "A study paper on forest fire detection using wireless sensor network." *International Journal of Psychosocial Rehabilitation*, vol. 23, no. 4, pp. 397–407, 2019, https://doi.org/10.37200/ijpr/v23i4/pr190199.

[3] X. Cui and G. Chen, "Application of improved ant colony optimization in vehicular ad-hoc network routing." In: *2021 IEEE 3rd Eurasia Conference on IOT, Communication and Engineering (ECICE)*, 2021, doi: 10.1109/ecice52819.2021.9645678.

[4] S. J. Wagh, M. S. Bhende, and A. D. Thakare, "Blockchain and IoT optimization." In: *Energy Optimization Protocol Design for Sensor Networks in IoT Domains*, pp. 205–224, 2022, doi: 10.1201/9781003310549-9.

[5] A. Bhavya, K. Harleen, and C. Ritu, *Transforming the Internet of Things for Next-Generation Smart Systems*. IGI Global, 2021.

[6] A. Kumar, P. S. Rathore, V. G. Diaz, and R. Agrawal, *Swarm Intelligence Optimization*. John Wiley & Sons, 2021.

[7] U. Kaur and Shalu, "Blockchain- and deep learning-empowered resource optimization in future cellular networks, edge computing, and IoT: open challenges and current solutions." In: *Blockchain for 5G-Enabled IoT*, pp. 441–474, 2021, doi: 10.1007/978-3-030-67490-8_17.

[8] Introduction to Internet of Things (Basic Concept, Challenges, Security Issues, Applications & Architecture). Nitya Publications, 2020.

[9] M. A. R. Khan, S. N. Shavkatovich, B. Nagpal, *et al.*, "Optimizing hybrid metaheuristic algorithm with cluster head to improve performance metrics on the IoT." *Theoretical Computer Science*, vol. 927, pp. 87–97, 2022, https://doi.org/10.1016/j.tcs.2022.05.031.

[10] K. Gulati, R. S. Kumar Boddu, D. Kapila, S. L. Bangare, N. Chandnani, and G. Saravanan, "A review paper on wireless sensor network techniques in

Internet of Things (IoT)." In: *Materials Today: Proceedings*, 2021, doi: https://doi.org/10.1016/j.matpr.2021.05.067.

[11] N. N. Srinidhi, S. M. Dilip Kumar, and K. R. Venugopal, "Network optimizations in the Internet of Things: a review." *Engineering Science and Technology, an International Journal*, vol. 22, no. 1, pp. 1–21, 2019, doi: https://doi.org/10.1016/j.jestch.2018.09.003.

[12] Y. Zhang, and S. Sun. "Real-time data driven monitoring and optimization method for IoT-based sensible production process." In: *2013 10th IEEE International Conference on Networking, Sensing and Control (ICNSC)*. IEEE, 2013.

[13] P. Ramezani, Y. Zeng, and A. Jamalipour, "Optimal resource allocation for multiuser Internet of Things network with single wireless-powered relay." *IEEE Internet of Things Journal*, vol. 6, pp. 1–1, 2018, doi: https://doi.org/10.1109/jiot.2018.2879373.

[14] N. Balakrishnan, A. Rajendran, D. Pelusi, and V. Ponnusamy, "Deep belief network enhanced intrusion detection system to prevent security breach in the Internet of Things." *Internet of Things*, vol. 14, p. 100112, 2019, doi: https://doi.org/10.1016/j.iot.2019.100112.

[15] S. Barshandeh, M. Masdari, G. Dhiman, V. Hosseini, and K. K. Singh, "A range-free localization algorithm for IoT networks." *International Journal of Intelligent Systems*, vol. 37, no. 12, pp. 10336–10379, 2021, doi: https://doi.org/10.1002/int.22524.

[16] A. Mohamed, *Handbook of Nature-Inspired Optimization Algorithms*. Springer Nature, 2022.

[17] A. Reda and Z. C. Johanyák, "Survey on five nature-inspired optimization algorithms." *Gradus*, vol. 8, no. 1, pp. 173–183, 2021, doi: https://doi.org/10.47833/2021.1.csc.001.

[18] A. Thongprasert and A. Jiamsanguanwong, "New product development processes for IOT-enabled home use medical devices: a systematic review." *Engineering Journal*, vol. 25, no. 2, pp. 15–48, 2021, doi: https://doi.org/10.4186/ej.2021.25.2.15.

[19] L. Sciullo, L. Gigli, A. Trotta, and M. D. Felice, "WoT store: managing resources and applications on the web of things." *Internet of Things*, vol. 9, pp. 100164, 2020, doi: https://doi.org/10.1016/j.iot.2020.100164.

[20] Y. Chen, S. Hao, and H. Nazif, "IoT-enabled product development method to support rapid manufacturing using a nature-inspired algorithm." *Journal of Management & Organization*, pp. 1–23, 2022, doi: https://doi.org/10.1017/jmo.2022.62.

[21] Y. Chen, S. Hao, and H. Nazif, "A privacy-aware approach for managing the energy of cloud-based IoT resources using an improved optimization algorithm." *IEEE Internet of Things Journal*, vol. 99, pp. 1–1, 2021, doi: https://doi.org/10.1109/jiot.2021.3112474.

[22] P. Bujok, J. Tvrdik, and R. Polakova, "Nature-inspired algorithms in real-world optimization problems." *MENDEL*, vol. 23, no. 1, pp. 7–14, 2017, doi: https://doi.org/10.13164/mendel.2017.1.007.

[23] X. Wang and Y. LI, "Solving Shubert function optimization problem by using evolutionary algorithm." *Journal of Computer Applications*, vol. 29, no. 4, pp. 1040–1042, 2009, doi: https://doi.org/10.3724/sp.j.1087.2009.01040.

[24] A. Ghaedi, A. K. Bardsiri, and M. J. Shahbazzadeh, "Cat hunting optimization algorithm: a novel optimization algorithm." *Evolutionary Intelligence*, vol. 16, pp. 417–438, 2021, doi: https://doi.org/10.1007/s12065-021-00668-w.

[25] M. Emami, A. Amini, and A. Emami, "Stock portfolio optimization with using a new hybrid evolutionary algorithm based on ICA and GA: recursive-ICA-GA (Case Study of Tehran Stock Exchange)." *SSRN Electronic Journal*, 2012, doi: https://doi.org/10.2139/ssrn.2067126.

[26] Y. Gao and K. Zhu, "Hybrid PSO-Solver algorithm for solving optimization problems." *Journal of Computer Applications*, vol. 31, no. 6, pp. 1648–1651, 2012, doi: https://doi.org/10.3724/sp.j.1087.2011.01648.

[27] A. Majumder, "Termite alate optimization algorithm: a swarm-based nature inspired algorithm for optimization problems." *Evolutionary Intelligence*, vol. 16, pp. 1–21, 2022, doi: https://doi.org/10.1007/s12065-022-00714-1.

[28] S. Yi and S. Yue, "Study of logistics distribution route based on improved genetic algorithm and ant colony optimization algorithm." *Internet of Things (IoT) and Engineering Applications*, vol. 1, pp. 11–17, 2016, doi: https://doi.org/10.23977/iotea.2016.11003.

[29] G. Yu and L. Kang, "New evolutionary algorithm based on girdding for dynamic optimization problems." *Journal of Computer Applications*, vol. 28, no. 2, pp. 319–321, 2008, doi: https://doi.org/10.3724/sp.j.1087.2008.00319.

[30] G. G. Wang, S. Deb, and L. D. S. Coelho, "Earthworm optimization algorithm: a bio-inspired metaheuristic algorithm for global optimization problems." *International Journal of Bio-Inspired Computation*, vol. 1, no. 1, pp. 1, 2015, doi: https://doi.org/10.1504/ijbic.2015.10004283.

[31] M. Kumar, S. Kumar, P. K. Kashyap, *et al.*, "Green communication in the Internet of Things: a hybrid bio-inspired intelligent approach." *International Journal Sensors*, vol. 10, no. 22, pp. 3910, 2022, https://doi.org/10.3390/s22103910

[32] S. Arslan and S. Aslan, "A modified artificial bee colony algorithm for classification optimization." *International Journal of Bio-Inspired Computation*, vol. 1, no. 1, pp. 1, 2022, doi: https://doi.org/10.1504/ijbic.2022.10049021.

[33] X. S. Yang, "Firefly algorithm, stochastic test functions and design optimisation." *International Journal of Bio-Inspired Computation*, vol. 2, no. 2, pp. 78, 2010, doi: https://doi.org/10.1504/ijbic.2010.032124.

[34] D. Devassy, J. Immanuel Johnraja, and G. J. L. Paulraj, "NBA: novel bio-inspired algorithm for energy optimization in WSN for IoT applications." *The Journal of Supercomputing*, vol. 78, no. 14, pp. 16118–16135, 2022, doi: https://doi.org/10.1007/s11227-022-04505-4.

[35] S. Hamrioui and P. Lorenz, "Bio inspired routing algorithm and efficient communications within IoT." *IEEE Network*, vol. 31, no. 5, pp. 74–79, 2017, doi: https://doi.org/10.1109/mnet.2017.1600282.

[36] C. X. Mavromoustakis, G. Mastorakis, J. M. Batalla, and Springerlink (Online Service, *Internet of Things (IoT) in 5G Mobile Technologies*. Cham: Springer International Publishing, 2016.

[37] M. P. Raju and A. J. Laxmi, "IOT based online load forecasting using machine learning algorithms." *Procedia Computer Science*, vol. 171, pp. 551–560, 2020, doi: https://doi.org/10.1016/j.procs.2020.04.059.

[38] S. Dash, Subhendu Kumar Pani, A. Abraham, and Y. Liang, *Advanced Soft Computing Techniques in Data Science, IoT and Cloud Computing*. Springer Nature, 2021.

[39] H. Sounni, N. El kamoun, and F. Lakrami, "Load balancing algorithm based-SDN for the IoT applications." *Indonesian Journal of Electrical Engineering and Computer Science*, vol. 21, no. 2, pp. 1209, 2021, doi: https://doi.org/10.11591/ijeecs.v21.i2.

[40] O. Y. Abdulhammed, "Load balancing of IoT tasks in the cloud computing by using sparrow search algorithm." *The Journal of Supercomputing*, vol. 78, pp. 3266–3287, 2021, doi: https://doi.org/10.1007/s11227-021-03989-w.

[41] B. T. Geetha, P. Santhosh Kumar, B. Sathya Bama, S. Neelakandan, C. Dutta, and D. Vijendra Babu, "Green energy aware and cluster based communication for future load prediction in IoT." *Sustainable Energy Technologies and Assessments*, vol. 52, pp. 102244, 2022, doi: https://doi.org/10.1016/j.seta.2022.102244.

[42] D. Sharma and S. Jain, "Optimized LOADng routing protocol parameters using black widow optimization algorithm for IoT." *Webology*, vol. 19, no. 1, pp. 535–550, 2022, doi: https://doi.org/10.14704/web/v19i1/web19038.

[43] L. Kakkar, D. Gupta, and S. Tanwar, "Comparative analysis of various encryption algorithms used in IoT security." In: *2021 9th International Conference on Reliability, Infocom Technologies and Optimization (Trends and Future Directions) (ICRITO)*, 2021.

[44] D. J. Hemanth and J. Anitha, "Modified Genetic Algorithm approaches for classification of abnormal magnetic resonance brain tumour images." *Applied Soft Computing*, vol. 75, pp. 21–28, 2019, https://doi.org/10.1016/j.asoc.2018.10.054

[45] H. Kurdi, F. Ezzat, L. Altoaimy, S. H. Ahmed, and K. Youcef-Toumi, "MultiCuckoo: multi-cloud service composition using a cuckoo-inspired algorithm for the Internet of Things applications." *IEEE Access*, vol. 6, pp. 56737–56749, 2018, https://doi.org/10.1109/access.2018.2872744.

[46] R. C. H, V. D and V. R. K, "Comparative analysis of applications of identity-based crpto system in IoT." *Information Security Education Journal (ISEJ)*, vol. 5, no. 2, pp. 64, 2018, doi: 10.6025/isej/2018/5/2/64-70.

[47] L. Kakkar, D. Gupta, and S. Tanwar, "Comparative analysis of various encryption algorithms used in IoT security." In: *2021 9th International Conference on Reliability, Infocom Technologies and Optimization (Trends and Future Directions) (ICRITO)*, 2021, doi: 10.1109/icrito51393.2021.9596234.

[48]   O. Speck, D. Speck, R. Horn, J. Gantner, and K. Sedlbauer, "Biomimetic bio-inspired biomorph sustainable? An attempt to classify and clarify biology-derived technical developments." *Bioinspiration & Biomimetics*, vol. 12, no. 1, pp. 011004, 2017, https://doi.org/10.1088/1748-3190/12/1/011004.

[49]   O. Hegazy, O. S. Soliman, and M. Salam, "A comparative study between FPA, BA, MCS, ABC, and PSO algorithms in training and optimizing of LSSVM for stock market prediction." *International Journal of Advanced Computer Research*, vol. 5, no. 18, pp. 35, 2015.

[50]   S. Jabbar, R. Iram, A. A. Minhas, I. Shafi, S. Khalid, and M. Ahmad, "Intelligent optimization of wireless sensor networks through bio-inspired computing: survey and future directions." *International Journal of Distributed Sensor Networks*, vol. 9, no. 2, p. 421084, 2013, https://doi.org/10.1155/2013/421084.

Chapter 7

Optimization applications and implications in biomedicines and healthcare

Niharika Kulshrestha[1], Abhinav Kumar[2], Vinay Kumar[2] and Subodh Srivastava[2]

Optimization is a set of methods which provides the best possible solution for a given problem. In this chapter, the role of optimization in healthcare systems, medical diagnosis, biomedical informatics, biomedical image processing, ECG classification, feature extraction and classification, and intelligent detection of disordered systems have been discussed in detail. Approaches for predictive analytics in healthcare and innovations and technologies for smart healthcare have been discussed using various methods. Some of the issues and challenges while using optimization algorithms for smart healthcare and wearables have been demonstrated in this chapter.

7.1 Introduction

Computer vision (CV) is a branch of computer technology which includes image processing, image analysis, and image understanding [1]. Computer vision is related to the construction of the 3D world from the observed 2D images. Figure 7.1 shows the different branches of image processing [2] which include digital image processing, CV, computer graphics, and artificial intelligence (AI). In a CV, input is an image, and output is a description. When input is a description, output is an image in computer graphics, whereas in AI, input is a description, and output is also a description.

Figure 7.2 shows the steps to be followed in digital image processing. First, an input image is acquired using either ultrasound or magnetic resonance imaging (MRI) or mammography or any other imaging modalities [3] and then preprocessing of the input image is done, which includes the denoising of the image followed by the image restoration [4]. Image enhancement is the next step to highlight the

[1]Department of Physics, GLA University, India
[2]Department of Electronics and Communication Engineering, National Institute of Technology – Patna, India

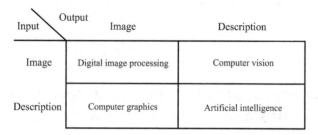

Figure 7.1   Branches that are correlated with digital image processing

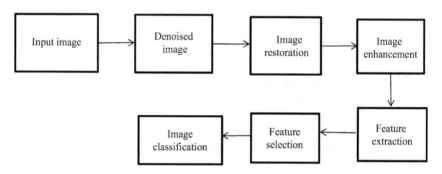

Figure 7.2   The steps to be followed in digital image processing

feature of the image and then these features are classified called features classification [5]. These features are then selected, this step is known as feature selection and then selected features are extracted called feature extraction to give the resultant output to find the abnormality in the image [6]. This image processing is used in the healthcare system widely for the early detection of chronic and harmful diseases such as heart disorders [7], lung cancer, breast cancer [8], and brain cancer [9].

These branches of digital image processing can be processed using machine learning (ML) [10] or deep learning (DL) [11] method. ML is an important advanced technology in health informatics. ML is a growing technology used to mine knowledge from data, i.e., automatic learning from volumetric data. ML implies proposing algorithms which can learn and progress over time and can be used for predictions [12]. Various applications of ML [13] are machine vision, biometric recognition, handwriting recognition, medical diagnosis, alignment of biological sequences, drug design, speech recognition, text mining, natural language processing (NLP), fault diagnostics, load forecasting, control and automation, and business intelligence. In this chapter, ML is discussed for the early detection of disorders or diseases in the human body. It can also be used in smart healthcare systems and technologies. The main objective of the ML system is to determine the accuracy. It provides patients' safety and healthcare quality [14]. DL [15] techniques are the advanced version of ML techniques. This technique reduces the need of solving the problem manually. Deep learning allows the computer to build complex concepts out of simpler concepts. One of the examples of a DL model is the feed-forward deep network or multilayer perceptron (MLP) [16]. An MLP is just a mathematical function mapping some set of input values to output values. The function is formed by composing many simpler functions [17].

Optimization algorithm (OA) [18] is the utilization of the minimum resources to obtain the best result. Although optimization may not seem like a task for machine learning, optimization techniques are frequently used in machine learning algorithms. Evolutionary computation is a branch of evolutionary biology that creates search and optimization techniques to aid in the completion of challenging tasks and issues. Genetic algorithm (GA) [19], evolution methods, evolutionary programming, and genetic programming are the main branches of evolutionary computation. These all are fundamental characteristics of the evolution process. The objective of the optimization is to minimize the different types of constraints to upsurge the performance of the proposed algorithm for getting the high performance, efficacy, and accuracy of the system [20]. OA can be applied anywhere and there are various kinds of optimization algorithms such as cuckoo search [21], ant colony [22], honey bee [23], fruit fly [24], a particle swarm [25], random search [26], and halving interval [27].

7.2 Role of optimization algorithms in healthcare systems

In healthcare systems, the role of OAs is rigorously significant that includes operational level, scheduling decisions as well as the design of healthcare plans [28]. In developed countries, expenditures in healthcare and its system account for a substantial portion of the gross domestic product (GDP). For instance, GDP in France is 12.2% and Germany is 12.8%, of the UK is about 9%, and the highest in USA is about 18% [29]. Healthcare delivery involves high cost and so efficient distribution of healthcare is crucial. In spite of spending huge amount in healthcare, USA is lagged behind other industrialized countries. The advantages of applying optimization algorithms are that.

(I)   It can improve the distribution and supply of healthcare providers.
(II)   It can reduce in traveling of patients.
(III) It can maximize the number of facilities and healthcare access equality.

In the modern smart healthcare system; the OA imparts a key role in the data delivery to end users. The emerging fields of analytics and machine learning, as well as traditional health economic analysis approaches, can all connect with optimization methodologies. Several healthcare systems need advanced technologies like the Internet of Things (IoT) [30], Big Data, Cloud Computing, and AI to make the healthcare system intelligent and realizable [31]. As IoT assists in data collection, Big Data gives out data analysis, Cloud Computing provides computing, and AI enables predictive analytics. But, these all technologies need efficient optimization algorithms to improve reliability in the modern healthcare system [32]. Moreover, the optimization has a major role in modeling and solving the healthcare operations management problems, too. For example, decision-making problems in healthcare delivery, which could be appointment scheduling, operation room scheduling, workforce scheduling, capacity planning, etc. [33]. Such kind of operational management optimization could maximize time used in operation theatre and matches nursing skills toward appropriate cases of patients for the day. In addition to these, population health issues like matching organ donors and recipients or developing radiation therapy protocols that limit patient harm could be addressed clinically via optimization [34].

Decision-making is necessary when using optimization algorithms in the delivery of healthcare, and this involves scheduling appointments, operating rooms (OR), capacity, and manpower. A key consideration factor in healthcare delivery systems, appointment scheduling, is made up of appointment times for each service at which the necessary resources will be made available, such as when planning procedures in an OR. The main challenges in designing optimal appointment schedules are uncertainty in service time such as patient hang around time, healthcare expertise inactive time, and over limit of the time are not specific [35]. Patients do not have complete information about their preferences, so a more realistic framework has been proposed that gets automatically updated when an appointment is done [36]. OR scheduling, often known as surgery scheduling, takes into account resources such ORs, surgeons, and surgical equipment. OR three tiers of scheduling decisions are made sequentially [37]. In order to plan surgeries in ORs on a daily basis, available OR time must first be assigned. Once this is done, a block schedule is created. This stage involves determining the number of surgeries, their order, and scheduled start times (appointment times).

Due to the requirement for reaching high service levels, high costs, and specialized resources, capacity planning is a significant concern in the healthcare industry. Bed capacity planning is also a type of capacity planning [38]. This is important because the factors like unexpected arrival of patients, indefinite time of patient's stay, and preplanned patient's stay can affect the availability of bed capacity. With a specific number of "virtual beds" and the ability for "virtual patients" to arrive, stay, and depart at rates that correspond to the actual historical trends, a simulation model is proposed in PASCAL utilizing a three-phase simulation shell (or any other patterns as required) [39]. Workforce scheduling refers to the planning of staff schedules based on the management of the staff required for healthcare facilities at both the operational and aggregate levels. It mainly deals with the management of nurses involved in workforce scheduling. Direct care and indirect care are the two types of nursing care. Indirect care refers to the time nurses spend on other tasks while providing direct care, which is a face-to-face interaction between nurses and patients. Nurse has a larger impact on patient health negatively due to their lack of time toward patient's intensive care. GA can be used for workforce scheduling [40]. Tabu search [41] is used as the primary technique, while knapsack and flow models are imposed in the pre-processing and post-processing models to create a software tool [42]. Ant colony optimization has also been proposed for nurse scheduling programs [43]. A mixed integer programming (MIP) model can also be used for workforce scheduling [44].

The primary function of an optimization algorithm is to support the location of medical facilities, organ transplantation, vaccine development, and disease screening. GA has been used for Human resource (HR) planning. Fuzzy Delphi is used to identify the factor influencing HR planning. This strategy encourages 36% of the talents and includes recognizing the competencies that could be in demand in emergencies [45].

7.3 Optimization algorithms in medical diagnosis

AI is the invention of fast as well as advanced computer technology. In the present time, AI has been frequently used in clinical purposes. Significant means in AI is the concept of machine learning, proposed by Arthur Samuel in 1959, which refers to employing algorithms to make machines learn from a vast amount of data in order to develop new methods for data analysis and study [46]. All kinds of medical examinations of human body are done using some kind of machines, which use some computing tools. These computer-aided tools diagnose diseases using auto-mated processes for higher performance and better cure of the disease. To refine the results of these automated processes and for the early-stage detection of disease; some optimization algorithms are used for feature extraction and selection of the disease. Some highly used OAs are cat swarm [47], flower pollination [48], glow worm swarm [49], genetic [19], gray wolf [50], particle swarm [51], whale [52], lion [53], grasshopper [54], moth flame [55], crow search [56], elephant search [57], social spider [58], ant colony [22], chimp [59], bees optimization algorithms, and many more [60].

Swarm intelligence [61] is a characteristic of systems of non-intelligent agents that exhibit collectively intelligent behavior despite having insufficient individual intelligence. Ant colony optimization (ACO) [22] and particle swarm optimization (PCO) [61] are the two main types of optimizations used in swarm intelligence. ACO is based on social insects and PCO follows the ability of human societies to process knowledge. Both ACO and PCO depend on the population of individuals. ACO is derived from ants, which are obviously significant creatures that are cap-able of finding effective solutions to issues that are well beyond their individual colony members' capabilities, such as the most efficient route to a food source. The emulation of human social behavior, or the ability of human society to process knowledge, is what drives PSO. A population of individuals having the ability to interact with their surroundings and one another is taken into account in particle swarm theory. Thus, interactions between individuals will affect the population level. Although some animal societies' collective behavior and particle systems served as the approach's first sources of inspiration, the algorithm's main focus is on its social adaptation of information.

In medical diagnosis, various features of a disease are extracted using a spe-cified algorithm or automated process. Then to reduce the extracted features for the selection of the disease; any of the OA is used. One of the most common cancers that affect roughly one million people worldwide is skin cancer. Its early detection can initiate early treatment and cure for the patients. Thermal exchange OA is used to detect skin cancer at its early stages [62]. A hybrid system is proposed to identify various diseases with an optimizing classifier parameter for the support vector machine (SVM) [63] and MLP. A hybrid intelligent system has been proposed considering the objectives like prediction accuracy [64], sensitivity, and specificity [65]. Global optimization-based techniques have been used to improve the diagnosis of breast cancer in patients [66]. Computer-aided diagnosis (CAD) [67] is designed with the aid of SVM where parameters are altered by optimization algorithms [14]. Over a decade, computer-aided diagnostics have proven to be effective and accurate for diagnosis. It has been suggested to use deep learning techniques along with supervised machine learning and meta-heuristic algorithms to conduct an accurate diagnosis [68]. For feature extraction mainly convolutional neural network (CNN) [69] is used and for feature selection, ant colony optimization is used [68]. Accuracy of more than 99% is obtained for the diagnosis of brain tumors and COVID-19. Cancer [70], diabetes, and heart disease can all be detected using an artificial neural network (ANN) that has been tuned using the directed bee colony (DBC) algorithm [71]. For the diagnosis of diseases including Alzheimer's disease, brain disorders, diabetes, liver diseases, COVID-19, etc., metaheuristic optimization algorithms have been utilized [60]. Cancer classification and automatic detection from 1,000 microscopic have been proposed for biopsy images [6]. It has four essential tissues: connective, epithelial, muscular, and nervous.

7.4   Optimization algorithms in biomedical informatics

Bioinformatics is an interdisciplinary field that combines physics, chemistry, biology, computer science, information engineering, mathematics, and statics and develops software for understanding large and complex biological data [14]. In essence, biomedical informatics is an application of information science to the field of biomedicine. According to Musen and Van Bemmel [72], techniques and systems for the collection, processing, and interpretation of patient data in medical informatics are designed and evaluated with the use of scientific knowledge. Biomedical data are a resource for comprehending fundamental research and helping with healthcare decisions based on evidence. The creation of contemporary analytical approaches, such as optimization algorithms and machine learning techniques, was motivated by the fact that it was historically very challenging to convert complicated and vast data sets into useful knowledge. Methods like trend reporting, data statistical modeling, and visualization techniques like association and correlation analysis are used to evaluate historical data. Also, pay attention to prediction and decision-making applications that construct predictive models using a known training dataset that comprises input data attributes and response values [73]. The GA [19], ACO [22,74], PSO [75], and other metaheuristic algorithms are effective solutions to optimization issues. The swarm intelligence algorithm is a solution for the complex problems of bioinformatics [51]. This algorithm provides fast and reasonably accurate solutions to such problems [25]. ACO and cuckoo algorithms [76] are computationally intensive and too complex where as meta-heuristic algorithm is quite simple [21]. Gradient descent optimization [77] is a traditional minimization optimization technique that determines how the weights are changed. Least Mean Square algorithm (LMS) [78] is the computation of weight to minimize the mean square error (MSE) between desired and actual outputs. Probabilistically, the LMS algorithm's solution and the MSE optimization's solution are equivalent.

7.5 Optimization algorithms in biomedical image processing

The enormously broad topic of biomedical image processing encompasses signal acquisition, image synthesis, image processing, image representation, and medical diagnosis based on features retrieved from images. Some fundamental image processing techniques include outlining, deblurring, noise cleaning, filtering, searching, classical analysis, and texture analysis [79]. There are mainly two kinds of imaging techniques, namely, radiological imaging and microscopic imaging. Radiological imaging includes ultrasound, X-ray, MRI, nuclear, and computer tomography (CT). Capsule endoscopy (CE) is used to detect gastrointestinal tract lesions called ulcers. Though the time of CE is about 6–8 h and can produce 60,000 images that become a difficult task for the medical practitioner to analyze such a large number of images for the optimization algorithm can be used such CAD tools can be used [80]. Biomedical image segmentation is a significant constituent of image analysis and diagnosis. The largest problem in image processing is resilience, hence optimization techniques have been employed to boost the effectiveness of earlier research on medical image segmentation. In the imaging modalities like X-rays, CT, and mammograms, researchers are interested in a certain region of the image such regions are extracted using image segmentation [81].

7.6 Optimization algorithms for ECG classification

Basically, the ECG assists to detect the motion of the heart rate. For the accurate classification of various kinds of arrhythmias in the ECG, some optimization is needed [82]. Feature extraction is the main feature in ECG classification. Preprocessing, feature extraction, GA optimization, and classification constitute the classification technique. The original ECG signals are preprocessed to eliminate noise. The WPD-statistical approach is used for feature extraction to acquire ECG characteristics. The feature dimensions are reduced, and the weights and biases of the BPNN are optimized using GA. The term "classification" refers to the division of ECG signals into the six categories of N, L, R, P, V, and A. Furthermore, it can be also achieved by using a swarm optimization algorithm that combined with classifiers to search the best-fitted classification parameters [82].

7.7   Feature extraction and classification

The first major decision in object recognition is to decide the set of features that is helpful for classification [83]. The feature can be defined as the characteristics and attributes of the object [5]. Image feature is the characteristics of an object that helps to distinguish an object from another object. Features can be artificial or natural. Natural features are the visual appearance of an image that is natural to the object such as brightness and texture. Artificial features are derived from image manipulations the examples are amplitude histograms and frequency spectra. A feature vector is a vector that contains n measured values as:

$$x = [x_1, x_2, x_3 \ldots x_n] \tag{7.1}$$

The classifier [83] takes the feature vector as input and performs the classification. Any pattern recognition task such as classification or clustering can be done to detect the object. The essential characteristics of good features are as follows:

(i)   Robustness – the property of a feature's invariance to operations such as translation, rotation, noise, and illumination is called robustness.
(ii)   Shift invariance – the capability to maintain its state during when shift operations are performed.
(iii) Rotation invariance – this is the capability to maintain its state originally stated when it is rotated.
(iv)   Size invariance – this is the ability to hold steady as its size changes.
(v)   Mirror shear and affine invariance – features hold true when mirroring, shearing, and affine transformation are applied.
(vi)   Occlusion invariance – the attribute of the features that do not change when all or a portion of the item is obscured is referred to as occlusion invariance.
(vii) Discrimination – there should not be any overlapping features and the properties should be able to tell one object apart from another.
(viii) Reliability – similar objects should have comparable values; hence, the values should be reliable.
(ix)   Independence – if two traits are statistically uncorrelated from one another, they are said to be independent. In other words, changing the value of one attribute does not change the value of the others.
(x)   Resistance to noise – an effective feature should be impervious to noise, artifacts, etc.
(xi)   Compactness – the features must be few in number in order to be displayed in a short space.

All features do not exhibit these properties. Hence, suitable parameters that distinguish the object uniquely should be identified and extracted. The feature can be classified as shown in Figure 7.3.

After image segmentation, the next step is featuring extraction. The technique of extracting and creating features to help in object classification is known as feature extraction [80]. This stage is crucial since the features' quality affects how

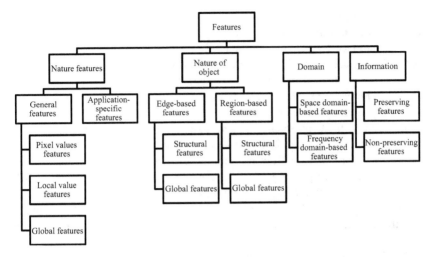

Figure 7.3   Classification of features

well they perform the categorization task. The feature vector is a vector that stores the expanded set of features. The categories of feature extraction include histogram-anchored characteristics like mean, median, variance, skewness, kurtosis, and first- and second-order moments, as well as texture features, also known as Harlicks features, which can be smooth or rough, etc. [5]. Area, perimeter, orientation, equivalent diameter, circularity, eccentricity, image curvature, and wavelet features [84] are some examples of geometric features, also referred to as shape features, that are used for the detection of transient changes in abnormalities like microcalcification and spiculated masses, among others.

7.7.1   Case study 1: feature extraction in mammography

For the purpose of identifying brief alterations in anomalies such microcalcification, spiculated masses, etc. in mammogram classification can be seen using a feature hybrid set that includes all feature categories [85]. Mean square energy and mean amplitude, or orientation, are recovered for the given image at three levels of Gabor wavelet decomposition, resulting in six orientation features, and are employed for improved categorization. In statistics, histogram, z-score, gradient information, etc. come under the statistical feature category. Since the hybrid feature set contains both redundant and non-redundant features, feature selection must be done after feature extraction of the spatial frequency, mean of the z-score, normalized gray level variance, the mean energy of the gradient, and threshold gradient. The difference between the image's maximum and minimum gray level values is known as the histogram range. The median of the absolute deviations from the median of the data is known as the median absolute deviation (MAD).

The z-score, also known as the standard score, shows how many standard deviations above or below the mean an observation or datum is. The population's mean, or z-score, is equal to the raw score's x value plus the population's standard deviation. The ratio of variation to an image's mean is known as the normalized gray level variance (Nvar). The gradient of an image gives information about fine edges and structures in an image. The mean energy of the gradient measures the energy of the gradient of image. Texture characteristics are crucial in the classification of mammograms. Haralick's texture features have been obtained from the gray level co-occurrence matrix (GLCM) probabilities as follows: homogeneity or angular second moment, contrast, correlation, variance1, variance2, standard deviation1, standard deviation2, dissimilarity measure, local homogeneity or inverse difference moment, energy, entropy haralick's correlation, cluster shade, cluster prominence, sum average, sum entropy, sum variance, difference variance, difference entropy, information measure1, and information measure2. Geometric features or geometric shape feature describe the geometric properties of the masses. Geometric elements are crucial to medical diagnostics for breast cancer detection.

7.7.2   Features are extracted by discrete wavelet transform

In the analysis of mammograms, wavelet-based [86] features include their effective de-correlation behavior, ease of spotting useful local and transient features, the capability of multi-resolution analysis, and accessibility of quick and reliable algorithms to compute the discrete wavelet transform (DWT) and its inverse. After performing a 2D discrete on the images, the wavelet characteristics are extracted. The main energy components of an image are measured by the group of coefficients known as approximation coefficients. The three remaining wavelet coefficients, abbreviated as cA, cH, cV, and cD, are referred to as approximation and detail coefficients. It is measured as variation in intensity or gray level along the horizontal, vertical, and diagonal axes, respectively. The average value of gray level fluctuations in an image in the three directions of horizontal, vertical, and diagonal is determined by adding the wavelet coefficients, which are specified as follows. The mean value of the detail coefficients obtained at the first level of decomposition to the mean value of the sum of the approximation coefficients obtained at the first, second, and third level wavelet decomposition is known as the wavelet ratio.

7.7.3   Features are extracted by the Gabor filter

It is a linear filter which is used to extract local image features like edge detection. Given that Gabor filters' [87] representations of frequency and direction are comparable to those of the human visual system, they are suitable for texture representation and discrimination. For the purpose of drawing out useful features from an image, a collection of Gabor filters with various frequencies and orientations may be useful. The two main important Gabor features extracted from the given mammographic images are mean square energy (Gabor Energy) and mean amplitude i.e., orientation. These two features have been extracted from the given images. The Gabor energy is defined as the responses of the linear symmetric and anti-symmetric image. The mean square energy in a window of fixed size.

7.7.4 Case study II: feature extraction in speech and pattern recognition

Speech feature extraction is in charge of converting speech signals into a stream of feature vector coefficients that only contains the data needed to identify a particular utterance. Typically, spectral analysis methods like Mel-frequency cepstral coefficients [88], linear predictive coding [89], and wavelet transforms are used to extract the feature vector of speech data. The required phonetic features can be acquired using the feature extraction technique, which provides good distinction, little correlation among coefficients, and is not based on linear attributes. In a situation where speech is continuous, a frame cannot hold information from two phonemes that follow one another. It only offers a limited depiction because it only considers the power spectrum and ignores the phase spectrum. Linear predictive coding (LPC) [89], a low-dimension feature vector is used for speech recognition. The advantages of LPC are listed as:

(I)   Speech production and perceptual representation require more than linear scales, so with the help of PLC, a strongly related feature set is created.
(II) It is able to separate the source from the vocal tract.
(III) It is not being able to incorporate a priori knowledge for the speech signal under test.

The features that are frequently utilized in automatic speech and pattern recognition are Mel frequency cepstral coefficients (MFCC) [90]. MFCC feature extraction processing steps are shown in Figure 7.4.

Mel frequency Cepstral coefficients is given as:

$$C[r] = \sum_{k=0}^{k-1} 2y[k]\cos\left(\frac{\pi}{2k}r \ (2k+1)\right) \tag{7.2}$$

where $C[r]$ is the MFCC coefficient and $y[k]$ is the input signal.

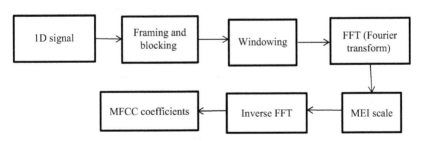

Figure 7.4   MFCC feature extraction process in speech processing

7.7.5   Feature selection

Feature selection is done after feature extraction and it is an optimizing set [91]. A statistical approach called feature selection can be used to trim the extracted features into a manageable number of features. Feature selection is an optimization step that removes unwanted features to create optimal feature set. It is based on the performance study of the extracted features. The main goal of feature selection is to choose a small set of features from which to create a pattern classifier with less complexity and thus enhance classification performance. Figure 7.5 shows the feature selection process after the extraction of features.

One of the most important operations in feature selection methods is evaluating the discrimination power of the individual feature. A significant stage in classification is feature selection because it directly influences a CAD [92] system's overall effectiveness. The feature selection algorithms may be categorized as filter based, wrapper based, and embedded [93]. The wrapper-based feature selection methods are proposed and examined to select minimum redundant and maximal relevant feature subset from original hybrid feature set. These are cross-validated lowest miss-classification errors of several supervised classifiers and forward sequential feature selection based on mutual information for unsupervised GA methods.

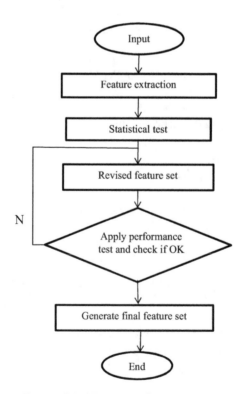

Figure 7.5   Feature selection process

7.7.6   Classification

A naive Bayes (NB) [83] classifier is based on classical Bayesian statistics and uses all the attributes and permits them to contribute to the decisions, taking into account the features as equally important and independent of each other, considering the class. Naïve Bayes algorithm is as follows:

$$y_{NB} = arg\ max_q P(y_q) \prod_j P(x_j|y_q) \tag{7.3}$$

where y_{NB} signifies the class output by the naïve Bayes classifier. $P(x_j|y_q)$ is the class-conditional probability, and $P(y_q)$ is the unknown probability.

K-nearest neighbor, also known as KNN, is a data-driven classifier that is straightforward and intuitive like NB classifier [94]. The K-NN algorithm is a non-parametric technique that makes no assumptions regarding the relationship between characteristics $[x_1, x_2, x_3 \ldots x_n]$ and class membership. The class-conditional densities, or $P(x_j|y_q)$, of the feature-vector distributions are necessary for classification.

Quantities that can have a wide range of values are ideally suited for estimation using logistic regression models. Because classification issues are so prevalent, statisticians have developed a method to use regression models for this problem. The method or model that is produced is known as the logistic regression method or model. For classification, Fisher's Linear Discriminant [95] can also be utilized. This n-dimensional classification challenge has been reduced to a potentially simpler one-dimensional problem. Rosenblatt [96] proposed the machine perceptron whose architecture encodes the structure of a linear discriminant function. Support vector regression is a logical progression from classification-based techniques. All the characteristics of SVM classifiers are retained through SVM regression analysis. SVM uses an optimization process that is effective for both the linearly separable and inseparable samples in order to get the weight vector that maximizes the margin. SVM hinges on these two mathematical operations:

(i)   Input nonlinear pattern is mapped into a high-dimensional space.
(ii) Building of the finest hyperplane for linear separating the feature vectors revealed in step (I).

Using previously undiscovered data, the SVM criterion function of the biggest margin offers a novel approach and ensures accurate classification. The criterion function is the most obvious for the purpose of classification and is the number of samples misclassified by the weight vector. Since this function is stepwise constant, it is naturally a weak candidate for gradient search. The Perceptron algorithm seems to be an alternative to the criterion function. Neural networks (NN) can be used to overcome the perceptron's limitations. The gradient approaches for minimization are not applicable since the perceptron criterion function takes into account incorrectly categorized data. The NN generally use gradient algorithms for minimization while solving regression problems, taking into account all samples and the minimal squared-error criterion.

7.8   Optimization algorithm-based intelligent detection of heart disorders

CNN can be used to monitor cardiac rhythms and anticipate heart illnesses by uncovering hidden links and patterns in the healthcare industry. CNNs have many hyperparameters and many particular designs, which are expensive and make it difficult to choose the optimal value out of all potential hyperparameter values. The CNN-JSO approach, which uses the JSO optimization process to adjust CNN hyperparameters, is used to predict cardiac disorders [97]. System for forecasting the level of heart disease risk using a fuzzy genetic algorithm, where first the dataset is preprocessed, then: (i) effective attributes are chosen using a variety of techniques, (ii) weighted fuzzy rules are developed using GA on the basis of the selected attributes, (iii) construct the fuzzy-based decision support using the generated fuzzy knowledge base, and (iv) predict heart disease.

The studies performed using real-world data sets demonstrate the efficacy of the suggested novel strategy [98]. Heart disease is diagnosed using a GA-based trained recurrent fuzzy neural network (RFNN), and the findings showed 97.78% accuracy [99]. With feature selection, one can choose the best subset of features and lessen the dimensionality of the data. It is suggested to use an enhanced version of the salp swarm algorithm (SSA) to overcome feature selection issues and choose the ideal feature subset in wrapper mode. The findings acquired over many types of datasets [100] confirm that the wrapper feature selection mode can be applied in a variety of expert and intelligent system applications. The present SVM classifier's parameters are proposed to be optimized using a hybrid optimization technique that combines the PSO and migration-modified biogeography-based optimization algorithms. This algorithm offers a better way to optimize the ECG signal's parameters. The suggested framework improves the automatic detection of different arrhythmias or rhythm irregularities, improving accuracy [101]. The choice of features is made using the Chimp optimization algorithm (CHOA) [59], which improves the classification accuracy of heart disease detection [102]. In this method, the cardiac image's noise is first cleaned out using a median filter. Finally, from the cardiac picture, GLCM characteristics are retrieved. The CHOA algorithm is used to select the best features from the extracted features. The classifier uses these chosen attributes as input. Support vector neural network (SVNN) is employed as the classifier in this method. The classifier assigns the image a normal or abnormal classification. According to simulation findings, the CHOA-based SVNN outperforms the traditional SVNN, ANN, KNN, and SVM in terms of accuracy [59]. Log-transformation is used to pre-process medical data, converting it to a uniform value range. The procedure of identifying important features to classify medical data is then carried out using sparse fuzzy-c-means (FCM). Although this sparse technique offers critical characteristics for detection and may be used to handle high dimensional data, incorporating sparse FCM for the feature selection process offers extra advantages for interpreting the models. The deep belief network (DBN), which is trained using the suggested Taylor-based bird swarm method (Taylor-BSA) for detection, is then given the chosen features. Here, the Taylor series and the bird swarm algorithm (BSA) are combined to create the Taylor-BSA [103].

7.9   Using predictive analytics in healthcare

Increased long-term investment in developing new technologies that use artificial intelligence and machine learning to foresee future events (potentially in real-time) to enhance people's health is a reflection of the present interest in predictive analytics for enhancing healthcare. Clinical prediction models, as they are sometimes known as predictive algorithms, aid in the diagnosis and prognosis of patients who are more likely to develop a disease. Predictive algorithms are used to provide patient counseling and to make clinical treatment decisions based on unique patient features rather than population averages in the era of personalized medicine. With the growing accessibility of Big Data, medical imaging, routinely gathered electronic health records, and national registry data [104], the rate at which new algorithms are published doesn't seem to be slowing down.

Any healthcare application must manage enormous amounts of data in various ways. The foundation for knowledge generation today is big data. Big data is a word used to describe data that possess specific qualities such as volume, velocity, value, truthfulness, and variability. Such enormous data must be saved, handled, and analyzed in order to produce the desired outcomes. Medical data is more difficult to interpret and anticipate results from, making them more important to patient care. Due to its importance, it is necessary to provide effective and higher-performing algorithms, methodologies, and tools to analyse big data in medicine. Traditional algorithms, however, are unable to analyze such complicated data. These types of data and analytics are highly suited for machine learning techniques. Big data analytics is explored in important facets of healthcare, including EHR upkeep, disease diagnosis, and patient emergency condition prediction [105]. The finest technique for handling massive amounts of data to perform predictive analysis or pattern identification is ML.

The healthcare business is facing challenges in key areas such as electronic record management, data integration, and computer-assisted diagnostics and disease predictions due to the need to lower healthcare costs and the shift to individualized treatment. To deal with these issues, machine learning provides a variety of tools, methods, and frameworks [106]. Healthcare's use of complex predictive analytics also raises moral and legal questions [58]. By allowing for more individualized healthcare delivery, predictive analysis has the potential to reduce health risks at both the population and individual levels [107]. The deployment of e-HPA must protect patient privacy, create a team to monitor the health system, include predictive analytics in medical education, and guarantee that electronic technologies do not supplant or obstruct physician and patient decision-making [108]. The decision-tree method is used to forecast chronic renal illnesses in the healthcare system [109]. Furthermore, crucial are predictive models, which must be enhanced with new strategies [110]. A potent method for analyzing predicted data is SVM regression analysis.

7.10   Optimization algorithm for smart healthcare: innovations and technologies

A framework known as "smart healthcare" makes use of technologies like wearables, the Internet of Medical Things (IoMT), sophisticated machine learning algorithms, and wireless communication technology to link people, resources, and organizations, provide seamless access to health records, and handle and respond to health environment demands intelligently [111]. In poor nations, the availability of ambulances, outdated infrastructure, and contemporary equipment make it difficult to provide healthcare services. The government institutions are unable to take on the thousands of competent professionals who have graduated from academic and training institutions, which creates problems with the availability of jobs for the trained health professionals who support health delivery. Thus, unemployment is a disease that threatens the prosperity of any country.

In some cases, industrialized countries offer excellent incentives to get competent healthcare professionals to work in their health sector, which causes an exodus of qualified healthcare workers in quest of better opportunities. In Africa, people frequently leave for a medical facility at the crack of dawn to escape the stress of waiting in line at public health facilities. Although there are private healthcare providers, one of the barriers keeping people from obtaining medical care in the private healthcare sector is the high cost of service. Because of the poor condition of the roads and the lack of adequate ambulance services, it is occasionally necessary to carry pregnant women, elderly people, and sick people on motorcycles and transport them to a medical facility. The system for delivering healthcare needs to be improved. Therefore, it is crucial that African healthcare systems are modernized. Using mobile technologies and applications to transform the delivery of health services is one method to accomplish this. This transition is anticipated to enhance service delivery and reduce the stress associated with waiting in lines, particularly for senior individuals.

How can we use mobile technology and its applications to provide healthcare services to the elderly is the fundamental topic driving this study. The elderly may not be computer literate, but a close relative or other trusted person can request basic healthcare services on their behalf. The "smart city" movement, a new technological paradigm, has some potential. In wealthy nations, the idea of a "smart city" [30] has significantly transformed society; nevertheless, emerging nations have not yet adequately investigated the idea. In order to give healthcare treatments in the quickest possible time, an algorithm is created to map the locations of the necessary locations. Smart mobile healthcare system is the term used to describe this system [112]. Transparency, easy and quick accessibility, security, efficiency, and other benefits are provided by a smart healthcare system that combines a blockchain data network with healthcare 4.0 operations [113,114]. Processes utilized in healthcare 4.0 that make data accessible are intended to be validated using statistical simulation-optimization techniques and algorithms. The Ethereum network implements the blockchain together with related programming languages, tools, and methodologies like solidity, web3.js, Athena, etc.

The performance of blockchain-based, decentralized apps for the smart health-care system is enhanced by this study of optimization algorithms applicable to trends in healthcare 4.0. For the proposed system, smart contracts and their designs are also ready to speed up the payment and trust-building processes. The outcomes of this work simulation demonstrate that the required gas value which represents block size and expenditure is within the current Ethereum network gas restrictions. Block utilization is above 80%, which indicates that the proposed system is operational [115]. When a patient has suffered a brain injury, a neurological disorder, or a mental illness, it is crucial to identify the patient's behavior. In traditional healthcare, the patient behavioral analysis presented considerably more of a challenge. The development of smart healthcare will allow for proper analysis of patient behavior. The IoT in healthcare is crucial for providing people with better medical facilities and supporting hospitals and clinicians. The suggested system consists of several medical devices that may gather and monitor a patient's medical information and health data as well as communicate with a doctor via network-connected devices, such as mobile-based apps and sensors. Through the use of machine learning algorithms, patient data are seen and exchanged over the Internet. In order to ascertain the patient's precise health status, the DBN analyses the patient's specifics from health data. The technology that was created demonstrated an average error rate of 0.04 and guaranteed an accuracy of 99% while evaluating patient behavior [116].

A Cloud of Things (CoT) [117] is produced by the combination of cloud computing and IoT. A new paradigm for pervasive and ubiquitous computing is created by this combination. Yet, energy-efficient CoT architectures are necessary for reliable CoT-based services, especially those that are very delay-sensitive, like healthcare. The efficiency of CoT structures in smart healthcare has received a lot of attention [118]. Smart healthcare can effectively lower the cost and risk of medical procedures, increase the efficiency of the use of medical resources, encourage collaboration and exchange between regions, advance telemedicine and self-service medical care, and ultimately make personalized medical services widely available [119].

7.11 Issues and challenges in using optimization algorithms for smart healthcare and wearables

Latency, limited computation power, interoperability, and security are some of the challenges that exist in the IoMT-based smart healthcare systems [111]. IoT challenges include related to security, privacy, and the sensitivity of health-related data. Electronic medical records, genetic data, and other sensitive and private information are all found in healthcare data and should be kept private. According to predictions, 72% of malicious traffic targets patient data [120]. So, it is crucial to defend against hackers by maintaining privacy and security, both physically and digitally. Low security, misconfigured hardware, and network configurations are further difficulties. Furthermore, because the nature of the data from these many types of devices is typically heterogeneous and is frequently managed by outside parties, it is difficult to ensure its governance, security, and privacy [121].

List of abbreviations

ACO	Ant colony optimization
AI	Artificial Intelligence
ANN	Artificial neural network
BSA	Bird swarm algorithm
CAD	Computer-aided diagnosis
CE	Capsule endoscopy
CHOA	Chimp optimization algorithm
CoT	Cloud of Things
CT	Computer tomography
CV	Computer vision
DBC	Directed bee colony
DBN	Deep belief network
DL	Deep learning
DWT	Discrete wavelet transforms
FCM	Fuzzy-c-means
GDP	Gross domestic product
GLCM	Gray level co-occurrence matrix
HR	Human resource
IoMT	Internet of Medical Things
IoT	Internet of Things
LPC	Linear predictive coding
MAD	Median absolute deviation
MFCC	Mel frequency cepstral coefficients
MIP	Mixed integer programming
ML	Machine learning
MLP	Multilayer perceptron
MRI	Magnetic resonance imaging
NB	Nïve Bayes
NLP	Natural language processing
NN	Neural networks
Nvar	Normalized gray level variance
OA	Optimization algorithm
OR	Operating room
PCO	Particle swarm optimization
RFNN	Recurrent fuzzy neural networks
SSA	Salp swarm algorithm
SVM	Support vector machine
SVNN	Support vector neural network

References

[1] G. Stockman and L. G. Shapiro, *Computer Vision*. Prentice Hall PTR, 2001.

[2] R. Szeliski, *Computer Vision: Algorithms and Applications*. Springer Nature, 2022.

[3] P. Kumar, S. Srivastava, and R. Srivastava, "Basic understanding of medical imaging modalities," in *High-Performance Medical Image Processing*, Apple Academic Press, pp. 1–17.

[4] S. Srivastava, N. Sharma, R. Srivastava, and S. K. Singh, "Restoration of digital mammographic images corrupted with quantum noise using an adaptive total variation (TV) based nonlinear filter," in *2012 International Conference on Communications, Devices and Intelligent Systems (CODIS)*, 2012, pp. 125–128.

[5] V. P. Singh, S. Srivastava, and R. Srivastava, "Effective mammogram classification based on center symmetric-LBP features in wavelet domain using random forests," *Technol. Heal. Care*, vol. 25, no. 4, pp. 709–727, 2017, doi: 10.3233/THC-170851.

[6] R. Kumar, R. Srivastava, and S. Srivastava, "Detection and classification of cancer from microscopic biopsy images using clinically significant and biologically interpretable features," *J. Med. Eng.*, vol. 2015, 457906, 2015.

[7] M. Nath, S. Srivastava, N. Kulshrestha, and D. Singh, "Detection and localization of S1 and S2 heart sounds by 3rd order normalized average Shannon energy envelope algorithm," *Proc. Inst. Mech. Eng. Part H J. Eng. Med.*, vol. 235, no. 6, pp. 615–624, 2021.

[8] A. Kumar, P. Kumar, and S. Srivastava, "A skewness reformed complex diffusion based unsharp masking for the restoration and enhancement of Poisson noise corrupted mammograms," *Biomed. Signal Process. Control*, vol. 73, no. August 2021, p. 103421, 2022, doi: 10.1016/j.bspc.2021.103421.

[9] R. R. Kumar, A. Kumar, and S. Srivastava, "Anisotropic diffusion based unsharp masking and crispening for denoising and enhancement of MRI images," in: *2020 International Conference on Emerging Frontiers in Electrical and Electronic Technologies (ICEFEET 2020)*, pp. 0–5, 2020, doi: 10.1109/ICEFEET49149.2020.9186966.

[10] T. M. Mitchell, *Machine Learning*, vol. 1. McGraw-Hill New York, 2007.

[11] Y. LeCun, Y. Bengio, and G. Hinton, "Deep learning," *Nature*, vol. 521, no. 7553, pp. 436–444, 2015.

[12] B. Nithya and V. Ilango, "Predictive analytics in health care using machine learning tools and techniques," in *2017 International Conference on Intelligent Computing and Control Systems (ICICCS)*, 2017, pp. 492–499.

[13] J. G. Carbonell, R. S. Michalski, and T. M. Mitchell, "An overview of machine learning," *Mach. Learn.*, pp. 3–23, 1983.

[14] E. V Bernstam, J. W. Smith, and T. R. Johnson, "What is biomedical informatics?," *J. Biomed. Inform.*, vol. 43, no. 1, pp. 104–110, 2010.

[15]   I. Goodfellow, Y. Bengio, and A. Courville, *Deep Learning*. MIT press, 2016.

[16]   P. Kumar, S. Srivastava, R. K. Mishra, and Y. P. Sai, "End-to-end improved convolutional neural network model for breast cancer detection using mammographic data," *J. Def. Model. Simul.*, p. 1548512920973268, 2020.

[17]   L. G. Kabari and E. O. Nwachukwu, "Neural networks and decision trees for eye diseases diagnosis," *Adv. Expert Syst.*, pp. 63–84, 2012.

[18]   X.-S. Yang, *Nature-Inspired Optimization Algorithms*. Academic Press, 2020.

[19]   S. Forrest, "Genetic algorithms," *ACM Comput. Surv.*, vol. 28, no. 1, pp. 77–80, 1996.

[20]   H. Chen and W. Ser, "Design of robust broadband beamformers with pass-band shaping characteristics using Tikhonov regularization," *IEEE Trans. Audio. Speech. Lang. Processing*, vol. 17, no. 4, pp. 665–681, 2009.

[21]   M. Mareli and B. Twala, "An adaptive Cuckoo search algorithm for optimisation," *Appl. Comput. informatics*, vol. 14, no. 2, pp. 107–115, 2018.

[22]   M. Dorigo and G. Di Caro, "Ant colony optimization: a new meta-heuristic," in *Proceedings of the 1999 Congress on Evolutionary Computation – CEC99 (Cat. No. 99TH8406)*, 1999, vol. 2, pp. 1470–1477.

[23]   M. Fathian, B. Amiri, and A. Maroosi, "Application of honey-bee mating optimization algorithm on clustering," *Appl. Math. Comput.*, vol. 190, no. 2, pp. 1502–1513, 2007.

[24]   W.-T. Pan, "A new fruit fly optimization algorithm: taking the financial distress model as an example," *Knowledge-Based Syst.*, vol. 26, pp. 69–74, 2012.

[25]   Y. Zhang, S. Wang, G. Ji, *et al.*, "A comprehensive survey on particle swarm optimization algorithm and its applications," *Math. Probl. Eng.*, vol. 2015, 2015.

[26]   J. Bergstra and Y. Bengio, "Random search for hyper-parameter optimization," *J. Mach. Learn. Res.*, vol. 13, pp. 281–305, 2012.

[27]   T. A. Jundale and R. S. Hegadi, "Skew detection and correction of devanagari script using interval halving method," *Commun. Comput. Inf. Sci.*, vol. 709, pp. 28–38, 2017, doi: 10.1007/978-981-10-4859-3_3.

[28]   Z. A. Abdalkareem, A. Amir, M. A. Al-Betar, P. Ekhan, and A. I. Hammouri, "Healthcare scheduling in optimization context: a review," *Health Technol. (Berl).*, vol. 11, pp. 445–469, 2021.

[29]   I. Papanicolas, L. R. Woskie, and A. K. Jha, "Health care spending in the United States and other high-income countries," *Jama*, vol. 319, no. 10, pp. 1024–1039, 2018.

[30]   A. Kumar and V. Nath, "Study and design of smart embedded system for smart city using Internet of Things," in: V. Nath and J. Mandal (eds), Nanoelectronics, Circuits and Communication Systems. Lecture Notes in Electrical Engineering, vol. 511, 2019, pp 397–408, Springer, Singapore.

[31]   R. K. Kodali, G. Swamy, and B. Lakshmi, "An implementation of IoT for healthcare," in *2015 IEEE Recent Advances in Intelligent Computational Systems (RAICS)*, 2015, pp. 411–416.

[32] L. M. Dang, M. J. Piran, D. Han, K. Min, and H. Moon, "A survey on internet of things and cloud computing for healthcare," *Electronics*, vol. 8, no. 7, p. 768, 2019.

[33] S. Batun and M. A. Begen, "Optimization in healthcare delivery modeling: Methods and applications," in: *Handbook of Healthcare Operations Management Methods and Application*, Springer, pp. 75–119, 2013.

[34] A. Reddy and D. Scheinker, "The case for mathematical optimization in health care: building a strong foundation for artificial intelligence," Heal. Aff. blog, 2020.

[35] P. P. Wang, "Static and dynamic scheduling of customer arrivals to a single-server system," *Nav. Res. Logist.*, vol. 40, no. 3, pp. 345–360, 1993.

[36] W.-Y. Wang and D. Gupta, "Adaptive appointment systems with patient preferences," *Manuf. & Serv. Oper. Manag.*, vol. 13, no. 3, pp. 373–389, 2011.

[37] A. Jebali, A. B. H. Alouane, and P. Ladet, "Operating rooms scheduling," *Int. J. Prod. Econ.*, vol. 99, no. 1–2, pp. 52–62, 2006.

[38] Y.-J. Gong, J. Zhang, H. Chung, *et al.*, "An efficient resource allocation scheme using particle swarm optimization," *IEEE Trans. Evol. Comput.*, vol. 16, no. 6, pp. 801–816, 2012.

[39] J. C. Ridge, S. K. Jones, M. S. Nielsen, and A. K. Shahani, "Capacity planning for intensive care units," *Eur. J. Oper. Res.*, vol. 105, no. 2, pp. 346–355, 1998.

[40] U. Aickelin and K. A. Dowsland, "An indirect genetic algorithm for a nurse-scheduling problem," *Comput. & Oper. Res.*, vol. 31, no. 5, pp. 761–778, 2004.

[41] S. Topaloglu, "A shift scheduling model for employees with different seniority levels and an application in healthcare," *Eur. J. Oper. Res.*, vol. 198, no. 3, pp. 943–957, 2009.

[42] K. A. Dowsland and J. M. Thompson, "Solving a nurse scheduling problem with knapsacks, networks and tabu search," *J. Oper. Res. Soc.*, vol. 51, no. 7, pp. 825–833, 2000.

[43] W. J. Gutjahr and M. S. Rauner, "An ACO algorithm for a dynamic regional nurse-scheduling problem in Austria," *Comput. & Oper. Res.*, vol. 34, no. 3, pp. 642–666, 2007.

[44] J. A. Castillo-Salazar, D. Landa-Silva, and R. Qu, "Workforce scheduling and routing problems: literature survey and computational study," *Ann. Oper. Res.*, vol. 239, pp. 39–67, 2016.

[45] A. Apornak, S. Raissi, A. Keramati, and K. Khalili-Damghani, "Human resources optimization in hospital emergency using the genetic algorithm approach," *Int. J. Healthc. Manag.*, vol. 14, no. 4, pp. 1441–1448, 2021.

[46] A. L. Samuel, "Some studies in machine learning using the game of checkers," *IBM J. Res. Dev.*, vol. 3, no. 3, pp. 210–229, 1959.

[47] S.-C. Chu, P.-W. Tsai, and J.-S. Pan, "Cat swarm optimization," in: *PRICAI 2006: Trends in Artificial Intelligence: 9th Pacific Rim International*

Conference on Artificial Intelligence Guilin, China, August 7–11, 2006 Proceedings 9, 2006, pp. 854–858.

[48]   X.-S. Yang, "Flower pollination algorithm for global optimization," in: *Unconventional Computation and Natural Computation: 11th International Conference, UCNC 2012, Orléan, France, September 3–7, 2012. Proceedings 11*, 2012, pp. 240–249.

[49]   C. Puttamadappa and B. D. Parameshachari, "Demand side management of small scale loads in a smart grid using glow-worm swarm optimization technique," *Microprocess. Microsyst.*, vol. 71, p. 102886, 2019.

[50]   S. Mirjalili, S. M. Mirjalili, and A. Lewis, "Grey wolf optimizer," *Adv. Eng. Softw.*, vol. 69, pp. 46–61, 2014.

[51]   D. Wang, D. Tan, and L. Liu, "Particle swarm optimization algorithm: an overview," *Soft Comput.*, vol. 22, pp. 387–408, 2018.

[52]   S. Mirjalili and A. Lewis, "The whale optimization algorithm," *Adv. Eng. Softw.*, vol. 95, pp. 51–67, 2016.

[53]   M. Yazdani and F. Jolai, "Lion optimization algorithm (LOA): a nature-inspired metaheuristic algorithm," *J. Comput. Des. Eng.*, vol. 3, no. 1, pp. 24–36, 2016.

[54]   B. Suits, *The Grasshopper: Games, Life and Utopia*. Broadview Press, 2014.

[55]   S. Mirjalili, "Moth-flame optimization algorithm: A novel nature-inspired heuristic paradigm," *Knowledge-based Syst.*, vol. 89, pp. 228–249, 2015.

[56]   A. Askarzadeh, "A novel metaheuristic method for solving constrained engineering optimization problems: crow search algorithm," *Comput. Struct.*, vol. 169, pp. 1–12, 2016.

[57]   G.-G. Wang, S. Deb, and L. dos S. Coelho, "Elephant herding optimization," in *2015 3rd International Symposium on Computational and Business Intelligence (ISCBI)*, 2015, pp. 1–5.

[58]   E. Cuevas, M. Cienfuegos, D. Zaldívar, and M. Pérez-Cisneros, "A swarm optimization algorithm inspired in the behavior of the social-spider," *Expert Syst. Appl.*, vol. 40, no. 16, pp. 6374–6384, 2013.

[59]   M. Pradhan, A. Bhuiyan, and B. P. Baliarsingh, "Chimp optimization algorithm-based feature selection for cardiac image-based heart disease diagnosis," in: *Ambient Intelligence in Health Care: Proceedings of ICAIHC 2022*, Springer, 2022, pp. 61–70.

[60]   S. Kaur, Y. Kumar, A. Koul, and S. Kumar Kamboj, "A systematic review on metaheuristic optimization techniques for feature selections in disease diagnosis: open issues and challenges," *Arch. Comput. Methods Eng.*, vol. 33, pp. 1–33, 2022.

[61]   J. Kennedy and R. C. Eberhart, "A discrete binary version of the particle swarm algorithm," in: *1997 IEEE International Conference on Systems, Man, and Cybernetics. Computational Cybernetics and Simulation*, 1997, vol. 5, pp. 4104–4108.

[62]   L. Wei, S. X. Pan, Y. A. Nanehkaran, and V. Rajinikanth, "An optimized method for skin cancer diagnosis using modified thermal exchange optimization algorithm," *Comput. Math. Methods Med.*, vol. 2021, 2021.

[63] S. K. Tripathy, R. Sudhamsh, S. Srivastava, and R. Srivastava, "MuST-POS: multiscale spatial-temporal 3D atrous-net and PCA guided OC-SVM for crowd panic detection," *J. Intell. & Fuzzy Syst.*, no. Preprint, pp. 1–16, 2022.

[64] P. Kumar, A. Kumar, S. Srivastava, and Y. Padma Sai, "A novel bi-modal extended Huber loss function based refined mask RCNN approach for automatic multi instance detection and localization of breast cancer," *Proc. Inst. Mech. Eng. Part H J. Eng. Med.*, p. 09544119221095416.

[65] M. R. Nalluri, D. S. Roy, K. Kannan, *et al.*, "Hybrid disease diagnosis using multiobjective optimization with evolutionary parameter optimization," *J. Healthc. Eng.*, vol. 2017, Article ID 5907264, 2017.

[66] A. Bagirov, A. Rubinov, and J. Yearwood, "Using global optimization to improve classification for medical diagnosis and prognosis.," *Top. Health Inf. Manage.*, vol. 22, no. 1, pp. 65–74, 2001.

[67] S. Srivastava, N. Sharma, S. K. Singh, and R. Srivastava, "Quantitative analysis of a general framework of a CAD tool for breast cancer detection from mammograms," *J. Med. Imaging Heal. Informatics*, vol. 4, no. 5, pp. 654–674, 2014, doi: 10.1166/jmihi.2014.1304.

[68] Y. A. Kadhim, M. U. Khan, and A. Mishra, "Deep learning-based computer-aided diagnosis (CAD): applications for medical image datasets," *Sensors*, vol. 22, no. 22, p. 8999, 2022.

[69] K. Jani, R. Srivastava, S. Srivastava, and A. Anand, "Computer aided medical image analysis for capsule endoscopy using conventional machine learning and deep learning," in: *2019 7th International Conference on Smart Computing & Communications (ICSCC)*, 2019, pp. 1–5.

[70] A. Saber, M. Sakr, O. M. Abo-Seida, and A. Keshk, "Automated breast cancer detection and classification techniques – a survey," in: *2021 International Mobile, Intelligent, and Ubiquitous Computing Conference (MIUCC)*, 2021, pp. 200–207.

[71] S. Agrawal, B. Singh, R. Kumar, and N. Dey, "Machine learning for medical diagnosis: a neural network classifier optimized via the directed bee colony optimization algorithm," in: *U-Healthcare Monitoring Systems*, Elsevier, 2019, pp. 197–215.

[72] J. H. Van Bemmel, "The structure of medical informatics: bibliography on educational courses at the Free University, Amsterdam," *Med. Informatics*, vol. 9, no. 3–4, pp. 175–180, 1984.

[73] S. Huang, J. Zhou, Z. Wang, Q. Ling, and Y. Shen, "Biomedical informatics with optimization and machine learning," *EURASIP Journal on Bioinformatics and Systems Biology*, vol. 2017, no. 1, pp. 1–3, 2016.

[74] M. Dorigo and T. Stützle, *Ant Colony Optimization: Overview and Recent Advances.* Springer, 2019.

[75] S. Das, A. Abraham, and A. Konar, "Swarm intelligence algorithms in bioinformatics," *Comput. Intell. Bioinforma.*, pp. 113–147, 2008.

[76] R. Rajabioun, "Cuckoo optimization algorithm," *Appl. Soft Comput.*, vol. 11, no. 8, pp. 5508–5518, 2011.

[77]   S. Ruder, "An overview of gradient descent optimization algorithms," *arXiv Prepr. arXiv1609.04747*, 2016.

[78]   W. Liu, P. P. Pokharel, and J. C. Principe, "The kernel least-mean-square algorithm," *IEEE Trans. Signal Process.*, vol. 56, no. 2, pp. 543–554, 2008.

[79]   H. K. Huang, "Biomedical image processing," *Crit. Rev. Bioeng.*, vol. 5, no. 3, pp. 185–271, 1981.

[80]   K. K. Jani, S. Srivastava, and R. Srivastava, "Computer aided diagnosis system for ulcer detection in capsule endoscopy using optimized feature set," *J. Intell. Fuzzy Syst.*, vol. 37, no. 1, pp. 1491–1498, 2019.

[81]   T. Khin, K. Srujan Raju, G. R. Sinha, K. K. Khaing, and T. M. Kyi, "Review of optimization methods of medical image segmentation," in: *Proceedings of the Third International Conference on Computational Intelligence and Informatics: ICCII 2018*, 2020, pp. 213–218.

[82]   S. Dalal and V. P. Vishwakarma, "GA based KELM optimization for ECG classification," *Procedia Comput. Sci.*, vol. 167, pp. 580–588, 2020.

[83]   S. Srivastava, N. Sharma, S. K. Singh, and R. Srivastava, "Design, analysis and classifier evaluation for a CAD tool for breast cancer detection from digital mammograms," *Int. J. Biomed. Eng. Technol.*, vol. 13, no. 3, pp. 270–300, 2013.

[84]   S. Srivastava, N. Sharma, S. K. Singh, and R. Srivastava, "A combined approach for the enhancement and segmentation of mammograms using modified fuzzy C-means method in wavelet domain," *J. Med. Phys.*, vol. 39, no. 3, pp. 169–183, 2014, doi: 10.4103/0971-6203.139007.

[85]   V. P. Singh, S. Srivastava, and R. Srivastava, "An efficient image retrieval based on fusion of fast features and query image classification," *Int. J. Rough Sets Data Anal.*, vol. 4, no. 1, pp. 19–37, 2017.

[86]   R. K. Senapati, S. Srivastava, and P. Mankar, "RST invariant blind image watermarking schemes based on discrete tchebichef transform and singular value decomposition," *Arab. J. Sci. Eng.*, vol. 45, pp. 3331–3353, 2020.

[87]   V. Kumar and S. Srivastava, "Performance analysis of reshaped Gabor filter for removing the Rician distributed noise in brain MR images," *Proc. Inst. Mech. Eng. Part H J. Eng. Med.*, vol. 236, no. 8, pp. 1216–1231, 2022.

[88]   V. Tiwari, "MFCC and its applications in speaker recognition," *Int. J. Emerg. Technol.*, vol. 1, no. 1, pp. 19–22, 2010.

[89]   Y. Sharma and B. K. Singh, "Prediction of specific language impairment in children using speech linear predictive coding coefficients," in: *2020 First International Conference on Power, Control and Computing Technologies (ICPC2T)*, 2020, pp. 305–310.

[90]   S. Gupta, J. Jaafar, W. F. W. Ahmad, and A. Bansal, "Feature extraction using MFCC," *Signal Image Process. An Int. J.*, vol. 4, no. 4, pp. 101–108, 2013.

[91]   S. Srivastava, N. Sharma, and S. K. Singh, "Empirical analysis of supervised and unsupervised filter based feature selection methods for breast cancer classification from digital mammograms," *Int. J. Comput. Appl.*, vol. 88, no. 8, 2014.

[92] G. Kumar, N. Kulshrestha, and S. Srivastava, "Analysis of different fuzzy c-means membership functions for the design of cad tool of early breast cancer detection," in: *Proceedings of 2nd International Conference on Advanced Computing and Software Engineering (ICACSE)*, 2019.

[93] M. Tahir, A. Tubaishat, F. Al-Obeidat, B. Shah, Z. Halim, and M. Waqas, "A novel binary chaotic genetic algorithm for feature selection and its utility in affective computing and healthcare," *Neural Comput. Appl.*, pp. 1–22, 2020.

[94] R. Kumar, R. Srivastava, and S. Srivastava, "Microscopic biopsy image segmentation using hybrid color K-means approach," *Int. J. Comput. Vis. Image Process.*, vol. 7, no. 1, pp. 79–90, 2017.

[95] D. M. Witten and R. Tibshirani, "Penalized classification using Fisher's linear discriminant," *J. R. Stat. Soc. Ser. B (Statistical Methodol.*, vol. 73, no. 5, pp. 753–772, 2011.

[96] F. Rosenblatt, "The perceptron: a probabilistic model for information storage and organization in the brain.," *Psychol. Rev.*, vol. 65, no. 6, p. 386, 1958.

[97] A. A. Samir, A. R. Rashwan, K. M. Sallam, R. K. Chakrabortty, M. J. Ryan, and A. A. Abohany, "Evolutionary algorithm-based convolutional neural network for predicting heart diseases," *Comput. & Ind. Eng.*, vol. 161, p. 107651, 2021.

[98] A. K. Paul, P. C. Shill, M. R. I. Rabin, and M. A. H. Akhand, "Genetic algorithm based fuzzy decision support system for the diagnosis of heart disease," in *2016 5th International Conference on Informatics, Electronics and Vision (ICIEV)*, 2016, pp. 145–150.

[99] K. Uyar and A. Ilhan, "Diagnosis of heart disease using genetic algorithm based trained recurrent fuzzy neural networks," *Procedia Comput. Sci.*, vol. 120, pp. 588–593, 2017.

[100] M. Tubishat, N. Idris, L. Shuib, M. A. M. Abushariah, and S. Mirjalili, "Improved Salp Swarm Algorithm based on opposition based learning and novel local search algorithm for feature selection," *Expert Syst. Appl.*, vol. 145, p. 113122, 2020.

[101] M. Kaliappan, S. Manimegalai Govindan, and M. Kuppusamy, "Automatic ECG analysis system with hybrid optimization algorithm based feature selection and classifier," *J. Intell. Fuzzy Syst.*, no. Preprint, pp. 1–16, 2022.

[102] L. Ali, A. Rahman, A. Khan, M. Zhou, A. Javeed, and J. A. Khan, "An automated diagnostic system for heart disease prediction based on χ^2 statistical model and optimally configured deep neural network," *IEEE Access*, vol. 7, pp. 34938–34945, 2019.

[103] A. M. Alhassan and W. M. N. Wan Zainon, "Taylor bird swarm algorithm based on deep belief network for heart disease diagnosis," *Appl. Sci.*, vol. 10, no. 18, p. 6626, 2020.

[104] B. Van Calster, L. Wynants, D. Timmerman, E. W. Steyerberg, and G. S. Collins, "Predictive analytics in health care: how can we know it works?," *J. Am. Med. Informatics Assoc.*, vol. 26, no. 12, pp. 1651–1654, 2019.

[105] I. Goyal, A. Singh, and J. K. Saini, "Big Data in healthcare: a review," in: *2022 1st International Conference on Informatics (ICI)*, 2022, pp. 232–234.

[106] S. K. Reddy, T. Krishnaveni, G. Nikitha, and E. Vijaykanth, "Diabetes prediction using different machine learning algorithms," in: *2021 Third International Conference on Inventive Research in Computing Applications (ICIRCA)*, 2021, pp. 1261–1265.

[107] V. Dhar, "Big data and predictive analytics in health care," *Big Data*, vol. 2, no. 3. New Rochelle, NY, pp. 113–116, 2014.

[108] R. Amarasingham, R. E. Patzer, M. Huesch, N. Q. Nguyen, and B. Xie, "Implementing electronic health care predictive analytics: considerations and challenges," *Health Aff.*, vol. 33, no. 7, pp. 1148–1154, 2014.

[109] B. Boukenze, H. Mousannif, A. Haqiq, and others, "Predictive analytics in healthcare system using data mining techniques," *Comput Sci Inf Technol*, vol. 1, pp. 1–9, 2016.

[110] A. Ray and A. K. Chaudhuri, "Smart healthcare disease diagnosis and patient management: innovation, improvement and skill development," *Mach. Learn. with Appl.*, vol. 3, p. 100011, 2021.

[111] G. Muhammad, F. Alshehri, F. Karray, A. El Saddik, M. Alsulaiman, and T. H. Falk, "A comprehensive survey on multimodal medical signals fusion for smart healthcare systems," *Inf. Fusion*, vol. 76, pp. 355–375, 2021.

[112] E. Freeman, I. E. Agbehadji, and R. C. Millham, "Nature-inspired search method for location optimization of smart health care system," in *2019 International Conference on Mechatronics, Remote Sensing, Information Systems and Industrial Information Technologies (ICMRSISIIT)*, 2020, vol. 1, pp. 1–9.

[113] G. L. Tortorella, F. S. Fogliatto, A. Mac Cawley Vergara, R. Vassolo, and R. Sawhney, "Healthcare 4.0: trends, challenges and research directions," *Prod. Plan. Control*, vol. 31, no. 15, pp. 1245–1260, 2020.

[114] K. Ashok and S. Gopikrishnan, "Statistical analysis of remote health monitoring based iot security models and deployments from a pragmatic perspective," *IEEE Access*, vol. 11, pp. 2621–2651, 2023.

[115] A. Kumar, R. Krishnamurthi, A. Nayyar, K. Sharma, V. Grover, and E. Hossain, "A novel smart healthcare design, simulation, and implementation using healthcare 4.0 processes," *IEEE Access*, vol. 8, pp. 118433–118471, 2020.

[116] R. M. K. Mohamed, O. R. Shahin, N. O. Hamed, H. Y. Zahran, and M. H. Abdellattif, "Analyzing the patient behavior for improving the medical treatment using smart healthcare and IoT-based deep belief network," *J. Healthc. Eng.*, vol. 2022, 2051642, 2022.

[117] M. M. E. Mahmoud, J. J. P. C. Rodrigues, K. Saleem, J. Al-Muhtadi, N. Kumar, and V. Korotaev, "Towards energy-aware fog-enabled cloud of things for healthcare," *Comput. & Electr. Eng.*, vol. 67, pp. 58–69, 2018.

[118] M. M. E. Mahmoud, J. J. P. C. Rodrigues, S. H. Ahmed, *et al.*, "Enabling technologies on cloud of things for smart healthcare," *IEEE Access*, vol. 6, pp. 31950–31967, 2018.

[119] S. Tian, W. Yang, J. M. Le Grange, P. Wang, W. Huang, and Z. Ye, "Smart healthcare: making medical care more intelligent," *Glob. Heal. J.*, vol. 3, no. 3, pp. 62–65, 2019.

[120] W. Li, Y. Chai, F. Khan, *et al.*, "A comprehensive survey on machine learning-based big data analytics for IoT-enabled smart healthcare system," *Mob. Networks Appl.*, vol. 26, pp. 234–252, 2021.

[121] P. A. H. Williams and V. McCauley, "Always connected: the security challenges of the healthcare Internet of Things," in: *2016 IEEE 3rd World Forum on Internet of Things (WF-IoT)*, 2016, pp. 30–35.

Chapter 8

Applications and challenges of optimization in industrial automation

Devarani Devi Ningombam[1]

8.1 Factory digitalization

The word "automation" can be used for a lot of different things and refers to a wide range of modern technologies that can work without constant human interaction or supervision [1]. The first benefit that comes from this change is that people will have less work to do. If we use an automated system or software at several points in our workflow, we will have more time for other projects and access to more resources. This will allow you to save time. Automation technology not only lowers operating costs by letting fewer people make the same or more products with the same or fewer people, but it also improves consistency and efficiency by making it impossible to make mistakes while the machine is running.

Industrial digitization is driven in large part by the need to respond quickly to changing consumer needs and market conditions [2]. If businesses time their production runs to match the seasons, they will waste less and have fewer unhappy customers. By replacing manual tasks with automated ones, you can get rid of rework, downtime, mistakes, and bottlenecks. You can also improve procedures, performance monitoring, and making decisions. Hence, you could save money, time, and manpower. Using intelligent technologies like artificial intelligence (AI) and the Industrial Internet of Things (IIoT) to automate manufacturing means turning analog processes into digital ones, automating human activities and knowledge into actions, making decisions for the system, and performing constant optimization [3].

"Factory digitalization" is the process of using cutting-edge technology to improve old ways of making things. Smart technologies, data analytics, and linked devices are helping industrial manufacturing practices greatly improve their efficiency, productivity, and accuracy as part of the industry's ongoing digital revolution. The operations, methods, and energy footprint of industries and supply chains are all being altered as a result of digitalization. In the context of manufacturing, "digital transformation" is the process of replacing analog activities with

[1]National Institute of Technology Patna (NITP), India

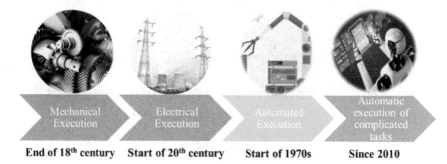

Mechanical Execution	Electrical Execution	Automated Execution	Automatic execution of complicated tasks
End of 18th century	**Start of 20th century**	**Start of 1970s**	**Since 2010**

Figure 8.1   Evolution of factory digitalization

digital infrastructure and processes to minimize complexity, boost efficiency, lessen the number of errors handled, and cut costs across the board [4]. The practically definite increase in an industry's profitability is the most persuasive argument in favor of the widespread use of digital technology by industrial enterprises. Product engineers can acquire a better understanding of future product enhancements by combining numerous technologies, such as an enterprise resource planning (ERP) system and product sensors.

8.1.1   Birth of factory automation

During the Industrial Revolution of the 1800s, automated techniques and technologies were used to increase manufacturing output (ISO 2003). This gave rise to today's version of automation, which continues to be in use. Around the same time, industries began utilizing relay logic and were electrified, which is the process of obtaining power from electricity [5].

In the 1920s, this caused the development of industrial automation to speed up very quickly. The use of centrally located power plants and the installation and use of new high-pressure boilers, electrical substations, and steam turbines have increased the need for instruments and controls. Putting electricity into factories in the 1920s made them more productive and changed how things worked on the factory floor. Production factories started using electric motors, and as time went on, fewer and fewer places still used steam engines to power shaft and belt drives at the front of the line. During this time of transition, industrial production increased by around 30 percent. This was because electric motors were substantially more efficient than steam engines, required less maintenance, and lacked the huge friction losses generated by line shafts and belts.

The Industrial Automation Initiative started in 2006 as part of a high-tech German strategic plan that focused the country's research and innovation policy on a few projects that would lead to scientific and technical breakthroughs in the next 10–15 years [6]. It uses computer, software, and Internet technologies to make its idea of an integrated industry a reality. In order to build stronger links between knowledge and skills, the German approach puts a lot of emphasis on collaboration between business and science [5]. They make it possible to set up networks that cover the whole process of making something, turning factories into smart places. Intelligent equipment, warehousing systems, and production facilities that provide end-to-end integration constitute the links. Its integration includes inbound logistics, production, marketing, outbound logistics, and service. Factory automation is projected to enhance tighter collaboration between business partners such as suppliers and customers and among employees, hence creating new opportunities for all parties involved to profit from one another. Figure 8.1 depicts the evolution of factory digitalization.

As a result of industrial digitization, we can expect to see new business models and big opportunities. Already, we can see the beginnings of this trend. Direct metal laser sintering (DMLS), an additive method like 3-D printing that deposits melted metal powder layers by laser, is used by some businesses to fabricate low-volume metal products from digital 3-D models. These components are made of a totally dense metal that has superior mechanical qualities. The DMLS process is intriguing because it can create intricate geometries that cannot be made using conventional machining techniques.

Implementing a digitization plan that considers how the organization's operations and structure will change is very important. On a cultural level, it can be hard to accept change, and leaders and other important people may be resistant. Because of this, it is important to set digitalization goals, create a digitalization strategy, choose the right technological enablers, build technology leadership, train your staff, and create a digital culture. All of these tasks should be done at the same time.

8.2   Product flow monitoring

The term "production monitoring" refers to the process of inspecting your products on-site every single working day of your production. An inspector will look at your manufacturing facility to make sure it meets your requirements. They will pick random units for inspection and look for and fix any flaws they find [7].

Monitoring production gives you information about the whole manufacturing process, makes you aware of any mistakes that might have happened at any point, and helps you avoid delivery delays. With production monitoring, we can keep an eye on several parameters at the spindle, machine, and factory levels at the same time. Automated and real-time data collection makes it possible to look at the data and find bottlenecks and other useful information. In the context of production monitoring, tracking entails keeping tabs on information in order to analyze the health of machinery. By analyzing production data, we can monitor and improve our processes more effectively. Enterprise ERP systems have the potential to incorporate monitoring technologies that expand their scope and improve their precision across the organization.

Nowadays, it is highly motivated to automate all monitoring operations. When we refer to automated monitoring, we mean a system of continuous monitoring. This sort of system is intended to notify a certified operator through an alarm, dialer, or pager in the event that a water treatment facility or water distribution system fails during regular operation. Automation reduces expenses and time spent on problem-solving, resulting in more productive teams overall. Due to the lessened need for manual intervention in the detection of failures, automation of monitoring results in not only improved alarms but also accelerated problem resolution.

The necessity of automated monitoring increases when a microservices architecture-based scenario is involved [8]. Monitoring microservices can be several orders of magnitude more complicated than monitoring traditional apps if monitoring tasks are not automated. Due to the fact that multiple systems operating on a range of technical platforms are connecting with one another and increasing or decreasing the number of instances they run, it is vital that adequate monitoring mechanisms for applications be created and not left as an option [9]. In this section, some of the best practices for automating monitoring are discussed, as follows.

8.2.1   Creating applications with monitoring in mind from the start

Monitoring frameworks should be built right into the codebases of projects so that they can deliver better metrics. For instance, a great number of monitoring frameworks include methods for capturing metrics, which can then be shown in a dashboard. For example, Micrometer is a Java framework that was developed specifically for microservices. It has the ability to capture parameters by making use of a wide variety of various formats. Customers will not be able to see these metrics unless the app was built on a framework that gives you access to them. For the same reason, it may be hard to add certain monitoring features to older systems: the code may not be easy to build to gather useful information about the software [10]. In addition, new monitoring frameworks may necessitate updated library versions, while obsolete systems may require prior releases of the same library to function well. In such a situation, refactoring is the only way to enable the use of sophisticated monitoring metrics on such antiquated systems.

8.2.2   Organize products into several categories

Product organization is vital because it allows people to specialize their skill sets to better serve a clearly defined product. It has the ability to alleviate difficulties in areas such as communication, product creation, and sales that a business may encounter [11]. On the basis of the features of the products and the variables affecting the purchase, the product can typically be classified into one of the following four primary groups:

(i)   Convenience products: Convenience products are easy to obtain and readily available at a variety of retailers, making them more important than product uniqueness or special features.
(ii) Shopping products: Shopping products are not bought as often as convenience products, but you can still find them in certain stores or online. They require research and comparing things like price, durability, reputation of the brand, features, and compatibility. There is a lot of competition, and customer or technical support after a purchase can make the time between the customer and the company longer.

(iii) Specialty products: Specialty products are often status or prestige purchases, so it is important to use messaging to build brand loyalty and keep customers through new product launches, feature updates, future directions, and brand innovations.

(iv) Unsought products: Promoting brand recognition can help customers get to know a company's product and image, which can build trust and keep customers for longer. For example, a pest control company may use a catchy musical jingle on local radio and television stations to increase the likelihood that customers think of the company before another.

Product classification can help you understand how different products fit into the greater context of making purchases in a certain market, which is why product category research is so crucial. There are numerous types of products and services currently available on the market. Due to the fact that the conditions surrounding the purchase of each type of product are distinct, it is feasible to build marketing strategies that are adapted to the product, the consumer, and the purchasing style in order to increase sales.

When used on products that are already in high demand, aggressive marketing methods that are meant for products that are not selling well may be unnecessary or even harmful. Similarly, you may not want to invest money from a marketing budget on a widespread advertising campaign for a highly specialized product that is only likely to appeal to a portion of the market. Spending some time considering product categories can help you make more efficient use of advertising resources by providing a more focused, precise message and rooting it in the customer behavior insights that are related to product classification. This might help you make better use of your advertising budget.

8.2.3 Include real-time tracking technologies

The monitoring system makes sure that a quick response can be made, that data can be kept safe and collected, and that the system as a whole is in great shape. Even if monitoring does not solve problems, it makes computer systems more reliable and stable in the long run. Monitoring factories enables businesses to manage and optimize their equipment assets more efficiently. With a production monitoring platform such as Machine Metrics, manufacturers are able to discover and optimize equipment capacity [12]. Moreover, producers can better identify the processes that surround machinery. It also gives information about the whole manufacturing process, makes aware of any mistakes that might have happened at any point, and helps to avoid delivery delays. And knowing and controlling every step of the manufacturing process can only mean two things for your business: better products and happy customers.

8.3 Inventory management

The Institute for Supply Management (ISM) recently conducted a survey that revealed record-long lead times, the unavailability of vital basic supplies, rising commodity prices, and difficulty transferring across industries due to the unprecedented spike in client demand [13]. Depending on how production processes work, digital transformation and the Internet of Things (IoT) could be both helpful and harmful. Because of this, some technological advances, like AI, robotics and drones, electric cars, and on-demand delivery, could change the way we look at the traditional supply chain. There are a number of different ways that this could be accomplished. Even if their long-term goal is to increase the efficiency and cost-effectiveness of e-commerce processes, one of the most difficult aspects of accomplishing this goal is integrating these systems and services across all of a company's existing supply chain activities. This is one of the components that must be accomplished [14].

Inventory management is important for almost all business owners, but it is even more important if we have more than one way to sell our products (or even a physical store). Attempting to manually balance all of these variables raises the probability of making mistakes. Not to mention the length of time required. What if, however, it is informed that a team could use that time to focus on more important tasks while still managing the inventory? At this stage, automated inventory management comes into play. By using the features of a retail operating system, we may reduce the amount of time spent on inventory management each year while also improving the accuracy of those procedures.

Both retailers and wholesalers can keep an eye on their stock in real-time thanks to automated inventory management systems. As a result of the systems, workflows are simpler and more effective. By creating your retail automation with pre-built circumstances, we will be able to focus on other crucial responsibilities with the assurance that the inventory will be managed automatically. This will give us an extra time to complete tasks. The majority of modern businesses, whether or not they specialize in e-commerce, employ automated inventory management to track and organize their stock, suppliers, and sales. Using an automated system enables merchants to monitor stocks in real-time and make timely business-critical choices. The main features of the automated inventory management are listed in Figure 8.2.

For instance, if one of our products has reached the lowest possible stock level and it is, therefore, necessary to reorder, the software that manages our inventory will tell us automatically (or even reorder for us). Our inventory automation should also work with other retail management systems, like your point-of-sale (POS) software and order management system. In order to achieve real-time accuracy in inventory management, we must keep track of sales across all channels. Only then can we hope to achieve that objective. The main benefit of automated inventory management is that we will know exactly which items sell better than others, which products sell poorly, how well each product is doing, and how much profit you are making. When we add this information to your demand projections, risk management, cash-flow projections, and expected profit margins, we can make plans that are more accurate and solid [15].

In the next section, the primary advantages of automated inventory management are highlighted in Figure 8.3.

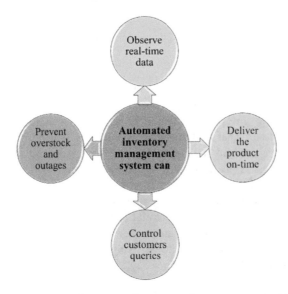

Figure 8.2　Main features of automated inventory management

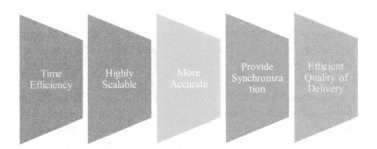

Figure 8.3　Main benefits of automated inventory management

8.3.1　Time efficiency

Traditional inventory management and control systems rely on manually analyzing data from multiple locations, which is inefficient and time-consuming. It is probable that forecasting future sales, calculating inventory levels, and generating reports will all be inaccurate and inefficient. Integration of point-of-sale systems and software for demand forecasting are two examples of sophisticated automated solutions. These technologies continuously update data and produce significant insights, resulting in the optimization of time. Reducing the number of hours spent manually inputting data can have a favorable influence on customer retention by minimizing inventory issues.

For example, consider all the hours spent manually updating spreadsheets with inventory data. With an automated system, the stock levels will be precisely and automatically updated across all channels. The automation engine will automatically register and update the system whenever an item is sold, returned, or received, freeing up the time to focus on what truly matters.

8.3.2   Scalability

Using cutting-edge software makes it much easier for a company to expand its operations and improve its products. With the help of automated inventory systems, businesses can be sure that building new warehouses will be profitable without hiring more people or spending more money on tracking and sending purchase orders by hand. This is made possible by automated inventory management systems. Real-time inventory data connected with other management systems ensures the accuracy of decisions regarding the expansion of the firm.

In the end, automation has the potential to bring about a lot of scalability and growth opportunities. Software that automates inventory management saves time, makes it more accurate, and makes it less likely that mistakes will be made while processing thousands of transactions per day.

8.3.3   Accuracy

Automated inventory management software provides retailers and producers with accurate, real-time stock data. This enables the system to automatically replace supplies in the event that they run out. In addition, by analyzing stock data patterns, organizations may make more precise and thorough predictions and suggestions regarding recruiting, optimal reordering points, arranging shifts to meet anticipated demand, changing targets, and eventually increasing sales. These forecasts and suggestions can be derived from an analysis of data trends.

When data is entered manually, there is a much higher chance of human error occurring. What is the answer? Do away with any and all requirements for manually entering inventory data. When we choose to automate the operations involved in inventory management, the software will handle the administration of data entry on its own. This includes adding, deleting, forecasting, and restocking stock in real-time.

8.3.4   Synchronization

Seventy-two percent of stock-outs were caused by mistakes in the way stores ordered and restocked items, according to a study that looked at 600 stores in 29 counties. All of these things can hurt a company's reputation: when demand forecasts are made by hand, they are often wrong, wrong orders can lead to lost sales, and not having enough goods in the warehouse can make customers unhappy. With automated inventory control software, stores, warehouses, and manufacturers are always aware of what needs to be reordered. This helps them fulfill their duties without delay, which reduces the number of errors made.

When talking to factories that use several distribution networks, the most common problem they wish to fix is managing inventory availability. Having to manually type in inventory availability as purchases are made, all while trying to avoid out-of-stocks and cancellations, is not only stressful but also expensive and resource intensive. Errors are likely to occur when orders are entered manually from one system into another. It is vital to regularly monitor and oversee sales across all channels in order to have a complete understanding of the situation and synchronize all data. All of this data can be synchronized in one central location so that reports can be generated to prevent underselling and overselling. This will ultimately result in cost savings and improved customer satisfaction.

8.3.5   Quality of delivery (QoD)

A study of 600 retail stores in 29 counties found that faulty in-store ordering and restocking procedures were to blame for 72% of stock-outs. All of these issues harm the company's reputation. The automated inventory control software regularly notifies retailers, warehouses, and manufacturers of the need for reordering. This allows them to do their jobs without delay, thereby decreasing the number of errors.

8.4   Safety and security

The opportunities for intelligent manufacturing and industrial automation continue to expand, evolve, and amaze. It is interesting to watch how new technical solutions may be deployed to improve the management and productivity of factory floors. This category includes inventions that enhance security, optimize process management, streamline edge computing, and coordinate motion.

The first step in doing the individual assignment is to stop people or things from going into areas that could be dangerous. Safety laser scanners, light curtains, and safety mats are all important parts of the process of turning off devices automatically and finding intruders without human intervention. Safety systems assist in ensuring people, plants, and equipment keep functioning safely. Improved process control could introduce higher levels of throughput and eliminate disruptions. Terminal management systems include any form of application in a terminal storage market to combine your operations [16].

Safety through EtherNet/IP protocol-based automation safety solutions boosts diagnostic data accessibility, boosts productivity, and reduces wiring complexity, and the connected enterprise (CE) is responsible for providing the network connectivity. This new perspective on safety not only makes it simpler to keep people and processes risk-free but also significantly increases overall productivity [17]. Intelligent safety devices provide enhanced visibility into operations and aid users in developing a deeper comprehension of process states, environmental variables, and other factors that affect productivity and safety.

Moreover, in an effort to save expenses, a number of organizations have turned to automation. While the system's increased efficiency is undeniably persuasive, it is the system's enhanced security that establishes the argument for its implementation. Here are several examples:

• Processes and operations: With automation, the number of operational injuries can be kept to a minimum since workers no longer have to do tasks that could be dangerous.

- Actions to take in an emergency: In an emergency, automated systems can provide real-time monitoring, which lets people act more quickly. Problems that were formerly thought to be inevitable can now be solved before they even arise.
- Risk management: With the help of safety automation software, businesses can quickly and easily change safety procedures and come up with a plan for how to handle an accident. Furthermore, it can be accomplished in a timely and efficient fashion that causes minimal interference with ongoing activities.

Some of the main benefits of the safety and security of factory automation are:

- When automation is used, it often increases efficiency because it makes things go faster, makes better products, and reduces waste. Maintaining your system may require an initial investment, but it will be considerably cheaper in the long run than keeping up with your existing costs.
- The anticipated annual expenditures connected with occupational injuries and illnesses are decreased by automation.
- As a result of having more time to focus on intellectually interesting work, employees are happier now that the majority of manual labor has been automated. In addition to expressing care for their safety, removing personnel from a potentially hazardous situation indicates the company's dedication to that asset.
- Advantage automation makes operations more secure and efficient, which increases productivity and gives businesses an edge in the market.

Steps to be taken to ensure safety and security in optimizing the automation industry are shown in Figure 8.4.

- Training employees: Automated systems can be helpful, but only when they are effectively used. Training staff is therefore essential. One of the many benefits of training is the ability to identify and avoid potentially hazardous situations.

Figure 8.4   Steps to be taken to ensure safety and security in optimizing the automation industry

- Keeping to a regular schedule: Because long-term use can cause wear and tear, it is important to do regular maintenance checks on automated systems. The return on investment for your system may also improve.
- Risk analysis: Before doing maintenance on a system, you need to know everything there is to know about its risk profile. Knowing about safeguards and proper procedures can help you save a significant amount of money. To make progress, all involved parties must have a shared understanding of the situation.
- Lockout/tagout: When doing maintenance, it is best to follow the Lockout/ Tagout procedures for controlling dangerous materials. Locking and tagging involve isolating energy sources that could be dangerous and could lead to the sudden release of stored mechanical energy. It is advised that this method be utilized as frequently as feasible; but, due to the need for a power source for programming and software upgrades, this is not always practicable.
- Realizing obligatory legal standards: Keep in mind that there are regulations governing the standards that must be met by an organization in terms of worker safety and maintenance practices. You should stay current with any modifications that may occur.

8.5 Quality control

In the modern business world, there has always been a need to make and deliver products quickly and well. Long delays can cause money to be lost and waste resources that could have been used to get new business [18]. Liberalization and digitalization have changed how companies operate by letting them sell their goods in many different countries. In response, there is a lot more competition between brands, and companies are being held to the highest standards of customer satisfaction. In order to be viable in today's application world, industries must rely on experienced people, sophisticated tools, and dependable procedures that allow the company to deliver more commercial value in less time [19]. To execute slightly elevated development services in a timely and trouble-free manner, a modern product testing approach that makes efficient use of test automation capabilities is expected. A "digital technology known as automated quality control" helps to increase the quality of inspections by helping to reduce the number of mistakes made during the workflow. Businesses are able to increase their performance and get their items to market more quickly without sacrificing product quality if they eliminate the need for manual proofreading.

Automatic data quality control technology makes it possible for businesses to get products to market faster without lowering the quality of those products. These technologies accelerate the entire process of quality control and minimize the amount of time spent on proofreading by automating manual tasks that, without automation, would take hours to complete. In turn, inefficiencies like fatigue and human error can be minimized, allowing for the prospect of faster and more accurate error detection [20]. Controlling quality guarantees that consistency and high standards of business practices may be maintained across the many production processes that are carried out on a daily basis at your organization. Moreover, automatic quality control at multiple revision points can help you find deviations as soon as they happen, so you can fix them before the number of them gets out of hand. Your business will be able to make the most of its resources and the production of its employees if it makes use of the advantages offered by quality control. These advantages include the following:

- saves energy spent searching for faults in content;
- in comparison to hours spent manually reviewing files, it inspects files in seconds;
- it easily detects all types of faults at any point in the process;
- achieve faster turnaround times by expediting approvals and decreasing quality delays;
- can compare two files side by side to check whether there are any differences between them;
- can find out which of your company's touchpoints are prone to errors and eliminate them;
- it can make use of the time that you would have spent otherwise editing in order to bring jobs to market more quickly.

For optimizing manufacturing automation while retaining the quality of the data, we should focus on the following factors as shown in Figure 8.5. Moreover,

Figure 8.5   Data quality factors

here are five tips that will help you improve your quality assurance process and use the best methods and procedures in your company.

(i) Establish a work environment in which employees are encouraged to look for methods to enhance the service quality of the organization. A way to ensure that quality management remains at the forefront of employees' minds is to cultivate an environment that promotes continuous improvement in this area. Giving individuals extra money when they exhibit a commitment to quality is one approach to reinforcing this attitude in the workplace.

(ii) Keep the machinery and automated software in good working order by scheduling frequent servicing. Preventative maintenance of machinery is essential for reliable production and worker security. When preventive maintenance is neglected, faulty plastic parts are produced, which leads to the breakdown of the device.

(iii) Develop a comprehensive training program. The foundation of great quality management is a well-organized training program. During staff orientation, quality management and its significance should be introduced. Continuous training and the introduction of new processes and procedures are additional chances to emphasize adherence to quality standards.

(iv) Establish a comprehensive overview for verifying product quality. Accurate product design relies heavily on the results of the quality inspection phase of production. A comprehensive inspection procedure is essential since it is frequently the last chance for a manufacturer to identify any design problems before a product is shipped.

(v) Schedule regular audits of the business's processes. Internal audits of the supply chain can be used to assess the efficiency of the operation and whether or not all regulations are being followed. Component manufacturers can improve customer satisfaction and get ready for external safety and compliance evaluations by performing internal audits.

8.6 Packaging optimization

"Package optimization" refers to the use of intelligent packaging to secure, identify, and protect goods throughout their delivery from a factory, warehouse, or distribution center to a client. Automation is a significant benefit that companies have in today's competitive market, and it is often one of the most effective methods for lowering packaging [21]. To stay ahead of the competition in the face of rising demand and escalating customer expectations, such as the expectation of one- or two-day delivery, firms will need new resources and strategies. The quality of the product's packaging affects how long it lasts, how happy the end user is with it, and how it affects the environment. To optimize the packing of a product from top to bottom, one must consider not just one, but all of the various containers that will be utilized during shipment. Packing can be classified into primary, secondary, and tertiary. Primary packaging compartmentalizes the goods well and offers a positive experience for the user. Display packaging is intended to use as little retail space as feasible, whereas, secondary and tertiary packaging are the extra layers of protection that make it possible to ship a product anywhere. Several aspects must be considered while maximizing the packaging, which includes:

(i)   Choosing the right materials for packaging: It is necessary to test the product to see how fragile it is and if the materials will protect it enough during shipping. Its primary package should facilitate an appealing opening experience for consumers. By selecting the appropriate secondary and tertiary packing, protection from potential shipping-related handling and environmental problems can be ensured.

(ii)   Appropriate package design: The correct package design, employing the correct quantity and type of packing materials, is a crucial component that can have a variety of effects on your supply chain. Non-standard package forms that attract consumers' attention on store shelves may not be the most space-efficient way to package your product in order to maximize space in trucks and warehouses.

(iii) Choosing the right amount of packaging has a big impact on your supply chain and the environment. Underpackaging results in damaged products, which increase your costs through product returns and waste. In addition to introducing an excessive amount of garbage into the environment, excessive packaging also results in greater packing costs and waste. In addition to causing stress on the supply chain, overpackaging also necessitates extra room for storage and transit.

(iv)   Product count optimization: If we are bundling many things for shipping purposes, we may be able to reduce costs and increase productivity by reevaluating how we mix the products into packs and pallets.

When companies work hard to improve their packaging designs, customer satisfaction goes up because customers are impressed by how quickly their products arrive and how clean they are. If the company sends fragile goods to customers all over the world, customers should use packaging that can absorb shock, resist water, and keep people from opening it. Using an optimized packaging technique can help save money in the long run. Any organization can save money on shipping costs and labor by redesigning the packaging to make the most efficient use of available space in trucks and storage facilities. The benefits of optimizing packaging automation are discussed as follows:

(a)   The number of packages from the packaging bridge can be significantly boosted by integrating automated procedures to supplement human labor. To meet the demands of single-line and multi-line orders, third-party logistics providers might use techniques that enable them to manufacture up to 1,000 unique packages every hour. These configurations can alleviate the workload of staff and help a corporation react to demand variations. This can be a major source of competitive advantage as the e-commerce business evolves and client expectations increase.

(b)   Automation is a cost-effective way for any merchant or logistics provider to improve operations and make them better fit the current market. Typically, businesses benefit most from solutions that help them avoid bottlenecks and save on labor expenses. Depending on the business's size, packaging needs, and the disruption a new solution may cause, systems that manage the entire packaging process or handle a specific task may be beneficial.

In any case, the success of a business will depend on how well a new automated technology or solution is put into place. Best practices will help a business integrate new procedures with the equipment and processes already in place, which will save time and money. So, automated packaging can have a big and good effect on business, and companies that want to get ahead of the competition should strongly consider using it.

8.7   Logistics and supply chain optimization

The process of making sure that orders are filled on time and in full (OTIF) is called logistics optimization. This is accomplished through streamlined logistics and distribution. The main goal of supply chain optimization is to make supply networks work better and more efficiently. This enables companies to deliver customers precisely what they want, when they want it, while also being lucrative and sustainable [22]. A company can do end-to-end quality control with an optimized supply chain, from getting the raw materials to delivering the finished products to customers. With this level of control, a company can cut down on waste and better manage key performance indicators (KPIs), which leads to better business results.

People usually think of the logistics operation and the supply chain as functions that help with other business tasks. But this view is slowly changing, and senior management is starting to see that the supply chain is a crucial part of the organization's ability to stay competitive. This is because the quality of the product, the time it takes to get it to the customer, and the cost are all better when the supply chain is streamlined and planned. In many markets, both now and in the future, customers

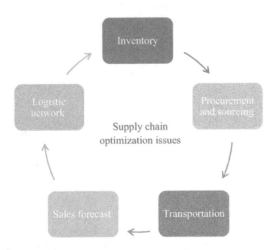

Figure 8.6   Supply chain optimization issues

want this [23–26]. So, every industry will have to make improving their supply chain a top priority if they want to reach operational excellence. Corporations must make the best use of their industrial and logistics capabilities, optimize and streamline flows throughout the supply chain, and get the most out of their resources if they want to keep their stock low while also being more responsive and reducing delivery times. Figure 8.6 depicts the issues faced during the optimization of supply chain.

While we are trying to optimize the supply chain, the primary challenges that we focus on are as follows:

(a)   Logistics network design
(b)   Procurement and sourcing optimization
(c)   Inventory optimization
(d)   Transportation planning and optimization
(e)   Sales forecasting

References

[1]   Nitzan, D. and Rosen, C. A. Programmable industrial automation. *IEEE Transactions on Computers*, C-25(12), 1259–1270, 1976.

[2]   Atack, J., Margo, R., and Rhode, P. Automation of manufacturing in the late nineteenth century: the hand and machine labor study. *Journal of Economic Perspectives*, 33, 51–70, 2019. Doi:10.1257/jep.33.2.51.

[3]   Wollschlaeger, M., Sauter, T., and Jasperneite, J. The future of industrial communication: automation networks in the era of the internet of things and industry 4.0. *IEEE Industrial Electronics Magazine*, 11.1, 17–27, 2017.

[4]   Lu, Y., Xu, X., and Wang, L. Smart manufacturing process and system automation – a critical review of the standards and envisioned scenarios. *Journal of Manufacturing Systems*, 56, 312, 2020.

[5]   Kagermann, H., Wahlster, W., and Helbig, J. Recommendations for implementing the strategic initiative INDUSTRIE 4.0. *Final Report of the Industrie 4.0*, 2013, p. 82.

[6]   Mabkhot, M. M., Al-Ahmari, A. M., Salah, B., and Alkhalefah, H. Requirements of the smart factory system: a survey and perspective. *Machines*, 6.2, 23, 2018.

[7]   Edrington, B., Zhao B., Hansel A., Mori M., and Fujishima M. Machine monitoring system based on MTConnect technology. *Procedia CIRP*, 22, 92–97, 2014.

[8]   Wang, L., Xu, S., Qiu, J., *et al.* Automatic monitoring system in underground engineering construction: review and prospect. *Advances in Civil Engineering*, 5, 1–16, 2020.

[9]   Doukas, C., Chantzis, D., Stavropoulos, P., Papacharalampopoulos, A., and Chryssolouris, G.. Monitoring and control of manufacturing processes: a review. *Procedia CIRP*, 8, 421–425, 2013. Doi:10.1016/j.procir.2013.06.127.

[10] Nour, M. and Hussain, M. A review of the real-time monitoring of fluid-properties in tubular architectures for industrial applications. *Sensors, 20* (14), 3907, 2020. https://doi.org/10.3390/s20143907.

[11] Cheng, C.-Y., Pourhejazy, P., Hung, C.-Y., and Yuangyai, C. Smart monitoring of manufacturing systems for automated decision-making: a multi-method framework. *Sensors*, 21, 6860, 2021. https://doi.org/10.3390/s21206860

[12] Sridharan, M., Devi, R., Dharshini, C.S., and Bhavadarani, M. IoT based performance monitoring and control in counter flow double pipe heat exchanger. *Internet of Things*, 5, 34–40, 2019.

[13] Kidonge, K.K., Automation of Inventory Management Process, Project Report, submitted to Makerere University (Uganda), 2006. Obtained from: https://silo.tips/download/automation-of-inventory-management-process

[14] Mascarenhas, M., Lamani, A. Matkar, C. Dessai, A.R., and Kotharkar. A. An automated inventory management system. *International Journal of Computer Applications*, 176, 21–23, 2020.

[15] Eswari, P. and Praveena, S.M. Optimization of Efficacy in Industrial Automation Control and Monitoring System using IIOT. 9001. ISO, ISO. "14649-1, 2008. Industrial automation systems and integration – Physical device control – Data model for computerized numerical controllers – Part 1: Overview and fundamental principles." *International Organization for Standardization*, 2003.

[16] Macher, G., Armengaud, E., Brenner, E., and Kreiner, C. A review of threat analysis and risk assessment methods in the automotive context. *International Conference on Computer Safety, Reliability, and Security*, pp. 130–141, 2016. Doi:10.1007/978-3-319-45477-1_11.

[17] Kriaa, S., Bouissou, M., Piètre-Cambacedes, L., and Halgand, Y. A survey of approaches combining safety and security for industrial control systems. *Reliability Engineering & System Safety*, 139, 156–178, 2015. Doi:10.1016/j.ress.2015.02.008.

[18] Winkler, D. and Biffl, S. Improving quality assurance in automation systems development projects. In M. Savsar (ed.), *Quality Assurance and Management. InTech*, pp. 379–398, 2012. Doi:10.5772/33487.

[19] Buzatu, C. and Orzan, I.A. Product quality control optimization for selection of measurement and control devices. In Chiru, A. and Ispas, N. (eds.), *CONAT 2016 International Congress of Automotive and Transport Engineering. CONAT 2016*. Springer, Cham, 2017. https://doi.org/10.1007/978-3-319-45447-4_69.

[20] Lönnroth, V. Improving Quality Control in Automation Projects Using Simulation Systems (Dissertation), 2021. Retrieved from http://urn.kb.se/resolve?urn=urn:nbn:se:kth:diva-293928

[21] Perez-Vidal, C., Gracia, L., Paco, J., Wirkus, M., Azorin, J., and Fernández, J. Automation of product packaging for industrial applications. *International Journal of Computer Integrated Manufacturing*, 31, 1–9, 2017. Doi:10.1080/0951192X.2017.1369165.

[22] Sathyamyla, K. and Bengt L. Modeling and optimization of synchronous behavior for packaging machines, *IFAC Proceedings*, 47(3), 1684–1691, 2014.

[23] Braccesi, L. Monsignori, M., and Nesi, Paolo. Monitoring and optimizing industrial production processes. In *Proceedings of the IEEE International Conference on Engineering of Complex Computer Systems, ICECCS*, pp. 213–222, 2004. Doi:10.1109/ICECCS.2004.1310920.

[24] Kusiak, A. Smart manufacturing. *International Journal of Production Research*, 56(1–2), 508–517, 2018.

[25] Plósz, S., Schmittner, C., and Varga, P. Combining safety and security analysis for industrial collaborative automation systems. In *Proceedings of the International Conference on Computer Safety, Reliability, and Security*, pp. 187–198, 2017. Doi:10.1007/978-3-319-66284-8_16.

[26] Xu, X. Machine Tool 4.0 for the new era of manufacturing. *The International Journal of Advanced Manufacturing Technology*, 92, 1893–1900, 2017.

Chapter 9

Expectations from modern evolutionary approaches for image processing

R. Srikanth[1] and V. Rajagopal[2]

Nature-inspired optimization algorithms (NIOAs) are a class of algorithms that are designed to solve complex optimization problems by emulating the natural processes of various biological and physical systems. These algorithms have been extensively studied and applied in various fields, including engineering, computer science, physics, economics, and biology, among others.

In recent years, there has been an increasing interest in the application aspects of NIOAs, as researchers and practitioners seek to harness their power and potential to solve real-world problems. This is due to the fact that NIOAs have several advantages over traditional optimization algorithms, including their ability to handle non-linear and non-convex problems, their ability to explore large solution spaces efficiently, and their ability to adapt to dynamic environments.

There are several types of NIOAs, including genetic algorithms, particle swarm optimization, ant colony optimization, and many others. Each of these algorithms is inspired by a different natural process, and they differ in terms of their implementation, strengths, and weaknesses. Applications of NIOAs are diverse and range from engineering design problems, such as structural optimization and control system design, to data mining and machine learning applications, such as clustering and classification problems. NIOAs have also been successfully applied in financial engineering, robotics, transportation, and energy management, among other fields.

Despite their potential, NIOAs are not a panacea for all optimization problems, and their performance can be highly dependent on the problem characteristics and the algorithm parameters. Therefore, researchers and practitioners need to carefully evaluate and tune NIOAs to ensure their effectiveness and efficiency. In summary, NIOAs are a promising class of optimization algorithms that have shown great potential in solving complex real-world problems. With ongoing research and

[1]Department of Electronics & Communication Engineering, Kakatiya Institute of Technology and Science, India
[2]Department of Electrical & Electronics Engineering, Kakatiya Institute of Technology and Science, India

development, NIOAs are likely to become even more powerful and versatile, paving the way for new applications and solutions in various fields.

Types of nature-inspired optimization algorithms

The list of nature-inspired optimization algorithms along with their descriptions and acronyms:

1. **Particle swarm optimization (PSO):** PSO is a computational method that uses the collective intelligence of a group of particles to move through the search space in search of the best solution. The particles exchange information with one another and adjust their positions and velocities to find the global optimum. PSO has been used successfully to solve a variety of optimization problems.

2. **Genetic algorithm (GA):** GA is a search and optimization algorithm inspired by the natural selection process. It starts with a population of candidate solutions, each encoded as a string of parameters. These candidate solutions evolved over successive generations by applying genetic operators such as mutation, crossover, and selection. The fittest individuals from each generation are selected to produce the next generation, eventually leading to an optimal solution. GA is widely used in optimization problems, machine learning, and artificial intelligence.

3. **Ant colony optimization (ACO):** ACO is a population-based optimization algorithm that is inspired by the behavior of ant colonies. In ACO, a population of artificial ants moves through a search space to find the optimal solution. The ants deposit pheromone trails to communicate with each other and adjust their movement based on the pheromone levels. Ants deposit pheromones on their path to a food source, which other ants can follow to reach the same source. ACO mimics this behavior by depositing virtual pheromones on the search space to guide the search toward the optimal solution.

4. **Artificial bee colony algorithm (ABC):** ABC is a population-based optimization algorithm inspired by honeybee colony behavior. A population of artificial bees moves through a search space to find the best solution in ABC. Bees communicate with one another and adjust their movements based on the quality of food sources.

5. **Firefly algorithm (FA):** FA is a population-based optimization algorithm inspired by the flashing behavior of fireflies. In FA, a population of artificial fireflies moves through a search space in search of the best solution. Fireflies use their light to attract potential mates, and their flashing patterns are influenced by the flashing patterns of nearby fireflies. FA mimics this behavior by adjusting the brightness and position of the fireflies to optimize the objective function.

6. **Cuckoo search algorithm (CS):** CS is a population-based optimization algorithm that is inspired by the brood parasitism behavior of some bird species. In CS, a population of artificial cuckoos lays eggs in other cuckoos'

nests to find the optimal solution. The cuckoos adjust the quality of their eggs and the host cuckoo discards eggs with lower quality.

7.   **Differential evolution (DE):** DE is a population-based optimization algorithm that is inspired by the process of natural selection. In DE, a population of solutions is evolved through differential mutation and crossover operations. The fittest individuals are selected to create the next generation of solutions.

8.   **Genetic algorithm (GA):** GA is an optimization algorithm inspired by the process of natural selection. It uses a population of candidate solutions to evolve better solutions through selection, crossover, and mutation.

9.   **Ant colony optimization (ACO):** ACO is a metaheuristic algorithm based on ant behavior that uses pheromone trails to determine the shortest path between a food source and the nest. It is frequently employed in the way to solve of optimization problems such as the traveling salesman problem.

10.   **Harmony search algorithm (HSA):** HSA [1] is an optimization algorithm inspired by the process of music improvisation. It generates new solutions by improvising new melodies, with the aim of finding the optimal solution. It is a metaheuristic optimization algorithm inspired by the process of musical improvisation. The algorithm was developed by Geem *et al.* in 2001 and has since been applied to various optimization problems, including engineering design, water resource management, and image processing. In HSA, a set of decision variables is represented as musical improvisation, and the optimization process is modeled as a process of generating better improvisations. The improvisations are evaluated using an objective function, and the better ones are used to create new improvisations through a process of improvisation memory, pitch adjustment, and harmony memory. Improvisation memory involves storing the best improvisations encountered so far, while pitch adjustment involves changing the decision variables of an improvisation. Harmony memory involves selecting the best improvisations from the improvisation memory and using them to generate new improvisations. HSA has been shown to be effective in solving a wide range of optimization problems, including function optimization, parameter tuning, and feature selection. It has several advantages over other optimization algorithms, such as its ability to handle discrete, continuous, and mixed-variable problems, and its fast convergence rate.

11.   **Differential evolution (DE):** DE is an optimization algorithm that uses the difference between two solutions in the population to generate a new candidate solution. It is based on the principles of evolution and natural selection.

12.   **Cuckoo search (CS):** CS is an optimization algorithm inspired by the behavior of cuckoo birds. It uses a population of cuckoos to lay eggs in host nests, with the aim of finding the optimal solution.

13.   **Glowworm swarm optimization (GSO):** GSO is an optimization algorithm inspired by the behavior of glowworms. It uses the bioluminescent behavior of glowworms to search for the optimal solution.

14. **Cat swarm optimization (CSO):** CSO is an optimization algorithm inspired by the behavior of cats. It uses the social behavior of cats to search for the optimal solution.

15. **Bat algorithm (BA):** BA is an optimization algorithm inspired by the echo-location behavior of bats. It uses the frequency and loudness of bat calls to find the optimal solution.

16. **Whale optimization algorithm (WOA):** WOA is an optimization algorithm inspired by the hunting behavior of humpback whales. It uses the bubble-net hunting behavior of whales to search for the optimal solution.

17. **Gray wolf optimizer (GWO):** GWO is a metaheuristic algorithm inspired by humpback whale hunting behavior. It enhances a given objective function using search agents and is commonly used for optimization problems like function optimization, data clustering, and feature selection.

18. **Grasshopper optimization algorithm (GOA):** GOA is an optimization algorithm inspired by the jumping behavior of grasshoppers. It uses the jumping and searching behavior of grasshoppers to find the optimal solution.

19. **Flower pollination algorithm (FPA):** FPA is an optimization algorithm inspired by the pollination behavior of flowers. It uses the pollination behavior of flowers to find the optimal solution.

20. **Moth flame optimization (MFO):** MFO is an optimization algorithm inspired by the navigation behavior of moths. It uses the natural behavior of moths to move toward the optimal solution.

21. **Dragonfly algorithm (DA):** DA is an optimization algorithm inspired by the hunting behavior of dragonflies. It uses the swarming behavior of dragonflies to find the optimal solution.

22. **Artificial ecosystem-based optimization (AEBO):** AEBO is an optimization algorithm inspired by the principles of ecological systems. It uses the principles of co-evolution, symbiosis, and ecological niches to find the optimal solution.

23. **Monkey algorithm (MA):** MA is a nature-inspired optimization algorithm that is based on the foraging behavior of monkeys. The algorithm was proposed in 2012 by Mirjalili and Lewis to solve complex optimization problems. The MA algorithm is designed to mimic the behavior of monkeys as they search for food in the forest. Monkeys use a combination of random exploration and memory to find food sources. They remember locations where they have found food in the past and use this information to guide their search for new food sources.

These are just a few examples of natural-inspired optimization algorithms, but there are several others in the literature.

9.1 Application domains of nature-inspired optimization algorithms

Nature-inspired optimization algorithms [2] are a type of optimization technique that resembles the characteristics of natural systems. Examples include GA, PSO, ACO, and simulated annealing. Because of their ability to solve complex optimization problems that traditional optimization techniques struggle with, these algorithms are gaining popularity. Because of their ability to solve complex problems efficiently, bio-inspired optimal algorithms have found uses across a broad spectrum of domains.

Here are some application domains where nature-inspired optimization algorithms are commonly used.

Engineering design: Nature-inspired optimization algorithms can be used to optimize engineering designs for products, processes, and systems, such as aerospace design, automotive design, and structural engineering. For example, particle swarm optimization has been used to optimize the design of airplane wings.

Finance: These algorithms can be used in finance for portfolio optimization, risk management, and stock price prediction. For instance, ant colony optimization has been used to solve the portfolio optimization problem, which involves selecting a mix of assets to maximize returns while minimizing risks.

Machine learning: Optimization algorithms that take inspiration from nature are widely employed to enhance the performance of various machine learning models, including but not limited to neural networks, decision trees, and support vector machines. As an illustration, genetic algorithms have been utilized to optimize the architecture of neural networks.

Image and signal processing: These algorithms can be used in image and signal processing to optimize parameters in image segmentation, filtering, and feature extraction. For example, particle swarm optimization has been used to optimize the parameters in image segmentation algorithms.

Robotics: NIOAs can be used to optimize the control of robotic systems. For example, ant colony optimization has been used to optimize the path planning of mobile robots.

Energy systems: These algorithms can be used to optimize energy systems such as power generation, transmission, and distribution. For instance, particle swarm optimization has been used to optimize the placement of wind turbines to maximize energy output.

Engineering design optimization: NIOAs are used to optimize various engineering designs, such as structural designs, mechanical designs, and electronic designs, for improved performance and efficiency.

Power system optimization: NIOAs are applied to optimize the operation and control of power systems for improved energy efficiency, reliability, and stability.

Transportation system optimization: Algorithms are used to optimize transportation systems, including routing, scheduling, and resource allocation, for reduced congestion and improved performance.

Robotics and automation: NIOAs are used to optimize robot behavior, motion planning, and control for improved performance in various applications such as manufacturing, logistics, and space exploration.

Image and signal processing: Algorithms are applied to optimize image and signal processing techniques for improved image quality, noise reduction, and signal extraction.

Data mining and machine learning: Algorithms are used to optimize machine learning algorithms and data mining techniques for improved accuracy, efficiency, and scalability.

Financial optimization: Bio-inspired algorithms are applied to optimize financial models, portfolio selection, and risk management strategies for improved financial performance.

Biomedical engineering: Bio-inspired algorithms are used to optimize various biomedical engineering applications, such as prosthetics, implants, and drug delivery systems, for improved efficiency and effectiveness.

Agriculture and environmental optimization: NIOAs are applied to optimize agricultural and environmental systems for improved crop yields, water management, and environmental sustainability.

Game theory and optimization: NIOAs are used to optimize game strategies and outcomes in various fields such as economics, psychology, and computer science.

Disaster management and emergency response: NIOAs are applied to optimize disaster management and emergency response strategies for improved disaster preparedness, response time, and resource allocation.

Social network analysis and optimization: Bio-inspired algorithms are used to optimize social network analysis and management for improved communication, collaboration, and information sharing.

Bioinformatics and genomics: NIOAs are applied to optimize bioinformatics and genomic data analysis for improved accuracy, efficiency, and scalability.

Smart grid optimization: Algorithms are used to optimize the operation and control of smart grids for improved energy efficiency, reliability, and stability.

Multi-objective optimization: Algorithms are applied to optimize multiple objectives simultaneously, such as cost, performance, and environmental impact, for improved decision-making.

Quality control and assurance: NIOAs are used to optimize quality control and assurance techniques for improved product quality, defect detection, and efficiency.

Supply chain optimization: Optimization algorithms are applied to optimize supply chain management for improved efficiency, responsiveness, and cost-effectiveness.

Chemical engineering: Bio-inspired algorithms are used to optimize chemical processes and systems for improved efficiency, cost-effectiveness, and environmental sustainability.

Construction and project management: NIOAs are applied to optimize construction and project management processes for improved cost-effectiveness, efficiency, and quality.

Energy management and optimization: NIOAs are used to optimize energy consumption, production, and management for improved energy efficiency and sustainability.

Overall, nature-inspired optimization algorithms have a wide range of application domains and can be applied to a wide range of optimization problems.

Nature-inspired optimization algorithms have resolved complex optimization problems in these and many other application domains. These algorithms could even find near-optimal solutions in a reasonable amount of time and have proven to be extremely effective in solving complex optimization problems that are difficult to solve using traditional optimization methods.

9.1.1 Implementation

To discuss the process of implementation of a naturally inspired algorithm, an optimization technique is considered and discussed its features and procedure of implementation. The harmony search optimization algorithm is selected to study how to implement an naturally inspired optimization algorithm to find an optimized solution by maximizing or minimizing a given objective function.

Image segmentation method based on a multilevel thresholding technique is considered for the explanation of the implementation of optimization techniques.

9.1.2 Finding optimized threshold level using harmony search optimization algorithm

The procedure of image segmentation is partitioning an image into its constituent parts, and a significant approach for extracting interesting features from images. Over a couple of decades, many efficient image segmentation approaches were formulated for various applications. Still, it is a challenging and complex issue, especially for color image segmentation.

To compute the optimized threshold values, Otsu's variance and Kapur's entropy [1] are deployed as fitness functions; both values should be maximized to locate optimal threshold values. In both Kapur's and Otsu's methods, the pixels of an image are classified into different classes based on the threshold level selected on the histogram. Optimal threshold levels give higher efficiency of segmentation.

Digital image segmentation is a technique of partitioning the image into regions to extract information about features of an image with homogeneous features in terms of intensity level, texture structure, color information, etc. Image segmentation schemes available from the literature, multi-level thresholding [1] of grayscale on the histogram of an image is a highly established method and used in various applications from satellite image segmentation to medical images. The important multilevel thresholding-based segmentation techniques are Kapur's and Otsu's methods [3]. The segmentation can be used often as a preprocessing step in object recognition, computer vision, image analysis, and so on in different applications like medical, agricultural, industrial, fault detection, and weather forecasting. In general, the majority of segmentation techniques are based on discontinuity and similarity, among abundant methods available thresholding is the most important technique for both grayscale and color images.

In general, to find out the optimized threshold values, two types of computational techniques are called parametric and nonparametric [4]. In the case of parametric techniques, statistical parameters are used, depending on initial conditions, and hence are inflexible to be applied. In the case of nonparametric techniques, thresholds are computed based on some criteria like Otsu's inter-class variance and Kapurs's entropy functions [5–9]. The thresholding method holds the properties like simplicity, accuracy, and robustness, which can be classified into two major categories: bi-level and multilevel [1,7], the pixels of an image are classified into different classes based on the threshold level selected on the histogram. In the case of bi-level thresholding, all pixels are classified into two groups based on threshold level. Pixels in the second category of multilevel thresholding are classified into more than two classes. Nonetheless, the primary constraint in multilevel thresholding is accuracy, stability, and execution time, among many other things.

In the case of color images [10], each pixel consists of three components (red, green, and blue) [10], due to this heavy load, segmentation of color images might be more exigent and intricate. Accordingly, it is essential to find the optimal thresholds by using optimization algorithms by maximizing the inter-class variance in Otsu's and the histogram entropy in the case of Kapur's on a histogram of an image. As per the no-free-lunch (NFL) principle [11], no algorithm can solve all types of optimization problems, one optimization algorithm may be useful well in one type of application and not succeed to solve other kinds of applications; thus, it is indispensable to devise and transform new algorithms.

Techniques with histogram plots are incapable of owning spatial contextual information to compute optimized thresholds. To conquer these drawbacks, a novel methodology is presented in this chapter, a curve which is having similar characteristics that of the histogram, and considers spatial contextual information of image pixels is named "Energy Curve" [3] can be used in the place of the histogram, HSA [1] used to select optimized gray levels, energy curve characteristics are similar to a histogram. For each value in an image, energy is computed in the grayscale range of that image. The threshold levels can be computed based on the values and peak points on the energy curve. In the literature, numerous optimization techniques along with the efficiencies and applications in particular fields are available; a few of them mentioned are PSO [12], ACO [13], BFO [14], ABC [15], GWO [16], MFO [17], SSA [18], FA [19], WOA [20], SCA [21], KHO [22], BA [23], FPA [24], and MVO [25]. Moreover, several customized algorithms are used in multilevel thresholding. For example, Chen *et al.* [26] proposed an improvised algorithm (IFA) to segment compared with PSO [27], and other methods [10,27–29].

9.1.2.1   Image segmentation with multilevel thresholding

Otsu method

This technique [2,5,6] is used for multi-level thresholding (MT), in which gray levels will be partitioned into different regions or classes; in this process, thresholding (*th*) levels need to be selected, and the set of rules to be followed for bi-level thresholding are

$$C1 \leftarrow p \ if \ 0 \leq p < th, \ C2 \leftarrow p \, if \, th \leq p < L - 1 \tag{9.1}$$

where $C1$ and $C2$ are two classes, p indicated pixel value for the gray levels $\{1, 2, 3, \ldots, L - 1\}$ in an image, and $L - 1$ has indicated the maximum gray level.

If the gray level is below the threshold th, then that pixel is grouped into class $C1$, else grouped into class $C2$. The set of rules for MT are

$$C1 \leftarrow p \text{ if } 0 \leq p < th1$$
$$C2 \leftarrow p \text{ if } th1 \leq p < th2$$
$$Ci \leftarrow p \text{ if } thi \leq p < thi \tag{9.2}$$
$$Cn \leftarrow p \text{ if } thn \leq p < thn + 1$$

From (9.2), $C1, C2, \dots Cn$ indicates different classes, and threshold levels to find objects are represented by $\{th1, th2, \dots, thi, thi + 1, thn\}$; these thresholds can be computed based on either a histogram or an energy curve. By use of these threshold levels, the entire pixels will be classified into different regions ($C1$, $C2 \dots Cn$). The significant methods of segmentation of images based on threshold levels are Otsu's and Kapur's methods, and in both cases, threshold levels can be computed by maximizing the cost function (interclass variance). In this chapter, optimized threshold levels thn are computed by Otsu's method th values [17]. In this method, interclass variance is considered the objective function, also called a cost function. For experimentation, grayscale images are considered. The below expression gives the probability distribution for each gray level:

$$Ph_c^i = \frac{h_c^i}{NP}, \sum_{i=1}^{NP} Ph_c^i = 1 \tag{9.3}$$

From (9.3), pixel value is denoted by, range of grayscale is $(0 \leq i \leq L - 1)$, where $c = 1, 2, 3$ for RGB and $c = 1$ for grayscale image, the total image pixels are represented by NP, and the histogram of considered images is represented by h_c^i. In bi-level thresholding, the total pixels in the image are grouped into two classes.

$$C1 = \frac{Ph_1^c}{w_0^c(th)}, \dots \frac{Ph_{th}^c}{w_0^c(th)}, C2 = \frac{Ph_{th+1}^c}{w_1^c(th)}, \dots \frac{Ph_L^c}{w_1^c(th)} \tag{9.4}$$

Whereas $w_0(th)$ and $w_1(th)$ are the probability distributions for $C1$ and $C2$, as it is shown below

$$w_0^c(th) = \sum_{j=1}^{th} Ph_i^c, \quad w_1^c(th) = \sum_{j=th+1}^{th} Ph_i^c \tag{9.5}$$

The mean or average of two classes μ_0^c and μ_1^c to be computed, the variance between classes σ^{2c} is given by (9.6) and (9.7)

$$\mu_0^c = \sum_{i=1}^{th} \frac{iPh_i^c}{w_0^c(th)}, \quad \mu_1^c = \sum_{i=th+1}^{L} \frac{iPh_i^c}{w_1^c(th)} \tag{9.6}$$

$$\sigma^{2c} = \sigma_1^c + \sigma_2^c \tag{9.7}$$

Notice that for both (9.6) and (9.7), c determined by the type of image, where σ_1^c and σ_2^c in (9.8) are the variances of classes C_1 and C_2

$$\sigma_1^c = w_0^c \left(\mu_0^c + \mu_T^c\right)^2, \sigma_2^c = w_1^c \left(\mu_1^c + \mu_T^c\right)^2 \tag{9.8}$$

where $\mu_T^c = w_0^c \mu_0^c + w_1^c \mu_1^c$ and $w_0^c + w_1^c = 1$. Based on the values of σ_1^c and σ_2^c, (9.8) gives the objective function:

$$J(th) = \max\left(\sigma^{2^c}(th)\right), 0 \le th \le L - 1 \tag{9.9}$$

From (3.9), $\sigma^{2^c}(th)$ is the total variance between two various regions after segmentation by Otsu's scheme for given th, optimization techniques required to compute the threshold level (th) by maximizing the fitness function is shown in (9.9). Similarly, for MT, the objective (or fitness) function $J(th)$ (as shown in (9.10)) to segment an image into k classes, requires k variances.

$$J(TH) = \max\left(\sigma^{2^c}(th_i)\right), 0 \le th_i \le L - 1, \text{where } i = 1, 2...k \tag{9.10}$$

where TH is a vector, $TH = [th_1, th_2, th_3......th_{k-1}]$ for multi-level thresholding; the variances between classes can be computed from (9.11)

$$\sigma^{2^c} = \sum_{i=1}^{k} \sigma_i^c = \sum_{i=1}^{k} w_i^c \left(\mu_i^c - \mu_T^c\right)^2 \tag{9.11}$$

where i_{th} represents i class, w_i^c indicates probability of i_{th} classes, and μ_j^c is the mean of i_{th} class. For MT segmentation, these parameters are anticipated as

$$w_0^c(th) = \sum_{i=1}^{th_1} Ph_i^c, w_1^c(th) = \sum_{i=th_1+1}^{th_1} Ph_i^c \cdots w_{k-1}^c(th) = \sum_{i=th_k+1}^{th_1} Ph_i^c \tag{9.12}$$

And, the averages of each class can be computed as

$$\mu_0^c = \sum_{i=1}^{th_1} \frac{iPh_i^c}{w_0^c(th_1)}, \mu_1^c = \sum_{i=th_1+1}^{th_2} \frac{iPh_i^c}{w_0^c(th_2)} \cdots \mu_{k-1}^c = \sum_{i=th_k+1}^{L} \frac{iPh_i^c}{w_1^c(th_k)} \tag{9.13}$$

Multilevel thresholding with Kapur's method

Kapur's method [1,2], which uses entropy as an objective function, is an important nonparametric technique for determining optimal threshold values. This method focuses on finding the best thresholds by maximizing total entropy. Entropy is a measure of the compactness and separability of classes. Kapur's method's objective function for multilevel is defined as

$$J(TH) = \max\left(\sum_{i=1}^{k} H_i^c\right), 0 \le th_i \le L - 1, \text{where } i = 1, 2...k \tag{9.14}$$

where TH is a vector, $[th_1, th_2, th_3 \ldots \ldots th_{k-1}]$. Each entropy is calculated separately with its *th* value, given for k entropies

$$H_1^c = \sum_{i=1}^{th_1} \frac{Ph_i^c}{w_0^c} \ln\left(\frac{Ph_i^c}{w_0^c}\right) H_2^c = \sum_{i=1}^{th_1} \frac{Ph_i^c}{w_1^c} \ln\left(\frac{Ph_i^c}{w_1^c}\right) \cdots H_k^c$$

$$= \sum_{i=th_k+1}^{th_1} \frac{Ph_i^c}{w_{k-1}^c} \ln\left(\frac{Ph_i^c}{w_{k-1}^c}\right) \tag{9.15}$$

Ph_i^c is the probability distribution of the particular intensity levels, which is obtained using (9.3). The probability distribution values $(w_0^c, w_1^c, w_2^c \ldots \ldots w_{k-1}^c)$ of the k classes are obtained using (9.5). In the end, by using (3.3), classify the pixels into various classless.

Energy curve
To find effective optimized threshold levels, the energy curve [3] can be used as an alternative of the histogram of an image for various applications.

Equation of energy curve
Consider an image indicated as $I = x(i,j)$, where i and j are spatial coordinates, $i = 1, 2, \ldots N$ and $j = 1, 2, \ldots M$, and size of image is $X = M \times N$. For an image, spatial correlation among neighboring the pixels can be devised by devising the neighborhood system with N of order d of an image with spatial coordinates (i, j) as $N_{ij}^d = \{(i + u, j + v), (u, v) \in N^d\}$, various configurations of the neighborhood are described in Ref. [22]. Neighborhood systems with order 2 are calculated for the creation of an energy curve, i.e., $(u, v) \in \{(\pm1, 0), (0, \pm1), (1, \pm1), (-1, \pm1)\}$ (Figure 9.1).

The foremost step is to get the energy of each pixel of an image considered, generate a binary matrix $B_x = \{b_{ij}, 1 \leq i \leq M, 1 \leq j \leq N\}$, the $b_{ij} = 1$ if $x_{ij} > x$; else $b_{ij} = -1$. Let $C = \{c_{ij}, 1 \leq i \leq M, 1 \leq j \leq N\}$ is another matrix, where $c_{ij} = 1, \forall(i, j)$. At each pixel value x and the energy value E_x of the image, I can be computed with the below expression:

$$E_x = -\sum_{i=1}^{M}\sum_{j=1}^{N}\sum_{pq \in N_{ij}^2} b_{ij}b_{pq} + \sum_{i=1}^{M}\sum_{j=1}^{N}\sum_{pq \in N_{ij}^2} c_{ij}c_{pq} \tag{9.16}$$

From (9.16), its second term should be a constant; consequently, the energy associated with each pixel is $E_x \geq 0$. From the above equation, we can clear that the energy for a particular gray, level is zero if each element of B_x either 1 or -1, can be put forward in another way as all the pixels of image $I(i,j)$ with gray level either greater than x or less than x, otherwise energy level at a particular gray value x is positive as given in Figure 9.2.

Problem statement
The optimal threshold levels can be computed by (i) maximizing inter-class variance for Otsu's method and maximizing total entropy for Kapurs's method. For the

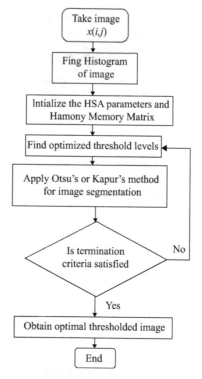

Figure 9.1   Flowchart to find optimized threshold levels using HSA

multilevel, the objective function of Kapur's method is defined as

$$J(TH) = \max\left(\sum_{i=1}^{k} H_i^C\right), 0 \le th_i \le L - 1, \quad \text{where } i = 1, 2 \ldots k$$

The inter-class variance for Otsu's method is given as

$$J(th) = \max\left(\sigma^{2^c}(th)\right), 0 \le th \le L - 1$$

9.1.2.2   Harmony search optimization algorithm

The HSA generates solutions, referred to as "harmonies," that are n-dimensional real vectors. Initially, random values are assigned to create the population and store them in the harmony memory (HM). The HM is then used to produce a new candidate harmony by adjusting the pitch or selecting random elements for updating. The worst HM vector is compared with the newly computed candidate harmony to update the elements in the HM. This process is repeated several times until the termination condition is met. Coupling HSA [1] and Otsu's algorithm can yield various segmentation algorithms.

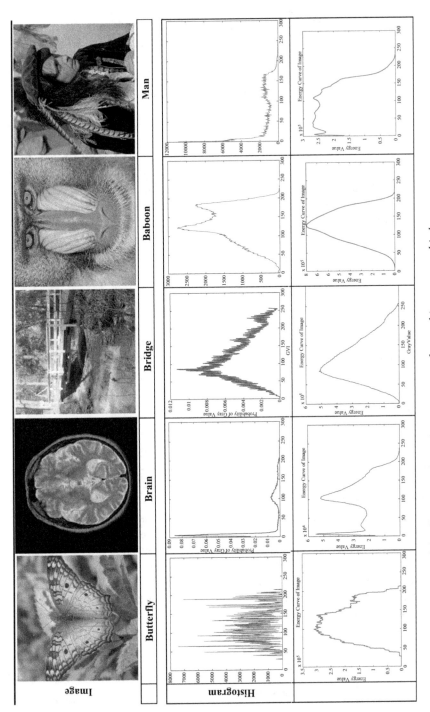

Figure 9.2   First row: input images; second row: histograms; third row: energy curves

Parameters of the algorithm

In the algorithm, the problem statement and variables can be summarized as the minimization or maximization of the function $(x), x = (x(1), x(2), \ldots \ldots x(n)) \in R^n$, The HSA aims to maximize the inter-class variance, which is expressed as the objective function in (9.11). The x indicates a set of variables to be designed.

$$\text{Where } x(k) \in [X_l(k), X_u(k)] \text{ for the range } k = 1, 2, \ldots .. n \tag{9.17}$$

The objective function, $f(x)$, is a cost function that is dependent on a set of variables denoted by x, where n is the length of the variable set. The upper and lower limits of the design variables, $x(k)$, are represented by $X_u(k)$ and $X_l(k)$, respectively. The HSA use several parameters, including the size of the harmony memory (HM), pitch adjusting rate (PAR), harmony-memory consideration rate (HMCR), and the number of iterations or improvisations (NI) distance bandwidth (BW).

Harmony memory initialization

In this stage, it is crucial to set up the initial components of the harmony search algorithm, known as the harmony memory (HM) vectors. Each HM vector denoted as $xi = \{xi(1), xi(2), \ldots xi(n)\}$ is generated randomly using the following equation: $xi(k) = X_l(k) + (X_u(k) - X_l(k)) * rand(0, 1)$ *for* $k = 1, 2, \ldots ., n$ and $i = 1, 2, \ldots .,$ HMS, that is length of HM, where HMS is the length of the HM. Here, $X_l(k)$ and $X_u(k)$ represent the lower and upper limits of the search space, respectively. These vectors are used to form the HM matrix, which contains HMS harmony vectors.

$$HM = \begin{bmatrix} x_1 \\ x_2 \\ \vdots \\ x_{HMS} \end{bmatrix} \tag{9.18}$$

Updating harmony memory and harmonic vector

The harmony search algorithm generates a new harmony vector, x_new, from the harmony memory (HM) matrix using three operations: memory consideration, random reinitialization, and pitch adjustment [1]. In the first phase, the initial decision value, $x_{new}(1)$, is selected randomly from the harmony memory set $\{x_1(1), x_2(1) \ldots . x_{HMS}(1)\}$. A random number, $r1$, is generated within the range [0,1], and if it is less than HMCR, then $x_{new}(1)$ is generated by memory consideration. Otherwise, $x_{new}(1)$ is selected from the search range $[X_l(k), X_u(k)]$. The remaining decision values, $x_{new}(2)$, $x_{new}(3)$, ..., $x_{new}(n)$, are selected similarly. The two operations, memory consideration, and random reinitialization can be summarized as follows:

$$x_{new}(k) = \begin{cases} x_i(k) \in \{x_1(k) \ldots \ldots \ldots \ldots . x_{HMS}(k)\} \\ X_l(k) + (X_u(k) - X_l(k)) * rand(0, 1) \\ \text{with probability of } 1 - HMCR \end{cases} \tag{9.19}$$

After generating each new decision value, x_{new}, the harmony search algorithm checks whether pitch adjustment is required or not. To do this, a PAR is defined, which is a combination of the frequency and bandwidth factor (BF). These two factors are adjusted to obtain a new x_{new} value from a local search around the HM. The pitch-adjusted solution, $x_{new}(k)$, can be calculated as $x_{new}(k)+/-rand(0,1)\cdot BW$ with a probability of PAR. This pitch adjustment process is similar to the mutation process in other bio-inspired algorithms. The range of pitch adjustment is restricted by the limits $[X_l(k), X_u(k)]$.

In the finishing stage, a new harmony vector, x_{new}, is computed and evaluated against the worst harmony vector, x_w, in the harmony memory. The fitness of x_{new} is compared with that of x_w, and if it is better, x_w is replaced by x_{new} and becomes part of the harmony memory. This process is repeated to maximize the objective function.

The optimization algorithm used in this study considers k variables, represented by threshold values th_k, to form a harmony or solution. For multilevel segmentation, the algorithm's population is represented by

$$\text{HM} = [x_1, x_2 ..., x_{1HMS}]^T, x_i = [th_1, th_2 ... ..., th_k] \qquad (9.20)$$

where each element x_i in the harmony memory represents a threshold value for each of the k variables. The HMS is the maximum size of HM. In this study, an 8-bit image with intensity values ranging from 0 to 255 is used, and the algorithm's parameters are set to HM = 50, HMCR = 0.5, PAR = 0.2, BW = 0.1, and NI = 3,500. The number of regions considered for segmentation ranges from 2 to 5.

Computing optimized threshold levels

The introduction section of this chapter outlines various multilevel thresholding techniques for image segmentation and highlights the limitations of the histogram-based methods. In the proposed method, an Energy Curve is utilized in place of the histogram, and the optimization of threshold levels is achieved using HSA. This is done by maximizing the inter-class variance for Otsu's method and entropy for Kapur's method, as shown in (9.10) and (9.14). The new approach is visually represented in Figure 9.1.

From the flow chart, take an image for experimentation $x(i,j)$ for multilevel thresholding-based segmentation, and plot the energy curve of the considered color image by using (3.1), then assign the design parameters of HSA, and the solution matrix values are filled with arbitrary numbers, initially denoted as x_i (set of threshold levels) as per (3.18), then divide the entire pixels in the image as per selected threshold levels into different classes or regions as per Otsu's technique and Kapur's method, then find the inter-class variance and entropy of the segmented image, as given in (9.14). Afterward, find the new set of threshold levels with (9.2) again, find the fitness and compare it with the previous fitness function, run this procedure until no improvement in the objective function or reach the specified number of iterations, and lastly find the optimized threshold valued (x_{new}) and classify the gray levels as (9.1) and (9.2) for the final segmentation of R, G, and B components separately for color images. The results of this scheme are compared with histogram-based techniques for evolution.

9.2   Results

This chapter introduces a novel technique for image segmentation that overcomes the limitations of methods that rely solely on image histograms. Such methods lack spatial contextual information and therefore may not yield optimal threshold levels. To address this issue, the proposed method utilizes energy curve, which captures the spatial relationship between pixels and their neighbors. The optimization of threshold levels for multilevel segmentation is achieved using harmony search algorithm (HSA) in combination with energy curve (Figures 9.3 and 9.4).

The primary objective of this article is to highlight the benefits of using the energy curve in comparison to the histogram. The research adopts a primarily quantitative approach for evaluating the proposed method, which involves analyzing nine images. To implement the proposed method, a MATLAB® code is developed, and the experiment is conducted on an eighth-generation Intel processor CORE i5-8250u with a clock speed of 1.60 GHz and 8 GB of internal memory. The MATLAB code is designed to generate energy curves and validation measures, which are then presented in tables. Some of the results presented in this chapter are taken from papers [30] authored by the authors of this chapter.

The resulting images are displayed in Figures 9.2–9.4, while comparative metrics are provided in Tables 9.1 and 9.2. The optimized threshold levels for $N = 2$–5 are indicated for five standard images, and the mean fitness of the proposed system is compared to various algorithms. The histograms and energy curves are displayed with their corresponding threshold levels denoted by red spots. In the tables, histogram is referred to as "H," the energy curve as "E," the number of regions as "N," and the threshold levels as "Th Levels." The segmentation efficiency improves with an increase in the mean value of the fitness function. Table 9.1 present the mean fitness function values for the proposed technique and algorithms based on histograms like Otsu's method with HAS (HAS_O) [1], Kapur's method based on HSA (HAS_K) [1], PSO with Otsu's method [31], Kapur's method with EMO (EMO_K) [32], and Otsu's method with EMO (EMO_O) for optimized threshold levels of $N = 2$–5 for five benchmark images. As shown in Table 9.1 for the bridge and butterfly images, the proposed method has a higher mean fitness function value than the other algorithms. Table 9.1 illustrates the proposed method's threshold levels and mean fitness function values for the baboon and man images, highlighting that the proposed method provides higher fitness values. In comparison to the proposed method, the HAS K and EMO K methods produce lower fitness function values. When $N = 2$, the mean object function for the bridge image is 2.06E+03 with the histogram and 1.58521E+11 with the energy curve.

Time taken for threshold level optimization and segmentation through histogram and energy curve approaches are presented in Table 9.2. The findings demonstrate that the proposed technique demands lesser time in comparison to other optimized algorithms. On an average, the proposed method takes 13.7813 seconds, which is lower than the time required for the EMO technique employing Otsu's method and Kapur's method. In summary, the threshold levels optimized using the HSA based on energy curve outperforms the ones obtained via

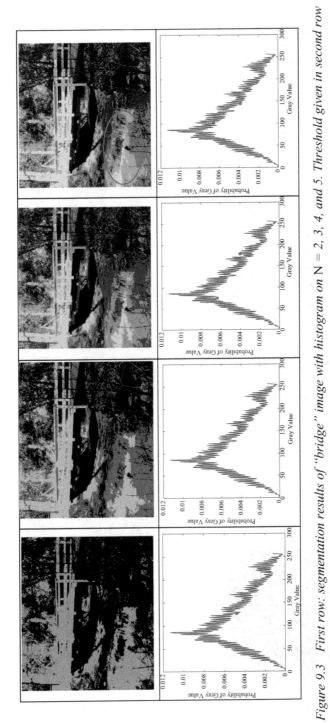

Figure 9.3   First row: segmentation results of "bridge" image with histogram on N = 2, 3, 4, and 5.   Threshold given in second row is indicated by red dots on histogram.

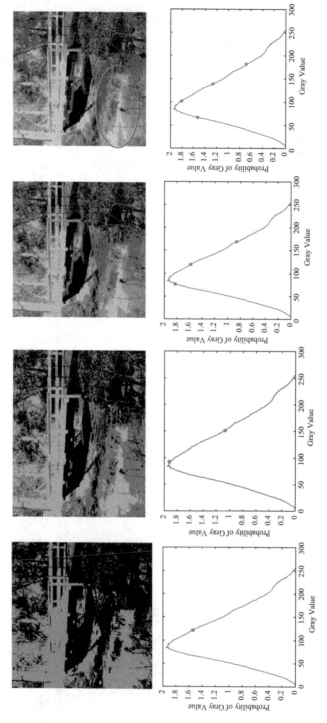

Figure 9.4   First row: segmentation results of "bridge" image with histogram on N = 2, 3, 4, and 5. Threshold given in second row is indicated by red dots on energy curve.

Table 9.1 Thresholding levels for different levels (N), and mean of fitness function with different segmentation methods

Image	N	HSA_O Th	Mean of fitness	HSA_K Th	Mean of fitness	PSO_O Th	Mean of fitness	EMO_O Th	Mean of fitness	EMO_K Th	Mean of fitness	Proposed method Th	Mean of fitness
Bridge	2	127	2.063e+03	116	13.5021	120	1.944e+03	126	1.944e+03	116	9.573	122	1.585E+11
	3	90, 157	2.532e+03	90, 161	12.678	95, 160	2.56e+03	95, 160	2.380e+03	92, 164	12.690	93, 152	1.45E+11
	4	76, 124, 182	2.720e+03	65, 126, 187	15.418	75, 123, 178	2.722e+03	74, 121, 177	2.560e+03	65, 126, 187	15.450	77, 120, 170	1.45E+11
	5	65, 105, 144, 192	2.78E+03	53, 98, 147, 199	17.803	61, 104, 144, 192	2.822e+03	66, 105, 146, 193	2.82e+03	57, 106, 155, 203	17.782	67, 102, 132, 182	1.45E+11
Butterfly	2	124	1.272e+03	213	12.040	122	1.272e+03	122	1.272e+03	213	12.040	122	3.195E+10
	3	99, 151	1.553e+03	27, 213	16.795	98, 150	1.553e+03	101, 153	1.552e+03	120, 213	16.662	99, 147	3.195E+10
	4	82, 118, 160	1.669e+03	27, 120, 213	21.417	81, 118, 159	1.669e+03	81, 119, 160	1.669e+03	27, 120, 213	21.417	84, 118, 157	3.698E+10
	5	83, 106, 129, 165	1.697e+03	27, 96, 141, 213	25.292	70, 97, 125, 160	1.711e+03	71, 99, 126, 162	1.711e+03	27, 96, 144, 213	25.295	78, 108, 135, 166	3.659E+10

(Continues)

Table 9.1 (Continued)

Image	N	HSA_O Th	HSA_O Mean of fitness	HSA_K Th	HSA_K Mean of fitness	PSO_O Th	PSO_O Mean of fitness	EMO_O Th	EMO_O Mean of fitness	EMO_K Th	EMO_K Mean of fitness	Proposed method Th	Proposed method Mean of fitness
Baboon	2	127	1.219e+03	201	13.100	127	1.2191e+03	128	1.2191e+03	193	13.100	123	4.395e+11
	3	97	1.547e+03	94	19.568	96	1.548e+03	77	1.548e+03	74	18.330	100	4.154e+11
		129		193		128		169		193		145	
	4	85	1.637e+03	69	22.8685	84	1.638e+03	85	1.638e+03	70	22.868	86	4.657e+11
		123		124		124		125		125		121	
		155		193		160		161		193		162	
	5	71	1.692e+03	54	26.962	71	1.692e+03	72	1.692e+03	54	26.9627	77	4.257e+11
		116		94		105		116		94		108	
		148		135		136		137		135		135	
		169		193		167		168		193		163	
Man	2	85	2.700e+03	101	15.358	82	2.700e+03	82	2.700e+03	189	13.256	80	3.092e+10
	3	51	3.064e+03	72	17.856	50	3.064e+03	51	3.064e+03	92	18.4609	57	3.092e+10
		120		169		115		116		189		115	
	4	36	3.213e+03	51	22.525	33	3.213e+03	33	3.2134e+03	70	23.2409	45	3.0922e+10
		87		117		85		85		151		89	
		137		163		134		134		199		135	
	5	30	3.267e+03	26	26.729	27	3.269e+03	31	3.269e+03	40	27.478	39	3.092e+10
		72		95		65		73		96		79	
		111		139		104		112		125		103	
		146		183		142		147		179		146	

Table 9.2   Time required for segmentation based on the proposed method and other methods

Image	N	Time (s)					
		HSA_O	HSA_K	PSO	EMO_O	EMO_K	Proposed
Bridge	2	10.125	18.0511	8.2658	50.51403	94.0337	6.1258
	3	16.2565	21.4523	12.566	104.4127	145.262	8.2365
	4	19.2365	20.5066	19.8609	155.0894	196.625	12.569
	5	24.369	79.7038	28.7158	218.9217	322.3668	16.547
Butterfly	2	7.8694	18.843	18.8806	64.44	94.9834	6.998
	3	14.8945	23.0062	20.7511	130.793	142.674	13.569
	4	19.658	23.0588	22.0223	182.19	291.81	16.458
	5	24.255	26.5361	23.0086	244.834	254.536	18.1675
Baboon	2	13.569	18.235	15.5688	60.6078	92.8163	10.257
	3	16.369	22.9658	19.9815	122.8779	145.5034	11.265
	4	18.6254	29.458	19.2624	268.2846	206.9632	13.524
	5	26.8027	41.8257	20.5374	261.3762	266.7319	16.654
Man	2	12.546	14.4032	11.8400	57.35	95.3515	9.657
	3	13.369	22.6598	14.7413	118.759	148.6318	10.894
	4	15.365	26.365	25.3560	181.8948	197.8918	12.324
	5	18.254	28.369	29.5827	244.309	248.3340	14.258
Average		**20.915**	**33.3438**	**22.9594**	**148.4578**	**179.811**	**13.7813**

histogram methods. Consequently, the segmentation process with the energy curve approach is superior to histogram techniques. This study predominantly utilized quantitative methods to scrutinize the results.

9.3 Parameter tanning

Bio-inspired optimization algorithms typically have several parameters that can be tuned to achieve better performance on different optimization problems. Some of the common running parameters of bio-inspired optimization algorithms are:

1. **Population size:** This parameter controls the number of candidate solutions generated and evaluated in each algorithm iteration. Larger population size may lead to superior solutions, but it also increases the computational cost.
2. **Mutation rate:** This parameter controls the rate at which mutations are introduced into the population. Mutations are random changes to the candidate solutions that allow the algorithm to explore new areas of the search space. A higher mutation rate can lead to more exploration, but may also reduce the convergence speed.
3. **Crossover rate:** This parameter controls the rate at which crossover is applied to the candidate solutions. Crossover is a genetic operator that combines two or more candidate solutions to create new solutions. A higher crossover rate can lead to more exploitation of good solutions, but may also reduce the diversity of the population.

4. **Selection strategy:** This parameter determines how the candidate solutions are selected for reproduction in each iteration of the algorithm. Common selection strategies include roulette wheel selection, tournament selection, and rank-based selection.

5. **Termination criteria:** This parameter specifies when the algorithm should be stopped. Reaching a maximum number of iterations, a minimum acceptable fitness value, or a specified amount of computing time all are common termination criteria.

6. **Initialization method:** This parameter controls how the first set of candidate solutions is generated. Random initialization, initialization based on domain-specific knowledge, and initialization based on previous successful solutions are all common initialization methods.

7. **Fitness function:** This parameter determines how the quality of candidate solutions is evaluated. The fitness function should be chosen carefully to accurately reflect the optimization problem being solved.

These parameters can be adjusted based on the distinctiveness of the optimization problem being solved to achieve better performance.

The GA and HSA are both population-based optimization algorithms that are devised to locate the optimal solution for the problem under test. While both algorithms have their own unique set of parameters, the most common parameters that need to be tuned for both algorithms are:

Parameters for genetic algorithm

1. **Population size:** The number of individuals in each generation of the algorithm.

2. **Selection method:** The method used to select individuals for the next generation (e.g., roulette wheel selection, tournament selection, etc.).

3. **Crossover rate:** The probability that crossover will occur between two individuals in the population.

4. **Mutation rate:** The probability that mutation will occur in an individual in the population.

5. **Fitness function:** The function used to evaluate each individual's fitness in the population.

Parameters for harmony search algorithm

1. **Harmony memory size:** The size of the harmony memory used in the algorithm.

2. **Pitch adjusting rate:** The probability that a pitch adjustment will occur in the algorithm.

3. **Harmony memory consideration rate:** The rate at which the algorithm considers the harmony memory when generating new solutions.

4. **Maximum improvisation iterations:** The maximum number of iterations the algorithm will perform before converging to a solution.

5. **Objective function:** The function used to evaluate the fitness of each generated solution.

It is important to note that the optimal values for these parameters may vary depending on the problem being solved. Therefore, it is recommended to experiment with different parameter values and analyze the results to determine the optimal set of parameters for a specific problem.

9.4   Constrained and unconstrained optimization

The two different types of optimization techniques used to find the maximum or minimum value of a function are constrained optimization and unconstrained optimization. Unconstrained optimization is the process of finding the smallest or maximum value of a function without any constraints. In other words, there are no restrictions on the variables' possible values. The goal of unconstrained optimization is to find the variable values that result in the function's minimum or maximum value.

Constrained optimization involves finding the minimum or maximum value of a function subject to one or more constraints. In other words, there are limitations on the values that the variables can take on. The goal of constrained optimization is to find the value of the variables that satisfy the constraints and result in the minimum or maximum value of the function.

There are several differences between constrained and unconstrained optimization techniques:

1. **Constraints:** The most obvious difference is the presence of constraints in constrained optimization problems. Unconstrained optimization has no constraints.
2. **Feasibility:** In constrained optimization, the solution must satisfy the constraints, making the solution feasible. In unconstrained optimization, there are no feasibility requirements.
3. **Objective function:** In both constrained and unconstrained optimization, the objective function is the function that we are trying to optimize. In constrained optimization, the objective function is subject to constraints.
4. **Solution:** Constrained optimization problems often have multiple solutions that satisfy the constraints, whereas unconstrained optimization problems usually have a unique solution.
5. **Optimization techniques:** Constrained optimization often requires more advanced optimization techniques, such as linear programming or nonlinear programming, whereas unconstrained optimization can often be solved using simpler techniques, such as gradient descent or Newton's method.
6. **Computational complexity:** Constrained optimization problems are generally more computationally complex than unconstrained optimization problems due to the presence of constraints.

Overall, the presence of constraints is the key difference between constrained and unconstrained optimization techniques.

The examples of constrained optimization problems in engineering are given below:

1. The optimal design of a truss structure is subject to constraints on the maximum stress, displacement, and weight.
2. Optimal control of a robotic arm is subject to constraints on the joint angles, velocity, and acceleration.
3. The optimal sizing of a heat exchanger is subject to constraints on the flow rate, pressure drop, and temperature difference.
4. The optimal allocation of resources in a manufacturing system is subject to constraints on capacity, lead time, and inventory level.
5. The optimal placement of sensors in a power grid is subject to constraints on the coverage, detection rate, and false alarm rate.
6. Optimal scheduling of production processes in a chemical plant is subject to constraints on the reaction rate, yield, and purity.
7. Optimal trajectory planning of a UAV is subject to constraints on the flight range, altitude, and speed.
8. The optimal placement of wind turbines in a wind farm is subject to constraints on the wind speed, turbulence, and wake effect.
9. Optimal design of a control system for a power plant subject to constraints on stability, response time, and energy efficiency.
10. The optimal routing of vehicles in a transportation network is subject to constraints on the traffic flow, capacity, and emissions.

These are just a few examples of the many constrained optimization problems in engineering. In each case, the goal is to find the optimal solution while satisfying a set of constraints that reflect the physical limitations and requirements of the system.

The examples of unconstrained optimization problems in engineering are given below:

1. Minimizing the weight of a cantilever beam subject to a fixed load and constraints on the stress and deflection.
2. Maximizing the efficiency of a heat engine is subject to constraints on temperature, pressure, and heat transfer.
3. Minimizing the power consumption of a motor subject to constraints on the torque and speed.
4. Maximizing the signal-to-noise ratio of a communication system is subject to constraints on bandwidth and power.
5. Minimizing the vibration of a mechanical system subject to constraints on the stiffness and damping.
6. Maximizing the output power of a photovoltaic system is subject to constraints on the irradiance and temperature.
7. Minimizing the total cost of a production process subject to constraints on the throughput and quality.
8. Maximizing the accuracy of a machine learning model is subject to constraints on the training time and complexity.

9. Minimizing the error of a control system subject to constraints on the stability and response time.
10. Maximizing the fuel efficiency of a vehicle subject to constraints on speed and acceleration.

In each case, the goal is to find the optimal solution to a single-objective or multi-objective optimization problem without any constraints or limitations on the decision variables.

The examples of constrained and unconstrained optimization problems in image processing are given below:

1. Unconstrained: Minimizing the distortion of a compressed image subject to no constraints.
2. Unconstrained: Maximizing the sharpness of an image subject to no constraints.
3. Unconstrained: Minimizing the noise level of an image subject to no constraints.
4. Unconstrained: Maximizing the contrast of an image subject to no constraints.
5. Unconstrained: Minimizing the computational cost of an image processing algorithm subject to no constraints.
6. Constrained: Minimizing the distortion of a compressed image subject to a maximum allowable bit rate constraint.
7. Constrained: Maximizing the sharpness of an image subject to a maximum allowable noise constraint.
8. Constrained: Minimizing the noise level of an image subject to a minimum allowable signal-to-noise ratio constraint.
9. Constrained: Maximizing the contrast of an image subject to a minimum allowable brightness level constraint.
10. Constrained: Minimizing the computational cost of an image processing algorithm subject to a maximum allowable processing time constraint.

In each case, the goal is to find the optimal solution to an optimization problem that optimizes a certain image processing task while satisfying certain constraints or limitations on the decision variables.

9.5 How to deal with constraints

Constraints in optimization algorithms refer to the limitations or restrictions on the variables or parameters of the problem being optimized. These constraints may arise due to physical, economic, or other real-world considerations. To deal with constraints in optimization algorithms, you can follow the following steps:

1. Formulate the constraints: First, you need to define the constraints that apply to the problem. The constraints can be of two types: equality constraints and inequality constraints.
2. Use appropriate optimization technique: There are various optimization techniques available to deal with constrained optimization problems. Some of the

popular optimization techniques include linear programming, quadratic programming, non-linear programming, and dynamic programming. Choose the appropriate technique based on the complexity and nature of the problem.

3. Convert constraints into penalties: One way to incorporate constraints in optimization algorithms is by converting them into penalties. This involves adding a penalty term to the objective function that is proportional to the violation of the constraint. The penalty function is designed in such a way that it becomes very large when the constraint is violated significantly.

4. Use Lagrange multipliers: Another way to incorporate constraints in optimization algorithms is by using Lagrange multipliers. This technique involves adding a new variable to the objective function for each constraint. The Lagrange multipliers are then used to ensure that the constraints are satisfied.

5. Use interior-point methods: Interior-point methods are a type of optimization technique that can be used to solve constrained optimization problems. This method works by transforming the original problem into an unconstrained problem and then solving it using iterative techniques.

In summary, dealing with constraints in optimization algorithms involves formulating the constraints, selecting an appropriate optimization technique, converting constraints into penalties, using Lagrange multipliers, and using interior-point methods.

Harmony search (HS) is a metaheuristic optimization algorithm that is commonly used to solve unconstrained optimization problems. However, there are situations where constraints are present in the problem being optimized. In such cases, the following methods can be used to deal with constraints in the harmony search algorithm:

1. Penalty function method: This method involves incorporating the constraints as penalty terms in the objective function of the harmony search algorithm. The penalty term is a function of the violation of the constraints and is added to the objective function. The penalty function is designed in such a way that it becomes very large when the constraints are violated significantly. The HS algorithm then minimizes the modified objective function that includes the penalty terms.

2. Dynamic bandwidth adjustment method: This method involves dynamically adjusting the bandwidth of the HS algorithm. The bandwidth is the parameter that controls the pitch adjustment of the harmony vectors. The bandwidth is adjusted such that the constraints are satisfied. The bandwidth adjustment is done iteratively until the constraints are satisfied.

3. Augmented Lagrangian method: This method involves adding the Lagrange multipliers to the objective function of the harmony search algorithm. The Lagrange multipliers are used to enforce the constraints in the optimization process. The augmented Lagrangian function is optimized using the HS algorithm to obtain the optimal solution.

In summary, the penalty function method, dynamic bandwidth adjustment method, and augmented Lagrangian method are three ways to deal with constraints in the harmony search optimization algorithm. These methods ensure that the optimal solution is found while satisfying the constraints of the problem.

9.6   Feature selection

The process of selecting a subset of relevant features or variables from a larger set of features available in a dataset is termed feature selection [33]. The goal of feature selection is to reduce data dimensionality, remove irrelevant or redundant features, and improve machine learning model accuracy and efficiency. In many real-world problems, datasets often contain a large number of features, but not all of them contribute equally to the predictive power of the model. In some cases, using all the available features can lead to overfitting, which means the method or model performs well on the training data but poorly on the test data. Feature selection can help to overcome this problem by selecting only the most informative and relevant features for the model.

The process of selecting a subset of relevant features or descriptors that capture important characteristics or patterns in an image is referred to as feature selection in image processing. The features selected can be used for a variety of tasks such as object recognition, image classification, and image segmentation.

Image feature selection is important because images can contain a large number of features, and not all of them may be useful or relevant to the task at hand. Moreover, using all the features can lead to overfitting or high computational complexity, which can affect the performance of the algorithm.

There are different techniques for feature selection in image processing, including:

1. SIFT (scale-invariant feature transform): This method extracts key features from images that are invariant to scale, orientation, and affine distortion. The SIFT features can be used for object recognition and image matching.
2. HOG (histogram of oriented gradients): This method extracts features that capture the local orientation information of an image. The HOG features can be used for pedestrian detection and human pose estimation.
3. SURF (speeded up robust features): This method extracts features that are invariant to scale, rotation, and illumination changes. The SURF features can be used for object recognition and image matching.
4. Deep learning: This involves using convolutional neural networks (CNNs) to learn features directly from the raw pixels of an image. The CNNs can be trained on large datasets to learn generic features that can be used for various image-processing tasks.

Nature-inspired optimization algorithms, such as genetic algorithms, particle swarm optimization, and ant colony optimization, can be used to perform feature selection in machine learning tasks. This process can help to reduce the dimensionality of the data and improve the accuracy and efficiency of the machine learning model.

Nature-inspired optimization algorithms can be used to perform feature selection by searching for the subset of features that maximizes the performance of the machine learning model. These algorithms work by iteratively evaluating candidate subsets of features and selecting the best subset based on a fitness function that measures the performance of the model.

For example, in a genetic algorithm approach, the candidate subsets of features can be represented as chromosomes, and the fitness function can depend on the accuracy of the machine learning model trained on the selected subset of features. The algorithm then evolves the population of candidate subsets over several generations, using selection, crossover, and mutation operators to generate new candidate solutions. Similarly, in a particle swarm optimization approach, the candidate subsets of features can be represented as particles that move through a search space of possible subsets, and the fitness function can be based on the accuracy of the machine learning model trained on the selected subset of features. The algorithm then updates the position of each particle based on its own best solution and the best solution of the swarm.

9.7   Advantages of using optimization techniques in engineering applications

Optimization techniques are widely used in engineering applications due to their numerous advantages.

Here are some of the key advantages of using optimization techniques in engineering applications:

1. **Improved efficiency:** Optimization techniques can help engineers to design and develop systems that are more efficient, reducing energy consumption and increasing productivity.
2. **Enhanced performance:** Optimization techniques can help engineers to optimize the performance of systems, improving the accuracy and reliability of results.
3. **Faster development:** Optimization techniques can help engineers to reduce the time it takes to develop new systems, allowing them to bring new products to market more quickly. Optimization techniques are often able to find the optimal solution faster than traditional methods. This is because they are designed to search the solution space more efficiently and effectively, which can save time and resources.
4. **Increased safety:** Optimization techniques can help engineers to design safer systems by identifying and addressing potential safety risks during the design phase.
5. **Improved sustainability:** Optimization techniques can help engineers to design systems that are more environmentally sustainable, reducing their carbon footprint and minimizing their impact on the environment.
6. **Flexible design:** Optimization techniques can help engineers to design systems that are more flexible and adaptable, allowing them to respond quickly to changing conditions and requirements.

7. **Improved performance**: Optimization techniques help to improve the performance of engineering systems by finding the optimal solution. This can lead to improved efficiency, reduced costs, increased productivity, and better quality of output.

8. **Increased robustness:** Optimization techniques can help to improve the robustness of engineering systems by identifying potential weaknesses and finding solutions to mitigate them. This can lead to systems that are more resilient to changes in the environment or unexpected events.

9. **Ability to handle complexity:** Engineering systems can be highly complex and difficult to analyze using traditional methods. Optimization techniques, however, are well-suited to handle complex systems and can help to identify the best solutions even in highly complex scenarios.

10. **Reduced costs**: Optimization techniques can help to reduce costs in engineering applications by identifying the optimal solution that meets the desired performance requirements at the lowest cost. This can lead to significant savings in material costs, manufacturing costs, and maintenance costs.

11. **Increased innovation:** Optimization techniques can help to promote innovation in engineering applications by exploring new design concepts and solutions that may not have been considered using traditional methods. This can lead to new and improved products, processes, and systems that are more efficient and effective.

12. **Improved image quality:** Optimization techniques can be used to improve the quality of images by optimizing the parameters of image processing algorithms. For example, optimization can be used to find the optimal set of parameters for image denoising, image segmentation, or image registration algorithms.

13. **Efficient feature selection:** In image processing, optimization techniques can be used to reduce the dimensionality of the feature space and improve the efficiency of subsequent processing steps. This can result in more precise and faster image analysis.

14. **Increased accuracy:** Optimization techniques can be used to improve the accuracy of image processing algorithms by finding the most efficient solution. For example, optimization can be used to find the best set of parameters for object detection, object recognition, or image classification algorithms.

15. **Automated optimization:** Optimization techniques can be used to automate the process of parameter tuning in image processing algorithms. This can save time and reduce the need for manual intervention, leading to increased efficiency and productivity.

16. **Robustness:** Optimization techniques can be used to improve the robustness of image processing algorithms by finding solutions that are less sensitive to changes in the input data or environmental conditions.

17. **Customization:** Optimization techniques can be used to customize image processing algorithms to specific applications and data types. This can lead to improved performance and accuracy in a variety of image-processing tasks.

Overall, optimization techniques are an essential tool for engineers in a wide range of applications. They provide a powerful means of improving the efficiency, performance, safety, and sustainability of engineering systems, while also reducing costs and accelerating the development process.

9.8 Conclusion

Nature-inspired optimized algorithms such as genetic algorithms, particle swarm optimization, and ant colony optimization have proven to be effective tools for solving complex optimization problems in a variety of fields such as engineering, finance, and healthcare. These algorithms are inspired by natural phenomena and biological systems, and they use natural selection and evolution to find the best solution. Constrained and unconstrained optimization algorithms have distinct advantages and are appropriate for a variety of problems. Constrained optimization algorithms take constraints into account when determining the best solution, whereas unconstrained optimization algorithms do not. When the problem has specific constraints, constrained optimization algorithms are more appropriate, whereas unconstrained optimization algorithms are faster and more efficient. Design is one of the engineering applications of optimization algorithms.

References

[1]   Oliva D, Cuevas E, Pajares G, Zaldivar D, and Perez-Cisneros M. Multilevel thresholding segmentation based on harmony search optimization. *J Appl Math* 2013;2013. doi:10.1155/2013/575414.

[2]   Abualigah L. Group search optimizer: a nature-inspired meta-heuristic optimization algorithm with its results, variants, and applications. *Neural Comput Appl* 2021;33:2949–2972. https://doi.org/10.1007/s00521-020-05107-y.

[3]   Patra S, Gautam R, and Singla A. A novel context-sensitive multilevel thresholding for image segmentation. *Appl Soft Comput J* 2014;23:122–127. doi:10.1016/j.asoc.2014.06.016.

[4]   Jia H, Ma J, and Song W. Multilevel thresholding segmentation for color image using modified moth-flame optimization. *IEEE Access* 2019;7: 44097–44134. doi:10.1109/ACCESS.2019.2908718.

[5]   Otsu N. A threshold selection method from gray-level histograms. *IEEE Trans Syst Man Cybernet* 1979;9:62–66. doi:10.1109/TSMC.1979.4310076.

[6]   Kwon SH. Threshold selection based on clustering analysis. *Pattern Recogn Lett* 2004;25:1045–1050. doi:10.1016/j.patrec.2004.03.001.

[7]   Resma KPB. and Nair MS. Multilevel thresholding for image segmentation using Krill Herd Optimization algorithm. *J King Saud Univ Comput Inf Sci* 2021;33(5):528–541. doi:10.1016/j.jksuci.2018.04.007.

[8]   Diego Olivaa EC, Gonzalo Pajares DZ, and Valentín Osuna. A Multilevel thresholding algorithm using electromagnetism optimization. *Neurocomputing* 2014;139:357–381.

[9]   Hammouche K, Diaf M, and Siarry P. A comparative study of various meta-heuristic techniques applied to the multilevel thresholding problem. *Eng Appl Artif Intell* 2010;23:676–688.

[10]   Bhandari AK, Kumar A, Chaudhary S, and Singh GK. A novel color image multilevel thresholding based segmentation using nature inspired optimization algorithms. *Expert Syst Appl* 2016;63:112–133.

[11]   Wolper DH and Macready WG. No free lunch theorems for optimization. *IEEE Trans Evol Comput* 1997;1(1):67–82.

[12]   Kennedy J and Eberhart R. Particle swarm optimization. *Proc IEEE Int Conf Neural Netw* 1995;4:1942–1948.

[13]   Socha K and Dorigo M. Ant colony optimization for continuous domains. *Eur J Oper Res* 2008;185(3):1155–1173.

[14]   Passino KM. Biomimicry of bacterial foraging for distributed optimization and control. *IEEE Control Syst Mag* 2002;22(3):52–67.

[15]   Karaboga D and Basturk B. A powerful and efficient algorithm for numerical function optimization: artificial bee colony (ABC) algorithm. *J Global Optim* 2007;39(3):459–471.

[16]   Mirjalili S, Mirjalili SM, and Lewis A. Grey wolf optimizer. *Adv Eng Softw* 2014;69:46–61.

[17]   Mirjalili S. Moth-flame optimization algorithm: a novel nature-inspired heuristic paradigm. *Knowl-Based Syst* 2015;89:228–249.

[18]   Yu JJQ and Li VOK. A social spider algorithm for global optimization. *Appl Soft Comput* 2015;30:614–627.

[19]   Yang X-S. Multiobjective firefly algorithm for continuous optimization. *Eng Comput* 2013;29(2):175–184.

[20]   Mirjalili S and Lewis A. The whale optimization algorithm. *Adv Eng Softw* 2016;95:51–67.

[21]   Mirjalili S. *SCA:* a sine cosine algorithm for solving optimization problems. *Knowl-Based Syst* 2016;96:120–133.

[22]   Gandomi AH and Alavi AH. Krill herd: a new bio-inspired optimization algorithm. *Commun Nonlinear Sci Numer Simul* 2012;17:4831–4845.

[23]   Yang X. A new metaheuristic bat-inspired algorithm. In *Proceedings of the Nature Inspired Cooperative Strategies for Optimization (NICSO)*, pp. 65–74, 2010.

[24]   Yang XS. Flower pollination algorithm for global optimization. In *Proceedings of the Unconventional Computing and Natural Computation*, pp. 240–249, September 2012.

[25]   Mirjalili S, Mirjalili SM, and Hatamlou A. Multi-verse optimizer: a nature-inspired algorithm for global optimization. *Neural Comput Appl* 2016;27(2):495–513.

[26]   Chen K, Zhou Y, Zhang Z, Dai M, Chao Y, and Shi J. Multilevel image segmentation based on an improved firefly algorithm. *Math Problems Eng* 2016;26:1–12.

[27]   Akay B. A study on particle swarm optimization and artificial bee colony algorithms for multilevel thresholding. *Appl Soft Comput* 2013;13(6):3066–3091.

[28]   Agarwal P, Singh R, Kumar S, and Bhattacharya M. Social spider algorithm employed multi-level thresholding segmentation approach. In *Proceedings of the 1st International Conference on Information Communication Technology for Intelligence Systems* vol. 2, pp. 249–259, 2016.

[29]   Khairuzzaman AKM and Chaudhury S. Multilevel thresholding using grey wolf optimizer for image segmentation. *Expert Syst Appl* 2017;85:64–76.

[30]   Srikanth R and Bikshalu K. Multilevel thresholding image segmentation based on energy curve with harmony Search Algorithm. *Ain Shams Eng J* 2021;12 (1):1–20.ISSN 2090-4479,https://doi.org/10.1016/j.asej.2020.09.003.

[31]   Chen Wei and Kangling F. Multilevel thresholding algorithm based on particle swarm optimization for image segmentation. In *2008 27th Chinese Control Conference, Kunming*, 2008, pp. 348–351, doi:10.1109/CHICC.2008.4605745.

[32]   Diego Oliva EC, Gonzalo Pajares, and Valentín Osuna DZ. A multilevel thresholding algorithm using electromagnetism optimization. *Neurocomputing* 2014;139:357–381.doi.org/10.1016/j.neucom.2014.02.020.

[33]   Abu Khurma R, Aljarah I, Sharieh A, Abd Elaziz M, Damaševičius R, and Krilavičius T. A review of the modification strategies of the nature inspired algorithms for feature selection problem. *Mathematics* 2022;10:464. https://doi.org/10.3390/math10030464

Chapter 10
Conclusion

Aakansha Garg[1], Varuna Gupta[2], Vandana Mehndiratta[2],
Yash Thakur[2] and Dolly Sharma[1]

10.1 Concluding remarks

With the advancement in technology, day-to-day life has become a lot easier. Resources requirement and task complexity are also increasing day by day. To imbibe these requirements with less effort, using minimum resources is the most adaptable solution. Optimization is performed to satisfy all these demands while reducing overall cost, complexity, and enhancing efficiency. Some problems are deterministic in nature like refrigerator cooling off mode, iron heating off mode, etc. Contrary to this, most of the real-world problems are stochastic processes for example traffic light controlling based on number of vehicles on the road, early diagnosis of heart diseases based on various parameters, identify number of cellular users who may demand network resources at same instance of time, image scenario like background, posture, etc., while using image processing and assuming human speed of working in a factory with automation processes and speed of other vehicles for an automated vehicle on the road. Maximum real-world problems are indeterministic in nature. Traditional methods like Newton's method, Secant method, Steffensen's method, Principal component analysis [1], and Brent's method [2]. These are computation methods to find only the exact solutions for real-world problems [3]. These methods always follow the traditional way only and are incompatible to any spontaneous changes.

Since the last few decades, researchers are more focused toward optimization. It may be done in different ways: *To analyze a random data* in much discrete way, machine learning algorithms are used. Some examples are K-means [4], K-nearest neighbor [5], reinforcement learning [6], Gaussian mixture model [7], Artificial neural networks [8], Hidden Markov Model [9], logistic regression [10], and support vector machine [11]. *To reduce the cost and latency* of transmission, compression algorithms like discrete cosine transform, discrete wavelet transform, and Lempel-Ziv-Welch (LZW) [12] are used. *To ensure security*, encryption algorithms

[1]ABES Institute of Technology, India
[2]Christ (Deemed to be University) – Delhi, India

like advanced encryption standard, data encryption standard, and triple data encryption standards are used [13]. *To optimize parameters* like energy consumption and other real-time requirements, numerous other algorithms have been used nowadays.

There are various problems to be solved in a specified steps or time. For example, an autonomous car path is difficult to design as the condition of the road, and other vehicles movements are non-deterministic. It is also difficult to predict the time when movement of vehicles will be predictable. Such problems are called NP-hard problems. To solve such problems, nature-inspired algorithms provide satisfactory solutions [14]. Based on the inspiration source, nature-inspired algorithms are categorized as follows. *Stochastic algorithms* are based on random search, for example, stochastic hill climbing and Tabu search. *Evolutionary algorithms* replicate the behavior of living organisms, for example, genetic algorithm and strength Pareto evolutionary algorithm. *Physical algorithms* are based on physical phenomena such as simulated annealing and harmony search. *Bio-inspired algorithms* are inspired by Darwin's theory of survival. *Swarm-based algorithms* are based on behavior of social creatures, for example, ant colony optimization and particle swarm optimization. *Chemistry-based algorithms* are based on optimization of chemical reactions, for example, grenade explosion method and river formation dynamics.

The nature-inspired algorithms has been adopted from different fields of science, i.e., physics, chemistry, biology, mathematics, social science, etc. These algorithms can be used to optimize single-objective problems and multi-objectives problems [15]. Due to the nature-inspired algorithms' precision, its application area has been increased a lot. Genetic algorithm along with heuristic and machine learning algorithm has been used to optimize various parameters like cost, energy consumption, and latency using D2D communication for an IoT, 5G, and 6G system[16]. A neoteric gravitational search algorithm for multi-constraint optimization problem has been used to optimize throughput of served users in UAV communication [17]. To automate a 3D packaging system, particle swarm optimization along with IoT has been designed [18]. The hill climbing algorithm has been used for maximum power point tracking in a photovoltaic power harvesting system for smart nodes of Internet of Things (IoT) [19]. An ensemble learning methods are used as base classifier to identify the cross-semantic and structural features of cloud to avoid massive data transmission in cloud computing systems [20]. Improved simulated annealing is applied to physiological detection and positioning of a visitor into the park [21]. The variety of bio-inspired algorithms is far beyond the scope of our explanation.

Particle swarm optimization (PSO) is a random search algorithm based on swarm, and it is simpler than other nature-inspired algorithms in terms of complexity and fast convergence [22]. PSO has been implemented to solve many real-time problems like, PSO with gradient descent method and support vector machine has been used to identify malicious data [23]. PSO has been used to allocate resources automatically to a distributed data computation for large data computations. It ensures that the subgroups will get resources directly proportional to computations [24]. The meta-heuristic PSO has been used to make decisions for node deployment fulfilling multiple objectives such as QoS for energy consumption, delay, and throughput, ensuring failure tolerance [25]. Since past two decades, PSO has been used in biomedical field and image processing. A single-particle optimizer-based local search has been used for DNA sequence compression [26]. It is evident that in some applications, performance of PSO has been further improved by integrating with some other algorithms. A hybridization of PSO with dragon fly optimization and gray wolf optimization has been used to find a feature set for early detection of Alzheimer's disease [27]. A multi-swarm technique further improves the overall outcomes for a problem. Initially, swarms are used for unconstrained local optimization. The results are further optimized globally using constrained PSO [28]. For optimum utilization of resources, PSO has been proposed. It optimizes routes based on arrival time and waiting tolerance of the passengers [29]. Thus, PSO is applied to solve a large set of engineering problems. To further improve the performance, these can be hybridized with other algorithms. PSO and its allies can be used for linear, non-linear, unconstrained, and constrained problem optimizations. These algorithms can be applied for solving single- and multi-objective problems.

Conventional nature-inspired algorithms and swarm optimization can be used for optimization. IoT, 5G, and 6G systems are becoming more and more complex. Conventional nature-inspired optimization algorithms like genetic algorithms, PSO, and simulated annealing improves overall performance of the system. To enhance it further, other optimization algorithms have been adapted. *Cat swarm optimization* algorithm and its allies versions can be applied in various fields like wireless sensor networks, electrical engineering, and communication engineering. These algorithms are based on cat lazy behavior contrary to her alert mode, and these are considered as seeking (local optimization) and tracing modes (global optimization) [30]. *Cuckoo optimization* algorithm is generally used for continuous problems, which are non-linear in nature. These are based on the cuckoo's habit to lay eggs in others' nests and selecting the best nest where her eggs can nurture without fail. This algorithm is used for complex problems, which are NP hard like data fusion in wireless networks, train neural network, manufacturing scheduling, and nurse scheduling [31]. *Mine blast optimization* algorithm (MBA) is based on clearing the mines field while targeting the most explosive (optimum) mine in which created pieces of shrapnel collide with other mines this is used as direction for further process [32]. This algorithm is good for constrained optimization problems. MBA, its hybrid, and advanced versions has been used to find solutions to various real-time problems. *Water cycle algorithm* (WCA) is based on the flow of the river, i.e., how the river is formed at high mountains due to snowfall, flows down to the valley, and ends up in the sea. This algorithm is widely used in various mechanical engineering design problems [33]. WCA and its various hybrid and advanced versions have been applied to solve a large number of engineering problems like spam e-mail detection, PI controller, and energy optimization [34].

The algorithms discussed till now can perform better but there is a limitation that if an algorithm is stuck into the premature stage of local optima, then an optimal value may not be obtained. This problem can be solved by using *anarchic society optimization algorithms* (ASA). It is based on the human behavior of a group of people who dislike stopping instead to keep visiting places which are less visited by them. In engineering, it is less popular till now. It has been used to assign various factories and machines to complete jobs in an area [35]. Teaching learning method is a population-based algorithm which optimize in the two phases, i.e., teacher's phase to teach students, student's phase, i.e., to learn by other students. It has been applied to many mechanical engineering design problems [36]. Another meta-heuristic algorithm is inspired by the *lion and ant* intelligence. A lion sets a trap for its prey and verifies the ant's movement in its trap, whereas ant tries to escape the trap by her intelligence. This algorithm can be applied to a large variety of engineering applications like in wireless sensor networks, signal processing, PV cells modeling, multilayer perceptron neural network, etc. [37]. *Crow search algorithm* is based on the fact that a crow follows another crow to steal it. It has a wide area of application in engineering like optimal power flow, feature selection, image processing, and cloud computing [38]. It is evident that these advanced meta-heuristic algorithms can be used to solve a wide range of engineering problems. Algorithms can be selected based on the problem type.

The nature-inspired algorithms are used in a large variety of application areas. IoT is one of the applications in which optimization of resources, data, time, network, battery, size of the device, etc. need to be optimized. Optimization helps to accommodate a greater number of users using the same resources which improves overall efficiency and cost of the system. Various algorithms like genetic algorithm, simulated annealing algorithm, differential evolution algorithm, particle swarm optimization, etc. are used to optimize position of access point has been implemented [39]. Crowd-based intelligence and genetic algorithms have been used to improve communication, caching and communication capacity the device correlation and distance for communication is optimized [40]. An discrete and evolutionary multi-objective method has been used to improve the throughput and energy efficiency of the system of a multi-UAV communication system [41]. The Hawk optimization algorithm, genetic algorithm, artificial bee colony algorithm, moth flame optimization, and whale optimization algorithms have been used to improve energy utilization in the Internet of Things (IoT) applications [42]. The swarm intelligence-based algorithms, i.e., flower pollination algorithm, slap swarm algorithm, and sine cosine algorithms are implemented to calculate docking points for efficient data collection UAV [43]. Thus, various algorithms have been used to optimize different parameters for several applications. The IoT technologies are further being used in various areas like medical science, smart cities, etc. In smart cities, expectation is to sense various data, software automation while using optimal usage of resources. A multi-swarm differential evolution particle swarm optimization is used to reduce energy utilization without altering the target task [44]. To implement smart healthcare systems in smart cities mobile cloud computing is used. This technology helps to reduce latency and resource consumption by offloading the task computation to nearby devices. Other optimization algorithms such as ant colony optimization and particle swarm optimization for optimal data offloading have been used [45]. Bat algorithm and fuzzy logic are used to optimize energy consumption and comfort index in the large cities [46].

Using other neighborhood devices for computation may fasten the process, but it may interfere with the user's privacy. Various security encryption algorithms are available to ensure user's privacy but ensuring privacy of user along with cloud-based power system results best. An identity-based encryption with equality test ensures no leakage of data to ensure user's security [47].

Apart from above various nature-inspired algorithms also finds applications in the fields of biomedical, healthcare, and industrial automation. For early detection of diseases various features have been incorporated in wearable devices like smartwatches and smart phones. Algorithms like GA, swarm intelligence, neural networks, and these elites are used for predictive analysis and to optimize the resource [48]. These algorithms are also widely used in industrial automations like warehouse replenishment where each time position allocations of a good is a new permutation which very well mimics the behavior of chromosomes. Fault diagnosis of rotation machinery is optimized by quantum genetic algorithm [49]. A robotic assembly planning has been implemented using GA, ant colony optimization, memetic algorithm, flower pollination algorithm, and teaching learning algorithms [50]. The scope is beyond mentioned areas, i.e., nature-inspired algorithms can be applied for optimization of a large variety of real-time problems.

10.2 Challenges and potentials of bio-inspired optimization algorithms for IoT applications

Bio-inspired optimization algorithms are computational methods that simulate natural biological processes to solve complex problems like mixed integer non-linear programming problems, constraint-based problems, and NP hard problems. These algorithms have shown great potential in various fields, including the IoT. However, some challenges and limitations need to be addressed to fully exploit their potential in IoT applications.

10.2.1 Challenges

Scalability: As IoT systems continue to grow in size and complexity, the scalability of bio-inspired optimization algorithms becomes a significant challenge. These algorithms may take a long time to converge or sometimes during local optimization, a wrong convergent point may lead to no convergence during global optimization. For smart applications, time and resource optimization is desirable.

Real-time constraints: Real-time applications require a flexible system which may adapt to real-time changes, which is a limitation as many bio-inspired optimization algorithms are computationally complex.

Robustness: IoT applications often operate in dynamic and unpredictable environments. Therefore, the robustness of bio-inspired optimization algorithms to changing conditions and perturbations is crucial.

Interpretability: Bio-inspired optimization algorithms are often considered as "black-box" approaches, which may limit their interpretability and applicability in certain IoT domains.

10.2.2   Potentials

Adaptability: Bio-inspired optimization algorithms are inherently adaptable and can dynamically adjust to changes in the environment, making them suitable for IoT applications that operate in dynamic and unpredictable environments.

Efficiency: Bio-inspired optimization algorithms are often highly efficient, making them suitable for IoT applications with limited computational resources.

Multimodal optimization: Many IoT applications involve the optimization of multiple objectives or criteria. Bio-inspired optimization algorithms can handle such problems efficiently, making them suitable for IoT applications with complex optimization objectives.

Diversity: Bio-inspired optimization algorithms can generate diverse solutions, making them suitable for IoT applications that require diverse solutions to be explored.

In summary, bio-inspired optimization algorithms have great potential for IoT applications, but they also face challenges that need to be addressed to fully exploit their potential. Researchers need to modify existing algorithms or propose new algorithms and techniques that can overcome these challenges while leveraging the potentials of these algorithms to address the optimization problems in IoT applications.

10.3   Challenges and opportunities of bio-inspired optimization algorithms for biomedical applications

Bio-inspired optimization algorithms are computational techniques that mimic natural processes to solve complex optimization problems. They have shown tremendous potential in a wide range of biomedical applications, including drug design, medical imaging, and bioinformatics. However, these algorithms also face several challenges that need to be addressed to realize their full potential.

Lack of transparency is one of the significant challenges in the optimization process. Bio-inspired optimization algorithms are often referred to as "black-box" algorithms, which means that the decision-making process is not transparent. This can be a challenge in biomedical applications where transparency is essential for regulatory compliance and ethical considerations. Therefore, it is crucial to develop explainable optimization algorithms that can provide a clear rationale for the solutions they generate.

Lack of reliability is another drawback as sometimes bio inspired algorithms are stuck into false local convergence which may lead to wrong global convergence. For critical applications, it may cause a great detriment. So, in spite of all virtues, it is difficult to adapt these algorithms for critical bio-medical applications.

Additionally, the optimization of biomedical problems often involves working with noisy and uncertain data. Bio-inspired optimization algorithms may not perform well when working with noisy data, and it may be challenging to distinguish between random noise and significant signal. Therefore, it is essential to develop optimization algorithms that can handle noisy and uncertain data effectively.

Accuracy of measured data is one of the important factors for response of nature inspired algorithms. As these are adaptable to dynamic changes. Any measured changes of data at any instance may mislead to a convergent point. It is difficult to determine the point where the device measured abrupt data.

Despite these challenges, bio-inspired optimization algorithms present numerous opportunities for biomedical applications. For example, they can be used to develop personalized medicine by optimizing treatment plans for individual patients based on their genetic and clinical data. They can also be used to optimize the design of medical devices and prosthetics, improving patient outcomes and quality of life. Additionally, bio-inspired optimization algorithms can help in the discovery of new drugs and therapies by searching vast chemical and biological spaces.

In conclusion, while bio-inspired optimization algorithms present numerous challenges in biomedical applications, they also offer significant opportunities. Addressing these challenges and developing more sophisticated algorithms will be crucial in realizing the full potential of bio-inspired optimization in the biomedical field.

10.4 Recent trends in smart cities planning based on nature-inspired computing

Nature-inspired computing is a new change in smart city planning that aims to use principles derived from natural systems to optimize and improve the efficiency of urban systems. Some recent trends in this area include:

Swarm intelligence: One of the key principles of swarm intelligence is to mimic the behavior of social insects, such as ants and bees. This idea is being used in smart city planning to improve waste management, make traffic flow better, and use less energy. For example, researchers are developing algorithms that mimic the foraging behavior of ants to optimize garbage collection routes in cities.

Genetic algorithms: Genetic algorithms are inspired by the process of natural selection and evolution. They are being used in smart city planning to optimize complex systems such as transportation networks, energy grids, and water management systems. For example, researchers are developing genetic algorithms to optimize the placement of electric vehicle charging stations in cities.

Artificial neural networks: Artificial neural networks are computational models that are inspired by the structure and function of biological neurons. They are being used in smart city planning to analyze data from sensors and other sources to identify patterns and optimize urban systems. For example, researchers are using artificial neural networks to optimize traffic light timings in cities.

Particle swarm optimization: Particle swarm optimization is a nature-inspired algorithm that is based on the behavior of social insects, such as flocking birds. It is being used in smart city planning to optimize a wide range of systems, including transportation networks, energy grids, and water management systems. For example, researchers are using particle swarm optimization to optimize the placement of renewable energy sources in cities.

Other algorithms: Cat optimization, flower pollination optimization, lion and ant optimization, etc. are nature-inspired algorithms that are based on some virtues of animals. For example, cat optimization uses the virtue of the cat being attentive while being in sleep mode for a large amount of time. These algorithms are used in smart city planning to optimize power consumption, network management resources, etc.

Overall, nature-inspired computing is an exciting and rapidly evolving field that is helping to drive innovation in smart city planning. By leveraging the principles of natural systems, researchers and planners are developing new algorithms and techniques that can help cities become more sustainable, efficient, and livable.

Although there are a number of algorithms in the IoT. IoT is a network of interconnected devices that collect and exchange data. IoT applications can range from smart homes and wearables to industrial monitoring and smart cities. To process and analyze the vast amount of data generated by these devices, efficient and effective algorithms are essential. Here are some of the most commonly used algorithms in IoT applications:

Machine learning algorithms: Machine learning algorithms are widely used in IoT applications for predicting, classifying, and clustering data. These algorithms use statistical models to analyze the data generated by IoT devices, enabling them to make accurate predictions and decisions.

Data compression algorithms: As IoT devices generate vast amounts of data, it is often necessary to compress this data to reduce storage and transmission costs. Data compression algorithms such as Huffman coding and Lempel-Ziv-Welch (LZW) compression are commonly used in IoT applications.

Encryption algorithms: With the increasing amount of sensitive data generated by IoT devices, encryption algorithms such as advanced encryption standard (AES) and RSA are crucial for securing data and protecting privacy.

Optimization algorithms: Optimization algorithms are used to improve the performance of IoT devices and systems. These algorithms aim to maximize efficiency while minimizing energy consumption and other resources.

Sensor data fusion algorithms: IoT applications often involve data from multiple sensors. Sensor data fusion algorithms are used to combine the data from these sensors and provide a more accurate representation of the physical environment.

Time series analysis algorithms: IoT applications often generate time series data, which can be analyzed using time series analysis algorithms. These algorithms can detect patterns, anomalies, and trends in the data, enabling more accurate predictions and decisions.

Overall, the algorithms used in IoT applications vary depending on the specific use case, but the ones mentioned above are some of the most commonly used.

10.5 Future perspectives of nature-inspired computing

Nature-inspired computing has already shown great promise in solving complex problems in various fields, including computer science, engineering, and biology.

As technology continues to advance, we can expect to see further developments and applications of this field. Some potential future perspectives of nature-inspired computings are:

Integration with AI and machine learning: Nature-inspired computing techniques, such as neural networks and genetic algorithms, can be combined with AI and machine learning to create more efficient and effective systems. This integration could lead to the creation of more intelligent machines capable of learning and adapting to new situations.

Advancements in robotics: Nature-inspired computing could also be used to improve the functionality of robots. For example, biomimicry could be used to create robots that move and behave like animals, making them better suited for tasks such as search and rescue missions.

Applications in healthcare: Nature-inspired computing could be used to develop new medical treatments and devices. For example, genetic algorithms could be used to optimize drug dosages for individual patients, while swarm intelligence could be used to develop algorithms for analyzing medical images. Early detection of disease is also possible using bio-inspired algorithms.

Sustainable development: Nature-inspired computing could also be used to help address environmental issues, such as climate change and pollution. For example, evolutionary algorithms could be used to optimize renewable energy systems, while swarm intelligence could be used to develop efficient transportation networks.

Cybersecurity: Nature-inspired computing could also be used to improve cybersecurity. For example, immune system-inspired algorithms could be used to detect and respond to cyber-attacks. An identity-based encryption with equality test ensures user's privacy [47].

Nature-inspired optimization techniques have become increasingly popular in the field of IoT due to their ability to optimize complex systems with large amounts of data. These techniques are based on the principles of natural selection, genetic algorithms, and swarm intelligence. They can be used to improve the efficiency and performance of IoT systems by optimizing various parameters such as energy consumption, network traffic, and data processing.

One example of nature-inspired optimization in IoT is swarm intelligence, which involves the use of algorithms inspired by the behavior of social insects, such as ants and bees. Swarm intelligence algorithms can be used to optimize the routing of data packets in IoT networks, resulting in more efficient and reliable data transfer.

Overall, the future of nature-inspired computing is exciting and holds great potential for solving some of the most pressing problems such as latency minimization for resilient responses are facing our world today.

10.6 Bio-inspired heuristic algorithms

Bio-inspired heuristic algorithms are computational techniques that draw inspiration from the principles of natural systems such as biological evolution, swarm intelligence, and neural networks to solve optimization problems. These algorithms have been widely used in various fields, including IoT systems, due to their ability to handle large and complex datasets.

In IoT systems, bio-inspired heuristic algorithms can be used for a wide range of applications, including network routing, resource allocation, and energy management. Here are some examples of bio-inspired heuristic algorithms used in IoT:

Ant colony optimization (ACO): ACO is a bio-inspired optimization algorithm that mimics the behavior of ants in finding the shortest path between their nest and food sources. In IoT, ACO can be used to optimize the routing path of data packets in wireless sensor networks.

Particle swarm optimization (PSO): PSO is a bio-inspired optimization algorithm that simulates the social behavior of a flock of birds or a swarm of bees. In IoT, PSO can be used to optimize the allocation of resources such as bandwidth, memory, and processing power among IoT devices.

Genetic algorithms (GA): GA is a bio-inspired optimization algorithm that mimics the processes of natural selection and evolution. In the IoT, GA can be used to optimize the configuration of IoT devices and sensors, such as the selection of the most suitable sensor parameters or the optimal placement of sensors.

Artificial neural networks (ANN): ANN is a bio-inspired algorithm that simulates the function of the human brain in processing information. In IoT, ANN can be used to predict the behavior of IoT devices and sensors based on historical data, which can help in optimizing energy consumption and reduce maintenance costs.

In conclusion, bio-inspired heuristic algorithms have shown great potential in solving optimization problems in IoT systems. As the complexity and size of IoT systems continue to grow, the use of bio-inspired heuristic algorithms will become even more important in ensuring the efficiency and reliability of these systems.

10.7   Probable future directions

There are several probable future directions in IoT optimization, some of which include:

Edge computing: IoT devices generate massive amounts of data, which can create network congestion and latency issues. Edge computing involves processing data closer to the source, reducing network traffic, and improving response times. In the future, IoT devices will increasingly incorporate edge computing capabilities to improve overall system performance.

Artificial intelligence and machine learning: AI and ML are already being used to optimize IoT systems by analyzing data patterns and identifying anomalies. In the future, AI and ML will become more sophisticated, enabling IoT systems to learn from data and adapt to changing conditions in real-time.

5G networks: The next generation of wireless networks, 5G, promises faster speeds and lower latency, which will significantly improve the performance of IoT devices. 5G will enable real-time data processing and support a much larger number of connected devices, making IoT systems more efficient and effective.

Blockchain: The distributed ledger technology behind cryptocurrencies like bitcoin, blockchain can be used to secure IoT data and transactions. In the future, blockchain will likely be used to create more secure and decentralized IoT systems, reducing the risk of cyber-attacks and data breaches.

Energy efficiency: IoT devices consume a significant amount of energy, which can be expensive and harmful to the environment. In the future, IoT devices will be designed to be more energy-efficient, incorporating features like low-power sensors and optimized communication protocols to reduce power consumption.

Overall, these trends suggest that the future of IoT optimization will be focused on making devices more intelligent, efficient, and secure, while also improving the performance and reliability of the overall system.

Bio-medical: Nowadays many people are suffering from various diseases. Some diseases result in sudden attack. An early detection of these diseases may be helpful. So it is a need of an hour to design a system with quick response, accurate with usage of minimum limited resources.

Localization of sensors: In smart cities, everything relates to IoT and to connect physical devices with IoT or to automate the processes sensors need to measure all kinds of data. During measurement, the position of the sensor plays an important in accurate measurement.

References

[1] B. A. Draper, K. Baek, M. S. Bartlett, and J. R. Beveridge, "Recognizing faces with PCA and ICA," *Comput. Vis. Image Underst.*, vol. 91, no. 1–2, pp. 115–137, 2003, doi: 10.1016/S1077-3142(03)00077-8.

[2] R. M. Morais and J. Pedro, "Machine learning models for estimating quality of transmission in DWDM networks," *J. Opt. Commun. Netw.*, vol. 10, no. 10, pp. D84–D99, 2018, doi: 10.1364/JOCN.10.000D84.

[3] M. Khajehzadeh, M. R. Taha, A. El-Shafie, and M. Eslami, "A survey on meta-heuristic global optimization algorithms," *Res. J. Appl. Sci. Eng. Technol.*, vol. 3, no. 6, pp. 569–578, 2011.

[4] M. R. McCall, T. Mehta, C. W. Leathers, and D. M. Foster, "Psyllium husk II: effect on the metabolism of apolipoprotein B in African green monkeys," *Am. J. Clin. Nutr.*, vol. 56, no. 2, pp. 385–393, 1992, doi: 10.1093/ajcn/56.2.385.

[5] P. Cunningham and S. J. Delany, "K-Nearest neighbour classifiers: a tutorial," *ACM Comput. Surv.*, vol. 54, no. 6, 2021, doi: 10.1145/3459665.

[6] M. Naeem, S. T. H. Rizvi, and A. Coronato, "A gentle introduction to reinforcement learning and its application in different fields," *IEEE Access*, vol. 8, pp. 209320–209344, 2020, doi: 10.1109/ACCESS.2020.3038605.

[7] J. Zambrano, *Gaussian Mixture Models – Method and Applications*, Presentation, FUDIPO project Machine Learning course, Oct-Dec 2017. doi: 10.13140/RG.2.2.32667.77602. https://www.researchgate.net/publication/321245699_Gaussian_Mixture_Model_-_method_and_application.

[8]   R. Dastres and M. Soori, "Artificial neural network systems," *Int. J. Imaging Robot.*, vol. 2021, no. 2, pp. 13–25, 2021, www.ceserp.com/cp-jour

[9]   L. Rabiner and B. Juang, "An introduction to hidden Markov models," in *IEEE ASSP Magazine*, vol. 3, no. 1, pp. 4–16, 1986. doi: 10.1109/MASSP.1986.1165342.

[10]   C. J. Peng, K. L. Lee, and G. M. Ingersoll, "An introduction to logistic regression analysis and reporting," *The Journal of Educational Research*, vol. 96, no. 1, pp. 3–14, 2002. doi: 10.1080/00220670209598786.

[11]   T. Evgeniou and M. Pontil, "Support vector machines: theory and applications." In: G. Paliouras, V. Karkaletsis, C. D. Spyropoulos (eds), *Machine Learning and Its Applications*, ACAI 1999. Lecture Notes in Computer Science, vol. 2049, 2001, Springer, Berlin, Heidelberg. https://doi.org/10.1007/3-540-44673-7_12 10.1007/3-540-44673-7.

[12]   G. Signoretti, M. Silva, P. Andrade, I. Silva, E. Sisinni, and P. Ferrari, "An evolving TinyML compression algorithm for IoT environments based on data eccentricity," *Sensors*, vol. 21, no. 4153, pp. 1–25, 2021. doi: 10.3390/s21124153.

[13]   I. Kuzminykh, M. Yevdokymenko, and V. Sokolov, "Encryption algorithms in IoT: security vs lifetime how long the device will encryption algorithms in IoT: security vs lifetime," preprint article, no. January 2022, 2021. https://www.researchgate.net/publication/353237519_Encryption_Algorithms_in_IoT_Security_vs_Lifetime _How_long_the_device_will_live.

[14]   Z. Wang, C. Qin, B. Wan, and W. W. Song, "A comparative study of common nature-inspired algorithms for continuous function optimization," *Entropy*, vol. 23(7), no. 874, pp. 1–40, 2021. doi: 10.3390/e23070874.

[15]   F. G. Mohammadi, F. Shenavarmasouleh, K. Rasheed, T. Taha, M. H. Amini, and H. R. Arabnia, "The application of evolutionary and nature inspired algorithms in data science and data analytics," in *2021 International Conference on Computational Science and Computational Intelligence (CSCI)*, 2021.

[16]   A. Garg, R. Arya, and M. P. Singh, "An integrated approach for dual resource optimization of relay-based mobile edge computing system," *Concurr. Comput. Pract. Exp.*, no. February, pp. 1–16, March 2023, doi: 10.1002/cpe.7682.

[17]   H. Li, J. Li, M. Liu, Z. Ding, and F. Gong, "Energy harvesting and resource allocation for cache-enabled UAV based IoT NOMA networks," *IEEE Trans. Veh. Technol.*, vol. 70, no. 9, pp. 9625–9630, 2021, doi: 10.1109/TVT.2021.3098351.

[18]   T. H. S. Li, C. Y. Liu, P. H. Kuo, *et al.*, "A three-dimensional adaptive PSO-based packing algorithm for an IoT-based automated e-fulfillment packaging system," *IEEE Access*, vol. 5, pp. 9188–9205, 2017, doi: 10.1109/ACCESS.2017.2702715.

[19]   X. Liu and E. Sanchez-Sinencio, "A highly efficient ultralow photovoltaic power harvesting system with MPPT for Internet of Things smart nodes,"

IEEE Trans. Very Large Scale Integr. Syst., vol. 23, no. 12, pp. 3065–3075, 2015, doi: 10.1109/TVLSI.2014.2387167.

[20] J. Zhang, P. Liu, F. Zhang, H. Iwabuchi, A. A. D. H. E. A. De Moura, and V. H. C. De Albuquerque, "Ensemble meteorological cloud classification meets internet of dependable and controllable things," *IEEE Internet Things J.*, vol. 8, no. 5, pp. 3323–3330, 2021, doi: 10.1109/JIOT.2020.3043289.

[21] C. C. Lin, W. Y. Liu, and Y. W. Lu, "Three-dimensional Internet-of-Things deployment with optimal management service benefits for smart tourism services in forest recreation parks," *IEEE Access*, vol. 7, pp. 182366–182380, 2019, doi: 10.1109/ACCESS.2019.2960212.

[22] A. Erturk, M. K. Gullu, D. Cesmeci, D. Gercek, and S. Erturk, "Spatial resolution enhancement of hyperspectral images using unmixing and binary particle swarm optimization," *IEEE Geosci. Remote Sens. Lett.*, vol. 11, no. 12, pp. 2100–2104, 2014, doi: 10.1109/LGRS.2014.2320135.

[23] J. Liu, D. Yang, M. Lian, and M. Li, "Research on intrusion detection based on particle swarm optimization in IoT," *IEEE Access*, vol. 9, pp. 38254–38268, 2021, doi: 10.1109/ACCESS.2021.3063671.

[24] Q. Chen, J. Sun, and V. Palade, "Distributed contribution-based quantum-behaved particle swarm optimization with controlled diversity for large-scale global optimization problems," *IEEE Access*, vol. 7, pp. 150093–150104, 2019, doi: 10.1109/ACCESS.2019.2944196.

[25] M. Z. Hasan and H. Al-Rizzo, "Optimization of sensor deployment for industrial internet of things using a multiswarm algorithm," *IEEE Internet Things J.*, vol. 6, no. 6, pp. 10344–10362, 2019, doi: 10.1109/JIOT.2019. 2938486.

[26] Z. Zhu, J. Zhou, Z. Ji, and Y. H. Shi, "DNA sequence compression using adaptive particle swarm optimization-based memetic algorithm," *IEEE Trans. Evol. Comput.*, vol. 15, no. 5, pp. 643–658, 2011, doi: 10.1109/TEVC. 2011.2160399.

[27] Y. F. Khan, B. Kaushik, M. Khalid Imam Rahmani, and M. E. Ahmed, "HSI-LFS-BERT: novel hybrid swarm intelligence based linguistics feature selection and computational intelligent model for Alzheimer's prediction using audio transcript," *IEEE Access*, vol. 10, no. November, pp. 126990–127004, 2022, doi: 10.1109/ACCESS.2022.3223681.

[28] Q. Zhao and C. Li, "Two-stage multi-swarm particle swarm optimizer for unconstrained and constrained global optimization," *IEEE Access*, vol. 8, no. 1, pp. 124905–124927, 2020, doi: 10.1109/ACCESS.2020.3007743.

[29] F. Chen, Y. Lu, L. Liu, and Q. Zhu, "Route optimization of customized buses based on optimistic and pessimistic values," *IEEE Access*, vol. 11, no. January, pp. 11016–11023, 2023, doi: 10.1109/ACCESS.2023.3241235.

[30] A. M. Ahmed, T. A. Rashid, and S. A. M. Saeed, "Cat swarm optimization algorithm: a survey and performance evaluation," *Comput. Intell. Neurosci.*, vol. 2020, Article ID 4854895, 2020, doi: 10.1155/2020/4854895.

[31] L. C. C. By, S. Date, P. Date, C. Verma, C. S. Algorithm, and O. Problems, *A Survey on Cuckoo Search Algorithm for Optimization Problems*, March, pp. 0–16, 2021, doi: 10.36227/techrxiv.14199221.

[32] A. Sadollah, A. Bahreininejad, H. Eskandar, and M. Hamdi, "Mine blast algorithm: a new population based algorithm for solving constrained engineering optimization problems," *Appl. Soft Comput. J.*, vol. 13, no. 5, pp. 2592–2612, 2013, doi: 10.1016/j.asoc.2012.11.026.

[33] H. Eskandar, A. Sadollah, A. Bahreininejad, and M. Hamdi, "Water cycle algorithm – a novel metaheuristic optimization method for solving constrained engineering optimization problems," *Comput. Struct.*, vol. 110–111, no. September 2012, pp. 151–166, 2012, doi: 10.1016/j.compstruc.2012.07.010.

[34] G. Al-Rawashdeh, R. Mamat, and N. Hafhizah Binti Abd Rahim, "Hybrid water cycle optimization algorithm with simulated annealing for spam e-mail detection," *IEEE Access*, vol. 7, pp. 143721–143734, 2019, doi: 10.1109/ACCESS.2019.2944089.

[35] A. Ahmadi-Javid, "Anarchic society optimization: a human-inspired method," in *2011 IEEE Congress of Evolutionary Computation (CEC)*, no. March, pp. 2586–2592, 2011, doi:10.1109/CEC.2011.5949940.

[36] D. Wu, S. Wang, Q. Liu, L. Abualigah, and H. Jia, "An improved teaching-learning-based optimization algorithm with reinforcement learning strategy for solving optimization problems," *Comput. Intell. Neurosci.*, vol. 2022, 2022, doi: 10.1155/2022/1535957.

[37] A. A. Heidari, H. Faris, S. Mirjalili, I. Aljarah, and M. Mafarja, "Ant lion optimizer: theory, literature review, and application in multi-layer perceptron neural networks," *Stud. Comput. Intell.*, vol. 811, no. August 2021, pp. 23–46, 2020, doi: 10.1007/978-3-030-12127-3_3.

[38] Q. Cheng, H. Huang, and M. Chen, "A novel crow search algorithm based on improved flower pollination," *Math. Probl. Eng.*, vol. 2021, pp. 1–26, 2021, doi: 10.1155/2021/1048879.

[39] X. Zhu, W. Qu, T. Qiu, L. Zhao, M. Atiquzzaman, and D. O. Wu, "Indoor intelligent fingerprint-based localization: principles, approaches and challenges," *IEEE Commun. Surv. Tutorials*, vol. 22, no. 4, pp. 2634–2657, 2020, doi: 10.1109/COMST.2020.3014304.

[40] K. Wang, Z. Yang, B. Liang, and W. Ji, "An intelligence optimization method based on crowd intelligence for IoT devices," *Int. J. Crowd Sci.*, vol. 5, no. 3, pp. 218–227, 2021, doi: 10.1108/IJCS-03-2021-0007.

[41] L. Liu, A. Wang, G. Sun, and J. Li, "Multiobjective optimization for improving throughput and energy efficiency in UAV-enabled IoT," *IEEE Internet Things J.*, vol. 9, no. 20, pp. 20763–20777, 2022, doi: 10.1109/JIOT.2022.3175712.

[42] K. Dev, P. K. R. Maddikunta, T. R. Gadekallu, S. Bhattacharya, P. Hegde, and S. Singh, "Energy optimization for green communication in IoT using Harris Hawks optimization," *IEEE Trans. Green Commun. Netw.*, vol. 6, no. 2, pp. 685–694, 2022, doi: 10.1109/TGCN.2022.3143991.

[43] E. Chen, J. Chen, A. W. Mohamed, B. Wang, Z. Wang, and Y. Chen, "Swarm intelligence application to UAV aided IoT data acquisition deployment optimization," *IEEE Access*, vol. 8, pp. 175660–175668, 2020, doi: 10.1109/ACCESS.2020.3025409.

[44] M. Sato, Y. Fukuyama, T. Iizaka, and T. Matsui, "Total optimization of energy networks in a smart city by multi-population global-best modified brain storm optimization with migration," *Algorithms*, vol. 12, no. 1, pp. 2186–2200, 2019, doi: 10.3390/a12010015.

[45] M. M. Islam, M. A. Razzaque, M. M. Hassan, W. N. Ismail, and B. Song, "Mobile cloud-based big healthcare data processing in smart cities," *IEEE Access*, vol. 5, pp. 11887–11899, 2017, doi: 10.1109/ACCESS.2017.2707439.

[46] A. S. Shah, H. Nasir, M. Fayaz, A. Lajis, I. Ullah, and A. Shah, "Dynamic user preference parameters selection and energy consumption optimization for smart homes using deep extreme learning machine and bat algorithm," *IEEE Access*, vol. 8, pp. 204744–204762, 2020, doi: 10.1109/ACCESS.2020.3037081.

[47] L. Wu, Y. Zhang, K. K. R. Choo, and D. He, "Efficient identity-based encryption scheme with equality test in smart city," *IEEE Trans. Sustain. Comput.*, vol. 3, no. 1, pp. 44–55, 2018, doi: 10.1109/TSUSC.2017.2734110.

[48] L. Kouhalvandi, L. Matekovits, and I. Peter, "Magic of 5G technology and optimization methods applied to biomedical devices: a survey," *Appl. Sci.*, vol. 12, no. 14, 2022, doi: 10.3390/app12147096.

[49] X. Zhu, J. Xiong, and Q. Liang, "Fault diagnosis of rotation machinery based on support vector machine optimized by quantum genetic algorithm," *IEEE Access*, vol. 6, pp. 33583–33588, 2018, doi: 10.1109/ACCESS.2018.2789933.

[50] A. Balamurali Gunji, B. B. B. V. L. Deepak, C. M. V. A. Raju Bahubalendruni, and D. Bibhuti Bhushan Biswal, "An optimal robotic assembly sequence planning by assembly subsets detection method using teaching learning-based optimization algorithm," *IEEE Trans. Autom. Sci. Eng.*, vol. 15, no. 3, pp. 1369–1385, 2018, doi: 10.1109/TASE.2018.2791665.

Index

Printed in the USA
CPSIA information can be obtained
at www.ICGtesting.com
JSHW011506221024
72173JS00005B/1225